SOCRATES' CHILDREN

SOCRATES' CHILDREN

Thinking and Knowing in the Western Tradition

Trudy Govier

broadview press

Canadian Cataloguing in Publication Data

Govier, Trudy
Socrates' Children

Includes bibliographical references and index
ISBN 1-55111-093-8
1. Philosophy – History. I. Title.

B72.G684 1997 190 C97-930774-0

Broadview Press
Post Office Box 1243
Peterborough, Ontario, Canada, K9J 7H5

in the United States of America
3576 California Road, Orchard Park, N.Y. 14127

in the United Kingdom
B.R.A.D. Book Representation & Distribution Ltd.
244A, London Road, Hadleigh, Essex SS7 2DE

Broadview Press gratefully acknowledges the support of the Canada Council, the Ontario Arts Council, the Ontario Publishing Centre, and the Ministry of National Heritage.

Cover design and book layout: Alvin Choong Design Studio

PRINTED IN CANADA
10 9 8 7 6 5 4 3 2 1 97 98 99

Contents

Preface

Philosophers are supposed to be "great thinkers," but they are often accused of restricting themselves only to critical thinking. Given a theory or argument, they can pose objections and take it apart. Is this the best we can get from philosophy – illustrations of how to destroy an idea? How did the great philosophers in the Western tradition think? Can we find in the history of Western philosophy any useful suggestions about how to think constructively or creatively?

It was an inter-disciplinary conference on Thinking in Boston in 1994 that led me to ask myself these questions. I was familiar with the criticism that Western philosophy has nothing to offer in the way of positive guidance about thinking, and I thought it would interesting to work through some philosophers central to the Western tradition to find out whether this was true. Men and women like Plato, Aristotle, Kant, de Beauvoir, and Wittgenstein, were nothing if not energetic and creative thinkers. What did they have to say about thinking? How did they think? Could we tell how they thought from what they wrote? When I described my ideas to Don LePan of Broadview Press, he was keenly interested in them and ultimately it was his encouragement which led me to write this book.

Soon after I began working on the book in the winter of 1995, I discovered the obvious: the theme of thinking cannot be treated by itself. It is not possible to understand or explain what a given philosopher had said about thinking without working through his or her ideas on a host of other subjects. Thus, more than I originally intended, this book turned into a selective general history – a presentation of some of the theories of knowledge, deliberation, meaning, and thinking central in the history of Western philosophy. To make sense of what various philosophers said or implied about thinking, I have had to describe what they thought about the sources of ideas, certainty, moral deliberation, doubt, belief, the moral life, religion, and many other topics. This book shows, I think, that the great philosophers did have some interesting things to say about thinking. And they thought in quite different ways. Socrates' style of thinking is different from Aristotle's; Hegel's differs from Hume's, which in turn is quite distinct from that of Descartes.

There are many histories of Western philosophy intended for students and general readers. What makes this one different from others? In addition to its development of themes pertaining especially to thinking, this book has several further differentiating features. I use quotations generously to provide a 'feel' for the philosophers described. I include two major women philosophers, Mary Wollstonecraft and Simone de Beauvoir. I often apply themes to contemporary examples. In the notes, I have included references to contemporary scholarship. The concluding chapter offers an overview of four current philosophical movements especially pertinent to thinking and knowledge: artificial intelligence research, the critical thinking-informal logic movement, deconstruction, and feminist epistemology. All the philosophers and trends discussed and described in an accessible and lively way.

This book is intended for every thoughtful reader who has wanted a better understanding of the history of Western philosophy but may be unable to start from a study of classic texts. In addition to those who are simply interested in philosophy and would like to know more about it, this group includes professionals in such fields as law, education, political science, psychology, and the sciences. Many people know that themes from philosophy past and present underlie their own work; they frequently encounter philosophical references which they would like to understand better. But they find the prospect of delving into Aristotle's *Metaphysics*, Kant's *Critique of Pure Reason*, or Hegel's *Phenomenology of Spirit* to be entirely daunting. I hope this book will provide easy access and interesting reading for such people, combining a sound background on central historical themes with practical and challenging advice about thinking itself.

This book is intended for students as well as for the general reader. It may be used as a sole text, or in conjunction with classic texts in a university or college introduction to the history of philosophy. The book is also suitable as a supplementary text in such courses as philosophy of education, philosophy of science, philosophy of law, women's studies, or anywhere else where it would be helpful to have available an accessible version of central philosophical views which are frequently alluded to, but not directly taught.

In the interest of readability, no formal footnotes were used. Notes following each chapter explain my sources, develop a few themes further, and offer suggestions for further reading.

In writing this book, I had to face many hard questions about whom to include and whom to exclude. To readers whose personal favorites were omitted, I can only say that including every worthwhile thinker was just not possible. The philosophical ideas are worth understanding in their own right, and all the philosophers discussed have made contributions to my ongoing theme of thinking. I regret not having space to include any medieval thinkers, and having to omit such important moderns as Locke, Leibniz, Rousseau, Berkeley, Spinoza, Mill, Russell, Moore, James, Peirce, Arendt, Husserl, Heidegger, Quine, Ayer, and Murdoch. Such thinkers could not be treated here, because the book had to be kept to a reasonable size.

I wish especially to thank David Gallop and Janet Sisson who both read virtually all chapters, offered many helpful criticisms, and have been extremely generous with their time. Thanks are also due to the anonymous reviewers for Broadview Press, to John Burbidge for reviewing the Hegel chapter, to Petra von Morstein for allowing me to audit her class on Hegel at the University of Calgary in the fall of 1995, and to my students in Philosophy 1000N at the University of Lethbridge in the summer of 1996 for their energy and interest. Nancy Heatherington Peirce offered useful comments on a late draft, and I am also endebted to Janet Keeping and Anton Colijn for ongoing moral support.

1

Socrates, the Sting Ray of Athens

Socrates (469 - 399 B.C.) is one of the most treasured personalities in the history of Western thought. He lived and worked in Athens, where he posed questions about virtue, knowledge, and understanding. Socrates was a well-known character in Athenian public life, noted for his capacity to ask probing questions and prove that people were not as wise as they thought themselves to be. In his day Athens was a major center of culture, allowing for democratic participation in government for male citizens, and considerable freedom of thought and expression.

Socrates left no written works; he philosophized through talking and arguing. What we know of Socrates comes from others who wrote about him. Plato, who was a student of Socrates in his later years, used Socrates as a main character in his philosophical dialogues. Plato's early dialogues are thought to portray Socrates' personality and style of thinking quite accurately. Other sources of information are the philosopher Aristotle, the chronicler Xenophon, and the comic playwright Aristophanes, who made fun of Socrates in his play *The Clouds*. The portrayal of Socrates here is based on Plato's early dialogues. For our purposes, Socrates is the character Plato described.

Short and stocky, with a snub nose, Socrates dressed shabbily and often went barefoot. Socrates was married and had three sons. Though of middle-class origins, he lived much of his life in poverty. Many people thought they had learned from Socrates, but he refused payment for his philosophical services, and insisted that he was not a teacher. Socrates was loved for his sense of humor, skill and persistence in argument, and willingness to engage in philosophical conversation and debate.

Because of his tenacious questioning of prominent citizens and his dismissal of common opinion as a reliable source of knowledge, Socrates eventually alienated influential Athenians. He was tried and convicted on charges of corrupting the youth and not respecting the gods of the city. Socrates was sentenced to death, and died drinking a poison, hemlock, in 399 B.C.

Socrates was no solitary thinker. His method of thinking involved talking, questioning, and arguing, typically in a small group. An issue would arise – usually some practical matter, such as educating the youth, running the government, understanding poetry, or conducting a legal case – and then, from questions and answers, the group would proceed in its discussion, either acknowledging errors and contradictions or moving on to fresh ideas. As a result of Socrates' persistent questioning, these new ideas were often contrary to the original ones.

Thinking, Questioning, and Arguing

People still use the phrase "Socratic method" in a way which preserves a connection with the historical Socrates. Today, the Socratic method is commonly understood as a means of teaching in which students are led forward by questions from the teacher. The approach is to work from the student's ideas; learning begins from what the student believes at the outset. In this sense, Socratic learning and teaching are based on an intense personal commitment. Despite his sense of humor and use of irony and sarcasm, Socrates was deeply serious about using philosophy to reflect on real problems of life and develop one's character. His mother Phaenarete was a midwife, and Plato said Socrates was a midwife too, in the sense that he was a person who helped ideas to be born. For Socrates, the goal of philosophical thought was knowledge: an enduring recognition and understanding of lasting truths. This understanding was to be sought in serious conversation and argument.

Socrates' seriousness and his concern to make sure that his fellow conversants agree with his starting points are illustrated in Plato's dialogue *Crito.* In this dialogue, Socrates is in prison under sentence of death and Crito is trying to persuade him that he should escape from jail, with the assistance of his friends. Against his friend Crito, Socrates argues that escaping his death sentence would be wrong, because it would be disloyal to the Laws of Athens. It is to those Laws that he owes his birth, upbringing, and life, and he has previously indicated commitment to them by his willingness to live out his life in Athens.

Before making this case to Crito, Socrates questions him to make sure they are starting the argument from the same point. Crito alluded more than once to what most people would think about Socrates if he were to escape and save himself. Socrates reminds Crito that they had not previously resolved questions by appealing to common opinion.

> Socrates: Was it always right to argue that some opinions should be taken seriously but not others? Or was it always wrong? Perhaps it was right before the question of my death arose, but now we can see clearly that it was a mistaken persistence in a point of view which was really irresponsible nonsense. I should like very much to inquire into this problem, Crito, with your help and to see whether the argument will appear in any different light to me now that I am in this position, or whether it will remain the same, and whether we shall dismiss it or accept it.
> Serious thinkers, I believe, have always held . . . that some of the opinions which people entertain should be respected, and others should not. . . . You are safe from the prospect of dying tomorrow, in all human probability, and you are not likely to have your judgment upset by this impending calamity. Consider, then, don't you think that this is a sound enough principle, that one should not regard all the opinions that people hold, but only some and not others? What do you say? Isn't that a fair statement?
> Crito: Yes, it is.
> Socrates: In other words, one should regard the good ones and not the bad?
> Crito: Yes.
> Socrates: The opinions of the wise being good, and the opinions of the foolish bad?
> Crito: Naturally.
> Socrates: To pass on then, what do you think of the sort of illustration that I used to employ? When a man is in training and taking it seriously, does he pay attention to all praise and criticism and opinion indiscriminately, or only when it comes from the one qualified person, the actual doctor or trainer?
> Crito: Only when it comes from the one qualified person.
> Socrates: Then he should be afraid of the criticism and welcome the praise of the one qualified person, but not those of the general public.
> Crito: Obviously.
> (*Crito*, 46d - 47b)

Crito agrees with Socrates: one should heed only the advice of a qualified person; for example, this is what people should do if they seek advice on physical training or physical health. The same policy should hold when moral questions are at stake.

> Socrates: Well, is life worth living with a body which is worn out and ruined in health?
> Crito: Certainly not.
> Socrates: What about the part of us which is mutilated by wrong actions and benefited by right ones? [Socrates is referring to the soul; he assumed that a person's soul is harmed if he acts wrongly.] Is life worth living with this part ruined? Or do we believe that this part of us, whatever it may be, in which right and wrong operate, is of less importance than the body?
> Crito: Certainly not.
> Socrates: It is really more precious?
> Crito: Much more.
> (*Crito*, 47e - 48a)

Crito had initially suggested that public opinion was a relevant and important factor to consider in making a choice. But Socrates has led him away from this belief; he changed Crito's mind by appealing to simple beliefs which they share. To move his argument forward, Socrates uses only statements that Crito is willing to accept. These include:

- Some opinions are better than others.
- The wise have better opinions than the foolish.
- A person training his body would pay attention only to the advice of a qualified advisor.
- Life with a ruined body would not be worth living.
- The soul is more precious than the body.

By implication, life with a ruined soul would not be worth living either. From these basic beliefs, Socrates leads Crito to the conclusions that a person should not ruin his or her soul, and should take advice only from a qualified person when deciding what to do. Common opinion about right and wrong is not an acceptable basis for making decisions about what to do.

Socrates was utterly committed to thinking by argument. In the *Crito* he acknowledges that the public, whose opinion he has dismissed on the basis of the above argument, has the power to put him to death. But Socrates feels sure that impending death – which most people would feel as an acute crisis – does not affect the merit of the rational argumentation. The most important thing is to live one's life rightly. Would it be right or wrong for Socrates to escape? The answer will depend on what he and Crito can best work out in conversation; it does not depend on the circumstance of whether there is a risk of death. What matters is what is right or wrong, and in no circumstance should one do something which is wrong. Socrates assumes that human beings have a soul which is distinct from the body and more important than the body, and that this soul will be harmed if we do wrong.

In this dialogue, the thinking and arguing are done mostly by Socrates. Crito's role is rather limited. He is apparently there to agree with the statements that Socrates uses as a basis for his argument and to grant that Socrates' conclusion is true. Thoughtful readers may feel that Crito should have been more active: Socrates moves, without justification, from the idea that the opinions of the wise are better than those of the foolish (which is true because of the way the words "wise" and "foolish" are defined) to the idea that there is some *one* qualified person whose advice is the best (a highly controversial view).

Discovering That We Do Not Know

In Plato's early dialogues, it is usually Socrates who raises provocative questions and pushes thought forward. Socrates often said that he was ignorant and did not know the answers to fundamental questions about justice, virtue, education, and knowledge. If his skill in argument made him sometimes seem superior to others, he insisted that it was an illusion. Any superiority Socrates might have lay in the fact that he *knew* he was ignorant, whereas other people tended to incorrectly believe that they were wise. According to Plato, Socrates argued quite seriously that he was the wisest person in the world, because he knew that he knew nothing. In contrast, other people thought they were wise, but lacked knowledge.

> You know Chaerephon, of course. . . . Well, one day he actually went to Delphi and asked this question of the god . . . He asked whether there was anyone wiser than myself. The priestess replied that there was no one. .. . I am only too conscious that I have no claim to wisdom, great or small. So what can he mean by asserting that I am the wisest man in the world?
> (*Apology*, 21a-b)

Socrates began to interview people renowned for their wisdom and found that few really knew the things they thought they knew. In the process he made himself rather unpopular. Finally, after talking with politicians, poets, craftsmen, and others, Socrates reached an interpretation of what the oracle had said.

> . . . real wisdom is the property of God, and this oracle is his way of telling us that human wisdom has little or no value. It seems to me that he is not literally referring to Socrates, but has merely taken my name as an example, as if he would say to us, The wisest of you men is he who has realized, like Socrates, that in respect of wisdom he is really worthless.
> (*Apology*, 23a-b)

There are several dialogues in which Socrates demonstrates that other people do not know what they think they know. In these dialogues, Socrates uses the tools of argument differently than in the *Crito*. In the *Crito*, we saw Socrates, with a small amount of participation from Crito, using argument to work out his own position. His argument proceeds from simple premises which strike Socrates as acceptable and are granted by Crito as a basis for carrying their thought forward. In other dialogues Socrates is shown using the tools of argument in a more negative way, to demonstrate that other people do not know what they think they know.

One prime example is the *Euthyphro*, still widely cited by philosophers interested in the relationship between religious belief and moral judgment. The *Euthyphro* discusses the relationship between piety (beliefs and attitudes toward the gods) and moral behavior. In this dialogue, Socrates, who has just been charged with impiety and corrupting the youth, meets Euthyphro at the entrance to the law courts and asks him what he is doing there. It turns out that Euthyphro is about to launch a prosecution against his own father on a charge of murder. Euthyphro's father had a domestic servant who had cut someone's throat; his father had bound the man, hand and foot, and left him in a ditch while waiting to find out what should be done about the case. The servant died lying in the ditch. Euthyphro believes that his father, being responsible for the death, should be charged with murder. Expressing amazement that anyone would prosecute his own father in a court of law, Socrates begins to question Euthyphro. Euthyphro is sure that he is acting rightly in bringing the prosecution, because he thinks he is doing what the gods would want him to do. He feels quite confident that he has an accurate knowledge of what the gods approve of – what is pious and impious, holy and unholy.

The question of piety and impiety is close to Socrates' heart: after all, he has himself been charged with impiety. He asks Euthyphro what piety is and how he knows about it.

> Socrates: State what you take piety and impiety to be with reference to murder and all the other cases. Is not the holy always one and the same thing in every action, and, again, is not the unholy always opposite to the holy, and like itself? And as unholiness does it not always have its one essential form, which may be found in everything that is unholy?
> Euthyphro: Yes, surely, Socrates.
> Socrates: Then tell me. How do you define the holy and the unholy?
> Euthyphro: Well then, I say that the holy is what I am now doing, prosecuting the wrongdoer who commits a murder or a sacrilegious robbery, or sins in any point like that, whether it be your father, or your mother, or whoever it may be. And not to prosecute would be unholy. And, Socrates, observe what a decisive proof I will give you that such is the law. . . . I tell them that the right procedure must be not to tolerate the impious man, no matter who. (*Euthyphro*, 5e)

Euthyphro goes on to mention tales of the gods and their quarrels. Socrates wonders aloud how people know what the gods are up to and what they think. But Euthyphro sees no need for scepticism about the gods.

> Euthyphro: . . . I will, if you wish, relate to you many other stories about the gods, which, I am certain will astonish you when you hear them.
> Socrates: I shouldn't wonder. . . . [but] you were not explicit enough before when I put the question. What is holiness? You merely said that what you are now doing is a holy deed – namely, prosecuting your father on a charge of murder.
> Euthyphro: And Socrates, I told the truth.
> Socrates: Possibly. But Euthyphro, there are many other things that you will say are holy.
> Euthyphro: Because they are.
> Socrates: Well, bear in mind that what I asked of you was not to tell me one or two out of all the numerous actions that are holy; I wanted you to tell me what is the essential form of holiness which makes all holy actions holy. I believe you held that there is one ideal form by which unholy things are all unholy, and by which all holy things are holy. Do you remember that?
> Euthyphro: I do.
> Socrates: Well then, show me what, precisely, this ideal is, so that

> with my eye on it, and using it as a standard, I can say that any action done by you or anybody else is holy if it resembles this ideal, or, if it does not, can deny that it is holy.
> (*Euthyphro*, 6d-e)

Euthyphro finds it hard to think about a general account and cannot offer a general definition of what is holy. He at first simply insists that he knows of many things that are holy. Socrates asks *why* – on what grounds – Euthyphro claims that these things are holy, and Euthyphro can only reply that they are holy "just because they are." Socrates again presses Euthyphro to offer a general definition. Finally Euthyphro says that what is pleasing to the gods is holy and what is not pleasing to them is unholy. Socrates goes on to explore the implications of this definition by testing its consistency with other beliefs that Euthyphro has about the gods. Tales of the gods depict them as quarrelling with each other. If they quarrel, they must disagree.

> Socrates: Accordingly, my noble Euthyphro, by your account some gods take one thing to be right, and others take another, and similarly with the honorable and the base, and good and bad. They would hardly be at variance with each other, if they did not differ on these questions. Would they?
> Euthyphro: You are right.
> Socrates: But . . . through disputing about these they are at variance and make war on one another. Isn't it so?
> Euthyphro: It would seem so.
> Socrates: And so, according to this argument, the same things, Euthyphro, will be holy and unholy.
> Euthyphro: That may be.
> Socrates: In that case, admirable friend, you have not answered what I asked you. . . . it seems that what is pleasing to the gods is also hateful to them. Thus, Euthyphro, it would not be strange at all if what you are now doing in punishing your father were pleasing to Zeus but hateful to Cronus and Uranus, and welcome to Hephaestus, but odious to Hera, and if any other of the gods disagree about the matter, satisfactory to some of them, and odious to others.
> (*Euthyphro*, 8a-b)

Now Euthyphro is in trouble with his definition of holiness as what is pleasing to the gods. Taken together with his other beliefs about the gods, it leads to a contradiction: Euthyphro is committed to asserting and denying the very same claim. Granting that the gods quarrel and disagree with one other, Euthyphro's definition implies that one and the same action can be both pleasing to some gods and displeasing to other gods. The very same action, then could turn out to be both holy and unholy – hardly a tolerable conclusion!

Euthyphro's confidence should be shaken, but he does not quite seem to get the point. After all, he feels that he is right in what he is doing and that the gods must agree with him. He tells Socrates that on the matter of prosecuting someone who has killed another, there will be no disagreement between the gods; if a person kills wrongfully, he ought to pay for it. At this point Socrates asks for proof that the gods would consider prosecuting one's father in such a case to be right. Euthyphro admits that he cannot provide any, though he is quite sure his view of what the gods would think is correct. After some energetic pursuit of the matter, Socrates turns their discussion in a slightly different direction. He argues that even if Euthyphro were (somehow) to demonstrate that the gods approved of his action, the original problem of saying what holiness is would remain unsolved.

> Socrates: . . . But suppose we now correct our definition, and say what the gods all hate is unholy, and what they love is holy, whereas what some of them love, and others hate, is either both or neither. Are you willing that we now define the holy and unholy in this way?
> Euthyphro: What is there to prevent us, Socrates? . . . (H)oliness is what the gods all love, and its opposite is what the gods all hate, unholiness. . . .
> Socrates: . . . Now think of this. Is what is holy holy because the gods approve it, or do they approve it because it is holy? (*Euthyphro*, 9c-d)

In this passage, Socrates works to get Euthyphro to explore his views further. He asks, in effect, whether the gods approve of things because of some property or quality these things have in themselves or whether, on the other hand, it is their very approval by the gods which makes those things holy. He has some trouble getting Euthyphro to comprehend this question. Eventually Socrates argues, and Euthyphro concedes, that what is holy is pleasing to the gods because of characteristics that make it holy. There is some quality or characteristic that makes for holiness. What is holy is not pleasing to the gods merely because it pleases them, or loved by them merely because they love it. If this were the case, the attitudes of the gods would be extremely arbitrary; they would have no reason for loving things, or finding them pleasing. Rather, the holy is pleasing, or loved, because of some quality that it has in its own right. Holiness, then, must exist independently of the attitudes of the gods, even though it evokes a response from them.

It is, perhaps, an *attribute* of holy actions and things that they are pleasing to the gods. But that fact does not *define* what is holy. When things please the gods, it is because there is something in their *essential character* that makes them pleasing to the gods. This is their (objective) holiness, and Socrates still wants to know what it is.

> Socrates: Consequently, Euthyphro, it looks as if you had not given me my answer . . . Say what the holy is, and never mind if the gods do love it, nor if it has some other attribute; on that we shall not split. Come, speak out. Explain the nature of the holy and unholy.
> (*Euthyphro*, 11b)

Euthyphro admits that he does not know how to explain his views to Socrates. He feels as though he is moving around in a circle. He had begun to launch the prosecution against his father, feeling sure that he was right in his attitude and his actions. When Socrates questioned him, he naturally appealed to his religious beliefs. He felt secure in his conviction that the gods approved of what he was doing. Euthyphro believed that he knew what piety (or holiness) was and made it the foundation of his practical moral decision-making. Now Socrates has upset all this. The dialogue ends with the implication that Euthyphro does not know what he thinks he knows, and therefore should not take his father to court.

> Socrates: If you did not know precisely what is holy and unholy, it is unthinkable that for a simple hireling you ever would have moved to prosecute your aged sire on a charge of murder. No, you would have feared to risk the wrath of the gods on the chance that you were not right, and would have been afraid of the talk of men. But now I am sure that you think you know exactly what is holy and what is not. So tell me, peerless Euthyphro, and do not hide from me what you judge it to be.
> Euthyphro: Another time, Socrates, for I am in a hurry and must be off this minute.
> (*Euthyphro*, 15d-e)

In his final statement Socrates ironically comments that he had had a "mighty expectation" of learning about piety and impiety from Euthyphro. But such was not to be. Both are ignorant of what piety, or holiness, is – but apparently only one of them knows that he does not know.

In the *Euthyphro*, a definition is questioned. But the dialogue is about much more than a definition. The character Euthyphro represents a certain attitude to life and moral problems – one still widely prevalent in our own time. Many people today, in considering moral issues such as abortion, euthanasia, and sexual morality, look to their religious beliefs and ideas about God's approval or disapproval. Euthyphro does the same; he attributes actions and attitudes to the gods, and appeals to them when he wants to resolve a moral problem. It is this attitude to religion, knowledge, and moral practise which is the real subject of the dialogue. Through his questions, Socrates shows not only that Euthyphro does not know what holiness or piety is, but that his attitude to moral problem-solving involves fundamental inconsistencies.

In the *Euthyphro*, Plato portrays Socrates as arguing that we cannot gain reliable moral knowledge by appealing to a religious being or beings. Three reasons are given to support this conclusion. First, we do not know what these beings do or think. Second, when there are several gods (as the Greeks believed) these gods might disagree with each other. (When it is believed that there is one God, as in Christianity, Judaism, or Islam, different texts and sects within each tradition interpret the word of God in different ways.) And third, the goodness (holiness) of actions must rest in their own characteristics and not merely in the attitudes divine beings have towards them. If there are gods or goddesses, or a God or Goddess, such beings would be morally righteous, and they would approve of good, or holy, actions because of some objective feature those actions have, and not as a matter of abitrary will. These features making for rightness or wrongness, goodness or badness, human beings could discover without appealing to speculative theories about divine beings. These conclusions from the *Euthyphro* retain their practical significance today, and are deemed to be correct by most moral philosophers.

As in the *Crito*, the Socrates of the *Euthyphro* is portrayed as thinking by arguing. In the *Crito* Socrates argued for his own conclusion: he should remain in Athens to undergo the punishment imposed on him by the court. In the *Euthyphro*, he argues against the view that religious belief can provide an adequate standard for moral judgment. In each context Socrates needs a place to start, something on which to base his case. Every argument, whether for a positive or a negative conclusion, must begin with premises which are granted by all of those arguing. In the *Crito*, Socrates worked from simple premises which were taken by him, and conceded by Crito, to be true. In the *Euthyphro*, Socrates worked from Euthyphro's own beliefs because he was showing that those beliefs about the gods and morality were logically inadequate. Socrates did not presume that those beliefs were true. He showed, rather, that they involved contradictions and inadequacies.

The Quest for Definition

Socrates was famous for his concern with general definitions. He believed that we do not know or understand what something is unless we can tell what it is, in a general statement of definition. Socrates believed that being virtuous requires knowledge, in the sense of having a general definition and account of what virtue is. One could not be courageous unless one knew what courage is; one could not be just unless one knew what justice is. In fact, Socrates believed that knowledge would guarantee virtue. He held – somewhat contrary to common sense – that no one does wrong knowingly. If a person drinks too much, or damages his or her health through sexual promiscuity, Socrates would insist that that person does not know, or does not "really" know, that these actions are harmful. The purpose of thinking was to achieve knowledge and understanding, especially knowledge of virtue which, he thought, would guarantee virtue itself.

Several of Plato's early dialogues show Socrates searching for definitions of fundamental moral concepts in the belief that an adequate general definition was essential for understanding and knowledge which, in turn, would guarantee morally right action and the preservation of one's soul. The *Laches* is a clear example. This dialogue portrays a discussion of courage, a topic which arises when two men, Lysimachus and Melesias, approach Socrates for advice about bringing up their sons. They wonder whether it would be a good idea to teach the boys to fight in armor. Plato sets the scene in such a way that, in a nice dramatic coincidence, two generals, Laches and Nicias, are also present. And Socrates himself had done military service in the Pelopponesian wars and shown considerable courage in battle.

Courage may be shown in other contexts – personal relationships, politics, sports, and daily life, for example. The discussion in the *Laches* tends, due to its context, to concentrate on courage in battle. Since the Greek city states were almost constantly warring amongst themselves at this time, the topic was a pressing one.

Would learning armored fighting make young men more courageous? This question leads Socrates and the others into a discussion of the nature of courage – despite warnings by Nicias.

> . . . anyone who is close to Socrates and enters into conversation with him is liable to be drawn into an argument, and whatever subject he may start, he will be continually carried round and round by him, until at last he finds that he has to give an account both of his present and past life, and when he is once entangled, Socrates will not let him go until he has completely and thoroughly sifted him.
> (*Laches*, 188a)

Perhaps it takes courage to argue with Socrates. But in any event, what is courage?

> Laches: Indeed, Socrates, I see no difficulty in answering. He is a man of courage who does not run away, but remains at his post and fights against the enemy [Definition One]. There can be no mistake about that.
> Socrates: . . . You would call a man courageous who remains at his post, and fights with the enemy?
> Laches: Certainly I should.
> Socrates: And so should I, but what would you say of another man who fights fleeing instead of remaining?
> (*Laches*, 190e-191a)

Laches has given only an *example* of courage, not an adequate *definition*. If courage, by *definition*, were to be remaining at one's post to fight with the enemy, then people who leave their post could not be courageous. And yet courageous soldiers could flee their post on horseback and come round from another angle to attack the enemy. Surely in doing so, they are courageous. Socrates wants a definition of courage and cowardice in general, not merely an example of one sort of courage. Definition One is too narrow. Socrates urges Laches to try again.

> Laches: I should say that courage is a sort of endurance of the soul [Definition Two]. . .
> Socrates: . . .And yet I cannot say that every kind of endurance is, in my opinion, to be deemed courage. Hear my reason. I am sure, Laches, that you would consider courage to be a very noble quality.
> Laches: Most noble, certainly.
> Socrates: And you would say that a wise endurance is also good and noble?
> Laches: Very noble.
> Socrates: But what would you say of a foolish endurance? Is not that, on the other hand, to be regarded as evil and hurtful?
> Laches: True.
> Socrates: And is anything noble which is evil and hurtful?

> Laches: I ought not to say that, Socrates.
> Socrates: Then you would not admit that sort of endurance to be courage – for it is not noble, but courage is noble?
> Laches: You are right.
> Socrates: Then, according to you, only the wise endurance is courage [Definition Three]?
> Laches: It seems so.
> (*Laches*, 192c-e)

Definition Two allows too many things to count as courage; it is too broad. Courage is not any and every endurance of the soul, because some endurance could be foolish. Courage, which is a virtue, could not be foolish. If courage is an endurance of the soul, it must be a *wise* endurance of the soul. This amendment to Definition Two yields Definition Three. But Definition Three poses problems of its own, because it raises the whole question of wisdom. When is endurance wise and when is it unwise?

With three definitions proposed and defeated, the inquiry has become quite frustrating. But Socrates urges Laches to continue. When discussing endurance, they should show endurance, and persist with their inquiry. They seem able to give examples of courage; thus they must somehow know something about it. Socrates himself, and presumably the generals as well, displayed courage in military situations. Why can they not produce a satisfactory definition of courage?

Admitting that they seem to be "tossing on the waves of argument," Socrates asks Nicias to contribute another definition. Nicias proposes Definition Four: courage is the knowledge (or wisdom) of that which inspires fear or confidence in war or anywhere else. But Definition Four provokes objections from Laches.

> Laches: . . . surely courage is one thing and wisdom another.
> Socrates: That is just what Nicias denies.
> Laches: Yes, that is what he denies; that is where he is so silly.
> Socrates: Suppose we instruct him instead of abusing him?
> Nicias: Certainly, Socrates, but having been proved to be talking nonsense himself, Laches wants to prove that I have been doing the same.
> Laches: Very true, Nicias, and you are talking nonsense. . .
> (*Laches*, 195b)

At this point the philosophical discussion seems to be degenerating into a quarrel. Laches seems to be feeling hurt because what he said was so roundly refuted, and he expresses his frustration by insulting Nicias and accusing him of talking nonsense. Socrates shifts the conversation, suggesting instruction instead of abuse.

Nicias admits that the knowledge of a craftsman or doctor would not necessarily amount to courage, but clings to his view that courage is a kind of knowledge. He amends his definition of courage as knowledge by specifying what sort of knowledge it is: courage is the knowledge of the grounds of hope and fear (Definition Five). Does Definition Five exclude cases which are genuinely cases of courage? Is it too narrow? Socrates points out that animals do not have knowledge. If courage is a kind of knowledge, then beasts like the lion and the leopard cannot be courageous. But this objection strikes Nicias as unimportant, and Socrates, hearing Nicias' response, agrees. Animals without knowledge are fearless, not courageous. A leopard may be fearless but it has no knowledge and thus no courage.

Socrates then poses another objection, based on an argument about knowledge and time. Hope and fear have to do with the future, and this seems right for courage; courage seems to concern the future, as it is a matter of how we respond to fearful things that might happen to us. But knowledge is unitary. There is not one knowledge for the future, another for the past, and another for the present. In medicine, for instance, one knows about health and sickness in general, not just health and sickness in the future.

> Socrates: And the same science has to do with the same things in the future or at any time?
> Nicias: That is true.
> Socrates: Then courage is a science which is concerned not only with the fearful and hopeful, for they are future only. Courage, like the other sciences, is concerned not only with good and evil of the future, but of the present and past, and of any time.
> Nicias: That, as I suppose, is true. . . [By implication, courage will turn out to be knowledge.]. . .
> Socrates: But then, Nicias, courage, according to this new definition of yours [Definition Five], instead of being only a part of virtue, will be all virtue?
> Nicias: It would seem so.
> Socrates: But we were saying that courage is one of the parts of virtue.
> Nicias: Yes, that was what we were saying.
> Socrates: And that is in contradiction with our present view.
> Nicias: That appears to be the case.
> Socrates: Then, Nicias, we have not discovered what courage is.
> Nicias: It seems not.
> (*Laches*, 199f)

Now they have reached contradictory conclusions. (Courage is a part of virtue; courage is knowledge, which is all of virtue. To know what to fear and what not to fear, one would have to know past, present, and future. Courage seems to turn into knowledge. But then it seemed knowledge was necessary for every virtue.) The dialogue ends on a note of scepticism. It would appear that none of the participants know what courage is.

Observations: The Legacy of Socrates

Unlike many other philosophers, including some who had preceded him, Socrates put forward no general theory of change, time, space, or matter. So far as we know, he did not speculate on the origins of the physical universe or the nature of the earth and the stars. Socrates was most concerned to raise questions about the meaning and purpose of human life and to reflect on fundamental moral concepts. Socratic thinking often led to more questions than answers. In another Platonic dialogue, the *Meno*, the character Meno compares Socrates to a sting ray, a fish whose sting makes people feel numb. Socratic questioning often had a numbing effect on people, making them feel almost helpless in their ignorance. But Socrates did not only ask questions; apparently he had reached some conclusions about virtue and knowledge. These are decidedly contrary to common sense, and are often referred to as the Socratic paradoxes.

> Virtue is knowledge.
> Nobody does harm (or wrong) willingly.
> No harm can come to a good person.

Socrates emphasized logic, argument, and reason, but understood these as techniques to be disciplined and directed towards a goal – the goal of understanding what it is to lead a virtuous human life. He spoke out against the Sophists, philosophical teachers who accepted payment and were willing to teach by means of argument and debate without subordinating these to serious moral goals. Unlike Socrates, the Sophists regarded logic, argument, and the art of speaking as techniques which could be put to any use, depending on what one wanted to do. Socrates was generally opposed to reaching decisions and conclusions purely on the basis of intuition or emotion. Interestingly, however, he is portrayed by Plato as having had a spiritual side. Socrates claimed to hear a "voice" which from time to time warned him not to do things he had been intending to do; despite his rationalism, he took that "voice" very seriously. Another spiritual aspect of Socrates' thinking is that he saw his pursuit of philosophy as a mission which he had been assigned by a god. But despite these aspects of his personality, Socrates' deepest commitment was to thinking through argument and conversation. He regarded emotion and intuition as a poor basis for making decisions and reaching conclusions.

At one point in another Platonic dialogue, the *Phaedo*, Socrates warns against "misology," a distrust of argument. He says that some people trust entirely in another person, only to find out that their trust has been misplaced, and as a result come to be *misanthropic*. That is, they come to despise humankind, because one person they trusted turns out to be untrustworthy. In a similar way, some people who are not very good at constructing and assessing arguments may put their entire trust in an argument, only to become seriously disillusioned when that argument turns out to contain a mistake. In an extreme reaction they may become *misologic*. This "misology" would be wrong, being based on a hasty generalization from one misleading case, and on a failure to appreciate that there are arguments of all degrees of merit – good, bad, mediocre, indifferent.

> . . . it would be a pitiful fate, if there were in fact some true and secure argument, and one that could be discerned, yet owing to association with arguments of the sort that seem now true and now false, a man blamed neither himself nor his own lack of skill, but finally relieved his distress by shifting the blame from himself to argument, and then finished out the rest of his life hating and abusing argument, and was deprived both of the truth and of knowledge of the things that are.
> . . . let's not admit into our soul the thought that there's probably nothing sound in arguments; but let's far rather admit that we're not yet sound ourselves, but must strive manfully to become sound. . .
> (*Phaedo*, 90e)

Even if discussion showed some arguments to be misleading and wrong, that would be no demonstration that there was anything wrong with *argument* as such. It might indicate only that the people arguing lacked skill or insight.

As portrayed by Plato, Socrates represents values which have been cherished throughout the history of Western thought: the values of reflection and understanding, of doing the right thing, and of leading the examined life. Plato wanted to show what sort of person Socrates had been, and did so by portraying him engaged in philosophizing. His early dialogues portray a Socrates who is a keen critical thinker and treasures his rational autonomy – that is, his independence and ability to think things through and reach his own conclusions. Socrates reflected on philosophical questions by discussing and arguing with others. But in the end, he accepted only those beliefs and ideas with which he, as an autonomous thinker, was rationally satisfied. Through questioning and conversation, Socrates sought to cultivate this same intellectual independence in other people.

There are still areas where Socrates' approach is relevant and useful today. Consider, for example, a recent newspaper article headlined, "Pronoia: Happiness may be hazardous to your health. That delicious feeling is actually a diagnosable mood disturbance that should be labelled a mental illness."

> In a *Journal of Medical Ethics* article titled, "A Proposal to Classify Happiness as a Psychiatric Disorder," Liverpool University psychologist Richard B. Bentall argues that the so-called syndrome of happiness is a diagnosable mood disturbance that should be included in standard taxonomies of mental illness. Happiness, he says, is "statistically abnormal, consists of a discrete cluster of symptoms, is associated with a range of cognitive abnormalities and probably reflects the abnormal functioning of the central nervous system.". . . In the journal *Social Problems*, Queen's College sociologist Fred H. Goldner applies the concept of pronoia – the antithesis of paranoia – to happy people. Instead of thinking others are saying horrible things behind his back, the pronoia sufferer believes others think well of him. Pronoids, according to the sociologist, live in a dangerously rose-tinted universe.

"Pronoia" is comparable to paranoia (which is commonly believed to be a mental disease), but is its emotional opposite. The paranoic thinks that everyone and everything are conspiring against him. So-called pronoids see reality as quite positive, and regard themselves as responsible for good things, which they are convinced are going to happen. If paranoia is a mental disorder, then pronoia is a mental disorder. So (apparently) happiness is a mental disorder.

The question which arises here is, at root, a Socratic one. Is it correct to regard pronoia as happiness? 'What is happiness?' we can almost hear Socrates asking. 'Whatever happiness is, is it not something good? And are not disorders of the mind something bad? Happiness is something good and it is not both good and bad, so happiness cannot be a *mental disease*.' To identify happiness with the newly diagnosed condition of "pronoia" is a mistake.

Happiness, surely, is not a matter of how we interpret the world or budget out responsibility for good or bad events. Then what is happiness? Is happiness a matter of experiencing pleasures? Of having fun? (What is pleasure? What is fun? What does it mean to have fun?) Perhaps fun is part of what makes people happy, but it cannot be the whole. Why not? There are happy people (for example, dedicated humanitarian workers) who seem to hardly ever have fun. But perhaps they have fun in different ways, peculiar to themselves. The same may be said of pleasure and happiness. Are there people who are happy and yet experience no pleasure? What is pleasure? What is happiness? It is, perhaps, a kind of overall satisfaction with our character and our lives, a kind of quiet general contentment. This definition, of course, is tentative and needs to be appraised further.

Many philosophers and others use thinking techniques similar to those of Socrates when such questions arise. Their background assumptions differ from those of Socrates – most take ordinary linguistic usage and common sense beliefs as the starting point for questions. (Happiness is something good; how then can it be a mental disorder – something bad?) But the approach is much the same, and it is applicable when a term incoporating central values is hard to pin down in words. What is a family? What does it mean to be a woman? To be a man? What is violence? What is terrorism? What is equality? We need understanding and accurate illuminating definitions, and we cannot get them merely by observation or by looking them up in the dictionary. We need thought and argument.

But thought and argument must start somewhere. For thinkers like Socrates who are critical and sceptical, that can be a problem. If we are sceptical about everything, we have no premises upon which to base arguments, no starting point for our thought. What was the basis for Socrates' thought? What did he use? Part of the answer is *logic* and *reason*. Socrates used basic logical reasoning, from *simple claims* deemed to be true. He drew out *implications* from suggestions and proposals made to him by others. For example,

If courage is x, then y.

Socrates had a basic commitment to *consistency*. If we reach inconsistent conclusions, we can be sure something is wrong. (For any statement, p, it can never be that both p and not-p are true.)

1. If courage is x, then courage is y.
2. It is not true that courage is y.
 Therefore,
3. It is not true that courage is x.

Such simple claims as premises (1) and (2) in this argument were granted both by Socrates and by his fellow arguers, in such dialogues as the *Crito* and the *Laches*.

In other cases, as in the *Euthyphro*, Socrates argues *from the beliefs of others*. Drawing out the implications of these beliefs, he arrives at a contradiction and thus shows that something is wrong. Sometimes Socrates argued on the basis of *analogy*: in the *Crito* he said that a person would take the best advice when caring for his body and so should take the best advice when caring for his soul.

Questions and objections can, of course, be raised against Socrates' method – and indeed these were almost certainly felt by Plato. One concern is the risk of generalized scepticism: if we apply the method in an absolutely general way, we may end up questioning everything. The method may seem unduly negative, capable of producing only negative results. Sometimes Socrates seems too harsh on others. Fellow citizens, invited to a chat, are asked to put forward suggestions and definitions, only to have these torn to shreds. The quarrelsomeness between Nicias and Laches hints that the Socratic method could set people against each other.

Another problem is that of selectivity. Why does Socrates choose to question definitions of piety and courage while other beliefs – that knowledge of health must be universal as to time (the *Laches*), or that remaining in a political state indicates support for its laws (the *Crito*) – remain unquestioned? Socrates was obviously convinced that there were universal and accurate definitions for conceptions like piety, courage, and justice. As Plato portrays him, he never doubted that the quest for these universal definitions made sense; nor did he question the existence of human souls or the gods. Had Socrates met another who was as adept at speaking and reasoning as himself, some of his own cherished beliefs might have been challenged.

In his middle and later dialogues, Plato continued to use Socrates as a central character, but he moved away from Socratic ideas to develop ambitious theories of his own.

2

Plato: The Shadows, the Cave, and the Dazzling Sun

Plato (427 - 347 B.C.) was a brilliant writer of philosophical dialogues. He came from a noble Athenian family and had considered a career in politics. Deeply shocked by Socrates' execution and deterred from engagement in politics by the sometimes violent competition for power in Greek city states, Plato left Athens for a period of travel to Italy, Sicily, and Egypt. He was later involved with practical politics, and attempted to influence Dionysius the younger, a ruler of Syracuse.

In addition to Socrates, Plato was influenced by other philosophical predecessors. One was Heraclitus, who lived around 500 B.C. and taught of constant change in a world of flux. Another was Parmenides, who lived around 480 B.C. and believed that not being was impossible, change was impossible, and reality was one unchanging thing. The attention to change and permanence in Plato's philosophy emerges from the contrasting teachings of Heraclitus and Parmenides. Plato was also influenced by Pythagoras, a mystic and a mathematical philosopher who saw the order in mathematics as the key to the order in the universe.

In Athens Plato established the Academy, a center for study and fellowship. The Academy included a garden, a grove of trees, a gymnasium, and other buildings. Participants had common meals – there was apparently quite an emphasis on healthy food – and enjoyed lectures and discussions on mathematics, geometry, harmonics, astronomy and some natural science, as well as philosophy. Ancestor of the Western university, the Academy lasted in one form or another in

Athens for some nine hundred years until it was destroyed by the Emperor Justinian in 529 A.D.

Though a highly theoretical thinker with a vivid imagination and mystical spirit, Plato's most cherished ambitions were deeply practical. His major goal in establishing the Academy was to train people so that they could acquire the understanding and values that would enable them to run a state properly. Plato believed that strenuous educational training for women and men of the highest abilities would enable them to be effective rulers in a just state.

Plato never appears as a character in his own dialogues. His dialogues convey a strong sense of Socrates' personality, but little of his own. He had considered being a poet or a playwright and these aspects of his talent are evident in his writings.

The Platonic dialogues are usually divided into three groups: the early ones (including the *Crito, Apology, Euthyphro,* and *Laches*) in which Plato portrays Socrates' character and ideas; the middle ones (including the *Meno, Phaedo, Republic,* and *Symposium*) in which he moves forward from the legacy of Socrates to develop his own theories; and the later dialogues (including the *Sophist, Theaetetus, Parmenides, Statesman,* and *Laws*), in some of which he expresses elaborate technical criticisms of his earlier ideas. The discussion here concentrates on the middle dialogues.

A major source of Plato's notions of thinking was his love and admiration for Socrates. Like Socrates, Plato sought absolute standards. He was unhappy with the shifting uncertainties of his time and with those who argued that human convention and decision determined right and wrong. Plato looked for fixed standards by which justice, truth, and beauty could be judged, seeking those standards as a stable basis for guiding human action. Socrates seems to have been confident that answers to his questions about the nature of justice, truth, and so on could be found; if anything, failure seems only to have strengthened his conviction that there were certainties to be discovered. One might fail to discover a good argument, or a solution to a problem on one particular occasion; one might even fail over a lifetime, but the answers were there to be discovered – somehow. Like Socrates, Plato stopped short of any dogmatic claim that he knew the answer to the essential natures of justice, truth, and the like; his philosophy was written in dialogues, allowing for the expression of several different viewpoints on the same topic. The purpose of thought, especially philosophical thought, was the quest for certain knowledge, not the absolute claim that such knowledge had been found.

To ask 'What is Courage?' or 'What is Virtue?,' as Socrates had, was to assume that the words "courage" and "virtue" had a single meaning which did not vary from one context to another. It seemed also to assume that there was such a thing as the essence, or definable core, of Courage or Virtue. All of this cried out for an explanation. What could be the basis for answers to questions about courage, virtue, beauty, life, and death? What could explain those answers and our access to them? Plato sought an account of the world which would render absolute standards and human awareness of them *intelligible.* In his quest for intelligibility, Plato began to reason and theorize, constructing a theory of reality and knowledge that went far beyond the thinking of Socrates.

Paradox and Recollection

In his dialogue the *Meno*, Plato portrays Socrates and Meno having a discussion about what virtue is and whether it can be taught. (In this and other middle dialogues, it is generally assumed that Socrates speaks for Plato.) Along the way, a central question about Socratic philosophizing is raised.

> Socrates: . . . So with virtue now. . . I am ready to carry out, together with you, a joint investigation and inquiry into what it is.
> Meno: But how will you look for something when you don't in the least know what it is? How on earth are you going to set up something you don't know as the object of your search? To put it another way, even if you come right up against it, how will you know whether what you have found is the thing you didn't know?
> Socrates: I know what you mean. Do you realize that what you are bringing up is the trick argument that a man cannot try to discover either what he knows or what he does not know? He would not seek what he knows, for since he knows it there is no need of the inquiry, nor what he does not know, for in that case he does not even know what he is to look for.
> Meno: Well, do you think it is a good argument?
> Socrates: No.
> (*Meno*, 80d-e)

The problem Meno describes has been called the paradox of inquiry. Inquiry does not make sense if we already know what we are trying to find out. But nor, apparently, does inquiry make sense if we do not know what we are trying to find out. People do inquire into things, so surely, somehow, inquiry must make sense. But how does it make sense?

Plato responds to the problem of inquiry by inventing a third possibility. We may have a kind of latent knowledge, a knowledge which we are not yet able to express, which is based on previous experience. Thinking, arguing, and reflecting can make us aware of this latent knowledge. Learning, Plato suggests, is possible because it is really recollection. The soul is distinct from the body and existed apart from the body in a previous life, where it possessed knowledge that we in our human lives have mostly forgotten. We can *recollect* that knowledge. Our recollecting of it is what we call learning. Socrates (representing Plato's own views at this point) speculated that the soul is immortal and has been born many times. In another world it had knowledge, which it can recall in this world, if it searches in the right way.

Meno expresses some doubts about the view that knowledge is recollection. Socrates then seeks to demonstrate this theory by working with a slave boy, and getting him to solve a problem in geometry by asking him questions. The boy initially gives a wrong answer to the problem of how to construct a square which is double the area of a given square. But by Socrates' questions he is able to reason about the problem and understand that his first answer was wrong. He does not know what he thought he knew. He is then led forward, again by careful questioning, to the correct answer.

> Socrates: At present these opinions, being newly aroused, have a dreamlike quality. But if the same questions are put to him on many occasions and in different ways, you can see that in the end he will have a knowledge on the subject as accurate as anybody's.
> Meno: Probably.
> Socrates: This knowledge will not come from teaching but from questioning. He will recover it for himself.
> (*Meno*, 85d)

The process of recovery is one of recollection. The story of the soul's life in another world, told by priests and priestesses, is admittedly open to doubt. Yet to Plato it seems to be a constructive and fruitful hypothesis – a better hypothesis on which to guide one's quest for knowledge and understanding than the pessimistic view that learning and knowledge are impossible. On the hypothesis that the soul has knowledge before birth and can recollect knowledge in this life, the search for knowledge makes sense. Unencumbered by the body and its pains and pleasures, the soul would achieve direct and pure knowledge, perhaps a sort of "vision."

In the other world, Plato theorized, the soul would know, or behold, timeless entities called the Forms. Plato introduced the Forms to point to concepts which transcend sense experience. He wanted to replace unreliable opinion by firmly grounded knowledge, and give an account of what would be known by those who found answers to the Socratic questions. Various individual actions may be holy or unholy; various individual things may be beautiful or ugly. But none of these individual items can give us an understanding of the general nature of holiness, unholiness, beauty, or ugliness. Things that are beautiful in one context may be ugly in another. The abstract quality, or essence, of holiness or beauty is not to be identified with variable particular actions or things. Somehow, we have concepts and standards that were not gained merely from our experience of this world, and these concepts guide our thought. If we are to understand what holiness is, or what beauty is, we must know an abstract concept that is independent of experience. And that is a Form.

Some of the clearest arguments for the existence of the Forms are found in the *Phaedo*, a moving dialogue set on the day of Socrates' death. In this dialogue Socrates is depicted discussing the immortality of the soul with his friends Phaedo, Simmias, Cebes, and several others. In the *Phaedo* the doctrine of recollection is linked directly with the existence of Forms. What the soul knows in a previous life, and what explain its ability to learn and recognize truths in this world, are timeless entities which perfectly embody standards or conceptions that are imperfectly imitated in the material world. One example is that of equality. Socrates argues that we do know equality and that we did not get our idea of equality solely from things like logs and stones.

> - 'We say, don't we, that there is something *equal*? I don't mean a log to a log, or a stone to a stone, or anything else of that sort, but some further thing beyond all those, the equal itself: are we to say that there is something or nothing?'
> - 'We most certainly are to say that there *is*' said Simmias, 'unquestionably.'
> - 'And do we know what it is?'
> - 'Certainly.'
> - 'Where did we get the knowledge of it? Wasn't it from the things

> we were just mentioning: on seeing logs or stones or other equal things, wasn't it from these that we thought of that object, it being different from them? Or doesn't it seem different to you? Look at it this way: don't equal stones and logs, the very same ones, sometimes seem equal to one, but not to another?'
> - 'Yes, certainly.'
> - 'But now, did the equals themselves ever seem to you unequal, or equality inequality?'
> - 'Never yet, Socrates.'
> - 'Then those equals, and the equal itself, are not the same.'
> - 'By no means, Socrates, not in my view.'
> - 'But still, it is from those equals, different as they are from that equal, that you have thought of and got the knowledge of it?'
> - 'That's perfectly true.'
> (*Phaedo*, 74a10 - c10)

Things in the world are not the Forms, but they help us to know the Forms. Things like logs are equal to one thing, not equal to another. Their equality is, in this sense, relative to something else; thus they cannot provide us with an *absolute* standard of equality. They help us to recollect something else, "the equal itself." We implicitly know a standard of equality, and are able to use it. By using that standard we can judge objects like logs to be equal or to be unequal. This world could not give us a fixed unambiguous standard of equality. So we must have become aware of the standard or Form in some other way – perhaps in a previous existence when the intellect was not distracted by the senses, and we were not handicapped by our bodies.

This argument can be generalized. Nowhere in the world is there a perfect circle, a perfect triangle, or a perfectly straight line. Nor, for that matter, is there in this world an example of perfect courage, a perfectly just state, or absolute beauty or holiness. Yet we have ideas of these things. What are these conceptions, and where did they come from?

> - 'Now if, having got it before birth, we were born in possession of it, did we know, both before birth and as soon as we were born, not only the equal, the larger and the smaller, but everything of that sort? Because our present argument concerns the beautiful itself, and the good itself, and the just and holy, no less than the equal; in fact, as I say, it concerns everything on which we set this seal, "*what it is*" in the questions we ask and in the answers we give. And so we must have got pieces of knowledge of all those things before birth.'
> (*Phaedo*, 75c8 - d5)

The Forms are unique conceptual entities which are ideal exemplars, or paradigms, of things in this world. Earthly things can be regarded as imitations of these perfect concepts – the just state is an imperfect imitation of the Just State, a circle of the Perfect Circle, a triangle of the Ideal Triangle, beauty of Absolute Beauty, and so on.

We must think carefully in order to prevent ourselves from being distracted by incidental things when we try to understand what is essential in our concepts or standards. Consider, for example, geometry. Geometric proofs fascinated Plato because they could provide certain knowledge which, while grounded in sense, was about mathematical objects. In doing geometry, a person has to know what to pay attention to. Diagrams are used, but in a geometric proof diagrams do not represent sensory things; they represent geometric conceptions which, strictly speaking, are conceptions of reason. To use a diagram properly a person must know what to attend to and what to ignore. A drawing of a circle may be in chalk or in the sand; it may have occasional wriggles or variations in the thickness of the line; it may seem interesting or uninteresting. But all these experienced incidentals are irrelevant from the point of view of understanding the geometric properties of a *circle*. Plato argued that understanding what is essential and what is merely incidental presupposes that we know what a circle is, and such knowledge involves considerable abstraction from sense experience. Similarly, beauty, justice, equality, and other absolutes are not understood in experiencing the changing things of the everyday world, but rather by appropriately abstracting from our mundane experience.

The absolute Form of Beauty is discussed in the *Symposium*, a dialogue set at a feast where the guests are giving speeches about love. Plato portrays Socrates as giving an unusual speech in which he talks movingly about the Form of Beauty. Socrates attributes his knowledge to Diotima, "a woman of wisdom," and reports what Diotima said to him. Passion and appreciation for the beauties of human bodies, he says, may lead to an appreciation of the beauty of human souls and ultimately to the Form of Beauty. Beauty Itself is changeless and stable. It is not beautiful in one respect and ugly in another, nor beautiful to some people and ugly to others. It is nonphysical, not of this world.

> It is not anywhere in another thing, as in an animal, or in earth, or in heaven, or in anything else, but itself by itself with itself; it is always one in form; and all the other beautiful things share in that, in such a way that when those others come to be or pass away, this does not become the least bit smaller or greater nor suffer any

> change. So when someone rises by stages . . . and begins to see this beauty, he has almost grasped his goal. This is what it is to go aright, or be led by another, into the mystery of Love: one goes always upwards for the sake of this Beauty, starting out from beautiful things and using them like rising stairs: from one body to two and from two to all beautiful bodies, then learning beautiful things, and from these lessons he arrives in the end at this lesson, which is learning of this very Beauty, so that in the end he comes to know just what it is to be beautiful.
> (*Symposium*, 211A - D)

Physical beauty inspires our love and our passions, but it is imperfect because it passes. Beautiful young women and men will become middle-aged, then old; they will lose their rosy glow and physical beauty. But Beauty Itself will not change. If one were ever to experience Beauty Itself one would no longer measure beauty by earthly standards.

Plato was convinced that we can learn and acquire knowledge by recognizing absolute standards which are somehow real, though they do not derive solely from our experience of the changing physical world. Like other thinkers of his day – and many philosophers since – he was tremendously impressed by proofs in geometry. Geometric proofs offer certain knowledge, showing that for human beings who use their intellect and take care to reason correctly, secure and well-established knowledge is possible. There are absolutes, and human beings can come to know them. There must be an explanation for such knowledge. Plato believed that human beings could not gain knowledge of these absolutes from sensory experience in the ordinary world. Our senses are unreliable; standards are relative to different needs and different contexts; people disagree; and the objects of sense are constantly changing. So how is our knowledge of absolute standards in mathematics to be understood? The answer, Plato theorized, lay in our being implicitly aware, and capable of recollecting, absolute conceptions known as the Forms. One explanation for our latent knowledge is that the soul existed before birth in a disembodied state, and in its previous existence gained such conceptions as Equality, Beauty, Triangularity, Circularity, Goodness, Holiness, and Justice.

> - 'Then let's go back to those entities to which we turned in our earlier argument. Is the Being itself, whose being we give an account of in asking and answering questions, unvarying and constant, or does it vary? Does the equal itself, the beautiful itself, *what each thing is* itself, that which *is*, ever admit of any change

> whatever? Or does *what each of them is* being uniform alone by itself, remain unvarying and constant, and never admit of any kind of alteration in any way or respect whatever?'
> - 'It must be unvarying and constant, Socrates,' said Cebes.
> - 'But what about the many beautiful things, such as men or horses or cloaks or anything else at all of that kind? Or equals, or all things that bear the same name as those objects? Are they constant, or are they just the opposite of those others, and practically never constant at all, either in relation to themselves or to one another?'
> - 'That is their condition,' said Cebes, 'they are never unvarying.' (*Phaedo*, 78c10 - e5)

The Forms do not change. Things in the world do change. So the Forms cannot be things in the world. The realm of experience is confusing and cannot provide us with fixed concepts and absolute standards. Knowledge, Plato reasoned, must be unchanging and clear, and must be of unchanging objects. Precision in knowledge and thought requires standards, which do not come from experience alone. Plato tended to draw a sharp contrast between thought and sensation, and believed that sensing was inferior to thinking.

Plato's emphasis on thought is again apparent in the *Phaedo*, where the topic of the soul and its immortality has poignant dramatic importance because Socrates is about to die. Socrates tries to persuade his companions that his bodily death is no tragedy. He will be leaving this world for a better one; his body is not his real self. The real and true Socrates is not the physical snub-nosed Socrates. It is the soul of Socrates, a soul only temporarily located in a body. Philosophy is another way in which a person can liberate the soul from the encumbrances of the body.

> . . . Lovers of knowledge recognize that when philosophy takes their soul in hand, it has been literally bound and glued to the body, and is forced to view the things that are as if through a prison, rather than alone by itself; and that it is wallowing in utter ignorance. Now philosophy discerns the cunning of the prison . . . As I say, then, lovers of knowledge recognize that their soul is in that state when philosophy takes it in hand, gently reassures it and tries to release it, by showing that inquiry through the eyes is full of deceit, and deceitful too is inquiry through the ears and other senses; and by persuading it to withdraw from these, so far as it need not use them, and by urging it to collect and gather itself together, and to be true to none other but itself, whenever alone by itself . . . and not to regard as real what it observes by other means, and what varies in various things; that kind of thing is sen-

> sible and seen, whereas the object of its own vision is intelligible and invisible.
> (*Phaedo*, 82d6 - 83b5)

In thought, the soul should be independent, trusting nothing but its own judgment, and refusing to be distracted by the varying objects of the material world.

The Divided Line

The contrast between knowledge and opinion was central in Plato's thought. Obviously, people can have opinions, or beliefs, which do not amount to knowledge. Sometimes those opinions are correct and quite useful. We may consider the contrast between a person who knows the way to Larissa (a Greek town) and another who merely has a correct belief or opinion about how to get there (perhaps someone else who knew told him). Either person could get to Larissa or guide other people there. But there is an important difference between knowledge and belief. Opinions, or beliefs, are not "tied down" the way knowledge is. If a person had a correct opinion about how to get to Larissa and then someone else came along and contradicted it, his initial opinion would be unsettled. He would now hold a different opinion, or perhaps none at all. Opinions or beliefs are unstable, whereas knowledge is fixed and stable.

> Socrates: . . . True opinions are a fine thing and do all sorts of good so long as they stay in their place, but they will not stay long. They run away from a man's mind; so they are not worth much until you tether them by working out the reason. That process, my dear Meno, is recollection, as we agreed earlier. Once they are tied down, they become knowledge, and are stable. That is why knowledge is something more valuable than right opinion. What distinguishes one from the other is the tether.
> (*Meno*, 98a-b)

Plato argued that what ties an opinion down is having an account, which provides reasons which show and explain why the opinion is true. (At that point it becomes more than an opinion.) To make an opinion reliable, we have to work out the reason for it – understand *why* things are as they are.

Plato stresses the contrast between knowledge and opinion again in the *Republic*. The *Republic* is about justice both within the state and within an individual person; it also contains a substantial discussion of education and knowledge. Plato considers objects of the material world to be inadequate, by themselves, as objects of knowledge. They are too changeable and are known only through the senses, which themselves are unreliable. To have knowledge, as opposed to opinion or belief, it is necessary to exercise the mind, abstracting from fluctuating sensory experience, and becoming aware of intelligible objects.

Plato contrasts the visible material world with the invisible intelligible world, seeing the former as a realm of which we characteristically have opinions or beliefs, and the latter as one of which we may hope for knowledge. The intelligible world is more clear than the visible world.

> - . . . You surely apprehend the two types, the visible and the intelligible.
> - I do.
> - Represent them then, as it were, by a line divided into two unequal sections and cut each section again in the same ratio – the section, that is, of the visible and that of the intelligible order – and then as an expression of the ratio of their comparative clearness and obscurity you will have, as one of the sections of the visible world, images. By images I mean first shadows, and then reflections in water and on surfaces of dense, smooth, and bright texture, and everything of that kind, if you apprehend.
> - I do.
> - As the second section assume that of which this is a likeness or an image, that is, the animals about us and all plants and the whole class of objects made by man.
> - I so assume it, he said.
> - Would you be willing to say, said I, that the division in respect of reality and truth or the opposite is expressed by the proportion – as is the opinable to the knowable, so is the likeness to that of which it is a likeness?
> - I certainly would.
> (*Republic*, 509d-510)

This passage describes the Divided Line, which Plato uses as an analogy for knowledge and belief, or opinion. Knowledge is clearer than Belief and its objects are more real. We may represent these Platonic views by drawing the line in such a way that the greater part represents Knowledge. If we make the area representing Knowledge (A) twice as large as that representing Belief (B) then the divisions within Knowledge (Aa and Ab) and Belief (Ba and Bb) should have the same proportion.

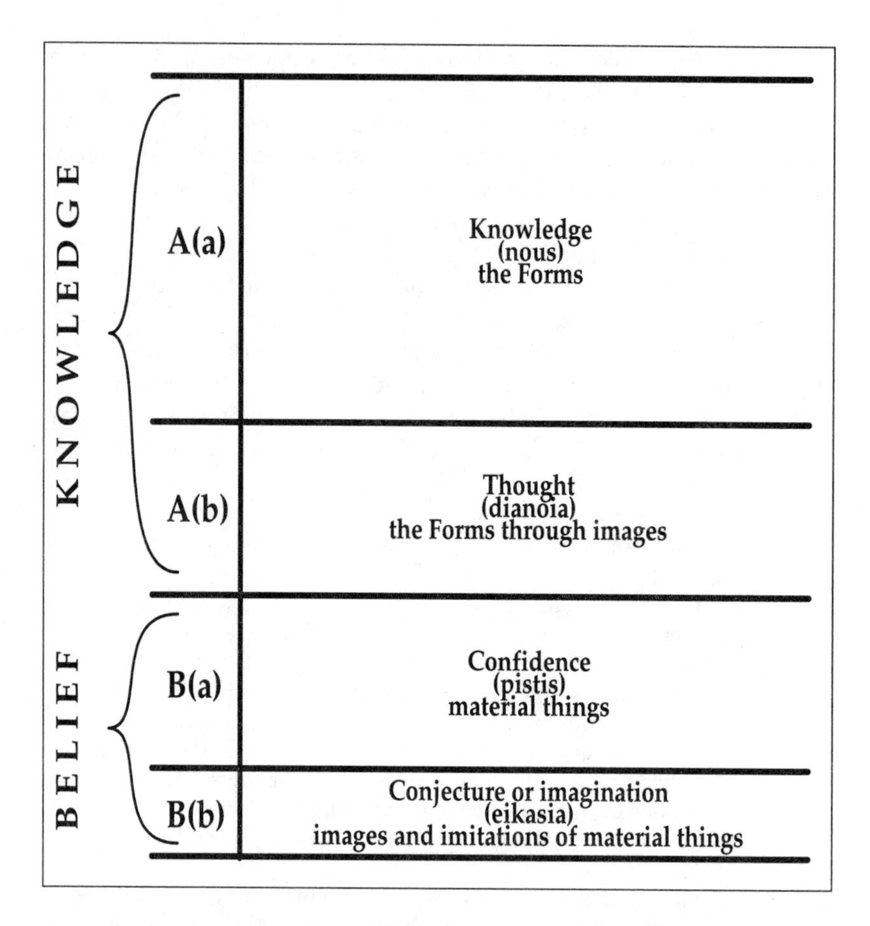

Of material objects in the physical world, Plato says here that we can have no knowledge when we do not know the Forms. Still, there are better and worse opinions or beliefs, and more and less stable objects of opinion. So far as the material world is concerned, we may have belief about material things (flowers, mountains, and so on) or only about shadows or imitations of those things (paper flowers, cardboard mountains, and so on). To represent this better quality of Belief, wherein we are at least able to distinguish between actual objects and imitations of them, the segment (Ba) is twice as long as (Bb). Ba represents the more reliable belief, *confidence* (*pistis*, in Greek) and Bb represents the shakier belief, *conjecture* or *imagination* (*eikasia*).

The A section of the line represents Knowledge. The proper objects of Knowledge are the Forms, but along segment A, a division can again be drawn. The highest type of Knowledge (Aa) is referred to as knowledge or understanding (*nous*) and the lower type (Ab) as thought (*dianoia*). The objects of thought are the Forms, yet at this stage knowledge is somewhat incomplete. We depend on some unproven assumptions and still have to use images to represent the Forms. Plato's example of this sub-segment is geometry. In geometry, images (for example a drawn circle) are used to represent abstractions (the form Circle), and unproven assumptions are used in proofs. With higher knowledge (*nous*) there is no need to rely on assumptions and no need to use images to represent Forms.

The Divided Line represents Plato's conviction that in the highest form of Knowledge, we would know timeless intelligible entities – the Forms – and we would know them so as to completely understand them, needing no unproven hypotheses and no sensory images to assist us in this understanding. This knowledge (Aa) would be superior to thought (Ab), confidence (Ba) and imagination (Bb).

Dialectic

How can we move beyond hypotheses so as to have no unproven assumptions, and reach the highest level of Knowledge? The process is one of dialectic – philosophical questioning, responding, arguing, and discussing. We may need to explore on the basis of hypotheses. Not having knowledge, we can still consider a hypothesis, explore its consequences and the reasons for it, and try to get somewhere. If we find that a hypothesis has false consequences, we reject it. If a hypothesis has no false consequences, it may be true. Thinking that it may be true, we can try to find reasons for it – seeking a higher hypothesis from which it could be derived. That higher hypothesis could be tested by examining its consequences. Then, if there were again no false consequences, we could move on to a still higher hypothesis, from which we could try to derive the second one and which we would test in turn.

This whole process is part of Plato's dialectic. To achieve *nous*, the highest Knowledge, we would have to have engaged in dialectic to such a point that our knowledge would depend on no unproven assumptions. Assumptions would be first treated as hypotheses and then, through the power of dialectic, we would rise to a fundamental starting point which did not depend on any assumption. Having reached the starting point, we could proceed downward to deduce a conclusion, using only knowledge of the Forms. Dialectic, then, is supposed to enable us to find a fundamental truth which needs no proof and from which all our assumptions can be derived.

But what is this dialectic? How do we practice it? How will we know when we have reached the fundamental point from which all our other knowledge will flow? Plato offers no complete answers to these questions. Apart from the method of hypothesis, it seems that dialectic is basically a matter of of arguing and meeting challenges to one's arguments. Typically, it is a social process of rigorous philosophical examination and counter-examination.

For Plato as for Socrates, the best thinking and reasoning was oral and done with others. To think alone or while reading was known to be possible but was not regarded as especially desirable. In the *Theaetetus*, a later dialogue on knowledge, Plato described a person thinking alone as being in dialogue with himself. Emerging from a largely oral culture, Plato believed that we should trust more in the results worked out with others in argument and discussion than in things we read. We cannot ask a book a question and get its response. Plato and Socrates trusted in spoken argument more than in written argument. Plato's preference for oral philosophizing was part of Socrates' legacy, and perhaps one reason that he wrote his philosophy in dialogues. One may sometimes have the impression, from the talk of the Forms, that Plato was some kind of dogmatic absolutist, claiming to possess the whole truth. However, such an impression is misleading. Plato was seeking absolute truth but was far from sure that he had found it. His dialogues contained many criticisms of his own views; sometimes, in fact, it is not even clear which character in a dialogue is speaking for Plato. The dialogue style is appropriate for Plato, who believed in the usefulness of dialectic. Reasoning dialectically means being aware of possible objections to our views and seeking to respond to them adequately. Plato believed that if this process is carried out skillfully by people of real talent, with sufficient dedication and energy, they may be able to reach the highest Knowledge, and an understanding of the Forms.

Dialectic and Thinking

In dialectic there are characteristically two distinct, apparently cogent, arguments for conclusions that are inconsistent with each other. Dialectic is based on pairs, or series, of arguments leading in incompatible directions. Sometimes dialectic is purely destructive: we are left with no knowledge, nor even any secure beliefs. But dialectic may be constructive as well: through a dialectical process we may establish a thesis by refutation. (Either A or B is right; B must be wrong because of C; therefore A is right.) Dialectic encourages us to grapple with puzzles and problems that we might not have perceived before. Typically, one argument in a dialectical process serves as a challenge to another, and the reader or listener is forced to reexamine his or her beliefs. Practicing the dialectic requires hard thinking.

If, like Plato, we consider thought to be a dialogue in the soul, we can think of opinions as various stages in that dialogue. When we hold an opinion, we may ask ourselves questions about it and sort through various objections and arguments that come to mind. When we do this, it is as though we are talking to ourselves, arguing with ourselves, back and forth. Here is an imaginary example, in which a thinker in dialogue with herself questions what was said at a funeral. In this example, "Point" and "Counterpoint" represent a point of view and objections raised against it.

> Point - At the funeral they said Betty would survive and be with Jesus. Her body is being cremated, so this must mean her mind, or soul, is supposed to continue without any body. Betty survives, then, as a mind or a soul. Even though her body has been cremated she exists somewhere else, in heaven, as a soul, and she can still feel and think and communicate.
> Counterpoint - But what and where is heaven? How do we know there is a heaven? We knew Betty as a person in a body. How can she be merely a soul? Could an immaterial soul be Betty, the Betty that I knew and loved? Her brain will be cremated. What is the relation between the brain and the soul? The body and the person? How can the person who was Betty survive as a soul?
> Point - I don't know what heaven is, what the soul is. Do I know she survives? Surely not! The priest is just saying this to reassure us. It doesn't make sense. How can it be true?
> Counterpoint - It must make sense to a lot of people, or they wouldn't be reassured. Presumably the priest believes this. Why should your (my) doubts be right? What's wrong with you (me)?

When we try to sort out such an emotional and perplexing topic, we are, in a way, in dialogue with ourselves. We *ask ourselves* what we truly believe and explore the reasons why. In a sense, we talk to ourselves, posing questions to ourselves, often realizing that we have no good answers, and sometimes revising our ideas on the basis of such a discovery.

The Sun and the Cave

In Book VII of the *Republic,* Plato introduces a further model for his theory of knowledge in the analogy of the Cave. Fundamentally, the story of the Cave is an image for education.

> - Next, said I, compare our nature in respect of education and its lack to such an experience as this. Picture men dwelling in a sort of subterranean cavern with a long entrance open to the light on its entire width. Conceive them as having their legs and necks fettered from childhood, so that they remain in the same spot, able to look forward only, and prevented by the fetters from turning their heads. Picture further the light from a fire burning higher up and at a distance behind them, and between the fire and the prisoners and above them a road along which a low wall has been built, as the exhibitors of puppet shows have partitions before the men themselves, above which they show the puppets.
> - All that I see, he said.
> - See also, then, men carrying past the wall implements of all kinds that rise above the wall, and human images and shapes of animals as well, wrought in stone and wood and every material, some of these bearers presumably speaking and others silent.
> - A strange image you speak of, he said, and strange prisoners.
> - Like to us, I said. For, to begin with, tell me do you think that these men would have seen anything of themselves or of one another except the shadows cast from the fire on the wall of the cave that fronted them?
> - How could they, he said, if they were compelled to hold their heads unmoved through life?
> (*Republic,* 514-515)

These strange prisoners are like us, Plato says. Trapped in our bodies just as these poor creatures are fettered in the Cave, we are, in our mundane lives, prevented from seeing anything but shadows and images. With no awareness of the Forms, imitations are all that we know, and we naturally mistake these imitations for the real thing.

A modern analogy for Plato's Cave is that of the movie theatre. At the movies, people sit facing forward to the screen, which they attend to avidly if the film is good. What they see on the screen is not reality, but only images that result from the work of the projectionist at the back of the theatre. If people had lived their whole lives in a movie theatre, and had never seen the world outside, they would find a move from the darkness into daylight extremely confusing.

Similarly, the prisoners in the Cave would experience confusion and disorientation were they to be released and move from darkness into light – just as people in Socrates' Athens had experienced disorientation when Socrates proved to them that they did not know what they had supposed themselves to know.

> - When one was freed from his fetters and compelled to stand up suddenly and turn his head around and walk and to lift up his eyes to the light, and in doing all this felt pain and, because of the dazzle and glitter of the light, was unable to discern the objects whose shadows he formerly saw, what do you suppose would be his answer if someone told him that what he had seen before was all a cheat and an illusion, but that now, being nearer to reality and turned toward more real things, he saw more truly? . . . [D]o you not think that he would be at a loss and that he would regard what he formerly saw as more real than the things now pointed out to him?
> - Far more real, he said.

Such a person could eventually learn to contemplate real things outside the Cave. He or she would understand imitations and shadows for what they were, recognize the sun, moon, and stars, and eventually gain the strength to gaze at the Sun itself. Such a person would see that the Sun provides the seasons of the year and is, in a sense, the cause of all things on earth. One who had left the Cave to see the real world instead of shadowy and dark imitations of it, would find the Cave gloomy and the preoccupations of the other prisoners petty and absurd. Nevertheless, Plato argues, such a man or woman has an obligation to go back into the Cave to apply new wisdom, teaching and leading those still captives of darkness. Having seen the Truth, such a person is a philosopher fit to be king or queen; he or she should return to the Cave and use his or her acquired wisdom to govern the state.

In this analogy, the Cave stands for the visible realm of images and objects, and the world outside the Cave for the intelligible realm of the Forms. The Sun represents one Form in particular, the Form of the Good.

> . . . in the region of the known the last thing to be seen and hardly seen is the idea of good, and that when seen it must needs point us to the conclusion that this is indeed the cause for all things of all that is right and beautiful, giving birth in the visible world to light, and the author of light and itself in the intelligible world being the authentic source of truth and reason, and that anyone

> who is to act wisely in private or public must have caught sight of this.
> (*Republic*, 517b-c)

Outside the Cave a former prisoner can eventually contemplate the Sun itself and understand it to be the fundamental support of the whole order of things. The Sun represents the Form of the Good, which is the highest Form and the one responsible for the order among all the others. After a long process of strenuous philosophical dialectic, some especially skilled men and women may achieve insight into the absolute structure of reality by apprehending the Forms and, in particular, the highest Form, the Form of the Good.

What sort of thinking is going on when someone apprehends the Form of the Good? Plato did not claim to explain the insight in words. He seems to have had a mystical vision which gave him a conviction of the oneness and order of things. Perhaps he sought insight into a single fundamental truth, from which all truths could be logically derived. Another possibility is that this final state of knowledge is one in which there is an understanding of the wholeness of things. All the hypotheses of earlier stages are fitted together, ordered, and justified with reference to each other.

Observations

Plato introduced into Western philosophy a series of related dualisms: soul/body, thought/sensation, reason/emotion, intellect/imagination, form/matter, knowledge/opinion, and others. These dualisms have been tremendously influential in Western philosophical thought and, indeed, in Western religion and culture. Sometimes Plato exaggerated contrasts, failing to notice a middle area where supposed opposites may be found in combination; reason and emotion, for instance, may work together. Interestingly, Plato's famous dualisms tended to imply more than distinctions; they were also the source of central judgments of value. One side of each duality is judged higher or better than the other: soul over body, thought over sensation, reason over emotion, intellect over imagination, form over matter, knowledge over opinion. These dichotomies, and the value judgments that accompany them, have been fundamental in much subsequent Western thought.

Plato's ideas about dialectic can stand independently of his theory of Forms. But his notion that thinking must be independent of sense and his model of the Divided Line are closely linked to the theory. Plato was convinced that we must transcend the world of sense and particulars in order to have genuine knowledge of universals. The theory of Forms was a response to the existence of standards – especially in the areas of mathematics and ethics – that appear not to be derivable solely from sense experience. Today, as in Plato's own time, the theory leads to as many questions as answers. Plato posited the theory of Forms in response to questions posed by human knowledge in mathematics and ethics. But that theory itself generated further questions of its own.

What exactly is a Form? Where and what is the realm in which Forms exist? How are the Forms related to each other, and to the material world? Are there forms for every quality and thing? Is there, for instance, a form for Mud? For Hair? For Dirt? Do Forms possess the qualities that they are posited to explain? For example, is the Form for Equality equal? If so, what is it equal to?

Is the Form for Beauty beautiful? Apparently so; it is Beauty sublime. Yet, as Plato himself came to recognize, this leads to a logical problem. Suppose, as Plato seems to have supposed in his middle dialogues, that things are beautiful because they "participate" in or "imitate" the form of Beauty Itself. Then suppose (as seems reasonable according to this theory) that Beauty Itself is also beautiful. Being beautiful is a matter of participating in a Form of Beauty. If that is the case, Beauty Itself must be beautiful because it participates in a further Form. We may call this further Form Beauty2, to distinguish it from the first Form, which we will call Beauty1. The same argument can be repeated for Beauty2. Is Beauty2 beautiful? If so there must be a further Form Beauty3, in which it "participates" and in virtue of which it is beautiful. The same logical problem will arise again and again. Thus an infinite number of Forms for Beauty will be needed. Thus, Plato's theory demands an infinite series of Forms, or an infinite regress.

This argument, usually referred to as the Third Man argument, implies a need for more and more entities to fulfill the demand for explanation. An infinite regress is not a satisfactory consequence. (We should not have to postulate the existence of an infinite number of entities in order to explain why two flowers are beautiful!) The theory of Forms seems to break down from a logical point of view – as was shown in arguments that Plato himself presented in his late dialogue, *Parmenides*.

Seeing that we rely on conceptions which are too exact to be based on sense experience alone, Plato pointed to problems about mathematical and ethical knowledge that are still being debated to

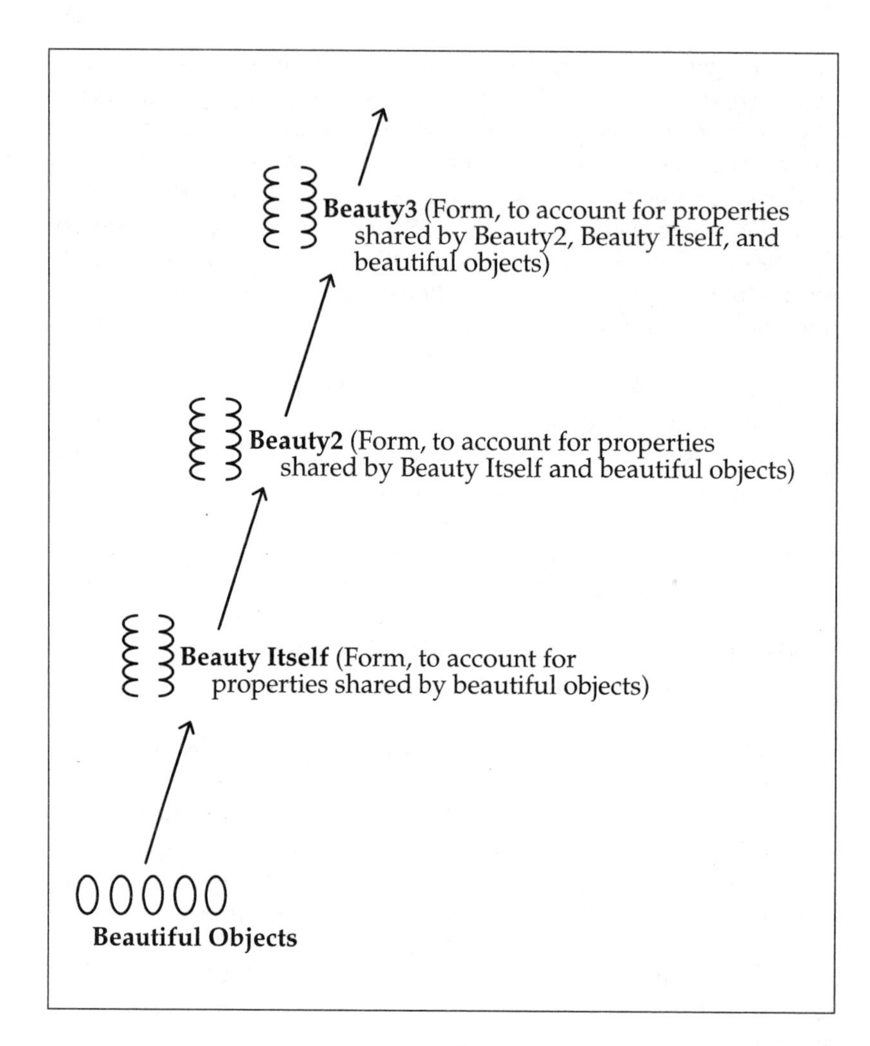

this day. Few modern thinkers believe in the Platonic Forms—though some, to be sure, still speak as though there are fixed concepts to be discovered. And few claim to have resolved the problems Plato was dealing with when he proposed his theory. Haunted by the Heraclitian description of the material world as constantly changing, and driven by his longing for absolute standards, Plato was led to posit entities and states of awareness in another realm. But he did not theorize in a dogmatic way. One aspect of Plato's legacy, his conception of thought as abstraction – moving away from sensation and the body to the purely intellectual – is open to the criticism of offering rationalistic temptations with too few checks on thought. Another aspect is Plato's myths, analogies, and stories.

Myth, Imagination, and Play

Quite apart from Plato's theory about Forms and the dialectic, there seems to be another message in his philosophical dialogues about a more imaginative and flexible style of thought. Writing in dialogues, Plato did not claim to possess the ultimate truth, still less to be able to put it into words. At points Socrates seems to have all the good lines in a dialogue, but elsewhere there are several strong speakers. Quite different points of view are put forward; often alternative ideas are stated and one theory is questioned from the point of view of another. For example, in the *Phaedo*, Simmias and Cebes raise important arguments against Socrates' view that the soul is immortal, and through Socrates, Plato offers detailed answers. The *Symposium* includes substantial speeches by Alcibiades, Aristophanes, and others. Particularly striking is Socrates' own speech, describing the ideas of Diotima, which at points portrays a world of flux, change, life, death, and a sense of immortality tied to birth and reproduction. The *Parmenides* depicts an older philosopher arguing quite convincingly against the young Socrates and the theory of Forms.

For all his emphasis on knowledge, changelessness and timelessness, Plato was unusually attentive to the fact that different people had different approaches to the truth. His dialogues reflect a variety of positions, a phenomenon which is entirely compatible with the Socratic emphasis on independent and autonomous thinking, and making up one's mind for oneself. Although Plato clearly believed that there is an ultimate reality and an ultimate truth, he did not claim to know it himself. Rather, he sought to depict different characters and theories, and different approaches to the truth. The dialogues were a tool for thought.

To inspire thought, Plato sometimes offers myths and stories unlikely to be true. Perhaps in a distant realm disembodied souls come to behold Platonic Forms like Equality and Beauty. Perhaps we will someday gain knowledge of absolutes. But that realm is not here and that day is not now. Nor had it arrived in Plato's day. To think about abstract problems we need all the help we can get and Plato tries to give it, using analogies, figures, and stories.

Some stories in Plato are used to illustrate and help argue a philosophical point. One such is the myth of Gyges in the *Republic*. Plato seeks to contrast a just person who wants to be good, with one who behaves in a just way only because he is concerned about his social reputation. To show how a man might only appear to be just, he tells the myth of Gyges. An ancestor of Gyges, a shepherd, got hold of a ring which could make him invisible. Able to commit wrongs without being detected, the shepherd killed the king, seduced the queen, and took over the kingdom. This shepherd was not a just man. Invisible, he could get away with anything, and invisible, he committed crimes – showing that if he had ever appeared to be a just person, the appearance was deceptive. There were no moral convictions underlying his just behavior; when he appeared to act well, this was only out of concern for his reputation and getting caught. A person who is truly just is concerned genuinely to be good, whatever the consequences.

At a number of points in Plato's dialogues, myths are introduced which seem to be of a religious origin. In the *Phaedo*, for instance, Socrates offers a lengthy description of the journey the soul would take after death. Another myth about life after death appears at the end of the *Republic*. Having argued at length that the just person is happier than the unjust person and justice will be its own reward, Plato moves on to introduce a story about what will happen to just and unjust souls after their life on this earth. The tale of "a warrior bold, Er, the son of Armenius," it is commonly referred to as the Myth of Er. Er was apparently slain in battle and his soul went to the afterworld, but later returned. His body revived on his funeral pyre. Returning to life, Er described a mysterious region where there were two openings side by side in the earth and two others in the heavens. Judges sent the righteous upward to heaven and the unjust downward into earth. In the depths of the earth unjust souls remained in suffering and squalour, while in heaven just souls were clean and pure. Having spent a thousand years in the appropriate place, souls returned to a central meadow and recounted their experiences. Those coming up from the earth had suffered agonies, while those who had been in heaven had experienced a beautiful and delightful world. Later, in a ceremony presided over by the maiden daughter of Necessity, the souls were asked to choose another life – animal or human, noble or peasant, male or female. The implication of the myth seems to be that the most important thing in life is to cultivate a wise soul which can make good choices. After having made their choices, the souls were led to the River of Forgetfulness where they drank water which made them lose their knowledge of the other worlds and the choice they had made. Er did not drink the water; somehow he recovered his sight to find himself at dawn lying on a funeral pyre and able to tell his story.

In the *Republic* Plato offers a sustained and complex argument to try to show that justice is its own reward. But the Myth of Er, right at the end of the dialogue, suggests that being just and cultivating a wise soul may have its rewards in a further world we experience after bodily death. Does the Myth of Er undermine the Platonic idea that being just is worthwhile in its own right? We might think so: if a person seems to be just and good but is cultivating his or her own soul merely in order to fare well in the after-life, then he or she is *not* virtuous for virtue's sake. Such a person is virtuous only because he or she hopes to benefit in heaven and in future lives. (Such a person seems no better than the shepherd in the myth of Gyges.) Alternately, we could interpret the Myth of Er as a supplement to Plato's argument, providing additional reasons for men and women to be just. Plato lets the myth stand at the end of the *Republic* as something for his readers to think about – not as something true but as important in the way that myths and stories can be. He ends a lengthy dialogue with a myth – not, it seems, to make a point or introduce a thesis of his own, but rather to give the reader something more to think about. There are many religions that hold that justice, or virtue, will somehow be rewarded after death – either in heaven, or in a better future life here on earth. Yet strict morality supports the Platonic idea that virtue should be its own reward. Such ideas are not easily reconciled.

Some tales in Plato seem to be offered purely for entertainment, yet are memorable and thought-provoking nevertheless. One such is that of Aristophanes in the *Symposium*, explaining why it is that people have such yearnings to be united with each other in love. At one time there were three kinds of human beings, and all were double. There were males, females and a third type, made up of male and female elements (hermaphrodites).

> . . .the shape of each human being was completely round, with back and sides in a circle; they had four hands each, as many legs as hands, and two faces, exactly alike, on a rounded neck. Between the two faces, which were on opposite sides, was one head with four ears. There were two sets of sexual organs, and everything else was the way you'd imagine it from what I've told you. They walked upright, as we do now, whatever direction they wanted. And whenever they set out to run fast, they thrust out all their eight limbs, the ones they had then, and spun rapidly, the way gymnasts do cartwheels, by bringing their legs around straight. (*Symposium*, 189E - 190B)

According to the myth, males were offspring of the sun, females of the earth, and hermaphrodites of the moon. They were spherical, and so was their motion – because they were like their parents in the sky. The hermaphrodites were so energetic and ambitious that they became holy terrors. Eventually Zeus split all the creatures in half so that each half had to walk upright on two legs.

> Now since their natural form had been cut in two, each one longed for its own other half, and so they would throw their arms about each other, weaving themselves together, wanting to grow together. In that condition they would die from hunger and general idleness, because they would not do anything apart from each other. Whenever one of the halves died and one was left, the one that was left still sought another and wove itself together with that. Sometimes the half he met came from a woman, as we'd call her now, sometimes it came from a man; either way, they kept on dying.
> (*Symposium*, 191B)

Zeus took pity on these pathetic creatures and altered their bodies so that the private parts were in the front and they could unite sexually. Some males would unite with females, some with other males and (presumably) some females with other females.

> This, then, is the source of our desire to love each other. Love is born into every human being; it calls back the half of our original nature together; it tries to make one out of two and heal the wound of human nature.
> (*Symposium*, 191D)

If a man united with a woman, the race could continue. But whether of the opposite sex or of the same sex, people crave an "other half." They are looking for completion; without another to unite with, they feel only half a being.

This story – "just a story" one might say – is part of an entertaining and sometimes bawdy speech. Yet the haunting allegory of the separated creatures points to something fundamental in human nature: our longing for another with whom to share physical and emotional love and, indeed, life itself. Plato himself had experienced intense and lasting love for another human being in his relationship with Dion, a male partner. Many of us need and search for a partner with whom to share our selves and our lives. It is as though we were halves of something larger than ourselves. The story of the hermaphrodites expresses a psychological truth – many human beings feel incomplete without an emotional, sexual, and intellectual partner – in an imaginative and poetic way.

Socrates' speech in the *Symposium* is unusual in that he claims to have gotten all his knowledge of love from "a Mantinean woman called Diotima – a woman who was deeply versed in this (love) and many other fields of knowledge." (This woman, probably a priestess, had been able to postpone a great plague in Athens for ten years by preparing a certain sacrifice.) Socrates spends much of his speech describing Diotima's teachings, which at points differ interestingly from ideas put forward elsewhere in the dialogues.

Diotima apparently tried to argue Socrates out of false dichotomies (oppositions that mistakenly assume there is no middle ground, such as knowledge OR ignorance, beauty OR ugliness) by reminding him that there are often intermediate states between two opposites. She also taught him that conditions and characteristics vary with different contexts; love is a different thing as it appears in different compartments of life. Apparently Diotima stressed change as a feature of life: people alter greatly through life, both in body and in mind, but nevertheless somehow retain their identity. And her thought about immortality was centered not around the persistence of a disembodied soul in another world but on the human quest for immortality through giving birth. Human beings die. But they long for immortality and try to achieve it in some way – some by giving birth to children, others by "giving birth" to intellectual products such as writings.

Socrates describes Diotima as his teacher and speaks as though she finds his amateurish efforts rather amusing. When Diotima seems to condescend to Socrates, it is as though Plato is making fun of himself.

> - "In that case, Diotima, who *are* the people who love wisdom, if they are neither wise nor ignorant?"
> - "That's obvious," she said. "A child could tell you. Those who love wisdom fall in between those two extremes. And Love [personified here as a god or spirit] is one of them, because he is in love with what is beautiful and wisdom is extremely beautiful. It follows that Love must be a lover of wisdom and, as such, is in between being wise and being ignorant. . . . My dear Socrates, that, then, is the nature of the Spirit called Love. Considering what you thought about Love, it's no surprise that you were led into thinking of Love as you did . . ."
> (*Symposium*, 204B)

Was Diotima a real woman? Why is this possibly mythical figure given such a prominent role in Socrates' speech at a banquet attended by no women save a flute girl? These questions have recently inspired considerable commentary and research, but the answers cannot be known for certain. The Diotima speech is another place in Plato's dialogues where we are offered food for thought, but no definite answer.

Plato was an extremely imaginative philosophical writer. His dialogues are full of vivid figures of speech, humor, ironic comments, analogies, stories, and myths. By no means is his whole philosophy expressed in the rigorous dialectic of philosophical argument, challenge, and response. Reading Plato and taking the Socrates of the middle dialogues as his spokesman, we might conclude that thinking is a purely intellectual thing, pursued for the sole purpose of reaching truths in a distant realm remote from bodily experience and daily life. Yet looking at all the different situations, characters, examples, analogies, myths, and stories in the dialogues suggests quite another view of thinking. The thinking shown in the dialogues is set in the context of the everyday world of Athens, with characters facing practical problems. It is flexible, imaginative, and playful – not always rigorously focused on a distant abstraction.

Plato, Socrates, Simmias, Phaedo, Cebes, and the others are long dead. But we, readers of Plato, live on to be challenged by his various puzzles and arguments. The dialogues are Plato's invitation to think, and think hard. Myths and allegories are important in Plato's philosophy, even though they are not put forward as true. Some of Plato's myths can be seen as implying a line of thought different from his own, offering simultaneously some truths and some falsehoods. Such myths offer a puzzle to be disentangled. To ask "What did Plato think?" is often inappropriate. Plato asks his readers to think, and to try to work their way out of the many inconsistencies, puzzles, myths, and arguments pointing in so many different directions, thus making sense of things for themselves.

In addition to puzzles and philosophical problems, Plato's dialogues bequeath a mixed legacy on the topic of thought itself. At points Plato seems to understand thought as a process of progressive abstraction, where we remove ourselves further and further from the familiar world to achieve knowledge of absolute standards fixed in another realm. Yet his dialogues display thought in this familiar world, as the interaction of people arguing against each other, enjoying analogies, drama, stories, and myths. In the dialogues, Plato's characters struggle with unsolved questions and puzzles in their quest for understanding, just as Aristotle, the most prominent student in the Academy, went on to do after Plato's death.

3

Aristotle: Finding the Golden Mean

Aristotle (384 - 322 B.C.) was born in Stagira, in Macedonia in northern Greece. His father was a court physician. At eighteen, Aristotle entered Plato's Academy in Athens, where he remained for twenty years as a student, scholar, and lecturer. Aristotle had extremely wide interests and loved to read; Plato is said to have called him the best reader and mind of the school. When Plato died, Aristotle left Athens to work and travel in Asia Minor. There he continued his studies in philosophy and did considerable biological research. In 342 B.C. King Philip of Macedonia asked Aristotle to come to tutor his son, Alexander, who later became the military conqueror, Alexander the Great. For three years Aristotle was tutor to Alexander. However, there is little connection between Aristotle's ideas about citizenship, ethics, and politics and those of Alexander.

In 339 B.C. Aristotle left Macedonia to return to Athens and found his own school, the Lyceum. It was located in a grove just outside Athens, at a spot which had been a favorite haunt of Socrates. The Lyceum was an energetic research center where ambitious surveys and studies were made of topics in biology, politics, history, and literature as well as in philosophy. It had its own library, including numerous manuscripts, maps, and historical objects. Aristotle gave extensive lectures at the Lyceum.

In 323 B.C. there was growing anti-Macedonian sentiment in Athens. Fearing persecution, Aristotle left to return to northern Greece. Recalling the tragedy of Socrates, he said he did not want Athens to sin twice against philosophy. Aristotle died the following year at the age of sixty-three.

It is estimated that Aristotle's written works extended to some 6000 pages, of which some 2000 pages survive today. The writings we have are not polished treatises; many were left in the form of lecture notes and working papers. This, together with the complexity and density of his thought, makes Aristotle's writings difficult to read. One poet remarked that reading Aristotle is like "eating chopped hay." Be this as it may, Aristotle's achievements were astounding. In philosophy, his ideas dominated four centuries of European thought in the Middle Ages, and they are still widely discussed today. Aristotle invented formal logic. In addition, he made key contributions to human knowledge in biology, chemistry, dynamics, psychology, sociology, and literary criticism.

Aristotle's written works reveal relatively little about his personality. He is said to have been bald, small-eyed and thin-legged, and to have spoken with a slight lisp. He was, apparently, noticeably well-dressed. Aristotle was married to Phythias and had a daughter; later, after the death of Phythias, he lived with another woman, Herpyllis, with whom he had a son. His will survives and its language and terms suggest that he was a kindly and generous family man.

Though Aristotle was strongly influenced by Plato, his approach to the world was quite different from that of his teacher and predecessor. Unlike Plato, Aristotle valued sense experience, which he believed to be the essential first stage of thought and knowledge. Aristotle believed that seeing, hearing, touching, tasting and smelling – all capacities human beings share with animals – provide the basic materials for thought. From perceptions, we gain memory; from memories, experience. Eventually, from experience, we are able to recognize patterns in things, and recognize the universal features of particular things.

Forms in the World

In nature, Aristotle thought no being or activity so lowly as to be unworthy of notice. He wrote about bees, wasps, snakes, horses, elephants, fish, and just about every creature imaginable.

> We therefore must not recoil with childish aversion from the examination of the humbler animals. Every realm of nature is marvellous; and as Heraclitus, when the strangers who came to visit

> him found him warming himself at the furnace in the kitchen and hesitated to go in, is reported to have bidden them not to be afraid to enter, as even in that kitchen divinities were present, so we should venture on the study of every kind of animal without distaste; for each and all will reveal to us something natural and something beautiful.
> (*Parts of Animals*, 645a15-20)

Even in a kitchen we might find something godly. Similarly in any animal, however humble and lowly it might appear, there is something natural and beautiful to be found.

> Absence of haphazard and conduciveness of everything to an end are to be found in nature's works in the highest degree, and the end for which these works are put together and produced is a form of the beautiful.
>
> If any person thinks the examination of the rest of the animal kingdom an unworthy task, he must hold in like disesteem the study of man.
> (*Parts of Animals*, 645a15-20)

Human beings too are animals. For Aristotle, what is beautiful is not Forms or entities outside the experienced world, but rather the orderliness and purposiveness of Nature itself. Nature shows life, development, and change; thought and contemplation begin when we try to understand its patterns. Like Plato, Aristotle sought knowledge and deemed that which is formal, necessary, and universal to be the highest knowledge. But unlike Plato, Aristotle believed that knowledge was grounded in sense experience – in our sensory awareness of individual things in particular situations in the physical world.

We move from an awareness and understanding of the *particular case* (e.g. the tree in the garden, a bird, or a single human being, like Socrates) to a recognition of the universal form or pattern that is contained within it (what a tree is, what a bird is, what a human being is). This process Aristotle called *induction*.

> . . . It is evident too that if some perception is wanting, it is necessary for some understanding to be wanting too –. . . and it is impossible to consider universals except through induction . . . and it is impossible to get an induction without having perception – for of particulars there is perception; for it is not possible to get understanding of them; for it [understanding] can be got neither from universals without induction nor through induction without perception.
> (*Posterior Analytics*, 81a38-b9)

In other words, understanding requires perception of particulars. This perception is necessary in order to know universals, which we are able to see, or intuit, in things that we perceive. Aristotle believed that particular things are not merely individual; they allow us to know universals because they are things of a type. Though individual, they have characteristics which are shared with other individual things.

Perceiving things does not explain them, but it is a necessary first step toward knowledge. An understanding of a pattern, or property common to many individuals is what we are seeking in speculative thought. We begin to gain that understanding by examining particular cases and particular things. Aristotle believed that this is true in the case of moral knowledge, just as it is true in the case of knowledge of physical things.

> I mean . . . if we were to seek what pride is we should inquire, in the case of some proud men we know, what one thing they all have as such. E.g. if Alcibiades is proud, and Achilles and Ajax, what one thing do they all have? Intolerance of insults; for one made war, one waxed wroth, and the other killed himself. Again in the case of others. e.g. Lysander and Socrates. Well, if here it is being indifferent to good and bad fortune, I take these two things and inquire what both indifference to fortune and not brooking dishonour have that is the same. And if there is nothing, then there will be two kinds of pride. . . . And it is easier to define the particular than the universal – that is why one should cross from the particulars to the universals.
> (*Posterior Analytics*, 97b16-30)

We must begin with what we can most easily know – particular things that we can sense and experience – and proceed from our perception of them to knowledge of the universal. What exists are individual things – bees, birds, horses, cedar trees, rocks, human beings, houses, beds, snakes, worms, and so on. These individual substances are self-contained objects which have a variety of properties, including those essential properties which make them the kinds of beings they are. These are forms, according to Aristotle. Considered in themselves, forms are the most knowable things, but they are not the things most easily known to us.

Aristotle did not *merely* observe when he was studying nature. He used organizing philosophical concepts to describe what he saw, and with them he sought to resolve the problems of change and permanence, universal and particular, that had been raised by Plato and his predecessors. Central Aristotelian concepts are potentiality and actuality, form and matter, genus and differentia, substance and attribute, and four kinds of cause. An acorn is potentially an oak; a mature oak tree is actually an oak. Using the notions of potentiality and actuality, Aristotle was able to describe development and change. An acorn is able to turn into an oak because, potentially, it already is one.

According to Aristotle, form and matter are combined in individual substances. An individual substance is made of something (matter) but has a determinate character that is essential to it (form). The wood in a tree is its matter; the structure and shape of that wood, which makes it into a living tree, is its form. Or we might consider a river. Water is its matter; where and how that water flows – to make it, say, the River Danube or the North Saskatchewan River – is its form. These examples of rivers and trees are natural entities, but the distinction between matter and form also applies to human artefacts. Consider, for instance, a table. Its wood is its matter and its shape – with a flat surface held above the ground, designed so that it can serve its function – is its form. The tree, the river, and the table are separate individual things. They are substances, which have various properties or attributes. The Danube flows south; the North Saskatchewan has water that is muddy brown.

Genus (overall category), species (sub-category), and differentia (differentiating feature) are also crucial classificatory terms in Aristotle's scientific and philosophical work. The genus of the species human being (called by Aristotle, *anthropos*) is animal. The differentia, the feature that distinguishes human beings as a species from other animals, is the capacity to reason.

In seeking explanations for things, Aristotle advises that we attend to four kinds of causes: the material cause, the formal cause, the efficient cause, and the final cause. The material cause of a table is the matter from which it is made – for example, wood. Its formal cause is its shape as a table – oval or rectangular, perhaps, with legs supporting a flat surface. Its efficient (or moving) cause is the carpenter who made it. Its final cause (or purpose or "end") is to serve as a surface on which things can be placed. When seeking understanding we typically ask "why?" and seek an answer that will tell us "because... ". In setting forth this view of the four causes Aristotle notes four different directions for explanation. The most common modern sense of "cause" is that of efficient cause. But we may ask about the matter, the form, or the purpose (final cause) of things as well.

> Knowledge is the object of our inquiry, and men do not think they know a thing till they have grasped the 'why' of it (which is to grasp its primary cause). So clearly we too must do this as regards both coming to be and passing away and every kind of natural change. . .
> In one way, then, that out of which a thing comes to be and which persists, is called a cause. e.g. the bronze of the statue, the silver of the bowl, and the genera (metal) of which the bronze and the silver are species.
> In another way, the form or archetype, i.e. the definition of the essence, and its genera, are called causes. . . and the parts in the definition.
> Again, the primary source of the change or rest: e.g. the man who deliberated is a cause, the father is the cause of the child, and generally what makes of what is made and what changes of what is changed. [Aristotle erroneously assumed that only males are causally active in reproduction. He believed that females were passive, supplying only the matter.]
> Again, in the sense of end or that for the sake of which a thing is done, e.g. health is the cause of walking about. ('Why is he walking about?' We say: 'To be healthy,' and having said that, we think we have assigned the cause.)
> (*Physics*, 194b24-35)

To think about nature and its many changing species, we must know what to look for and how to generalize. We must ask questions that will bring us to understanding and explanation, and understand the questions we are asking.

Aristotle and Plato

As a member of Plato's Academy for some twenty years, Aristotle was of course familiar with Plato's theory of Forms. He did not accept that theory. Aristotle understood Plato as having postulated Forms as things, or substances existing in a realm of their own, apart from the earth, and as believing that such postulated non-earthly entities could somehow explain numbers and properties. He believed that Plato's theory, on this interpretation, was mistaken. According to Aristotle, there are universal properties possessed by individual things; among these universal properties are some that constituted the "form" or essential characteristic(s) of things. But these universal characteristics do not exist as separate objects in their own right. Rather, they are inherent in individual substances. Aristotle believed that what it was to be a horse was something inherent in individual horses, not a separate entity or Form existing in a realm apart from the material earth.

> . . . it would seem impossible that the substance and that of which it is the substance should exist apart; how, therefore, could the Ideas [Forms], being the substances of things, exist apart?
> (*Metaphysics*, 991b1-3)

Aristotle regarded Platonic Forms as unnecessary entities that could not help in explaining the nature and development of beings in the material world.

> For the Forms are practically equal to – or not fewer than – the things . . . . For to each thing there answers an entity which has the same name and exists apart from the substances, and so also in the case of all other groups there is a one over many, whether the many are in this world or are eternal.
> . . . And in general the arguments for the Forms destroy the things for whose existence we are more zealous than for the existence of the Ideas [Forms] . . .
> (*Metaphysics*, 990b18-19)

For Aristotle what was primarily real was the physical world. By and large, he resisted postulating entities outside this world to try to explain objects and processes within it.

Aristotle shared with Plato the assumption that there are universal patterns which explain the order that exists in the world, and those patterns are knowable by thinking human beings. But he understood universals differently. Somewhat paradoxically, in the Aristotelian scheme of things the universal 'horse' is fully present in each individual horse.

Aristotle believed that forms gradually emerge in living beings – as when an acorn, developing in fertile soil, slowly turns into an oak. Rejecting part of Plato's theory left Aristotle with a problem: how to make sense of the reality of universal characteristics (properties such as beauty, humanity, or being a horse) without introducing separate entities such as Plato's Forms. Trying to explain mathematical and moral knowledge, Plato postulated abstract entities in an immaterial realm. He then faced the problem of what these entities were and how they were related to material things. Aristotle did not postulate Forms as eternal entities and thus did not face the troubling puzzles pointed out by Plato in the Third Man argument of the *Parmenides*. But he faced another problem: how something universal (what it is to be a horse, beauty, humanity) could exist in many different particulars without being anything separate from them.

Aristotle also differed from Plato in that his understanding of the soul was more naturalistic. Whereas Plato believed that the soul was captured in the body, Aristotle defined the soul as the form of the body. The soul is related to the body as form is related to matter. In sensation, memory, and imagination, the soul is reliant on the body and the natural world. Plants have nutritive souls which give them the capacity to grow, mature, and reproduce; animals have appetitive (desiring) souls, with the capacities of nutritive souls and additional abilities to perceive, remember, and move. Human beings have all this and more: souls with the capacity of reason. Aristotle believed that it is reason that "activates" the intelligible forms of sensible things, making what is potentially intelligible in them actually intelligible to us. Active reason illuminates things, bringing their universal and defining attributes to our attention in something like the way that the sun's light enables us to see colors. Because of active reason, our minds are able to assimilate and understand the order which is a real feature of the world.

Aristotle seems to have believed that active reason is not dependent on the body. He argued that there is no organ of the body which is needed for reason in the way that the eyes are needed for sight and the ears are needed for hearing. (Aristotle regarded the brain as a coolant; in the Aristotelian scheme of things, no single bodily organ was identified with reason or reasoning.) Passive reason depends on the senses, but active reason, Aristotle thought, could exist apart from the body. Active reason seems to be some kind of immaterial power which enters the human organism from without. To Aristotle, active reason, indispensable in our recognition of patterns in the world, was something divine. The *nous* or active reason in an individual person was related to that person in much the way God (or, the closest thing in Aristotle's system, the Unmoved Mover) was related to the cosmos.

According to Aristotle, human beings are essentially rational beings. To think and reason actively is our nature, our best and highest virtue, and it is by exercising our highest virtue that we can achieve happiness. Rational thought, and the contemplation of rational truths are the essence of happiness for Aristotle. He argued that happiness is a type of activity. It is not a matter of passively consuming entertainments (the way we passively watch television, for instance) or of being in a state of changeless bliss.

> . . . Relaxation, then is not an end; for it is taken for the sake of activity. The happy life is thought to be one of excellence; now an excellent life requires exertion, and does not consist in amusement. (*Nicomachean Ethics*, 1177a1-6)

In discussing happiness, Aristotle allowed that human beings will find pleasure in many kinds of activities, and have material needs that must be met. Human happiness cannot be based solely on contemplation or intellectual activities. Nevertheless, Aristotle held that for human beings, the highest activity is the exercise of reason. Our capacity to wonder, our thirst for understanding, and our ability to seek out and recognize universal patterns in nature are the best that is in us. The greatest and most appropriate happiness for human beings, therefore, is the happiness of intellectual contemplation.

> If intellect is divine, then, in comparison with man, the life according to it is divine in comparison with human life. . . we must so far as we can, make ourselves immortal, and strain every nerve to live in accordance with the best thing in us; for even if it be small in bulk, much more does it in power and worth surpass everything. (*Nicomachean Ethics*, 1177b29-33)

Practical Knowledge and Deliberation

Aristotle divided knowledge into three types: theoretical, productive, and practical. When we pursue theoretical knowledge, we are concerned to understand the nature of things; we search for universals and for explanations which show why things must be as they are. Theoretical knowledge includes theology (the study of eternal, unchanging things), mathematics, and the study of nature (physics and biology). Productive knowledge is the knowledge of the artist or craftsman, whose purpose is to make something. In practical knowledge, our concern is not so much understand as to *act*. We want to act appropriately, sensibly, and well. Practical knowledge includes ethics and politics.

Interestingly, logic – an area in which Aristotle was a profound innovator – does not appear in this scheme of things. Aristotle thought of logic as the *organon* or tool for all the other sciences.

Thought varies depending on what sort of knowledge we are pursuing. It is directed toward different goals in each case, and standards of precision vary with the subject matter.

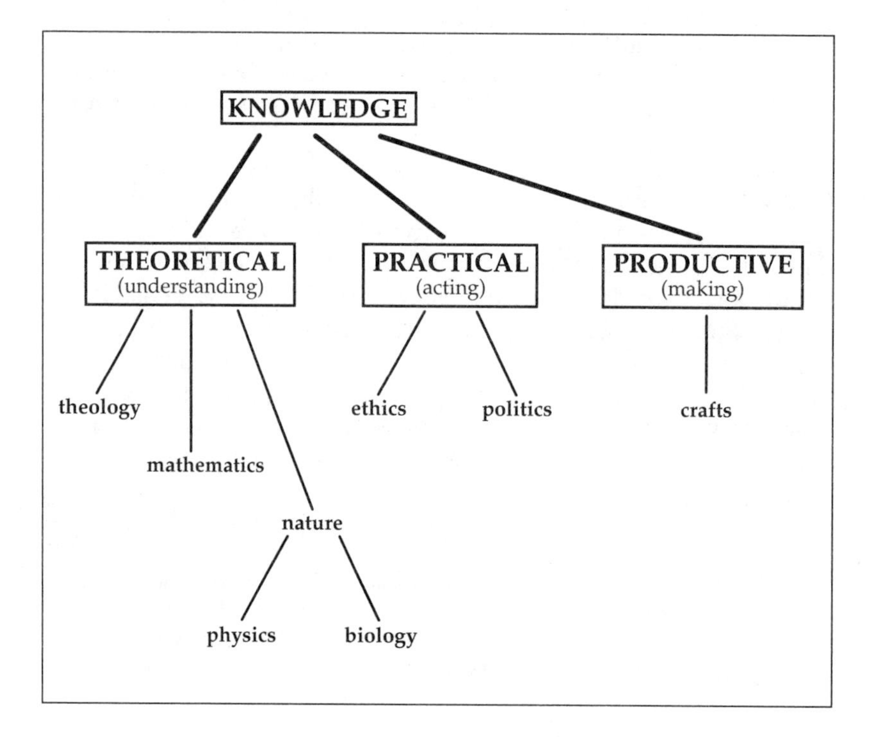

> Our discussion will be adequate if it has as much clearness as the subject matter admits of, for precision is not to be sought for alike in all discussions, any more than in all the products of the crafts. Now fine and just actions, which political science investigates, admit of much variety and fluctuation of opinion, so that they may be thought to exist only by convention, and not by nature. And goods also give rise to a similar fluctuation because they bring harm to many people, for before now men have been undone by reason of their wealth, and others by reason of their courage. We must be content, then, in speaking of such subjects and with such premises to indicate the truth roughly and in outline . . . . In the same spirit, therefore, should each type of statement be *received*; for it is the mark of an educated man to look for precision in each class of things just so far as the nature of the subject admits.
> (*Nicomachean Ethics*, 1094 12-28)

The issue of how best to live one's life is not a scientific or technical one. We should not expect to approach ethical or political questions mathematically, or to find a rigorous proof of a single correct response to questions about how to live.

A person of practical intelligence is one who can take the right steps to achieve the right goal. Practical intelligence is a matter of knowing what to do and being able to do it. It requires sensitivity to the situation one is in. Of paramount importance in life, practical wisdom (*phronesis*) is quite different from the sort of theoretical intelligence involved in being a good scientist, philosopher, theologian, or mathematician. The distinction between practical wisdom and theoretical wisdom recalls the ancient joke about Thales, who lived in the sixth century B.C. and is deemed to have been the first philosopher in the Western tradition. Thales was said to have been strolling along, thinking so hard about the nature of the universe that he did not notice where he was going, and fell into a well. If this story is true, Thales, however theoretically brilliant he might have been, lacked practical intelligence. A comparable modern stereotype is that of the absent-minded professor, preoccupied with abstruse researches and calculations, famed for his great intellect, but unable to respond to the emotional needs of family members, manage his bank account, keep a simple household tidy and functioning, or prepare basic nutritious meals.

Aristotle made many astute observations about practical knowledge. We must be sensitive to particular situations and seek to respond to them appropriately. Rules or laws will not tell us what to do. Rules are couched in general terms and for this reason are in a crucial sense incomplete. Circumstances and situations vary greatly, and no rule or general principle can include within itself a relevant description of every possible case. If, for instance, a person is seeking to improve her health, she might be told to exercise for at least an hour every day. But such a policy has to be followed with due respect for varying circumstances. If a family member is ill or in crisis, getting an hour every day for exercise may not be feasible.

The same sort of problem arises with moral principles. Consider the rule that what is borrowed should be returned. Even this simple moral rule should not be taken as standing with no exceptions; a reasonable person will understand it to mean that what is borrowed should be returned "other things being equal." Perhaps by returning something borrowed we would put a life at risk, as in the case when someone loaned a weapon and then returned in a state of absolute rage wanting it back. In such a case, we ought not to return the weapon – even though there is a general moral presumption that what we borrow we should return. Rules offer guidelines, but circumstances have to be taken into account. To have good judgment about cases requires experience; thus, Aristotle said, older people tend to have more practical knowledge than younger people. Practical knowledge is a matter of knowing what to do, being able to act and respond appropriately in a wide variety of circumstances. Rules do not tell us how to handle a particular case; we must know how to apply the rules. For this we need judgment.

How do we understand and respond to a particular case when there is a call for action? We may have to make judgments of prudence about how to take care of ourselves. Or we may have to make moral judgments, in cases where what we do significantly affects other people. Both in contexts of prudence and in contexts of morality, we must first sense that a situation requires action, attending to the circumstances and reflecting on what they indicate, to see whether there is something that calls for our response. In the area of prudence, this might mean noticing such things as that our gums are swollen and uncomfortable, or that the roof of our house needs repair. In the area of morality, it might be such a thing as seeing that a friend is upset or that we occupy a social role (parent, teacher, citizen) that gives us a special duty or responsibility. Being sensitive in practical ways and responding to situations appropriately may in time become a matter of habit. But it will never be purely routine: we need to keep an open mind and be reflective about how our goals should be pursued in concrete circumstances. Aristotle argued that practical wisdom requires an appreciation of what is good together with knowledge of the facts of experience, and the intellectual skill needed to efficiently and reliably apply general knowledge to a particular situation.

When deciding what to do, we *deliberate*. Deliberation is a kind of thinking which is appropriate only in a certain range. We deliberate when we have ends, or goals, and there is something we can do to move towards these goals – but we do not yet know what that is. Deliberating, we seek to find a means to our end. We may understand that an action Y leads to Z (our goal), that another action X will put us in a position to undertake Y, and that a further action, W – which is actually in our power to do – will put us in a position to undertake X. If we wish to achieve Z, we can begin by doing W. One of Aristotle's examples was that of health. For most people good health is a valued end; the question is what to do to obtain it. If a person learns that eating light meat is conducive to health, and that chicken is light meat, he may eat chicken in a quest to improve his health. (The example of chicken, light meat, and health is Aristotle's.)

To have practical wisdom, a person must have the right objectives and know how to carry them out. For example, it is a virtue to want to help the poor, but it takes practical wisdom to know how best to do this. Aristotle advocated moderation in action. To act virtuously, we must respond with the appropriate emotion and act in a way that fits the circumstances. To do so, we must seek "the mean," the response and action which is just right for this circumstance. This generally involves moderation and a sense of fit and proportion. There is a moderate and right way to display courage, generosity, kindness, and other virtues. To sense it we need to have the right sorts of habits, and then deliberate.

> . . . if excellence is more exact and better than any art, as nature also is, then it must have the quality of *aiming at the intermediate.* I mean moral excellence; for it is this that is concerned with passions and actions, and in these there is excess, defect, and the intermediate. For instance, both fear and confidence and appetite and anger and pity and in general pleasure and pain may be felt both too much and too little, and in both cases not too well; but to feel them at the right times, with reference to the right objects, towards the right people, with the right aim, and in the right way, is what is both intermediate and best, and this is characteristic of excellence. Similarly with regard to actions also there is excess, defect, and the intermediate.
> (*Nicomachean Ethics,* 1106b14-23)

One who gives away too much money is prodigal, or overly generous; one who gives away too little money is mean or stingy. The right thing is to be "liberal," to give away some money, but neither too much nor too little. But to find the mean, just the right intermediate response, is not simple. It is no easy matter to respond appropriately: sometimes getting angry is the right thing to do; on other occasions, it amounts to bad temper and is regarded as wrong.

Such comments are readily applicable to many contemporary situations. To speak firmly to an aggressive salesperson, telling him or her that we have no time to talk and cutting that person off abruptly, may be just the right thing to do in some circumstances (if, for instance, the salesperson is being very pushy and we are on our way to an important appointment). But to use a similar style with our mother or with a friend who is upset would not be appropriate. Common thinking about what is appropriate action seems to agree with Aristotle's view that action has to be tailored to fit particular agents and particular circumstances. In a military emergency, what a general should do, and what a foot soldier should do, are likely to be quite different.

Consistently with Aristotle's view that rules do not do all the work in practical thinking, the doctrine of the mean does not provide a general moral principle which we can automatically apply to every case. Perhaps of necessity, it is rather vague and unspecific. To say that we should respond to a person in particular circumstances in a way which is *right* and *appropriate* for those circumstances leaves open the basic question: what is the right way? As Aristotle recognized, the doctrine of the golden mean does not apply to all vices and virtues. Suppose that someone is tempted to commit a murder. It is not sensible to think that such a thing would be permissible provided he murders just the right person, at just the right time, in just the right manner!

In moral matters, Aristotle did not separate emotion from reason. He believed that our thinking about practical matters is profoundly connected to the way we feel. Thought should guide emotions, but emotions too, in their own way, do and should guide practical thought and action. Emotions are crucial aspects of our response to circumstances. Some circumstances merit certain emotions – such as anger or love – and feeling helps us respond appropriately to the situation. To feel strongly is in many cases natural and right. If, for example, we see a case where someone is being cheated of what is properly his, it is fitting and reasonable to feel angry; such anger may help us respond. A similar argument can be made for many cases of injustice. Determining what we should do in a given case requires the appropriate feelings, discretion, a sense of proportion, and judgment.

Strategies for Thinking

Aristotle believed that in order to explore a subject we should begin with an examination of what was generally thought about it by noteworthy people, as well as from the point of view of ordinary opinion and practice. We should take account of what has been accepted: what seems to be the case to most people, or to the people who are the most famous, celebrated, and wise. These beliefs he called the *endoxa*. From an examination of the *endoxa*, topics for thought, puzzles and problems, and clues to the true view will emerge. We might find contradictions between views held by prominent thinkers, as in the case when Heraclitus believed that everything was in a constant state of change and Parmenides argued that change was impossible. These views cannot both be true. Thinking and philosophizing, we try to resolve puzzles and problems which emerge from a survey of *endoxa*, using both theoretical arguments and an appeal to concrete evidence. On the other hand, we might find considerable agreement between thinkers, in which case we would be especially cautious about rejecting their shared beliefs.

In philosophy or any other subject, we do not commence thought and exploration just anywhere. The *endoxa* provide a place to begin. That certain ideas have been accepted is reason to pay some attention to them, to consider arguments put forward to defend them, and to reflect on what might be correct and incorrect about them.

> The investigation of the truth is in one way hard, in another easy. An indication of this is found in the fact that no one is able to attain the truth adequately, while, on the other hand, no one fails entirely, but everyone says something true about the nature of things, and while individually they contribute little or nothing to the truth, by the union of all a considerable amount is amassed. . . we should be grateful, not only to those whose opinions we may share, but also to those who have expressed more superficial views; for these also contributed something, by developing before us the powers of thought. . . for from the better thinkers we have inherited certain opinions, while the others have been responsible for the appearance of the better thinkers.
> (*Metaphysics*, 993a27-b19)

The appeal to the *endoxa* is sometimes criticized as being too conservative. If common opinion is superstitious, or ordinary moral practices gravely unjust, a theory beginning from *endoxa* may fail to reject them, even though there is a sound basis for doing so. In this regard it is noteworthy that Aristotle accepted slavery and regarded women as inferior to men. He was in these ways affected by the customs and beliefs of his time. However, in defense of the practice of *beginning* with *endoxa*, it can be said that criticism and philosophy have to start somewhere. The Aristotelian strategy for thinking is to begin by considering *endoxa*, but that does not mean that one must conclude one's thinking by accepting those beliefs. There is no need for thinking to end at the place where it begins.

Aristotle's practice of considering the views of his predecessors is apparent at many places in his written work. When he writes about the soul, for instance, he notes:

> For our study of soul it is necessary, while formulating the problems of which in our further advance we are to find the solutions, to call into council the views of those of our predecessors who

> have declared any opinion on this subject, in order that we may profit by whatever is sound in their suggestions and avoid their errors.
> (*On the Soul*, 404b20-25)

Aristotle then proceeds to discuss the theories of numerous philosophers who had proceeded him: Democritus, Anaxagoras, Protagoras, Plato, Heraclitus, and several others.

In addition to surveying relevant beliefs and opinions held by other people, Aristotle advises that we should take notice of appearances or phenomena – how things seem to be. Appearances must be accounted for. By appearances (*phainomena*), Aristotle did not mean scientific data or observations, but rather, ordinary beliefs about how things are. How do things strike us? How do they appear to us? The theory we offer must take into account appearances, what things seem to be, and explain why it is that they seem as they do. Even a dream or illusion – which is by no means a reliable guide to reality – is something experienced in life. Any sound account of human beings and the cosmos has to explain a wide variety of phenomena. At one point (when discussing ethics) Aristotle suggested that a measure of the correctness of an account is that it:

> (a) solves all the puzzles arising from commonly held opinions, while
> (b) retaining as many of these opinions as possible,
> (c) describing as many of the phenomena, or appearances, as possible.

Something close to this conception is used by some prominent moral philosophers today.

In such areas as logic, ethics, politics, and psychology some of Aristotle's data were taken from language. He paid considerable attention to the way in which words were used. Like many modern philosophers, Aristotle believed that distinctions incorporated in his own language were based on plausible beliefs about what is experienced. Accordingly, paying attention to language, distinctions, different meanings of words, and "what is said" is often an important first stage in Aristotle's thinking.

Aristotle did not raise the question as to whether patterns in the Greek language were a reliable guide to the structure of reality. He simply assumed that this was the case. Clearly such an assumption is questionable; it would not be accepted by most philosophers today. Patterns in a single language are not in themselves a reliable guide to patterns in physical and social reality because there are literally thousands of human languages and they emphasize different aspects of reality and may interpret the world quite differently from one another. Patterns in one's own language do not give definitive insight into philosophical problems. Nevertheless, this method of Aristotle's can again be defended as offering a strategy for thinking, a source of questions if not of answers. Attending to language is of crucial importance, because we think about things in our own language and are affected by its distinctions and conventions.

Often an important way to clarify thought is to make careful distinctions. Many words have a number of different senses ("words are said in many ways," as Aristotle put it), and understanding is considerably enhanced if we explore these. By doing this, we can avoid vagueness and misunderstanding and pose clearer questions to ourselves and others.

> It is useful to have examined the number of uses of a term both for clearness' sake (for a man is more likely to know what it is he asserts, if it has been made clear to him how many uses it may have), and also with a view to ensuring that our deductions shall be in accordance with the actual facts and not addressed merely to the word used. For as long as it is not clear in how many ways a term is used, it is possible that the answerer and the questioner are not directing their minds upon the same thing.
> (*Topics*, 108a17-24)

Often Aristotle seeks to resolve a problem by making a distinction. At one point, for example, he explores the question whether a person should love himself. There are arguments against this view, and arguments for it.

> Now if we grasp the sense in which each party uses the phrase "lover of self", the truth may become evident. Those who use the term as one of reproach ascribe self-love to people who assign themselves the greater share of wealth, honours, and bodily pleasures; . . . men who are lovers of self in this way are reproached for being so. [But] if a man were always anxious that he himself, above all things, should act justly, temperately, or in accordance with any other of the excellences, and in general were always to try to secure for himself the honourable course, no one will call such a man a lover of self or blame him.
> (*Nicomachean Ethics*, 1168b12-27)

The puzzle can be solved if we make a distinction. Self-love in the sense of greed and selfishness is bad; but if self-love means caring for one's own virtue, it is good.

Aristotle frequently made distinctions and then moved forward to explore connections. A favorite example was that of health. Exercise is healthy in the sense that it contributes to health; a complexion is healthy in the sense that it is a symptom of health; a city may be healthy in the sense that people who live there can readily preserve their health. These are distinct uses, but they are also connected. The primary, or focal, sense of health is that in which a person is healthy – a healthy person has a feeling of physical well-being and a body and organs functioning as they ought to. Aristotle thought that terms for being and existence were similar to health in this way.

> There are several senses in which a thing may be said to *be*, as we pointed out previously in our book on the various senses of words; for in one sense it means what a thing is or a 'this' [substance] and in another sense it means that a thing is of a certain quality or quantity or has some such predicate asserted of it. (*Metaphysics*, 1028a10-16)

There are different ways to be: to be a substance (an independently existing entity); to be a quality (a property of a substance); to be a quantity (a number of a substance); and so on. But being a substance is the most basic, for qualities and quantities are qualities and quantities of substances.

Logic, Argument, and Dialectic

The Syllogism

Aristotle's work on logic was highly original and profoundly important. Aristotle invented formal logic. He was the first person to conceive of representing thought by formal symbols and used these formal representations to describe and work out a system for evaluating inferences. Aristotle's formal logic offers a description of a kind of argument called the *syllogism*, which he was the first to describe. Aristotle defined the syllogism as discourse in which, when certain things are posited (assumed), something else necessarily follows.

Consider the following:

> A belongs to every B. (All B are A.)
> B belongs to every C. (All C are B)
> Therefore, A belongs to every C. (All C are A.)

In this example the unbracketed statements are worded as they are in most English translations of Aristotle's works, and the bracketed ones as would be common in most contemporary logic textbooks. In the interests of simplicity, the latter wording will be used here.

The form 'All B are A; All C are B; therefore all C are A' represents an argument which is a *valid syllogism,* in which the first two statements are premises and the third is the conclusion. The argument is a syllogism because the premises and conclusion are in *categorical form* as described by Aristotle – classes of things related using forms of the verb to be. It is *valid* because, if its premises are true, its conclusion must also be true.

Syllogistic logic is a *formal* logic because the same pattern may accurately describe many different arguments with different contents. The following two arguments, for instance, have the same form though their content is different.

> All birds are creatures that fly.
> All creatures that fly are creatures with wings.
> Therefore,
> All birds are creatures with wings.

> All whales are mammals.
> All mammals are creatures that give birth to their young alive.
> Therefore,
> All whales are creatures that give birth to their young alive.

Formalizing arguments allows us to achieve a simple representation which permits us to comment on the validity of an indefinite number of arguments at once, in a simple, rigorous, and elegant way. There are many valid patterns of syllogism, nearly all of which were described by Aristotle. Here is another example.

> No M are W. (For example, 'No logicians are evangelists.')
> All S are M. (For example, 'All syllogistic logicians are logicians.')
> Therefore,
> No S are W. (For example, 'No syllogistic logicians are evangelists.')

Aristotle was the first to investigate the conditions of the validity of arguments and draw up rules that could be used to evaluate inferences.

In every syllogism there are three categorical terms: a major term (the predicate in the conclusion), a minor term (the subject in the conclusion) and a middle term (which appears in both premises but not in the conclusion). In the argument about whales, for instance, the major term is 'creatures that give birth to their young alive' and the minor term is 'whales.' The middle term, which allows us to link the minor term and the major term, is 'mammals.' There are many arrangements of these three categorial terms which produce syllogisms. In his work *Prior Analytics*, Aristotle described all of these patterns and for each one either gave a proof that it was valid or showed, by counter-example, that it was not.

The Principles of Non-Contradiction and the Excluded Middle

Aristotle formulated and discussed two principles of tremendous importance in the history of thought and logic. These are the Principle of Non-Contradiction and the Principle of the Excluded Middle.

The Principle of Non-Contradiction is an absolutely fundamental presupposition of thought. It states that the affirmation and the denial of the same proposition cannot both be true at the same time and in the same respect. Consider, for example, 'The Danube is polluted.' This proposition affirms that a particular river, the Danube, has the property of being polluted. If it is true, then its denial, 'It is not the case that the River Danube is polluted,' must be false. For the river both to be and not to be polluted at the same time and in the same respect would be a contradiction, which is impossible.

The Principle of Non-Contradiction is presupposed in every study of anything at all. It is a principle of which we may be certain, one which is so basic that it makes no sense to call it a hypothesis. Aristotle put it this way:

> Evidently then such a principle is the most certain of all; . . . It is that the same attribute cannot at the same time belong and not belong to the same subject in the same respect; we must presuppose, in face of dialectical objections, any further qualifications which must be added.
> (*Metaphysics*, 1005b18-21)

To cite another example, if a table is large at a given time and with respect to a given purpose then, at that time and with respect to that purpose, it is not the case that that table is not large. A table might be large for a modest kitchen and not large for an elegant dining room. But this does not mean that it is, *without qualification* both large and not large. The Principle of Non-Contradiction rules out affirming and denying the same quality to the same subject *at the same time and in the same respect.*

People may sometimes speak as though they believe contradictory things. The ancient philosopher Heraclitus sometimes did so, as, for instance, when he said "in changing it is at rest." Such a way of talking is strong evidence that a person is not speaking literally (Heraclitus does not mean quite what one would normally mean by those words). Often in such cases, a person is using a contradictory combination of words to hint at another meaning. By saying "in changing it is at rest," Heraclitus seems to have meant that the condition of change is permanent in the sense that things are always changing. According to the Principle of Non-Contradiction, it is not possible for a thing both to have and lack the same property at the same time and in the same respect. Nor is it possible for anyone to literally believe both the affirmation and the denial of the same proposition.

> For it is impossible for anyone to believe the same thing to be and not to be, as some think Heraclitus says . . . if an opinion which contradicts another is contrary to it, obviously it is impossible for the same man at the same time to believe the same thing to be and not to be; for if a man were mistaken in this point he would have contrary opinions at the same time.

No one can literally hold contradictory opinions or beliefs.

> It is for this reason that all who are carrying out a demonstration refer to this [the Principle of Non-Contradiction] as an ultimate belief; for this is naturally the starting-point even for all the other axioms.
> (*Metaphysics*, 1005b12-33)

No demonstration or thought can proceed if we do not presume the soundness of the Principle of Non-Contradiction.

Because its truth is presupposed by every demonstration, and even by speech itself, we cannot demonstrate that the Principle of Non-Contradiction is correct – and Aristotle was well aware of this problem. We would need to use the Principle of Non-Contradiction in order to logically demonstrate its correctness, because this Principle underlies every logical argument. By using the Principle, we would be presupposing that it was correct; and in presupposing that it was correct, we would then not be demonstrating that it was correct. When one *presupposes* the truth of something which he or she is attempting to *demonstrate*, a logical mistake is made. This is the mistake of circular argument – arguing in a circle – sometimes called begging the question. Aristotle suggests that we can in a sense show negatively that the Principle of Non-Contradiction must be accepted, by considering the case of a person who seeks to deny it. For such a person, there are two possibilities. Either he says something, or he does not. If a person says nothing he merits no answer. (One might as well reply to a vegetable, Aristotle says.) If such a person says something meaningful, something of significance, then the words he uses have a definite meaning. This is to say they exclude their opposites. If the person who would deny the Principle of Non-Contradiction says, for instance, "I am a woman" and means something, what she says must exclude the meaning "I am not a woman." Meaningful speech requires significance, which in turn presupposes the Principle of Non-Contradiction. So the principle can be shown in a negative way: anyone who tries to deny it will not make sense.

In fact, action as well as speech can be shown to presuppose this principle.

> For why does a man walk to Megara and not stay at home thinking he ought to walk? Why does he not walk early some morning into a well or over a precipice, if one happens to be in his way? Why do we observe him guarding against this, evidently not thinking that falling in is alike good and not good? Evidently he judges one thing to be better and another worse. And if this is so, he must judge one thing to be man, and another to be not-man, one thing to be sweet and another to be not-sweet. For he does not aim at and judge all things alike . . .
> (*Metaphysics*, 1008b14-24)

People who act are like the man walking to Megara. They do something, indicating that they have a goal and think that a certain means, which they are undertaking, is the way to reach that goal. The man walking to Megara wanted to get to Megara; he did not want to go somewhere else. He sought his goal by walking towards Megara, not by walking in another direction, or falling into a well, or jumping off a cliff. We act because we believe certain things and have certain goals, which is to say that we do not believe the opposite things and have the oppose goals. In any particular action, we do not act as though things were anything and everything. Accordingly, action itself presupposes the Principle of Non-Contradiction.

The Principle of Excluded Middle is about the affirmation and denial of propositions. The denial of a proposition denies *exactly* what that proposition affirms. Consider:

(1) Socrates was born in Athens. (affirmation)
(2) It is not the case that Socrates was born in Athens. (denial)

The Principle of Non-Contradiction tells us that the affirmation and denial of a proposition cannot both be true, so according to it, statements (1) and (2) cannot both be true. The Principle of Excluded Middle tells us something else: that there is no half-way point between the affirmation of a proposition and its denial. One must be true and the other false; these are the only two possibilities. For example, either Socrates was born in Athens or he was not.

To apply the Principle of Excluded Middle, we must be sure that the two propositions considered genuinely stand in the relation of affirmation and denial. This can be tricky. Consider, for instance, these propositions:

(3) Athens is a beautiful city.
(4) Athens is an ugly city.

In a loose sense we might say that propositions (3) and (4) say "the opposite." Nevertheless, (4) does not deny what (3) affirms. Why not? Because there are many alternatives between being beautiful and being ugly. The denial of (3) is 'It is not the case that Athens is a beautiful city.' But to say this is NOT to say that Athens is an ugly city. (A city could fail to be beautiful because it had a rather mediocre appearance; this would not mean that it was ugly.) Between beautiful and ugly there are intermediate states; thus the "middle" cannot be excluded.

To apply the Principle of Excluded Middle properly, we have to be sure that we are really considering the affirmation and denial of the same proposition. The case has to be like (1) and (2), and NOT like (3) and (4). The Principle of Excluded Middle says that the affirmation of a proposition must be true, or its denial must be true, and there is no third possibility. The two possibilities divide the universe.

> For if one person says that something will be and another denies this same thing, it is clearly necessary for one of them to be saying what is true – if every affirmation is true or false; for both will not be the case together under such circumstances. . . . It is necessary for the affirmation or the negation to be true.
> (*De Interpretatione* 9, 18a34-b3)

There are two truth values for a clearly understood proposition, true and false, and the proposition must have one or the other. Whether we know or judge the proposition to be true or false is another question, but whatever the state of our knowledge, clearly formulated propositions must be either true or false and can be nothing in between. The "middle" is excluded.

Demonstration and the Complete Science

Aristotle had a conception of what a systematic complete body of scientific knowledge would look like if it were perfectly organized. He believed that it would consist of a hierarchy of demonstrative syllogisms. Aristotle described this conception of a completed science in his *Posterior Analytics*, using *demonstration* as his basic idea. Interestingly, however, Aristotle's own scientific writings consisted mostly of reports of observations and informal argument. There is scarcely one complete syllogism to be found in all of his scientific treatises. His observations were extensive and his theorizing considerable but he had not reached the stage of formalizing a completed science.

A demonstration is a valid syllogism in which the premises enable us to know and understand the conclusion. In a demonstration the premises must be "primary" – not known by virtue of anything else and prior to the conclusion. The premises are better known than the conclusion and knowledge is supposed to flow down from them to the conclusion. Fundamental premises would not be derived from any other more basic premises. Aristotle seems to have thought that fundamental premises or principles would be grounded in induction, or generalizations from experience.

In a demonstration the premises are not only supposed to prove the conclusion true; they are also supposed to describe the cause of the facts described in the conclusion and, in doing so, offer an explanation. (Such arguments have been called "syllogisms of the because.") Aristotle regarded the world as hierarchically organized into genus and species divisions. If we ask a question of the form

'Why do deer have antlers?' we should be able to find an answer of the form 'Because deer are in a sub-class of the more general class M, and all M's have antlers.' We could then formulate a valid syllogism:

> All deer are M's.
> All M's have antlers.
> Therefore,
> All deer have antlers.

Seeking this explanation, we assume that it is a fact that deer have antlers and that there is some explanation for this fact. The explanation can be discovered if we find the right middle term, M, which gives the reason why.

Sometimes Aristotle went so far as to describe scientific inquiry as a process of searching for middle terms. But judging from his scientific writing, he did not himself do science this way. Aristotle's syllogistic view of science should not be seen as a blueprint for inquiry. Rather, we should understand it as a model of what a completed and perfectly organized science would look like, if such a science were ever to exist.

Aristotle believed that in his extensive description of the syllogism, he had described all formally valid arguments in syllogistic form. He may have believed in addition that all valid arguments were syllogistic in form. (Because Aristotle used other forms of argument in his own writings, whether or not he believed this is debatable.) But whatever Aristotle himself thought about the matter, it is now recognized that syllogistic logic describes only some valid arguments, not all of them. It does not handle valid arguments based on *relations* (e.g., Susan is taller than Mary and Mary is taller than Angela; therefore Susan is taller than Angela) or on the connections between *propositions* as opposed to classes (e.g., Either Socrates is dead or Socrates is alive; Socrates is not alive; therefore Socrates is dead). Due to the influence of Aristotelian thought in the Middle Ages, syllogistic logic was for many centuries assumed by other philosophers to be the essence, and even the whole, of formal logic.

While perhaps mistaken about the scope of his logic, Aristotle avoided a mistake made by many contemporary logicians. He did not assume that every account of argument should be couched in formal terms. On the contrary: Aristotle had much to say about informal logic (general considerations about the merits of arguments not couched in formal terms) and rhetoric (techniques of persuasion). He did not think that demonstrations were the only arguments worthy of attention. Inductive arguments – probabilistic arguments based on premises from sense experience – are crucially important in the establishment of knowledge. Such arguments are not demonstrations in the Aristotelian sense.

Dialectic

Aristotle distinguished *demonstration* from *dialectic*. Some questions require a dialectical treatment, because there is no method other than arguing back and forth that can be used to address them. Examples of such questions are 'Should we pursue pleasure?' and 'Is the world eternal?'. On such questions, Aristotle said, people may have no opinion at all, or may disagree; in fact, even those who are supposed to be the most wise may disagree about these things. (One such contemporary example is that of a fundamental issue in the abortion debate: When does life begin?)

In dialectic, we do not have premises known to be true, upon which to base our arguments. We must use other starting points, such as the claims conceded by those people participating in a discussion. Premises in a dialectical argument are conceded by participants, and then there is a search for conclusions that can be derived from them. If the arguments are good and persuasive, those conclusions will also be conceded by participants, and progress can be made. As a member of Plato's Academy for twenty years, Aristotle was familiar with dialectic as practiced there. Perhaps because he assumed that his readers would share this familiarity, he did not offer a detailed description of the practice of dialectic. Arguments used in dialectic were supposed to be sound and non-deceptive. But they did not have to be syllogistic in form. Generally the activity of arguing back and forth was understood in a highly competitive way. People who argued opposite sides of the case apparently regarded each other as opponents; they attacked each other and tried to defend their own ideas, or positions, against attack. Dialectic was to be used to win arguments; in some of his writings, Aristotle sought to describe winning strategies. In this sense dialectic was almost a kind of sport – as are many contemporary debates in which the object seems to be to win, rather than to find out what is true about the subject under discussion.

There are two quite different perspectives on argument: we may argue to win our case, or we may argue in search of the truth. In different places and with respect to different topics, Aristotle takes both perspectives. For Aristotle, as for Plato and Socrates, dialectic also had its truth-seeking side, and important intellectual purposes were served. At one point Aristotle comments that in dialectic we have an eye only to common opinion, whereas in philosophy we treat things for their truth. But this contrast can be overstated: in philosophy too dialectic is used. Dialectic may be a kind of competitive intellectual sport in which people set out to win victories from their opponents, but it is not *only* that. The back-and-forth debate that characterizes dialectic can be genuinely illuminating. Pursuing arguments and counter-arguments, we are allowed to see both sides of a case. The dialectical process reveals puzzles and problems, and stimulates our curiosity as to how different views can be reconciled, or whether new theories can emerge from the old ones.

Aristotle accepted the Platonic idea that dialectic could enable thinkers to understand fundamental principles.

> It [dialectic] has a further use in relation to the principles used in the several sciences. For it is impossible to discuss them at all from the principles proper to the particular science in hand, seeing that the principles are primitive in relation to everything else; it is through reputable opinions about them that these have to be discussed, and this task belongs properly, or most appropriately, to dialectic; for dialectic is a process of criticism wherein lies the path to the principles of all inquiries.
> (*Topics*, 101a37-b4)

The fundamental principles of a science cannot themselves be demonstrated. To say that they are *fundamental* is to say that they cannot be demonstrated from other principles. Since they are basic to a science, they cannot be justified with reference to that particular science. Such a procedure would amount to arguing in a circle. Such principles may be investigated using general techniques of philosophical criticism – that is to say, by employing dialectical arguments.

Observations

Aristotle's views on thinking are difficult to summarize because of the breadth and complexity of his thought. He explored many subjects ranging from biology and physics to psychology, logic, ethics, politics, metaphysics, and literary criticism. Because Aristotle said so many different things about so many different subjects, his views are hard to state in just a few words. We can generalize that Aristotle valued observations, tended to think in quite concrete terms, attended to the beliefs and theories of others, and was a careful thinker, seldom neglecting relevant differences and distinct senses of terms. Perhaps because of his use of *endoxa*, Aristotelian views tend to be closer to "common sense" than those of many other philosophers and creative thinkers.

Aristotle believed and argued that different subjects demanded different styles and standards of thought. He was not a reductionist thinker; that is to say, he did not try to reduce good thinking to one single thing, as have some other thinkers who regard logic, mathematics, or physics, as the ultimate and best sort of knowledge. Aristotle believed that each area of study has its own problems, patterns, and styles of reflection. Appropriate and accurate thinking in logic is one thing; in psychology it is something else; in metaphysics and ethics something else again. There is no hierarchy of subjects in Aristotle – no sense that one type of knowledge, or one style of thinking, is highest and best and produces conclusions that dictate the rest of science. Theoretical understanding requires knowledge of universal and necessary propositions, which are organized so that the facts of the world are fully explained. Practical wisdom requires sensitivity, deliberation, and good judgment about subjects not susceptible to full proof.

Aristotle was nothing if not a highly original, subtle, and complex thinker. His philosophy left enduring contributions and problems, only some of which have been explored here.

For some time after Aristotle's death his writings survived only in a tattered and damaged form. Eventually they were published by Andronicus of Rhodes sometime between 43 and 20 B.C. Contemporary versions of Aristotle's treatises derive from this edition. Aristotle's influence continued at the Lyceum in the period immediately following his death. In Greek and Roman times there were many other noteworthy philosophical movements – including Platonism, Atomism, Epicureanism, Stoicism, Cynicism, and Scepticism. Athens continued as a major center for philosophy until 529 A.D., when the Emperor Justinian closed its philosophical schools. After that, philosophical activity continued in Constantinople.

Through Latin and Arabic translations, nearly all of the Aristotelian works that we now possess had become available to scholars in Europe between the ninth and twelfth centuries A.D. On the whole, they were received enthusiastically. In 1255 the university in Paris required students to study the *Organon*, *Physics*, *Ethics*,

Metaphysics and *On the Soul*. But there was some concern that Aristotle was not a properly Christian thinker. In the thirteenth century Thomas Aquinas (1224 - 1274) worked out an elaborate philosophical system in which he synthesized central themes from Aristotle's work with Christian beliefs. This system, highly original in many respects, established the respectability of Aristotle in the predominantly Christian Europe of the high Middle Ages. For centuries it was common to refer to him as "the Philosopher" – as though there was only one. The philosophy of Aquinas, who is often referred to as St. Thomas, is still an important force in the world because of its considerable importance for Catholic theology and moral teaching. Through Aquinas and Catholicism, Aristotelian ideas still have tremendous influence in the contemporary world.

In one sense Aquinas did a lot for Aristotle's philosophical reputation, attending to and explaining many details of his works and entrenching the position of Aristotelian philosophy in the universities and schools. In another sense, though, understanding and appreciation of Aristotle as a creative and original thinker was inhibited when he came to be regarded as an authoritative source of knowledge on virtually every topic. There was a strong tendency after the thirteenth century to treat Aristotle's work as dogma – to see only a fixed system and miss the subtleties, complexities, and problems emerging from Aristotle's thought. Eventually there was a strong reaction against the dogmatism of the scholastics. By the seventeenth century, many thoughtful Europeans were more than willing to dispute the Aristotelianism they had come to know because it was highly dogmatic. Among prominent rebels were Bacon, Hobbes, and Descartes.

4

Descartes: Are There Rotten Apples in that Basket?

Rene Descartes (1596 - 1650) was born at La Haye in France. His mother died a year after his birth. Descartes was a sickly child, pale, with a dry cough, and it was feared that he would not survive to adulthood. Descartes was sent to LaFleche, a liberal Jesuit school. The teachers appreciated his talent and allowed him to have his own room and sleep late because of his troubled health. Upon finishing the program at LaFleche, Descartes went to the University of Paris, where he studied law. Although he enjoyed studying history, literature, and various classics of the past, he was quite dissatisfied with the state of his knowledge on completion of his formal education. He felt that he lacked certainty.

In Descartes' time, the issue of finding a firm foundation for belief was an especially pressing one. As a result of the Protestant reformation, Catholic Christianity was challenged by new churches and sects. Within the Catholic Church, the Inquisition was a fearful institution, to which prominent thinkers such as Galileo had been forced to submit. There was intense, often violent, disagreement about religious doctrine and there seemed to be no reliable methods for resolving philosophical and theological disputes. In philosophy, the recovery of ancient manuscripts meant that Plato, Aristotle, and other ancient authors were being studied with great zeal. But these classic works offered a confusing array of doctrines.

After completing his studies, Descartes sought to expose himself to "the book of the world." He travelled with the military in Holland and Germany. In 1619, in a stove-heated room, he had an intellectual vision of a mathematical science of nature. In 1628 Descartes moved to North Holland, where he continued to live and work for the next twenty years. The atmosphere for thought and publishing was comparatively free in Holland, which had a strong tradition of tolerance. In 1635, Descartes' relationship with a woman in Amsterdam led to the birth of a daughter, Francine. Her death at the age of five was one of the great tragedies of his life.

Descartes had keen interests in science and mathematics. He invented Cartesian coordinates, which make it possible to represent algebraic relationships geometrically. He also invented the system for representing mathematical powers. It was Descartes' ambition to work out a complete science of physical nature, describing nature in mechanical laws that could be expressed mathematically. Philosophy he saw as establishing roots from which the tree of knowledge would grow. Descartes believed that philosophy would be a relatively small part of his work. Nevertheless, it is primarily as a philosopher that he is remembered and studied today.

Descartes was essentially a solitary thinker. Through most of his life he stayed in bed through the morning, reading and writing in peace and quiet. At the invitation of Queen Christina of Sweden, who was trying to bring arts and culture to the north, Descartes went to Stockholm in 1649. He found life there disappointing and difficult. His problems in Sweden were compounded by the fact that the queen wanted lessons on philosophy at five o'clock in the morning. The change in habits proved to be too shocking for Descartes, who died of pneumonia in Stockholm in 1650.

Descartes was an intellectual revolutionary. He valued clarity, certainty, and intellectual independence and these values led him away from the philosophy of the schools of thought that had come to dominate Europe during the Middle Ages. Plato and Aristotle had been great and original thinkers in their own time, but by the seventeenth century they had too many followers who had no proper philosophical method and did not seek to develop original doctrines.

> ... we shall never be philosophers, if we have read all the arguments of Plato and Aristotle but cannot form a solid judgment on matters set before us; this sort of learning would appear historical rather than scientific.
> (*Rules for the Direction of the Mind*, 154)

Descartes was determined to think independently, chop through the obscurities of the jargon that had come to dominate discussions of philosophy, and discover for himself simple and clear truths. He believed that thought should above all be clear and understandable, and that the foundations of knowledge should be worked out by each person for himself or herself. Because this was Descartes' goal, he had quite definite views as to how thinking should be conducted. Like Plato he regarded geometric proof as a model for philosophy and believed that philosophy and the sciences had to be grounded on first principles. He sought rigorous proofs, and valued reason above all else as the source of insight into the world. Descartes was a rationalist; he believed that human reason was the primary source of knowledge.

The Method of Doubt

Descartes wanted to strike forth on his own, to establish his own solid foundation for philosophy and science. His method was to begin with doubt and scepticism. For him, scepticism was a technique to be used in achieving knowledge that was beyond doubt. Beliefs come from many sources, none especially reliable. To have any hope of establishing certainty, we should begin philosophizing by doubting all our previous beliefs.

> ... since book-learning ... has been made up, and has developed gradually, from the opinions of many different men, it is therefore not so close to the truth as the simple reasonings that a man of good sense may perform ... Again, I reflected, we were all children before we were men; we must have been governed a long time by our own appetites on the one hand and our preceptors on the other; these two sides must frequently have been opposed, and very likely there have been times when neither side urged us to the best course. Thus it is practically impossible for our judgments to be so clear or so firm as they would have been if we had had the full use of our reason from the moment of birth, and had never had any other guide.
> (*Discourse on Method*, Part Two, 16)

Descartes rejected the Aristotelian approach of beginning with *endoxa* or common beliefs. Descartes thought that many of our ordinary beliefs are not reliable and that a person who does not wish to be misled should be very careful about what he or she believes. Many people of differing interests and opinions write books; books say many different things. Many of our beliefs were acquired when we were children and not rationally independent. We were born not as miniature versions of Socrates, but as helpless dependent beings having little option but to take on trust what other people tell us. For these reasons Descartes resolved to withold his assent from any opinion that was not "completely certain and indubitable." Belief that could survive the rigorous screening process imposed by this method of doubt would establish the basis for certainty in philosophy and science.

Descartes wrote in the first person and his use of "I" was a novelty in philosophy at the time. It is direct and appealing, compatible with his goal of establishing a secure starting point by his own clear thinking. Yet his philosophical works are not only about his own doubts and thoughts; Descartes is not merely recounting a story about how he personally came to doubt and later reasoned his way back to certainty. The "I" stands for any reader and thinker who is using Descartes' works as a basis for reflection. We all have beliefs based on the senses; we all have experienced sensory illusions and vivid dreams. We are supposed to think with Descartes and, by meditating upon these considerations, come to understand that there are grounds for doubting our beliefs.

We cannot simply decide to doubt all our previous beliefs and then do it – just like that. To apply this method requires careful thought, meditation, and the exercise of the will. Descartes' most famous work, *Meditations on First Philosophy*, contains an invitation to the reader to think and meditate. By concentrating on the reasonings in the *Meditations* we can come to understand the basis for doubt and seriously apply it to our beliefs.

The first stage in cultivating doubt is a negative evaluation of knowledge that comes from the senses.

> Whatever I have up till now accepted as most true I have acquired either from the senses or through the senses. But from time to time I have found that the senses deceive, and it is prudent never to trust completely those who have deceived us even once.
> (*First Meditation*, 12)

We have many beliefs based on seeing, hearing, touching, smelling, and so on. None of these sources is completely reliable. For instance, we may see in the distance a tower which looks rounded and then, on coming close to it, discover that it is square. If we are looking for *indubitability* (that which we cannot doubt) we cannot find it in beliefs acquired from the senses.

But what about sense-based beliefs that seem impossible to doubt?

> – for example, that I am here, sitting by the fire, wearing a winter dressing-gown, holding this piece of paper in my hands, and so on. . . . how could it be denied that these hands or this whole body are mine?
> (*First Meditiation*, 13)

Would a person not have to be mad in order to doubt such a thing? This would be the sort of person who would say he was dressed in purple when he was completely naked! How could immediate experience like that of sitting by the fire, or seeing one's own hand, be misleading?

Well, there is the matter of dreams. Like other human beings, Descartes has had dreams. In his dreams it has seemed to him that he was awake, holding paper, sitting by the fire and so on. Yet all the while he was asleep in bed. Could he be dreaming when he feels so sure he is sitting by the fire? Could even the most immediate and apparently obvious sensory impressions be unreliable because of the possibility of dreaming?

> . . . at the moment my eyes are certainly wide awake when I look at this piece of paper; I shake my head and it [the head] is not asleep; as I stretch out and feel my hand I do so deliberately, and I know what I am doing. All this would not happen with such distinctness to someone asleep.

It seems that Descartes must know that he is awake, because it feels to him that he knows; he seems "certainly" to be wide awake. But is this good enough?

> As if I did not remember other occasions when I have been tricked by exactly similar thoughts while asleep! As I think about this more carefully, I see plainly that there are never any sure signs by means of which being awake can be distinguished from being asleep. The result is that I begin to feel dazed, and this very feeling only reinforces the notion that I may be asleep.
> (First Meditiation, 13)

Anything we perceive in waking life could come to us also in a dream. In some dreams things seem very vivid and lifelike. A person who feels quite sure that he is awake and seated by the fire could nevertheless be dreaming. If this were the case for Descartes, he would falsely suppose that the fire and the paper are things in the world and not just ideas in his mind. There is reason to doubt even the most obvious things, if the evidence for them comes from the senses, given the possibility that we could be dreaming.

But not all beliefs are grounded in sense experience. What about the truths of arithmetic and geometry, which do not come from this source? Perhaps they are still certain.

> For whether I am awake or asleep, two and three added together are five, and a square has no more than four sides. It seems impossible that such transparent truths should incur any suspicion of being false.
> (*First Meditation*, 14)

Can these sorts of truths perhaps still be relied upon? How could we go wrong in believing something like this? Could our very reason deceive us?

Perhaps even our reason could deceive us: there is, after all, the possibility that an all-powerful being exists. If there is an omnipotent being, that being might have made all appearances deceptive, making us feel and see the way we do – even if there were no earth or sky or any other extended thing. Descartes – or anyone else – might be the sort of creature that goes wrong even when he is doing the simplest thing, even when he feels absolutely confident that he is right, as when he adds two and three to get five. Descartes himself is an imperfect being, because he has been deceived or mistaken. The same line of argument would apply to any other human being. As imperfect beings, it is all the more likely we should make mistakes, and it would seem all the more difficult to achieve certainty.

> I have no answer to these arguments, but am finally compelled to admit that there is not one of my former beliefs about which a doubt may not properly be raised; and this is not a flippant or ill-considered conclusion, but is based on powerful and well thought-out reasons. So in future I must withhold my assent from these former beliefs just as carefully as I would from obvious falsehoods, if I want to discover any certainty.
> (*First Meditation*, 15)

When the possibility of a deceiving omnipotent being [God being a deceiver] is added to the arguments from dreaming and the unreliability of sense perception, the scope of doubt seems universal. Even the most basic propositions of arithmetic can be doubted.

Doubt calls for effort because we usually accept our habitual opinions without reflection. To *doubt,* we need to suspend our judgment by exercising our freedom to not believe. We must struggle against our old beliefs and habitual opinions. Even after understanding cogent arguments which show that our customary beliefs are doubtful, we tend to lapse back into our old confidence. Descartes recommends that we struggle against our habitual beliefs by "pretending for a time that these former opinions are utterly false and imaginary." Employing this technique, we can seek to establish a kind of counter-balance to the weight of preconceived opinion in our minds. No harm will come from failing to endorse commonsense beliefs because the project is one of pure inquiry. It concerns only theoretical knowledge and certainty – not practical knowledge or action. Descartes said that his task in constructing a philosophical system did not involve action, but merely the acquisition of knowledge. Descartes did not propose walking through a fire on the supposition that fire is only an idea in his mind, or refuse to use ordinary arithmetic when calculating his grocery bills. In matters of practice, he was willing to conform to custom. But in matters of theory he proposed to doubt everything.

To maximize his doubt, Descartes supposes that some malicious demon or Evil Genius is employing all his energies in an effort to deceive. On this hypothesis, all external things are merely the delusions of dreams; Descartes would not even have a physical body. Doubt has become extreme or, as is often said, hyperbolic.

To defend universal doubt against a critic of his day, Descartes offers an analogy:

> Suppose he had a basket full of apples and, being worried that some of the apples were rotten, wanted to take out the rotten ones to prevent the rot spreading. How would he proceed? Would he not begin by tipping the whole lot out of the basket? And would not the next step be to cast his eye over each apple in turn, and pick up and put back in the basket only those he saw to be sound, leaving the others? In just the same way, those who have never philosophized correctly have various opinions in their minds which they have begun to store up since childhood, and which they therefore have reason to believe may in many cases be false. They then attempt to separate the false beliefs from the others, so as to prevent their contaminating the rest and making the whole lot uncertain. Now the best way they can accomplish this is to reject all their beliefs together in one go, as if they were all uncertain and false. They can then go over each belief in turn and re-adopt only those which they recognize to be true and indubitable. Thus I was right to begin by rejecting all my beliefs.
> (*Seventh Replies*, 63)

As rot will spread among apples in a basket, falsehood and uncertainty will spread among beliefs. Since our beliefs are logically related to each other, the falsehood or uncertainty of some will undermine the certainty of others.

Descartes was an *epistemic individualist*. That is to say, he wanted to start a system of knowledge by himself, using only propositions which he himself, in unclouded mental vision, could clearly understand to be indubitable. But can intellectual independence be taken to these lengths? Can a person really doubt everything, distancing himself or herself from all previous assumptions and opinions? There are many indications in the *Meditations* that Descartes did not shake off his religious beliefs. Nor did he entirely cease to employ the concepts and distinctions of the scholastic philosophy in which he had been trained – not to mention the assumptions embodied in the structures of the Latin and French languages in which he thought and wrote. Reflecting on the apple analogy, one might compare language to the basket in which the apples are contained. The apples are examined one by one before being put back in the basket, but the basket itself is never scrutinized.

Cogito Ergo Sum: I think, therefore I am.

In the *Second Meditation*, Descartes reflects on his strange situation.

> So serious are the doubts into which I have been thrown as a result of yesterday's meditation that I can neither put them out of my mind nor see any way of resolving them. It feels as if I have fallen unexpectedly into a deep whirlpool which tumbles me around so that I can neither stand on the bottom nor swim to the top. . . . Anything which admits of the slightest doubt I will set aside just as if I had found it to be wholly false; and I will proceed this way until I recognize something certain or, if nothing else, until I at least recognize for certain that there is no certainty. Archimedes used to demand just one firm and immovable point in order to shift the entire earth; so I too can hope for great things if I manage to find just one thing, however slight, that is certain and unshakeable.
> (*Second Meditation*, 16)

To clear his mind of past prejudices and careless assumptions, Descartes meditates on the possibilities that everything is an illusion, that there is no world outside his mind, that even his memory is deceiving him, and that perhaps there is not even a god.

But would it follow that he himself did not exist? If there were to be no physical world, Descartes would have no body. But even in such a circumstance, if he had convinced himself of anything at all, he would surely have to exist. Even if an Evil Genius were to deceive him, he would have to exist in order to be deceived.

> . . . let him deceive me as much as he can, he will never bring it about that I am nothing so long as I think that I am something. So after considering everything very thoroughly, I must finally conclude that this proposition *I am, I exist,* is necessarily true whenever it is put forward by me or conceived in my mind.
> (*Second Meditation*, 17)

And so there is a certainty. Whatever else may be doubtful, the being that doubts IS doubting. And that being must EXIST in order to do so. Even a deceiving God or Evil Genius could not undermine this certainty.

In the *Discourse on the Method* the insight was stated in French as "je pense, donc je suis" – I think, therefore I am. The Latin words are "cogito ergo sum" and the argument is often referred to simply as the *Cogito*. For any thinking being, "I exist" is indubitable. One may try to doubt it, but the very act of trying to doubt it will show that it is true. To doubt, or to think, one must exist. If I doubt, I exist. This is the foundation point Descartes was looking for, the beginning of a reconstruction of a system of knowledge after the universal doubt.

What, then, is this 'I' that exists? Descartes considers his previous opinions. Following the Aristotelian philosophy, he had once thought that he was a rational animal. He thought that he had a face, hands, arms, and a whole physical body, that he was able to perceive the external world through his senses, and that he could touch himself and other objects in the world. But if there is an Evil Genius, he could be deceived about any or all of these things. The Cogito establishes existence. But existence of what? Of a being that doubts and thinks; of a thinking thing.

> Thinking? At last I have discovered it – thought; this alone is inseparable from me. I am, I exist – that is certain. But for how long? For as long as I am thinking. For it could be that were I totally to cease from thinking, I should totally cease to exist. At present I am not admitting anything except what is necessarily true. I am, then, in the strict sense only a thing that thinks; that is, I am a mind, intelligence, or intellect, or reason – words whose meaning I have been ignorant of until now. But for all that I am a thing which is real and which truly exists. But what kind of a thing? As I have just said – a thinking thing.
> (*Second Meditation*, 18)

This thing which doubts is a thinking thing. Should it cease to think, it may well cease to exist.

There is a joke about this theme. – A man walks into a bar and the bartender asks him whether he wants a whiskey. "I think not," he says. He immediately disappears. – Descartes would not likely have appreciated this joke, which assumes that there is a normal world in which people have bodies, walk into bars, want drinks, and so on and so forth. As the joke illustrates, the Cogito with its notion that existence is bound to thinking is amusingly different from our common sense conception of persons. But then again, the *Second Meditation* is set not in the normal world of common sense, but in the context of hyperbolic doubt.

Descartes has adopted the policy of assenting only to beliefs he recognizes as indubitable. At this stage of the *Second Meditation*, he does not yet know he has a body. Knowledge of himself as a mind cannot, then, depend on knowledge of himself as a body. To understand what sort of being he is, he has to distinguish what he knows – thought – from what he does not yet know – body or extended things outside the mind.

> But what then am I? A thing that thinks. What is that? A thing that doubts, understands, affirms, denies, is willing, is unwilling, and also imagines and has sensory perceptions.
> This is a considerable list, if everything on it belongs to me. But does it? Is it not one and the same 'I' who is now doubting almost everything, who nonetheless understands some things, who affirms that this one thing is true, denies everything else, desires to know more, is unwilling to be deceived, imagines many things even involuntarily, and is aware of many things which apparently come from the senses? Are not all these things just as true as the fact that I exist, even if I am asleep all the time, and even if he who created me is doing all he can to deceive me? . . . The fact that it is I who am doubting and understanding and willing is so evident that I see no way of making it any clearer. But it is also the case that the 'I' who imagines is the same 'I.'
> (*Second Meditation*, 19)

Thinking includes doubting, understanding, willing and imagining. What a thinking being imagines may not be real, but his perceptions and his imagining (thought) of it quite definitely are.

At this stage, then, Descartes knows indubitably that he is a thinking being, and does not know (yet) that he has a body – or even that there are any physical things in the world. Things he seems to know about the physical world – for instance that wax smells like honey – might in a careless moment strike him as more certain and obvious than his knowledge of his own mind. But if they do, it is a mistake.

> Surely my awareness of my own self is not merely much truer and more certain than my awareness of the wax, but also much more distinct and evident. For if I judge that the wax exists from the fact that I see it, clearly this same fact entails much more evidently that I myself also exist. It is possible that what I see is not wax; it is possible that I do not even have eyes with which to see anything. But when I see, or think I see (I am not here distinguishing the two) it is simply not possible that I who am now thinking am not something.
> (*Second Meditation*, 22)

Beliefs about physical things like wax can be doubted, but a person's knowledge of his or her own immediate thought and existence cannot. It is this knowledge which is easiest and "most evident." With this theme, Descartes ends his *Second Meditation*.

How much has Descartes established about the mind and the body in this meditation? If he is arguing that because he knows his mind before he knows his body, his mind is something distinct from his body, he is surely committing a fallacy. From the fact that I can know A without yet knowing B, it does not follow that A is, in reality, distinct from B.

The materialist philosopher Pierre Gassendi (1592 - 1655) did not find Descartes' conclusions about himself as a thinking thing especially impressive.

> As regards the nature of the body, you have, O Mind, listed all the things we know: extension, shape, occupation of space, and so on. But what, after all your efforts, have you told us about yourself? You are not a bodily structure, you are not air, not a wind, not a thing which walks or senses, you are not this and not that . . . given that you are looking for knowledge of yourself which is superior to common knowledge . . . you must see that it is certainly not enough for you to announce that you are a thing that thinks and doubts and understands, etc. You should carefully scrutinize yourself and conduct a kind of chemical investigation of yourself, if you are to succeed in uncovering and explaining to us your internal substance.
> (*Fifth Objections*, 71)

Descartes was not convinced. He replied that Gassendi did not know how to ask the right questions about the mind.

> Nor do I see what more you expect here, unless it is to be told what colour or smell or taste the human mind has, or the proportions of salt, sulphur and mercury from which it is compounded. You want us, you say, to conduct 'a kind of chemical investigation' of the mind, as we would of wine. This is indeed worthy of you, O Flesh, and of all those who have only a very confused conception of everything, and so do not know the proper questions to ask about each thing.
> (*Fifth Replies*, 71-72)

From doubting and thinking, we know that we exist as thinking things, and we know this before we know the existence or nature of any physical body.

Proofs of God's Existence

The Cogito suggests a method for arriving at certain knowledge.

> In this first item of knowledge there is simply a clear and distinct perception of what I am asserting; this would not be enough to make me certain of the truth of the matter if it could ever turn out that something which I perceived with such clarity and distinctness was false. So I now seem to be able to lay it down as a general rule that whatever I perceive very clearly and distinctly is true.
> (*Third Meditation*, 24)

But is this rule acceptable? What about the hyperbolic doubt, the possibility that there is an Evil Genius deceiving him? For all he knows at this stage, Descartes might be a creature who could be wrong even when he feels most convinced. These grounds for wondering whether his own reason is reliable are "very slight and, so to speak, metaphysical." But the possibility of an Evil Genius remains; Descartes has, at this point, no conclusive argument against it. To dismiss this hyperbolic doubt, Descartes undertakes the task of exploring God's nature and existence.

> . . . in order to remove even this slight reason for doubt, as soon as the opportunity arises I must examine whether there is a God, and, if there is, whether he can be a deceiver. For if I do not know this, it seems that I can never be quite certain about anything else.
> (*Third Meditation*, 25)

At this point, Descartes has ideas of animals, corporeal objects, plants, angels, God, and other men. Where do these ideas come from? Perhaps he has made them up himself; he might have done so. But this would not be possible, Descartes argues, in the case of the idea of God. The idea of God is the idea of a perfect being, an infinite substance, eternal and unchanging, supremely intelligent and powerful, existing independently, a being which created Descartes and everything else – that is, if anything else exists. Whether or not God exists, Descartes is certain that he has a clear and distinct *idea* of God. This idea must come from somewhere; there must be a cause for it. That cause, Descartes argues, is God himself; it could not be anything else, since a cause must contain at least as much reality as its effect.

> Now it is manifest by the natural light that there must be at least as much reality in the efficient and total cause as in the effect of that cause. For where, I ask, could the effect get its reality from, if not from the cause? And how could the cause give it to the effect unless it possessed it? It follows from this both that something cannot arise from nothing, and also that what is more perfect – that is, contains in itself more reality – cannot arise from what is less perfect.
> (*Third Meditation*, 28)

When Descartes refers to the "natural light" he is alluding to his powers of reason, to principles that are self-evident and that he can logically intuit to be true. Such principles as 'everything has a cause;' 'the cause of a thing must be as real as its effect;' and 'what is more perfect cannot arise from what is less perfect' he takes to be basic self-evident truths of this kind.

Descartes doubts and is capable of being deceived; thus he is an imperfect being. As an imperfect being, he himself cannot produce an idea of a perfect being. Yet he does have an idea of God. God, therefore, must exist – as a perfect being, the author of Descartes' own existence, and the being who has produced in his creature, Descartes, the idea of a perfect being (God himself).

> Altogether then, it must be concluded that the mere fact that I exist and have within me an idea of a most perfect being, that is, God, provides a very clear proof that God indeed exists.
> . . . When I turn my mind's eye upon myself, I understand that I am a thing which is incomplete and dependent on another and which aspires without limit to ever greater and better things; but I also understand at the same time that he on whom I depend has within him all those greater things, not just indefinitely and poten-

> tially, but actually and infinitely, and hence that he is God. The whole force of the argument lies in this: I recognize that it would be impossible for me to exist with the kind of nature I have – that is, having within me the idea of God – were it not the case that God really existed.
> (*Fourth Meditation*, 35)

This argument is not convincing. Even granting that everything must have some cause, there are alternative possible causes for having the idea of a perfect being. It is entirely possible, for instance, that Descartes' idea of God came from his Jesuit teachers at LaFleche rather than from God himself.

Descartes now believes himself to have proven that God, a perfect being, exists. Having moved this far, he can dismiss the Evil Genius hypothesis and eliminate hyperbolic doubt.

> By 'God' I mean the very being the idea of whom is within me, that is, the possessor of all the perfections which I cannot grasp, but can somehow reach in my thought, who is subject to no defects whatsoever. It is clear enough from this that he cannot be a deceiver, since it is manifest by the natural light that all fraud and deception depend on some defect.
> (*Third Meditation*, 35)

God exists and God is, by definition, a perfect being. As such, He could not be a deceiver. Thus God would not create human beings, such as Descartes, in such a way that their powers of reason would be warped and misleading. Because God exists and is not a deceiver, human reason must be reliable. Now Descartes can again have full confidence in his own powers of reason. Those things which are clear from "the natural light" he can take to be certain and indubitable. The only reason for doubting them was the Evil Genius hypothesis, and he has now dismissed that hypothesis on the grounds that God exists and God is no deceiver.

What are these self-evident truths known by reason or "the natural light"? Examples are:

> From the fact that I doubt I can conclude that I exist.
> There must be at least as much reality in the efficient and total cause as in its effect. Fraud and deception necessarily proceed from some defect.
> Nothing can be the cause of nothing.
> The same thing cannot both be and not be. (A version of the Principle of Non-Contradiction)
> Two is even and three is odd.
> If equals are added to equals, the result is equal.

Most of these principles seem clear and self-evidently true. But the use of reason, and principles of reason, to prove God's existence is a problem when the context is one of hyperbolic doubt. The issue raised is that of the *Cartesian Circle.*

The Problem of the Cartesian Circle

A person is said to "argue in a circle" when he or she uses premises and assumptions that would not be appropriate unless the conclusion were true or accepted. Circular argument (also called begging the question) is a fallacy in logic. To justify a conclusion we cannot properly use premises that presuppose that that conclusion is true.

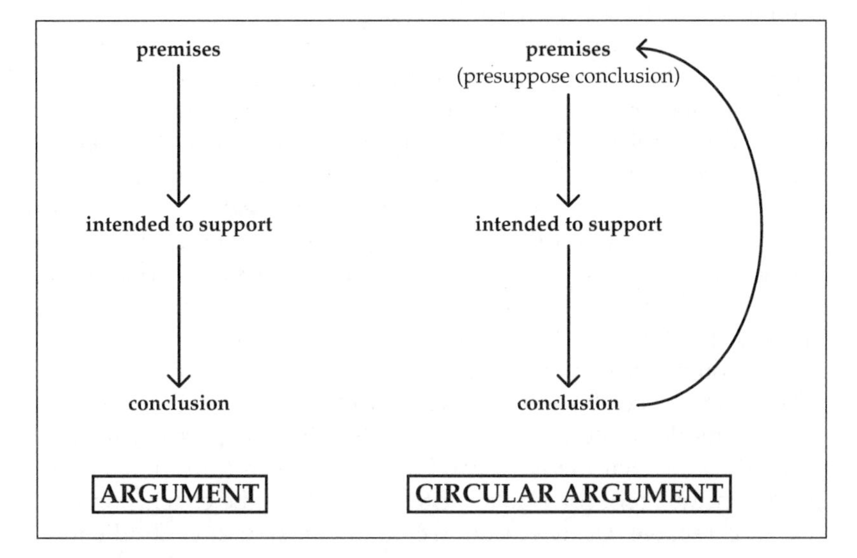

It has seemed to many readers and critics, both in his time and in our own, that Descartes is caught in a troublesome circle when he appeals to reason to prove God's existence, and then appeals to the existence and non-deceptiveness of God in order to show that reason is reliable. Descartes must rely on basic principles of reason in order to argue for God's existence. But having "proven" God's existence, he then appeals to God to justify relying on basic principles of reason. X is used to prove the existence of Y – but then Y is needed and used to justify relying on X. Isn't this a circular argument?

One critic who was convinced that the argument was circular was Antoine Arnauld (1612 - 1694), a theologian who wrote a set of objections to the *Meditations*. Arnauld said:

> The only remaining scruple I have is uncertainty as to how a circular reasoning is to be avoided in saying: "the only secure reason we have for believing that what we clearly and distinctly perceive is true is that God exists." But we can be sure that God exists, only because we clearly and evidently perceive that; therefore prior to being certain that God exists, we should be certain that whatever we clearly and evidently perceive is true.
> (Fourth Objections, 92)

Contemporary scholars still discuss the issue of whether Descartes inadvertently committed the fallacy of arguing in a circle. Some have tried to rescue Descartes from this charge.

It is hard to avoid being circular if one is trying to justify reason itself. (Aristotle recognized this problem when considering whether we could demonstrate that the Principle of Non-Contradiction was correct.) In order to set forth a justification in argument, one has to reason. Even disregarding the particular difficulty of proving God's existence, there seems to be a general problem of *reasoning* in order to justify *reason*. Wouldn't such reasoning necessarily be circular? The problem arises in a particularly acute way in Descartes because the hyperbolic doubt that he posits is so extreme that it applies or should apply to reason itself; hyperbolic doubt gives grounds for thinking that reason might be unreliable. Would anyone who takes this possibility seriously be able to escape circularity?

One modern interpreter has suggested that Descartes be regarded as showing that the most careful use of reason (presumably displayed in the proof for God's existence) leads to the conclusion that reason is reliable. Using reason, we do not encounter contradictions or arguments against reason. In that sense, reason is justified. On this interpretation, Descartes can be saved from the charge of arguing in a circle – though there are other criticisms of his argument for God's existence.

After the *Third Meditation*, Descartes proceeds from the conviction that God exists, is good, and is a non-deceiver. God would not make his creatures (human beings like Descartes) the sort of being that is systematically deceived. Because this is so, Descartes now feels confident that the physical world must exist. His ideas and inclinations make him strongly convinced that it does and since God is good, these ideas and inclinations should not be systematically misleading. The essence of the physical world is to be corporeal matter.

Matter, in the physical world, is extended, unthinking, and outside the mind. Descartes offers another proof for God's existence and further arguments that the mind must be absolutely distinct from the body.

Descartes argued that disciplined thought should be simple and clear – absolutely lucid, so that no step forward is taken without our clearly and distinctly understanding the reasons for it. We should move forward in simple steps, breaking down complex problems so that, with concentration, we can logically intuit every move at every stage. But it is hard to be convinced that the proof of God in the *Third Meditation* measures up to this standard. For most readers, the pivotal role of God in establishing the possibility of knowledge in the Cartesian system comes as a disappointment. Descartes' standards for lucidity and indubitability are so high that his own work is not able to measure up to them.

Thinking, Error, and Free Will

Assuming that God exists and is not a deceiver, why do Descartes and other human beings make mistakes? Descartes argues that God is not to be blamed when human beings make mistaken judgments. To show that human beings, not God, are responsible for intellectual errors, Descartes offers a theory about error and what we can do to avoid it. Error results because we tend to jump to conclusions. We make judgments too quickly, on imperfect evidence. We can avoid mistakes and achieve certainty if we hold back and assent only to those propositions which we clearly and distinctly perceive to be true.

When we make a judgment, two aspects or faculties of the mind are involved: the understanding and the will. It is the understanding which apprehends or perceives the various ideas or propositions which we will judge to be either true or false: 'I exist,' 'I have a pain in my knee,' 'Lemons are yellow,' 'God exists', 'God is all-powerful', or whatever. It is the will which pronounces the judgment, saying, in effect, "yes" or "no" to such propositions. Descartes believed that our understanding is limited, but our will is not. It is every bit as great as the will of God.

> . . . (N)evertheless it [God's will] does not seem any greater than mine when considered as will in the essential and strict sense. This is because the will simply consists in our ability to do or not do something (that is to affirm or deny, to pursue or avoid); or rather,

> it consists simply in the fact that when the intellect puts something forward for affirmation or denial or for pursuit or avoidance, our inclinations are such that we do not feel we are determined by any external force.
> (*Fourth Meditation*, 40)

When we make a judgment using the will, we can affirm or deny any proposition. If we do so without a clear and distinct understanding, we make mistakes. In such cases, the will rushes ahead of the understanding. It assents prematurely, "leaping to a conclusion." Our will is free: we can say "yes"; we can say "no"; or we can suspend judgment. To avoid error when we do not have a clear and distinct perception, we should suspend our judgment. Should we judge too quickly, the blame will be ours.

According to Descartes, there are two ways in which the will is free: it has the freedom of indifference, and the freedom of spontaneity. The *freedom of indifference* is a matter of having choices. This is the sort of freedom we have when we are considering a proposition for which there is no compelling evidence either that it is true or that it is false. Suppose we are considering the proposition 'The ceasefire will hold.' We can affirm it (believe that the ceasefire will hold) or deny it (believe that the ceasefire will not hold) or suspend our judgment. The proper thing to do when we do not have compelling evidence either way is to suspend judgment.

> If, however, I simply refrain from making a judgment in cases where I do not perceive the truth with sufficient clarity and distinctness, then it is clear that I am behaving correctly and avoiding error. But if in such cases I either affirm or deny, then I am not using my free will correctly. If I go for the alternative which is false, then obviously I shall be in error; if I take the other side, then it is by pure chance that I arrive at the truth, and I shall still be at fault, since it is clear by the natural light that the perception of the intellect should always precede the determination of the will.
> (*Fourth Meditation*, 41)

Freedom in the sense of choice or "indifference" is also involved when we make a decision whether or not to pay attention to something. We notice a drop of dew on a flower; we decide whether to pay attention to it or not. Making decisions about what we will pay attention to and controlling the focus of our attention is a crucial aspect of freedom of thought. When we do pay attention to something, if we wish to understand it and acquire knowledge, we must concentrate and not allow ourselves to become distracted. To achieve clarity and certainty Descartes advises that we should concentrate the mind on simple things and not let our attention wander.

The other sort of freedom, *freedom of spontaneity,* is a matter of assenting as we want to assent. This is something quite different from making choices under circumstances where we can go either way. When evidence is "compelling" we cannot help but believe, but we are nevertheless believing as we wish to. In the case of the *Cogito,* for instance, we clearly and distinctly understand that "I exist" is true, and we cannot help but believe it. In this case and others like it, we do not have a choice as to what to believe. We can only judge in one way, but this is not because any external force is compelling us. It is because there is "a great light in the intellect" followed by "a great inclination in the will." There is not choice, but for Descartes, that does not mean that the will is unfree. We are believing what we want to believe; we would not want things to be any other way.

Why do human beings make mistakes? This happens because we do not exercise our capacity to suspend judgment; we assent or dissent before we have enough evidence. Whenever we have insufficient evidence, we do not have clear and distinct perceptions, and in all such cases we can choose to believe, disbelieve, or suspend judgment. Some of Descartes' critics wondered about free will. How do we know that we have this free will? Descartes says:

> Let everyone just go down deep into himself and find out whether or not he has a perfect and absolute will, and whether he can conceive of anything which surpasses him in freedom of the will. I am sure everyone will find that it is as I say. It is in this [sense] then, that the will is greater and more godlike than the intellect. (*Conversations with Burman*, 21)

In this way Descartes replied to questions about free will by saying that we know our own selves and the nature of our own thought. He claimed that by "looking down deep in ourselves" we can know that we have a free will, a power of choice and decision. We are free to accept a proposition, to reject it, or to suspend judgment. When we do not have enough evidence that we are compelled to accept a proposition (when it is not clear and distinct) we should suspend our judgment. In this way, we can avoid error. Error occurs because we jump to conclusions: we make judgments prematurely, before we have enough evidence. When we judge prematurely, we misuse our freedom, affirming or rejecting claims on which we should suspend our judgment.

Descartes moves from his theory of error to a theory of knowledge. If we know how to avoid mistakes, then we know how to reach the truth. Every clear and distinct perception must have God for its author and thus it cannot be deceptive, because God is no deceiver. If we can attend to what is in our mind, and refrain from making judgments until we perfectly understand, we can come to know the truth.

> So today I have learned not only what precautions to take to avoid ever going wrong, but also what to do to arrive at the truth. For I shall unquestionably reach the truth, if only I give sufficient attention to all the things which I perfectly understand, and separate these from all the other cases where my apprehension is more confused and obscure. And this is just what I shall take good care to do from now on.
> (*Fourth Meditation*, 43)

The will is not indifferent in such cases; it has spontaneous freedom.

Mind and Matter

In the *Second Meditation*, it looks as though Descartes is arguing that because he can know his existence as a thinking thing before he knows that he has a body, his essence is that of a thinking thing. To many readers, this seemed to be an unsatisfactory argument, because it failed to establish that the mind can be separated from the body. (Being able to know the mind without the body does not, they argued, prove that the mind is distinct from the body. The order of knowledge may not reflect the nature of reality.) Descartes replied to his critics, insisting that he did not claim to establish the distinction between the mind and the body until the *Sixth Meditation*. In that meditation there are two arguments which purport to establish the distinction between mind and body.

The first such argument is as follows:

> First, I know that everything which I clearly and distinctly understand is capable of being created by God so as to correspond exactly with my understanding of it. Hence the fact that I can clearly and distinctly understand one thing apart from another is enough to make me certain that the two things are distinct, since they are capable of being separated at least by God .... on the one hand I have a clear and distinct idea of myself, in so far as I am simply a thinking, non-extended thing; and on the other hand, I have a distinct idea of body in so far as this is simply an extended non-

> thinking thing. And accordingly, it is certain that I am really distinct from my body and can exist without it.
> (*Sixth Meditation*, 55)

The idea of self or mind as a thinking thing is distinct from the idea of body as an extended thing (something that occupies space). Hence the mind could, in principle, be separated from the body. If two things can be thought of as distinct, then God could in principle separate them, and they are really distinct.

Descartes' second argument goes like this:

> . . . there is a great difference between the mind and the body, in as much as the body is by its very nature always divisible, while the mind is utterly indivisible. For when I consider the mind, or myself in so far as I am merely a thinking thing, I am unable to distinguish any parts within myself; I understand myself to be something quite single and complete. Although the whole mind seems to be united to the whole body, I recognize that if a foot or arm or any other part of the body is cut off, nothing has thereby been taken away from the mind. As for the faculties of willing, of understanding, of sensory perception and so on, these cannot be termed parts of the mind, since it is one and the same mind that wills, and understands and has sensory perceptions. By contrast, there is no corporeal or extended thing that I can think of which in my thought I cannot easily divide into parts; and this very fact makes me understand that it is divisible. This one argument would be enough to show me that the mind is completely different from the body, even if I did not already know as much from other considerations.
> (*Sixth Meditation*, 59)

The mind, as a thinking thing, is not divisible into parts. The body, as an extended material thing, is divisible into parts. Hence the mind is distinct from the body

Descartes' conception of matter had a profound effect on subsequent science and Western culture. Matter, according to Descartes, is extended substance. It operates in a purely mechanical way; the only thing it can do is move. What we take to be characteristics of material bodies – color, smell, and taste, for instance – are only sensations that their motion produces in our minds as a result of the mechanical actions upon our bodily senses. Descartes believed in a radical separation of mind and matter. As thinking beings, we can understand the operation of matter if the philosophical foundation is properly established. Goals, purposes, and values refer to consciousness, which characterizes only mind, not matter. Thus Descartes believed that value judgments and Aristotelian final causes had no proper place in science. Matter and its movements should be studied mathematically: matter is extended; its quantity and motion can be measured. Knowledge, predictability, and the control of natural processes are the goals of science, and we can attain these by approaching natural processes as mechanical and quantifiable and seeking simple objective laws to describe them.

In the seventeenth century, the shift to a mechanistic conception of nature and the use of mathematics in physics were tremendously productive from a scientific point of view. This way of understanding mind and matter marked Western science from the early modern period until very recently.

Interestingly, however, Descartes' mechanistic conception of nature is one of the aspects of his philosophy that is most strongly criticized today. Current science does not seem to support a radical rupture between consciousness and the physical world. At the micro-level of sub-atomic physics, basic physical states cannot be defined without a reference to an observer. If the quantum theory of sub-atomic particles is correct, the very foundations of matter require reference to an observer and, for that reason, reference to mind. For this reason, the mechanistic conception of nature, though tremendously progressive and productive in its own time, now appears to be scientifically obsolete. In addition, the notion that the natural world is something purely mechanical is open to ethical and political objections because it implies that nature is valueless in itself and is there simply as a "thing" for human beings to control, consume, and conquer. Many interpreters of Western cultural history believe that this attitude contributed significantly to the present-day environmental crisis. Unlike nature as conceived by Aristotle, Cartesian mechanical nature seems to be something dead – without vitality, purpose, life, or value. Just how far Descartes took this mechanical view of nature can be seen from his beliefs about animals.

According to Descartes, animals do not have souls or minds. Hence animals are incapable of consciousness and feel no pain or pleasure. Descartes believed that animals operate purely according to mechanical principles, as though they were "automata," or machines. If there were a machine with the organs and appearance of a monkey, Descartes speculated, such an entity would be indistinguishable from an animal. Both animal and machine would show us matter in motion; neither would have a soul or mind. On this view, animals are not thinking things because they are only material things.

Human beings use language and have a power of reasoning which is adaptable to a wide variety of circumstances. Magpies and parrots can utter words, but they are not conscious of what they are saying.

> And this does not merely show that the brutes have less reason than men, but that they have none at all, since it is clear that very little is required in order to be able to talk.
> (*Discourse on the Method*, 42)

The human characteristics of language use and flexible powers of reasoning provide evidence that human beings are conscious thinking creatures. God has given us minds or souls. The supposed souls of animals, on the other hand are "nothing but their blood." Any human activity that does not depend on thought (for instance the beating of the heart, or the digestion of food) is purely mechanical. Animals, as Descartes understood them, operate purely mechanically, instinctually. The actions of swallows in the spring, honeybees, cranes in flight, or apes in fighting are purely natural and mechanical and show no evidence of thought.

From Descartes' views on mind and matter, we have inherited what is now called the mind/body problem. If mind and matter are so different, how are human beings possible? Descartes acknowledged that human beings have minds and bodies which seem, in their persons, to be united. If a person's throat is dry, she is likely to feel thirst, and as a result take a drink of water. First a condition in the body affects the mind; then a decision (in the mind) brings about a movement (in the body) of the hand, arms, lips and throat. In ordinary life, such things happen all the time. Descartes acknowledged that in common experience, the body affects the mind and the mind affects the body.

> There is nothing that my own nature teaches me more vividly than that I have a body, and that when I feel pain there is something wrong with the body, and that when I am hungry or thirsty the body needs food and drink, and so on. . . . Nature also teaches me, by these sensations of pain, hunger, thirst and so on, that I am not merely present in my body as a sailor is present in a ship, but that I am very closely joined and, as it were, intermingled with it, so that I and the body form a unit. If this were not so, I, who am nothing but a thinking thing, would not feel pain when the body was hurt, but would perceive the damage purely by intellect, just as a sailor perceives by sight if anything in his ship is broken.
> (*Sixth Meditation*, 56)

So far as 'my' body is concerned, I am no mere neutral observer. When my body is affected one way or another, I *feel* its pains and pleasures. I do not merely observe them the way a sailor might observe damage to his ship.

But how does this happen? How can the 'I' which is an indivisible thinking thing intermingle with my body, which is a divisible extended thing? Intermingling sounds like a physical process. With his radically disparate conceptions of body and mind, Descartes created a problem. He separated mind and body so thoroughly that it seems impossible to understand how they come together in a human person. Descartes' friend and correspondent, the Princess Elizabeth of Bohemia (1618 - 1680), asked him how the soul can affect the body when it determines voluntary actions. Being immaterial, the soul cannot move. It cannot push or pull; it is not extended, so it cannot be in physical contact with the body. Elizabeth found herself

> . . . unable to comprehend, from what you had previously said concerning weight, the idea by which we should judge how the soul (nonextended and immaterial) can move the body; . . . And I admit it would be easier for me to concede matter and extension to the soul, than the capacity of moving a body and of being moved, to an immaterial being.
> (*Correspondence*, Atherton, 16)

Descartes replied that we do have a kind of notion of the union of body and soul. In fact, he said, this union is understood very clearly by ordinary people who have not constructed systems of philosophy, and who make use only of their senses. In an astounding concession, Descartes suggested that Elizabeth go ahead and attribute extension to the soul, "for that is nothing but to conceive it united to the body."

But Elizabeth was not satisfied with this response.

> I too find that the senses show me that the soul moves the body; but they fail to teach me (any more than the understanding and the imagination) the manner in which she does it. And, in regard to that, I think there are unknown properties in the soul that might suffice to reverse what your metaphysical meditations, with such good reasons, persuaded me concerning her inextension . . . . Although extension is not necessary to thought, yet not being contradictory to it, it will be able to belong to some other function of the soul less essential to her.
> (*Correspondence*, Atherton, 21)

Elizabeth suggested that the radical distinction between mind and body might have been a mistake. Had Descartes followed his own advice about how to avoid error, he would have suspended his judgment about the properties that a thinking thing was able to possess. By doing so he would have avoided a central problem in his own system and left quite a different heritage to his scientific and philosophical successors.

Observations: Cartesian Thought, Cartesian Problems

Descartes viewed thinking as directed to a single goal: obtaining certainty. To think in an accurate and proper way, we should break down questions and problems into simple parts, and concentrate our attention at the smallest, simplest level. In so doing, we may hope to arrive at clear and distinct perceptions. These clear and distinct perceptions will not lead us astray. If we exercise our free will and suspend our judgment until we have arrived at clear and distinct perceptions, we will be able to reach the truth. For Descartes, thought essentially involves reduction, analysis, logical insight, and deduction. We should reduce problems to their simplest elements, applying reason and the principles of "the natural light" to move small steps at a time. Eventually we can review all the parts and hold them together to deduce more substantial conclusions.

Descartes states four basic rules for thinking:

> The first was never to accept anything as true if I had not evident knowledge of its being so; that is, carefully to avoid precipitancy and prejudice, and to embrace in my judgment only what presented itself to my mind so clearly and distinctly that I had no occasion to doubt it.
> The second, to divide each problem I examined into as many parts as was feasible, and as was requisite for its better solution.
> The third, to direct my thoughts in an orderly way; beginning with the simplest objects, those most apt to be known, and ascending little by little, in steps as it were, to the knowledge of the most complex; and establishing an order in thought even when the objects had no natural priority one to another.
> And the last, to make throughout such complete enumerations and such general surveys that I might be sure of leaving nothing out.
> (*Discourse on Method*, 21)

To Descartes, it was more important to get an answer that was indubitably correct than to synthesize many different pieces of evidence or imagine something new. The most important things were to avoid error and to attain the truth – and avoiding error was most important of all. There is relatively little emphasis in the Cartesian account on synthesis in thought – that is, on drawing things together as opposed to taking them apart. The Cartesian method is reductionist: it breaks things down for analysis. One risk of such an approach is that we may miss aspects of interdependence between distinct elements. For instance, in understanding the biology of a rabbit, the reductionistic approach will lead us to examine the bone structure, cells, reproductive system, and so on, but it will not encourage us to look at the relationship between the rabbit and the natural environment. Nor is there any room in the Cartesian project for the more imaginative, playful, and creative aspects of thought so delightfully portrayed in some of the Platonic dialogues. For Descartes, the purpose of thought is to attain certainty. Knowledge did not have to be exciting, or original, or profound; it only had to be indubitable. Though inspiring in its own domain and impressive in its lucidity and single-mindedness, Cartesian thought is very narrowly focused.

This narrow Cartesian focus has both benefits and costs. As for benefits, we can appreciate Descartes' clarity and emphasis on paying close attention to a problem. In the context in which he worked, Descartes' desire to avoid jargon and appeals to authority, his appeal to the reasonableness and native talent of the common person, his frank autobiographical style, and the lucidity of much of his writing constituted a philosophical breakthrough. These innovations had a profound effect on subsequent philosophizing and writing. To this day, the use of "I" in academic papers in philosophy is acceptable, whereas it is regarded as inappropriate in virtually all other disciplines.

But there were costs too. The Cartesian emphasis on indubitability severely restricted the scope of philosophical achievement. After the *Cogito* Descartes went on to build up a system of knowledge. But critics who rejected his proofs for God's existence were not able to follow him, and seemed to be left only with doubt and the Cogito.

The method of doubt had a tremendous effect on subsequent European philosophy, particularly in the area of theory of knowledge. By attempting to doubt all his previous beliefs, Descartes led himself into solipsism, or what is called the Egocentric Predicament. After applying universal doubt, the thinker seeks to begin anew, to construct a system of knowledge. At this stage his or her vantage

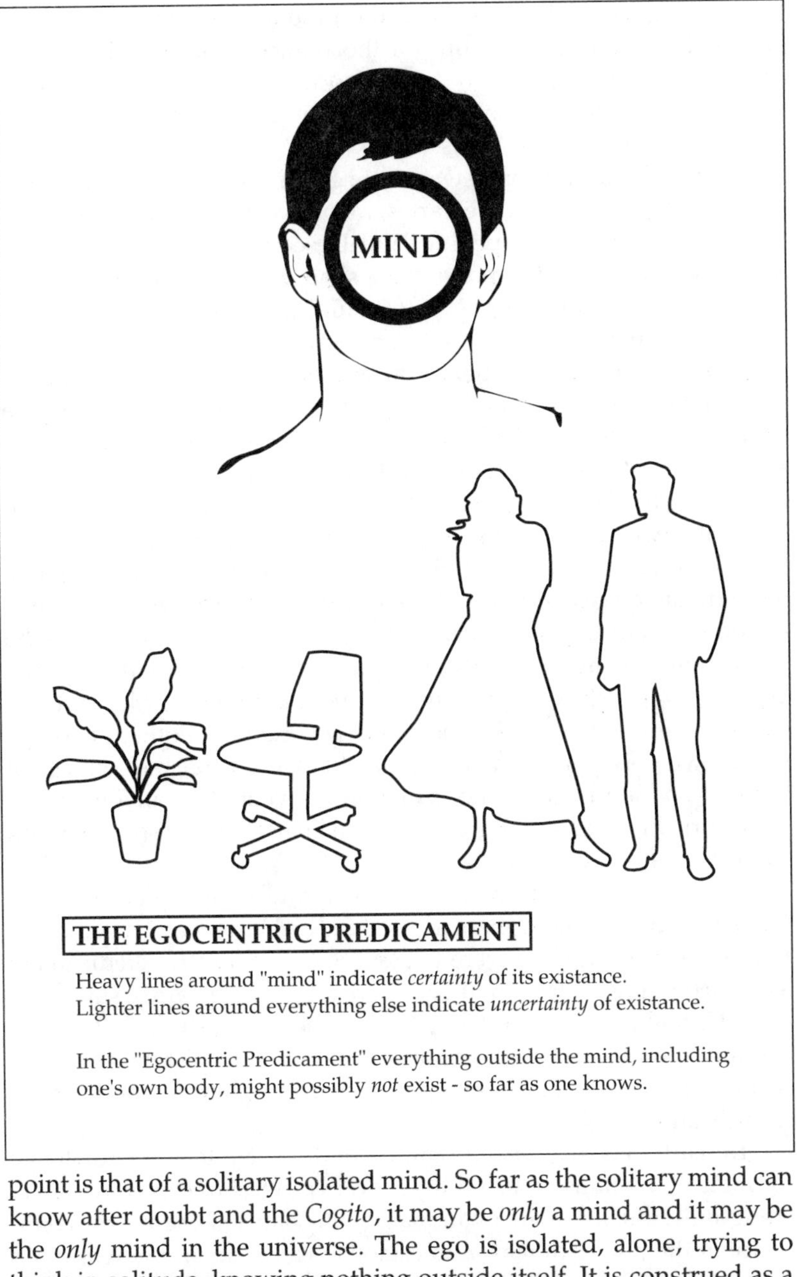

point is that of a solitary isolated mind. So far as the solitary mind can know after doubt and the *Cogito,* it may be *only* a mind and it may be the *only* mind in the universe. The ego is isolated, alone, trying to think in solitude, knowing nothing outside itself. It is construed as a mind only, a mind that may relate only to itself. This isolated mind has ideas about the material world and other people – but the material world and other people may not exist. In the Cartesian system, they are argued back into existence on the grounds that God exists and God is not a deceiver. But for those unconvinced by Descartes' arguments for God's existence, the Egocentric Predicament remains unresolved. The mind may well be alone in the universe, apparently accompanied only by its ideas.

Is this the only proper way to begin to philosophize? Is it the right way? After reading Descartes, many have thought so. The *First Meditation* is highly compelling, and Descartes' goal of certainty is one which many philosophers have shared. As a result, the notion that the task of philosophy is to build up knowledge from the Egocentric Predicament has been profoundly influential.

Despite this deep influence on western thought, many modern philosophers have devoted considerable energy to opposing the Cartesian approach to knowledge. Many argue that human beings are social creatures who know and learn as social beings – not as isolated minds. They question the individualistic way in which Descartes wanted to build up philosophical knowledge. (The idea that knowledge should be built up in this way is called epistemic individualism.) According to these influential critics, we are not able to doubt as radically as Descartes thought, because we are tied to the distinctions and assumptions presupposed by, and embodied in, the language in which we think. That language is public; we learn it and use it with other people. Furthermore, we often trust other people to tell us what is going on in the world. Language, the vehicle of thought and argument, is not something invented by anyone in the Egocentric Predicament. It may not even be usable by a solitary mind alone.

The notion that any person could find himself or herself in the egocentric predicament may, in the final analysis, be contradictory. Furthermore, even if we were to assume the egocentric predicament as a starting point for knowledge, if we employ Descartes' standards of indubitability, we are unlikely to move beyond the *Cogito*. Thought conducted on Cartesian principles will not go far. Aristotelian *endoxa* seem more realistic and sensible as a starting point for philosophy, science, and ethics.

Descartes believed that he could build up a system of knowledge for himself, by himself, using his powers of reason. He was an epistemic individualist and a rationalist. He had extraordinary confidence in the power of reason to establish truths about the world. As a rationalist, Descartes believed that truths about the mind, God, and the physical world could be *a priori*, that is to say, independent of (or prior to) sense experience. That I cannot doubt without existing is something I know without depending on my eyes, ears, nose, or touch. I know it by the natural light of reason *a priori* and I know with certainty that it is true. Logical insight, my "natural light," assures me that to doubt, I must exist. I do not rely on sense experience in order to work through the Cogito. And the Cogito becomes the model for other truths. Pure reason will provide insight into the mind and the world. With concentration and a proper exercise of will, suspending judgment when I do not perceive things clearly and distinctly, reason can establish truths, *a priori*, about the world. Descartes regarded the key ideas of thinking substance, extended substance, and God as *innate*. Like Plato, he believed such ideas could not be derived from sense experience. But instead of arguing, as Plato did, for Forms and recollection, Descartes contended that these innate ideas were implanted in our minds by God.

With its emphasis on innate ideas and *a priori* knowledge of the physical world, the rationalist tradition was continued after Descartes by Leibniz, Spinoza, and others who constructed remarkable philosophical systems of their own. But the rationalist tradition had its opponents in the empiricists, who stressed the role of sense perception in knowledge and denied the possibility of innate ideas. Most notable among the empiricists were three British philosophers: Locke, Berkeley, and Hume.

often have beliefs about things which we are not experiencing. Therefore, Hume concluded, belief must be an idea. Hume was thus led to define belief as a vivid and strong idea which holds us and affects our other ideas.

> But belief is somewhat more than a simple idea. 'Tis a particular matter of forming an idea: And as the same idea can only be vary'd by a variation of its degrees of force and vivacity; it follows upon the whole, that belief is a lively idea produc'd by a relation to a present impression, according to the foregoing definition. (*Treatise*, 97)

People know from experience the difference between believing something and merely imagining it. For example, to *believe* I own a castle in Spain is entirely different from *imagining* I own a castle in Spain. We seem to know, or feel, a difference between imagination and belief, but it is no easy matter to describe this difference in words. Ideas that are *believed*, Hume said, are felt in a different way from ideas that are merely considered or contemplated. What we believe is more firm, vivid, solid, and strong; it has a faster hold on our minds and a greater effect on our actions. The variety of terms, Hume admitted, was "rather unphilosophical" – but he felt that the phenomenon itself was well understood.

Hume offered various arguments in support of his contention that we cannot control our beliefs. Experience, he said, shows that we cannot believe whatever we like. We may choose to think about an animal with the body of a horse and the head of a human being, but we cannot simply *choose* to believe that such a creature exists. To believe, according to Hume, is to feel our ideas in a particular way. This *feeling* emerges from custom and experience. We cannot control what we are feeling, and this feeling of belief, like others feelings, is not within our rational or voluntary control. What we find in experience is that belief just happens to us. It "arises immediately"; there is no operation of the mind that we perform in order to achieve it. (We do not and cannot make ourselves believe things, Hume says.) Custom simply operates and, based on experience, we come to believe.

Descartes held the view that the *will* had an important role to play in *belief*. In fact, he claimed that we could know by looking inside ourselves that we had free will so far as belief was concerned. According to Descartes, we can know, by introspection, that we are free to believe or to suspend our judgment. Hume's view is very different. He denied that introspection reveals any such thing as free

5

Hume: Custom, the Cement of the Universe

David Hume (1711 - 1776) is the most eminent Scottish philosopher. He was born in Edinburgh. His father died when he was two and his mother, Katherine Hume, a strong and strong-minded woman, managed the estate and the family. As the third child in the family, Hume received a small inheritance which was not enough to live on. He lived frugally in his early adulthood, and earned his money variously from writing, tutoring, and secretarial positions. After studies at the University of Edinburgh, Hume briefly tried law and business as professions, but found that he had "an insurmountable aversion to anything but the pursuits of Philosophy and General Learning." As a young man, Hume lived for several years at La Fleche in France – the very place where Descartes had gone to school. (La Fleche was more affordable than Paris.)

Hume was brought up in a strict and rather gloomy Calvinist Christianity, against which he rebelled early. Although he censored himself so as not to express some of his agnostic views, his arguments and remarks about the Christian religion were known widely enough to cause him difficulty in his life. Religious objections to Hume and his ideas were one factor in his failing to get two university appointments for which he was eligible.

In 1746 Hume accepted a position as secretary to Lieutenant-General St. Clair, who was about to set forth on a military campaign against the French in Canada. The expedition went to Brittany instead. Hume later accompanied St. Clair to Vienna and Turin. He made valuable contacts and was able to become financially independent. In 1752, Hume visited Paris, where he was a great success. When he returned to Edinburgh in 1769, his financial situation was solid and he and his sister were able to live in a comfortable house.

Hume began to develop the ideas expressed in his longest philosophical work, *A Treatise of Human Nature*, when he was eighteen, and he was only twenty-seven when the book was published. To his great disappointment, it was not a success; Hume said it "fell dead-born from the press" and later came to think that he had published too soon. This poor reception was probably due to a lack of understanding. Hume had somewhat greater success with literary essays and a history of Great Britain.

In philosophy, Hume's major works after the *Treatise* were *An Inquiry Concerning Human Understanding*, *An Inquiry Concerning the Principles of Morals*, and *The Dialogues on Natural Religion*. All are widely read and debated today. The *Dialogues on Natural Religion* were the product of labor and love over twenty-five years. Because of the controversial arguments they contain, Hume arranged to have them published after his death.

Hume died in 1776 after an uncomfortable illness. Despite the fact that he did not believe in immortality, he faced death cheerfully and calmly. Hume enjoyed the company of women, but he never married and left no descendants. He was a plump, kindly, and good-natured person who disliked controversy. Hume enjoyed games and company as well as philosophizing. Intellectually he was disturbed at the sceptical conclusions of his arguments; he struggled intensely to reconcile his philosophical conclusions with his natural beliefs. These tensions are reflected in his writings.

Hume falls in the tradition of British *empiricism*. Contrary to rationalists such as Plato and Descartes, the empiricists believed that the source of human knowledge was sense experience (sometimes called sensory experience). Hume developed his philosophy in the context of the empiricism of the English philosopher John Locke (1632 - 1704) and the Irish philosopher George Berkeley (1685 - 1753). Locke and Berkeley disputed the rationalist claim that human beings could acquire *a priori* (or independent of experience) knowledge of the world and rejected the possibility of innate ideas, insisting that ideas have their source in sense experience.

Hume the Empiricist

Hume began his philosophizing with a strict expression of empiricism. When we think, we have ideas. Those ideas come from experience. When we see, hear, touch, taste, or smell something, we have a sensory impression of it. It is our sense experience which is the ultimate source of all our ideas and thoughts.

> All the perceptions of the human mind resolve themselves into two distinct kinds, which I shall call IMPRESSIONS and IDEAS. The difference betwixt these consists in the degrees of force and liveliness with which they strike upon the mind, and make their way into our thought or consciousness. Those perceptions, which enter with most force and violence, we may name *impressions;* and under this name I comprehend all our sensations, passions and emotions, as they make their first appearance in the soul. By *ideas* I mean the faint images of these in thinking and reasoning; such as, for instance, are all the perceptions excited by the present discourse, excepting only, those which arise from the sight and touch, and excepting the immediate pleasure or uneasiness it may occasion.
> (*Treatise*, 1)

When we experience or feel something, we have an impression; when we think about it later, we have an idea deriving from, and corresponding to, what we felt before.

> . . . we shall always find, that every idea which we examine is copied from a similar impression. Those who would assert that this position is not universally true nor without exception, have only one, and that an easy method of refuting it; by producing that idea, which, in their opinion, is not derived from this source.
> (*Inquiry Concernign Human Understanding*, 18)

If someone tries to produce such an idea, Hume will try to point out the impression(s) from which it has been derived.

Hume distinguished between simple and complex impressions and ideas. If an impression or idea can be distinguished as to aspects or parts, it is complex. Otherwise it is simple. A simple idea is derived from a simple impression that corresponds to it. The idea of the taste of pineapple is a simple idea; a person who has not tasted pineapple could not have acquired this simple idea. Nor will a person who has never experienced the passions of love have an idea of what it is to be in love. But a complex idea, such as the idea of a New Jerusalem with streets of gold and walls of rubies, does not require an impression which corresponds to it. A person could consider the idea of a New Jerusalem, though she had never experienced such a thing. She would have simple impressions (of streets, of walls, of gold, and so on) which would give simple ideas, and those simple ideas would provide the material for a complex idea. We associate various impressions and ideas, and our imagination can put them together in novel ways. A complex idea can be broken down into simple ones, and simple ideas have their source in corresponding simple impressions.

Hume drew a further distinction between impressions of *sensation* and those of *reflection*. Impressions of sensation come to us, apparently from things outside ourselves. When we taste a pineapple, see something blue, or hear a trumpet, we have an impression of sensation. Impressions of reflection arise from our response to our impressions and ideas of other things. They include pleasure, pain, hope, fear, pride, and shame – responses that we feel in response to some of our other impressions and ideas.

> An impression first strikes upon the senses, and makes us perceive heat or cold, thirst or hunger, pleasure or pain of some kind or other. Of this impression there is a copy taken by the mind, which remains after the impression ceases; and this we call an idea. This idea of pleasure or pain, when it returns upon the soul, produces the new impressions of desire and aversion, hope and fear, which may properly be called impressions of reflexion . . . These again are copied by the memory and imagination, and become ideas; which perhaps in their turn give rise to other impressions and ideas. So that the impressions of reflection are only antecedent to their correspondent ideas; but posterior to those of sensation and derived from them.
> (*Treatise*, 8)

Hume thought that seeking to trace ideas to their source in impressions would clarify them and would help to banish meaningless jargon. Ideas can become faint and obscure, whereas impressions are quite vivid and specific. If there is some philosophical term such as "substance" which seems obscure and hard to understand, we can seek to clarify it by asking what impression it comes from. If there is a plausible account, the idea will be better understood. If there is no plausible account, it is a pseudo-idea, something we do not really understand. Hume used his empiricist principles to argue against some of the conceptions of the rationalists.

> When we entertain, therefore, any suspicion that a philosophical term is employed without any meaning or idea (as is but too frequent) we need but enquire, *from what impression is that supposed idea derived*? And if it be impossible to assign any, this will serve to confirm our suspicion. By bringing ideas into so clear a light we may reasonably hope to remove all dispute, which may arise, concerning their nature and reality.
> (*Inquiry Concerning Human Understanding*, 21 - 22)

A clear example of the de-bunking use of empiricism is Hume's argument against the conception of *substance*.

> I wou'd fain ask those philosophers, who found so much of their reasonings on the distinction of substance and accident, and imagine we have clear ideas of each, whether the idea of *substance* be derived from the impressions of sensation or reflexion? If it be convey'd to us by our senses, I ask, which of them; and after what manner? If it be perceiv'd by the eyes, it must be a colour; if by the ears, a sound; if by the palate, a taste; and so of the other senses. But I believe none will assert that substance is either a colour, or sound, or a taste. The idea of substance must therefore be deriv'd from an impression of reflexion, if it really exist. But the impressions of reflexion resolve themselves into our passions and emotions; none of which can possibly represent a substance. We have therefore no idea of substance, distinct from that of a collection of particular qualities, nor have we any other meaning when we either talk or reason concerning it.
> (*Treatise*, 16)

Hume also used empiricist principles to address the issue of innate ideas, ideas that rationalist philosophers had thought were contained in the mind before any sense experience. Hume's view was that impressions may be called innate, if we mean by "innate" only that they are not derived from other perceptions. But because impressions come from experience, they are not innate in anything like the sense in which Descartes and other rationalists had supposed them to be. Since all ideas are derived from impressions, no ideas are innate in the rationalist sense.

What about abstract ideas or, as the ancients called them, Forms or universals? On this topic, Hume followed his predecessor Berkeley and argued that abstract or general ideas do not exist as such. Berkeley and Hume claim that what other philosophers had taken to be abstract ideas are really particular ones, attached to a general word and used in a general way. Their arguments seem to assume that ideas are *images*. The abstract idea of a tree could not be an idea of an oak or a pine or cedar, because the abstract idea of a tree must be capable of representing *any* tree. It would have to be an idea of tree-in-general or tree-as-universal. So apparently this "tree" could have no particular characteristics. But every thing in nature has particular characteristics. Because we experience it through our senses, everything which we experience is individual. We can see an oak tree or a cedar tree, but we can never see a tree-in-general. How, then, can we come to have an abstract idea of a tree – or any other abstract idea?

We experience only particular individual things. Berkeley, and Hume following him, argued that we have impressions of particulars and from these, derive ideas of particulars. We are able to use words, such as "tree," as general words. To go along with a general word there is an idea, and this idea is an idea of a particular, derived from a particular impression. Though the idea is of a particular, we use that idea in a general way, ignoring aspects which are irrelevant to our applications. For instance, when we use the word "tree" we may associate with it an idea of a tall oak standing in a clearing, but we can nevertheless use the word "tree" to represent a cedar tree in a grove in Athens.

> Abstract ideas are therefore in themselves individual, however they may become general in their representation. The image in the mind is only that of a particular object, tho' the application of it in our reasoning be the same, as if it were universal. . . . The word raises up an individual idea, along with a certain custom; and that custom produces any other individual one, for which we may have occasion.
> (*Treatise*, 20 - 21)

The mind is active; it has habits and customs, and it operates with its impressions and ideas in various ways. Hume appealed to the activity of the mind to address Plato's question about the source of mathematical ideas. He used the same example Plato had appealed to in the *Phaedo*, that of equality.

According to Hume, equality is a relation between objects. The idea of equality arises when the mind makes comparisons. We sometimes realize that our judgments need correction. We can correct and generate an improved standard of exactness. And we can do this repeatedly, or at least we can imagine doing so. Thus we progressively generate more accurate imaginary standards of equality. From these, our mind goes on to generate the "fiction" of absolutely exact equality.

> For as the very idea of equality is that of such a particular appearance corrected by juxta-position or a common measure, the notion of any correction beyond what we have instruments and art to make, is a mere fiction of the mind, and useless as well as incomprehensible. But tho' this standard be only imaginary, the fiction however is very natural; nor is any thing more usual, than for the mind to proceed after this manner with any action, even after the reason has ceas'd which first determin'd it to begin.
> (*Treatise*, 49)

We make one correction, then another; then our mind proceeds along this path, and we come to an "imaginary" or "fictional" standard of perfect equality. Like a ship set in motion, the mind tends to continue on the path it has begun. Thus we are able to produce from our sense experience ideas which do not precisely correspond to our sense experience. Hume believed that all this is a natural process, and something like it happens in many areas of human endeavor. According to Hume, the idea of equality is not a Platonic Form we can recollect because we knew it in a previous life. Rather it is an idea that the mind generates from sense experience.

A fundamental principle in Hume's philosophy is that simple impressions and ideas, which are distinct from each other, are capable of being separated from each other. They are not necessarily connected together. When we think of an apple, we think of a sweet, firm, roughly spherical fruit, typically red on the outside and white within. But the ideas of firmness, roundness, sweetness, redness, whiteness, and fruit are separable from each other. They need not be linked together as they are in our idea of apple. Each simple impression or idea is distinct from every other, and capable of existing without it.

However, impressions and ideas are clearly *associated* in our minds. They are related – and not merely by chance. The principles of association, according to Hume, are Resemblance, Contiguity in place or time, and Cause-and-Effect. Our imagination connects ideas according to these principles. If a picture resembles an original object (as a portrait might resemble its subject, for instance) we tend to think of the original when we think of the picture. If we see a portrait of Canadian Prime Minister Jean Chrétien, we will think of Jean Chrétien. Proximity in space or time is also a principle of association. If one apartment is next to another, we tend to think of the second when we see the first. Most of all, we associate things that are related as causes and effects. For instance, if we believe that mosquito bites are the cause of malaria, we will tend to think of malaria when we think of mosquitoes.

Though separable, impressions and ideas are associated, because this is the way human nature is. Hume saw the principles of association, in the mental sphere, as comparable to the principles of attraction in Newtonian physics. In Newtonian physics, masses attract each other because they exert gravitational force on each other. In Hume's philosophical psychology, impressions and ideas attract each other (or, more colloquially, "stick together") because of the ways in which they are associated.

> Here is a kind of ATTRACTION, which in the mental world will be found to have as extraordinary effects as in the natural, and to shew itself in as many and as various forms.
> (*Treatise*, 12)

Hume's Perplexing Arguments

Among the things we suppose ourselves to know, Hume made a fundamental division between *relations of ideas* (e.g. three times five is equal to half of thirty) and *matters of fact* (e.g. the sun will rise tomorrow). Relations of ideas we know by reason and they do not depend on the existence of objects outside the mind. Matters of fact could be otherwise. That the sun has risen today is a matter of fact. It is quite imaginable that it will not rise tomorrow. No contradiction would result if it did not – though we would all be alarmed and surprised.

Induction

Several of Hume's most perplexing arguments are about matters of fact and knowledge from experience – induction. (Hume's understanding of induction is different from that of Aristotle because, unlike Aristotle, Hume did not believe that we could recognize universals in particular objects.) Clearly all knowledge of matters of fact depends on sense experience. Yet in what we take ourselves to know, we go far beyond the immediate testimony of the senses.

> If you were to ask a man, why he believes any matter of fact, which is absent; for instance, that his friend is in the country, or in France; he would give you a reason; and this reason would be some other fact; as a letter received from him, or the knowledge of his former resolutions and promises. . . . And here it is constantly supposed that there is a *connexion* between the present fact and

> that which is inferred from it. Were there nothing to bind them together, the inference would be entirely precarious. The hearing of an articulate voice and rational discourse in the dark assures us of the presence of some person: Why? because these are the *effects* of the human make and fabric, and closely connected with it.
> (*Inquiry Concerning Human Understanding*, 26)

We depend on relations of cause and effect to link what we do perceive (the letter, or the voice) with things we do not perceive (the friend in France, or the person speaking) and that is how we come to believe matters of fact beyond the sensory impressions that are present to us. All knowledge of matters of fact going beyond immediate sense experience depends on relations of cause and effect, and relations of cause and effect depend on experience.

> When it is asked, *What is the nature of all our resasonings concerning matters of fact?* the proper answer seems to be, that they are founded on the relation of cause and effect. When again it is asked, *What is the foundation of all our reasonings and conclusions concerning that relation?* it may be replied in one word, Experience. But if we carry on our sifting humour, and ask, *What is the foundation of all conclusions from experience?* this implies a new question, which may be of more difficult solution and explication.
> (*Inquiry Concerning Human Understanding*, 32)

Hume pointed out that in ordinary life and in scientific reasoning, we apply *past* experience to the *future*. We believe that the sun will rise tomorrow because it has always risen in the past. Though reasoning in this inductive way, from past regularities to a conclusion about the future, is an absolutely fundamental human habit, the philosophical justification for it is uncertain. That is to say, we cannot prove by logic that this way of reasoning is correct. It is, after all, quite conceivable that the future should be unlike the past; there would be no contradiction in this.

Based on Hume's empiricist principles there are only two ways to prove things: by demonstrative reasoning and from experience. If we can reason demonstratively from a premise to a conclusion, then there would be a contradiction were the premise to be true and the conclusion false. For induction, demonstrative reasoning will not do the job. There is no *contradiction* implied in the supposition that the future does not resemble the past. For all that logic has to say, the past can be just what it is, and the future may be quite different. Nor can we appeal to experience for a "proof," because the reliability of experience is exactly what is at issue.

> To say it is experimental [based on experience], is begging the question. For all inferences from experience suppose, as their foundation, that the future will resemble the past . . . If there be any suspicion that the course of nature may change, and that the past may be no rule for the future, all experience becomes useless, and can give rise to no inference or conclusion. It is impossible, therefore, that any arguments from experience can prove this resemblance of the past to the future; since all these arguments are founded on the supposition of that resemblance.
> (*Inquiry Concerning Human Understanding*, 39)

We reason inductively, from experience, but not because we have compelling arguments showing that it is correct to do so. Rather it is because such is our custom and habit. Like animals and young children, who come to conclusions out of habit and instinct, adult human beings just are the sorts of creatures who think in this way.

Causation

Closely related to the problem of induction is that of causation. On this topic, Hume's favorite example came from billiards, one of the games he loved. If we see one billiard ball move toward another and strike it, we suppose that the movement of the first ball will cause that second ball to move. Further, we believe that the second ball *must* move when it has been struck by the first. Our idea of causation, then, contains an element of necessity. Where does this idea of necessity come from? According to Hume's empiricist assumptions, there must be some impression from which it is derived. But what can that be?

> When we look about us towards external objects, and consider the operation of causes, we are never able, in a single instance, to discover any power or necessary connexion; any quality, which binds the effect to the cause, and renders the one an infallible consequence of the other. We only find, that one does actually, in fact, follow the other. The impulse of one billiard-ball is attended with motion in the second. This is the whole that appears to the outward senses. The mind feels no sentiment or inward impression from this succession of objects: Consequently there is not, in any single, particular instance of cause and effect, anything which can suggest the idea of power or necessary connection.
> (*Inquiry Concerning Human Understanding*, 67)

We have a *feeling* of necessary connection. But our sense of necessity does not come from what we perceive about the external world. Nor, in a single case, is it based on an impression of reflexion we feel in ourselves.

What is this idea of necessary connection? And where does it come from? It is a *felt expectation*. When we have observed billiard balls repeatedly, or have observed similar sequences, we come to expect this sort of effect. When we have seen events regularly "conjoined," we come to expect certain sequences, and we then feel a necessity for the second to follow upon the first. The necessary connection, which we assume to be fundamental in causation, is only in our own minds. After repeatedly seeing a particular C-event followed by a particular E-event, we come so strongly to expect an E-event when we see a C-event that we believe the E-event *must* happen. That is the element of necessity.

> . . . after a repetition of similar instances, the mind is carried by habit, upon the appearance of one event, to expect its usual attendant, and to believe that it will exist. This connexion, therefore, which we *feel* in the mind, this customary transition of the imagination from one object to its usual attendant, is the sentiment or impression from which we form the idea of power or necessary connexion. . . . Contemplate the subject on all sides; you will never find any other origin of that idea.
> (*Inquiry Concerning Human Understanding*, 81)

From a commonsense point of view, we would attribute the necessary connection to something which lies in the events themselves. But it arises only from our expectation that the future will resemble the past, which amounts to a "felt determination of the mind." And this, though something we customarily suppose, cannot be proven either by reason or by experience.

The External World

When we think about matters of fact we assume that the objects of which we have knowledge exist outside our minds. The sun, billiard balls, France, our friend, an apartment – all these are things experienced in life, objects we assume to exist apart from ourselves. I suppose France to be a large country far away, existing outside my mind whether I am thinking about it or not. Consider another example, that of a white table.

> This very table, which we see white, and which we feel hard, is believed to exist, independent of our perception, and to be something external to our mind, which perceives it. Our presence bestows not being on it: our absence does not annihilate it. It preserves its existence uniform and entire, independent of the situation of intelligent beings, who perceive or contemplate it. (*Inquiry Concerning Human Understanding*, 169)

Or so I think, and so thinks almost every human being. It is an extremely powerful instinct of nature for human beings to believe such things as that tables exist outside our minds.

> But this universal and primary opinion of all men is soon destroyed by the slightest philosophy, which teaches us, that nothing can ever be present to the mind but an image or perception, and that the senses are only the inlets, through which these images are conveyed, without being able to produce any immediate intercourse between the mind and the object. . . . The existences which we consider, when we say, *this house* and *that tree*, are nothing but perceptions in the mind, and fleeting copies or representations of other existences, which remain uniform and independent. (*Inquiry Concerning Human Understanding*, 169-70)

It is a question of fact, Hume says, whether objects exist outside the mind and cause our perceptions, and it is by experience that we seek to know matters of fact. But all we experience are impressions and ideas, and these are "perceptions of the mind." How can they teach us of the existence of things outside the mind, and independent of the mind? Given a foundation only of impressions and ideas, we are in no position to know whether there are objects external to the mind or not. We commonly believe that objects are outside us, distinct from our minds, and independent of us, and that they continue to exist whether we are perceiving them or not. But these beliefs are apparently not supportable by philosophical arguments.

So far as the existence of an external world is concerned, philosophical reasoning and commonsense instincts pull us in opposite directions. Philosophically, we seem to have proven something we are incapable of believing or acting upon in common life: that what we take to be objects are no more than impressions and ideas in our minds. Sceptical arguments "admit of no answer and produce no conviction," Hume said. We cannot help believing in objects outside the mind, existing independently of us and our perceptions. It is human nature to believe this. And yet experience, the only thing which could tell us whether there are such objects or not, apparently cannot give us any information about them. What we experience, impressions and ideas, are perceptions of the mind. As such, they indicate nothing about what is supposed to be distinct from and independent of the mind. If all the qualities of matter exist only as perceptions in the mind, where and what is matter?

What, then, are we to say about the basic commonsense belief that there is a world outside the mind?

> . . . such an opinion, if rested on natural instinct, is contrary to reason, and if referred to reason, is contrary to natural instinct, and at the same time carries no rational evidence with it, to convince an impartial enquirer.
> (*Inquiry Concerning Human Understanding*, 173)

The issue presents a terrible dilemma for thought and action. To act, we rely on instincts and arrive at beliefs contrary to reason. When we think rationally, we are led to conclusions our instincts will not allow us to believe.

The Self

Descartes was one of many philosophers who assumed that he could be intimately conscious of the existence and continuance of his own self, which he understood to be a mental thing, or mental substance. Descartes believed that he could discover his own existence as a thinking thing, a mind, through the Cogito. Hume's view of the self stands in sharp contrast to that of Descartes. Just as Hume debunked the conception of material substance, he rejected the conception of mental substance. And the grounds were the same: he could find no impression from which the idea of a mental substance could be derived. Hume's reasonings on this issue follow straight from his empiricist principles.

> It must be some one impression, that gives rise to every real idea. But self or person is not any one impression, but that to which our several impressions and ideas are suppos'd to have a reference. If any impression gives rise to the idea of self, that impression must continue invariably the same, thro' the whole course of our lives; since self is suppos'd to exist after that manner. But there is no impression constant and invariable.
> (*Treatise*, 251)

I suppose that all my impressions and ideas belong to me – to *my self* – and I suppose that I have been the same person, or self, ever since birth, that I am something which endures and which is conscious of my various impressions and ideas. But the problem is, I, who am supposed to have these impressions and ideas, can find no impression or idea that represents my self.

> For my part, when I enter most intimately into what I call *myself* I always stumble on some particular perception or other, of heat or cold, light or shade, love or hatred, pain or pleasure. I never can catch *myself* at any time without a perception, and never can observe any thing but the perception.
> (*Treatise*, 252)

Hume would argue that even when Descartes was thinking through the Cogito, he did not have an impression of *himself*. In arriving at the Cogito, he had some particular impression, to be sure – that of doubting or thinking. Hume would call that impression an impression of reflexion.

What we tend to think of as a unitary, persisting self or mental substance, conscious of various impressions and ideas, is nothing of the kind. What, then, is the self? It is

> . . . nothing but a bundle or collection of different perceptions, which succeed each other with an inconceivable rapidity, and are in a perpetual flux and movement. Our eyes cannot turn in their sockets without varying our perceptions. Our thought is still more variable than our sight; and all our other senses and faculties contribute to this change; nor is there any single power of the soul which remains unalterably the same, perhaps for one moment. The mind is a kind of theatre, where several perceptions successively make their appearance; pass, re-pass, glide away, and mingle in an infinite variety of postures and situations.
> (*Treatise*, 253)

People, it seems, are nothing but bundles or collections of different perceptions. But what makes a bundle into the bundle it is? This is quite a problem. What we are conscious of, what we find if we "look into ourselves" is continual change, a flux of impressions and ideas. We don't find any ties; we do not find those impressions and ideas tied into bundles. The mind, Hume says, is a kind of theatre in which impressions and ideas are constantly passing through. But there is one crucial qualification: there is no theatre!

> The comparison of the theatre must not mislead us. They are the successive perceptions only that constitute the mind.
> (*Treatise*, 253)

In the Appendix to the *Treatise*, Hume returned to the topic of self and personal identity. He admitted that he found himself in "a labyrinth" with the problem. Hume offered the imaginary example of a mind "reduc'd even below the life of an oyster" and having only one perception. If we consider such a mind, we are in effect considering only that single perception; there is no *self* or *substance* to be found in the case. The addition of other perceptions will not change the matter. It is because our various perceptions resemble each other and are related to each other that we think of ourselves as having one and the same persisting mind or self. It is a mistake to suppose that the self is a continuing, unchanging mental substance. Nevertheless, in some sense a person does have personal identity. The identity arises because of the "bundle" or "collection"; changing perceptions are connected through resemblance and cause and effect. It is the principles of association (Resemblance, Proximity in Space and Time, and Cause-and-Effect) that tie the impressions and ideas together.

> Our impressions give rise to their correspondent ideas; and these ideas in their turn produce other impressions. One thought chases another, and draws after it a third, by which it is expell'd in its turn. In this respect, I cannot compare the soul more properly to anything than to a republic or commonwealth, in which the several members are united by the reciprocal ties of government and subordination, and give rise to other persons, who propagate the same republic in the incessant changes of its parts. And as the individual republic may not only change its members, but also its laws and constitutions; in like manner the same person may vary his character and disposition, as well as his impressions and ideas, without losing his identity.
> (*Treatise*, 261)

In a political state, there are many different people, but they are connected in various ways, and some people produce others. Similarly, Hume suggests, in a mind there are many different perceptions, but they are connected in various ways and some produce others.

Thomas Reid (1710-1796), Hume's best contemporary critic, found Hume's conclusions on personal identity utterly paradoxical. Reid sought to construct a philosophical system from a foundation of common sense. To Reid, what Hume seemed to be saying just did not make sense.

> I am, therefore, that succession of related ideas and impressions of which I have the intimate memory and consciousness. But who is the *I* that has this memory and consciousness of a succession of ideas and impressions? Why it is nothing but the succession itself. Hence I learn that this succession of ideas and impressions ultimately remembers and is conscious of itself . . .
> (*Works*, 444)

Reid asked: in Hume's theory are the impressions conscious of the ideas? Or the ideas of the impressions? Or both of both?

> [T]his succession of ideas and impressions not only remembers and is conscious, but that it judges, reasons, affirms, denies – say, that it eats and drinks, and is sometimes merry and sometimes sad. If these things can be ascribed to a succession of impressions and ideas, in consistency with common sense, I should be very glad to know what is nonsense.
> (*Works*, 444)

Reid argued, in effect, that Hume's system broke down because it was based on impressions and ideas which were supposed to be perceptions of the mind, and yet it could make no sense of the mind.

In an Appendix to the *Treatise*, Hume admitted that he was not satisfied with his account of the mind or self. How are there to be enough connections to constitute a self, without a continuing substance to hold the impressions and ideas together? How is the *activity* of the mind to be understood when the mind is nothing but a bundle or collection of impressions and ideas?

Hume on Scepticism, Belief, and the Will

Hume has, apparently, shown us that on empiricist principles there is no good justification for believing that the future will resemble the past, that events have any necessary connection with each other, that there is an external world outside the mind, or even – for that matter – that the mind itself exists. It would seem, then, that he was led by his empiricist assumptions and methods to very radical scepticism. But there was an intense dialectic within Hume's own mind on these issues. Surprisingly, despite all the strands of scepticism in his work, Hume was a strong critic of scepticism. He was a sceptic only in a qualified sense.

Hume regarded many of his philosophical conclusions as literally and simply *unbelievable*. Human nature, he thought, would prevent us from believing the philosophical conclusions for which he seemed to have compelling arguments. After a long and complex discussion of our knowledge – or lack of knowledge – of a world independent of perceptions in the *Treatise*, Hume says:

> As the sceptical doubt arises naturally from a profound and intense reflection on those subjects, it always encreases, the farther we carry our reflections, whether in opposition or conformity to it. Carelessness and in-attention alone can afford us any remedy. For this reason I rely entirely upon them; and take it for granted, whatever may be the reader's opinion at this present moment, that an hour hence he will be persuaded there is both an external and internal world . . .
> (*Treatise*, 218)

This is a puzzling passage. Is Hume really advising us to solve our problems by ignoring his arguments, and by being careless and inattentive? Such comments are baffling!

At points, Hume seems to agonize over the paradoxes his empiricist logic has revealed.

> I am first affrighted and confounded with that forelorn solitude, in which I am plac'd in my philosophy, and fancy myself some strange uncouth monster, who not being able to mingle and unite in society, has been expell'd [from] all human commerce and left utterly abandon'd and disconsolate. . . . When I look abroad, I foresee on every side dispute, contradiction, anger, calumny and detraction. When I turn my eye inward, I find nothing but doubt and ignorance.
> (*Treatise*, 264)

When Hume followed his impulse to philosophize, he came to conclusions contrary to what he had to believe in ordinary life. The tension tormented him.

> Where am I, or what? From what causes do I derive my existence, and to what condition shall I return? Whose favour shall I court, and whose anger must I dread? What beings surround me? and on whom have I any influence, or who have any influence on me? I am confounded with all these questions, and begin to fancy myself in the most deplorable condition imaginable, inviron'd with the deepest darkness, and utterly depriv'd of the use of every member and faculty.
> (*Treatise*, 269)

Hume found solace only in turning away from philosophical reasoning to enjoy the company of friends – wining and dining and playing games like billiards and backgammon. This was his recreational escape from scepticism.

The Pyrrhonists were sceptics of ancient Greece; their movement was founded by Pyrrho, who lived just after Socrates. Pyrrhonists had claimed to be able to give arguments both for and against any proposition, and for this reason, they recommended that we *suspend our judgment* on all matters. Hume criticized the Pyrrhonists sharply on the grounds that they were recommending something *impossible*. Believing and suspending judgment, Hume contended, are not actions we can undertake as we choose; our beliefs are not under our control. Nature, Hume insisted, *causes* us to believe just as it causes us to think and feel. Thus Hume rejected Descartes' method of universal doubt.

> The Cartesian doubt . . . were it ever possible to be attained by any human creature (as it plainly is not) would be entirely incurable; and no reasoning could ever bring us to a state of assurance and conviction upon any subject.
> (*Inquiry Concerning Human Understanding*, 167)

Hume argues that Cartesian doubt is impossible because we cannot control our beliefs. On this matter, Descartes and Hume differ absolutely. Descartes assumed that when we cannot doubt something, we know it, and that when we do not know something, we can doubt it. But Hume denies this supposed equivalence between knowing and not being able to doubt. On his account, we are naturally compelled to hold many beliefs which we do not know to be true and for which there is no systematic justification. But that does not mean that we can doubt them.

Descartes held that in the absence of clear and distinct ideas, we can *choose* to suspend our judgment. Hume, by contrast, saw belief as emerging from human nature, from custom and habit, and thus as not being within our control. We are simply not capable of believing contrary to the inductive assumption that past experience is a guide to the future – or of accepting that tables, horses, apartments, and France are entities existing only in our minds.

Hume's account of belief was restricted by his empiricist view that all the contents of the mind must be either impressions, or ideas derived from impressions. What is belief? Hume struggled with the question, which he said was "a great mystery of philosophy" ignored by previous thinkers. Belief cannot be an impression, because we

will; according to Hume, we cannot look inside our mind and discover free will. We do not have any internal impression of deciding to believe, or choosing to believe. And even if we were to have such an impression, we could not show that it "produced" our belief. In the mind, as in the external world, we experience one thing, then another – and we never experience a necessary connection between them.

Unlike Descartes, Hume thought of human beings as continuous with nature, and granted that animals have feelings and beliefs. In defense of his conception of belief as involuntary, he offers several arguments of a somewhat evolutionary nature. Even in infancy, human beings need beliefs based on experience, simply in order to survive. We do not reason as infants and small children. Later, when we do reason, many of our reasonings are fallacious. If we depended on abstract and general reasoning to get us through the day, we would not survive as animal creatures. Furthermore, if there is any rationally compelling argument to justify our natural beliefs, it would take a philosophical genius to discover it. (Hume himself had certainly not been able to do so!) Life cannot rest on the faint possibility that such a genius will come forth. We must believe by nature.

Hume says that we are made as the sorts of creatures we are, having the customs and habits we do, in order that we are able to survive.

> Animals, therefore, are not guided in these inferences by reasoning: Neither are children: Neither are the generality of mankind, in their ordinary actions and conclusions: Neither are philosophers themselves, who, in all the active parts of life, and, in the main, are the same with the vulgar [ordinary people] and are governed by the same maxims. Nature must have provided some other principle, of more ready, and more general use and application; nor can an operation of such immense consequence in life, as that of inferring effects from causes, be trusted to the uncertain process of reasoning and argumentation.
> (*Inquiry Concerning Human Understanding*, 116-117)

Custom makes animals – including human beings – form their expectations and beliefs according to what they have experienced in the past. Thus human nature helps protect us from our fallible reasonings. Hume says that human beings by instinct avoid fire after being once burned by it, just as birds by instinct build nests, incubate their eggs, and care for their young.

Only a qualified or – as Hume says – "mitigated" scepticism is feasible. Mitigated scepticism is based on caution and moderation, an awareness of how fallible we are, and an avoidance of superstition and dogmatism. Such scepticism Hume heartily recommends. But he argues that wholehearted scepticism – the Cartesian suspension of judgment about any proposition we cannot absolutely prove to be indubitable – is not only psychologically impossible, but absurd.

Practical Implications

If we ask for Hume's advice on the matter of thinking, it is hard to get a clear answer. Hume was an empiricist. He clearly believed that thought arose from sense experience and was bounded by it. Yet his empiricist principles led him to radically sceptical conclusions which he (and other human beings) could not believe, and those sceptical conclusions tormented him. The ability to escape those conclusions came only in "carelessness and inattention." Just what are we to conclude from such remarks? It is scarcely plausible to think that Hume – a probing critic and skillful arguer if there ever was one – is advising us to ignore general arguments, turn our attention away from serious problems, and believe whatever comes into our minds or heads.

At the end of the *Inquiry Concerning Human Understanding,* Hume claimed that his distinction between relations of ideas and matters of fact could be put to good use in critical thinking.

> When we run over libraries, persuaded of these principles, what havoc must we make? If we take in hand any volume; of divinity or school metaphysics, for instance; let us ask, *Does it contain any abstract reasoning concerning quantity or number*? No. *Does it contain any experimental reasoning concerning matters of fact and existence*? No. Commit it then to the flames; for it can contain nothing but sophistry and illusion.

In these famous but unusually strident remarks, Hume anticipated the logical positivists of the twentieth century. The logical positivists were scientifically minded philosophers who rejected as *meaningless* any statements that were not either empirical or purely logical.

Hume's constructive recommendations for human thought become more apparent when we turn to his writings on religion. In the *Inquiry Concerning Human Understanding* Hume wrote substantially about miracles and religious and secular attitudes to life. His posthumously published *Dialogues on Natural Religion* contain a sustained examination of an important argument for the existence of God. This argument goes as follows:

1. The world is ordered and organized, much as a watch or an intricate mechanism is.
2. A watch or any other intricate mechanism has been created by an intelligent being.

Therefore,

3. The world must have been created by an intelligent being.

And

4. That being is God.

This type of argument for God's existence is called the Argument from Design. In Hume's *Dialogues on Natural Religion* the Argument from Design is defended by a character called Cleanthes and criticized by another character, Philo. Philo claims that many other analogies apart from that of a watch or intricate mechanism are possible. (For instance, the world resembles an organism, and organisms result from sex and birth; thus it could equally well be argued that the world is the offspring of two other worlds, also organisms.) We have no experience which could tell us whether the world as a whole is more like a mechanism or an organism, so we have no experience which allows us to judge one analogy better than the other. Thus, Hume argues, the Argument from Design provides an insufficient justification for belief in an intelligent God who created the world.

In his writings on religion and immortality, Hume urges that we *conform our reasonings to experience*, where our nature has equipped us to reason and survive. If there is no basis in experience for a belief, we cannot reasonably hold it. Although we cannot philosophically justify our reasonings from experience in any definitive sense, we are the sorts of beings who do *by nature* reason from experience; reasoning in this fashion is what we are equipped to do, and it is the best we can do.

The basis of reasoning from experience is the fact that we notice similarities between events and form our expectations accordingly. If events of type C have always been followed by events of type E, we fully expect an E-event when we experience a C-event. In such a case, custom leads us to believe that C- events cause E-events, so that a C-event will "produce" an E- event. Another possibility is that C-events are usually, but not always, followed by E-events. If this is the case, then after a C-event we would tend to expect an E-event with some degree of probability. In such a case, C-events are not the sole cause of E-events, but may one of many causes required in bringing E-events about.

> A wise man, therefore, proportions his belief to the evidence. In such conclusions as are founded on an infallible [completely regular] experience, he expects the event with the last degree of assurance, and regards his past experience as a full *proof* of the future existence of that event. In other cases, he proceeds with more caution: He weighs the opposite experiments: He considers which side is supported by the greater number of experiments: to that side he inclines, with doubt and hesitation; and when at last he fixes his judgement, the evidence exceeds not what we properly call *probablilty.*
> (*Inquiry Concerning Human Understanding*, 122)

If E-events happen from time to time, but we have noted no regular relation between them and any sort of preceding event, we will think that they happen by chance.

But suppose that some new event, X, should occur. What might this mean? No matter what an X-event is, it does not make sense to think that X-events are literally, *absolutely*, new. Resemblance is a matter of degree, and X is bound to resemble other events in some way or other. Things which strike us as new are nevertheless similar in some respects to things within our experience. For that matter, things which strike us as similar also differ in some ways. No things are so alike as eggs, Hume remarks. Yet if we look carefully at two eggs, we can always find some difference between them. When we think of *types* of events (sunrises, the movement of billiard balls, and so on) we gloss over some differences and attend to similarities. It is in virtue of the similarities, the "resemblances", that we associate events and come to have such categories as "sunrise", "the movement of billiard balls", and so on.

For any two events, we can always find some differences between them and some similarities between them. Thus to suppose that an absolutely novel event should occur does not make sense. The novel event, X, will be relatively new, not absolutely new. We are creatures made to reason on the basis of resemblance, experience, and cause and effect. We would respond to X, a novel event, by trying to relate it to other events which are within our experience to try to find out what it is *like,* and then we would think about it, on the basis of these resemblances. Such thought would be reliable only to the extent that an X-event does resemble other events within our experience. To the extent that an X-event is unique, we can know nothing about its causes or effects. These would be matters of fact about which we cannot gain knowledge *a priori*, so we would have no relevant experience or custom to guide us.

Thus, in the end, Hume does offer some advice about how we should think. His advice is consistent with his empiricism, and it can be stated in two maxims.

> 1 We should conform our beliefs to experience insofar as it is possible.
> 2 We should restrict our beliefs to the realm of experience.

On matters of fact for which we have no relevant experience, we have no proper basis for beliefs.

There are matters we cannot know by experience, such as how the universe began, whether a God exists, whether God could intervene in human history to produce miraculous events, what the nature of God might be, whether there is a heaven, whether the whole world resembles a machine or an organism, whether we might experience a future life after death, and so on. Such questions are so far from ordinary life that our experience of vaguely similar matters is no reliable guide. In the Argument from Design, people reason from the analogy that because a watch, which is intricately ordered, has an intelligent designer and maker, so too must the world; it is also intricately ordered. But the similarity between a watch and the world is too remote to make this argument plausible. Besides, as Hume showed brilliantly in his *Dialogues on Natural Religion*, there are too many possible analogies for the creation of the world. Like a web, it might have been spun by a spider; like a living animal, it might be the offspring of other beings, and so on. No one of these analogies is good enough to give us any well-grounded belief about how the world was created. We cannot know about God, the beginning or ending of the world, or the nature of heaven, because we do not have the relevant experience.

To see earth and earthly experience as a mere passage to a remote but somehow better world, as Plato did, is, according to Hume, a perverse and irrational reversal of the natural direction of thought.

> But what must a philosopher think of those vain reasoners, who instead of regarding the present scheme of things as the sole object of their contemplation, so far reverse the whole course of nature,

> as to render this life merely a passage to something farther; a porch, which leads to a greater, and vastly different building; a prologue, which serves only to introduce the piece, and give it more grace and propriety? Whence, do you think, can such philosophers derive their idea of the gods? From their own conceit and imagination surely.
> (*Inquiry Concerning Human Understanding*, 150)

The world we experience is the world we know and it is the only world we know; of other worlds we can only speculate. Life is here; we should not denigrate or de-value the world we experience by regarding it as a mere introduction to a grander life in an unknowable other realm.

Nature ensures our survival. By nature we are creatures who believe that trees and chairs are stable objects existing outside ourselves, that we ourselves have a stable personal identity, and that the future will resemble the past. We believe these things despite the fact that there is no philosophical demonstration proving that they are true; we are led to believe them by the experience we have, and we have to believe them to survive. Nature has not similarly guaranteed that we will hold the beliefs of the Christian religion – or of any other religion, for that matter.

Hume said that beliefs on religious matters have been dangerous in promoting superstition and violent controversy. In this area, Hume urged agnosticism.

> . . . philosophical decisions are nothing but the reflections of common life, methodized and corrected. But they [philosophers] will never be tempted to go beyond common life, so long as they consider the imperfection of those faculties which they employ, their narrow reach, and their inaccurate operations. While we cannot give a satisfactory reason why we believe, after a thousand experiments, that a stone will fall, or fire burn; can we ever satisfy ourselves concerning any determination, which we may form, with regard to the origin of worlds, and the situation of nature, from and to eternity?
> (*Inquiry Concerning Human Understanding*, 181)

Philosophical reasonings are fallible but nearly always harmless – or so Hume thought. Reasonings in religion are not only more unreliable, they can cause tremendous damage. "Generally speaking the errors in religion are dangerous; those in philosophy only ridiculous," Hume said.

Observations: Hume's Problems

Hume's philosophy has long been perplexing to students and commentators. His intense personal dialectic about scepticism and natural belief, his apparent rejection of some of his own most eloquent and famous arguments, and his tendency to use in one part of his philosophy an idea that he has roundly rejected in another are only some its puzzling aspects.

In the end, Hume does make recommendations about how we should think. We should think according to what experience teaches, and restrict our thought to matters on which we have enough relevant experience to have some real evidence. Then, we should conform our beliefs about matters of fact to the evidence. In giving this advice, Hume has implicitly (and probably unconsciously) assumed that there *is* some sense in which we can control what we believe. All this sounds fine, but in saying it, Hume contradicts his own view that belief is beyond our control. If thinking and believing are truly beyond our control, it makes no sense to make *recommendations* as to how they should be conducted. How, whether, when, and why we have control over believing and suspending judgment is a question left over at the end of Hume's philosophy – and one not answered satisfactorily by philosophers to this very day.

A closely related question is that of the nature and activity of the mind. Hume came to regard the mind as nothing but a collection or bundle of impressions and ideas. Yet he nevertheless frequently appeals to the activity of the mind. It is hard to understand how impressions and ideas could *act* in the way Hume needs the mind to act.

Thomas Reid, who understood Hume far better than other critics of his day, found his arguments acute but rejected his conclusions. Reid contended that Hume's empiricist starting point had led him to such bizarre conclusions that the starting point itself must have been wrong. To reason on empiricist principles and discover that neither the material world nor the mind itself can be known to exist constitutes a refutation of those very principles. It reduces them to absurdity. Thus, against Hume, Reid said that his conclusions amounted to a refutation of the type called *reductio ad absurdum*. A *reductio ad absurdum* argument is of the following type:

> From ABC we are able to prove E and F.
> But E and F are absurd and clearly false.
> Therefore,
> There is something wrong with ABC.

Reid claimed that Hume's philosophy constituted a refutation of his own empiricist principles, because the conclusions he was led to when he reasoned from those principles were absolutely intolerable.

For all their various disagreements with rationalism, the British empiricists, including Hume, had unwittingly followed Descartes in accepting the Egocentric Predicament as the starting point for philosophy. They assumed that ideas "in the mind" are known first, and that the rest of human knowledge and belief must be built up from there. In common life people naturally believe that they see such things as the sun and moon, and that these are far away from them. But, said Reid, philosophers following "the way of ideas" have subtly and harmfully led them away from this sort of commonsense starting point.

> But how are we astonished when the philosopher informs us that we are mistaken in all this; that the sun and moon which we see are not, as we imagine, many miles from us, and from each other, that they are in our own mind; that they had no existence before we saw them, and will have none when we cease to perceive them; because the objects we perceive are only ideas in our own minds, which can have no existence a moment longer than we think of them?
> (*Works*, 298)

In the "way of ideas," philosophers introduce their students and readers to a whole new world in which everything is an idea which can be annihilated with the twinkling of an eye. The process is insidious. It is hard to spot an error in Hume's reasoning. But what has happened, Reid noticed, is very peculiar indeed. Ideas, which were supposed to *represent* objects, perversely came to *replace* them and then – still more perversely – to replace even the minds in which those ideas had originally been thought to exist. Hume fell into the Egocentric Predicament because he sought to base his whole philosophical system on impressions and ideas, and those, by definition, are mental. In this way, Reid argued that Hume, for all his brilliance, had based his philosophy on erroneous principles. Hume's work revealed crucial gaps in the understanding of such notions as self, matter, substance, causation, and identity. If his paradoxical conclusions showed something to be wrong with his empiricist starting point, what should replace that starting point? Was rationalism a better view? Was common sense an adequate starting point?

In his own time, Hume was not fully understood by critics. Even Reid did not fully appreciate that Hume had given his own reasons for saying that we *must* accept commonsense beliefs about the world. Hume's question was not about whether to believe in induction, causation, and a material world, but rather about how to reconcile our natural beliefs with the philosophical problems that emerged when these beliefs were carefully scrutinized. It was the German philosopher Immanuel Kant who understood and appreciated Hume. Kant did not read English, but he had read the full *Inquiry Concerning Human Understanding* in translation, and he had access to selections from the *Treatise* through a German translation of James Beattie's *Essay on the Nature and Immutability of Truth: In Opposition to Sophistry and Scepticism.* Though popular and successful in his time, Beattie was not much of a philosopher. But he quoted Hume at length, and the German translation of Beattie's work extended Kant's access to Hume's thought. Hume's problems were a major inspiration for Kant's original philosophical system. In 1783, seven years after Hume's death, Kant wrote:

> But Hume suffered the usual misfortune of metaphysicians, of not being understood. It is positively painful to see how utterly his opponents, Reid, Oswald, Beattie, and lastly Priestley, missed the point of the problem;. . . they were forever taking for granted that which he doubted, and demonstrating with zeal and often with impudence that which he never thought of doubting. . .
> (*Prolegomenon*, 6)

Kant, who appreciated the depth of the problems Hume had discovered, sought to resolve them in his own way. But before considering Kant's response to Hume, we pause to examine the provocative views of another highly original philosopher of the eighteenth century, Mary Wollstonecraft.

6

Wollstonecraft: The Oak that Braved the Storm

Mary Wollstonecraft (1759 - 1797) was an English political journalist, travel writer, and political philosopher. She is best remembered today for her *Vindication of the Rights of Woman*. Wollstonecraft's life and work reflect central themes of the eighteenth–century Enlightenment, with its stress on the power of reason to achieve human progress, and the passionate individuality of the Romanticism that began to develop in the late eighteenth century. Wollstonecraft was a determined, energetic, and fiercely independent woman who was unique in her time, living alone and supporting herself by writing. Her life was one of hardship, adventure, and tragedy. As one who experienced life's difficulties firsthand, she wrote knowingly and passionately about oppressive institutions and prospects for reform.

Wollstonecraft's family was not wealthy and her older brother, as the first son, stood to inherit everything the family had. As a child, Wollstonecraft was painfully aware of her low status in her own family; and the injustice of preferring sons to daughters. Determined to make her own way in the world, she left her family at the age of nineteen to work as a ladies' companion. Several years later she worked with her sisters and her friend Fanny Blood to establish a school for girls. Wollstonecraft made contact with the Dissenters, liberal–minded thinkers who stood outside the established Church of England. Prominent in this circle was the moral philosopher Richard Price, who became a close friend. Price's philosophical ideas about the relation between reason and moral knowledge influenced Wollstonecraft's political and philosophical writings.

By 1786 Blood had married and died in childbirth, the school was failing, and Wollstonecraft was struggling to support herself and help her two sisters. Her economic need was one reason that she began to write; she published *Thoughts on the Education of Daughters*, earning some modest payment. Determined to support herself without marrying, Wollstonecraft took a position as governess to Lord and Lady Kingsborough, near Cork, in Ireland. Leaving that position several years later, she was assisted by her publisher, Joseph Johnson; she came to live in London where she did translations and reviews for his journal, *The Analytical Review*. She published a novel, *Mary*, based on her own life, and a collection for children, *Original Stories*, illustrated by William Blake, who later became one of England's most famous Romantic poets. Blake admired Wollstonecraft and later wrote a poem about her.

Wollstonecraft and her colleagues were moved and inspired by the French Revolution of 1789, which they regarded as an upsurge of popular revolt against a long-entrenched regime of tyranny, injustice and inequality. Some observers feared that the tumult of the Revolution would spread, upsetting English life and traditions. The philosopher Edmund Burke expressed his anxieties and intellectual doubts about the Revolution in his *Reflections on the Revolution in France*.

Outraged by what she regarded as Burke's complacent conservatism, Wollstonecraft wrote a reply entitled *Vindication of the Rights of Men*, published in 1790. In this work she defended the rights of men of all social classes. Wollstonecraft argued that desperate poverty, hardship, and injustice resulted from the traditions that Burke was so concerned to preserve. In France efforts to have the education of girls recognized along with the education of boys seemed to be failing. Wollstonecraft realized that people who spoke of the rights of men really meant *men*, and men only. Even among social critics and radicals, it was common to regard women as beings who existed solely in order to please men. Convinced that women had as much claim to political and moral rights as men, and hoping to influence developments in France, Wollstonecraft wrote the *Vindication of the Rights of Woman* which was published in 1792.

In 1792 Wollstonecraft went to France to witness revolutionary developments first hand. By that time the Revolution was becoming increasingly violent, the more moderate

Girondins group was outlawed, and the more fanatical Jacobins, under Robespierre, were taking over. Many of Wollstonecraft's friends and colleagues were arrested and blood was literally flowing in the streets of Paris. Among the many liberal thinkers killed were several prominent women, including the outspoken French feminist Olympe de Gouges, who was guillotined.

During this tumultuous period, Wollstonecraft fell in love with an American writer and author, Gilbert Imlay, who registered her as his wife, giving her American status in France and the right to remain there in a turbulent period after most of the other English in Paris had been arrested. She became pregnant and in 1794 their daughter Fanny Imlay was born. Some months later Imlay left for England and Wollstonecraft and her daughter Fanny followed. Deeply saddened by the fact that Imlay had taken up with another woman, Wollstonecraft attempted suicide. She was rescued and revived. Seeking some outlet for Wollstonecraft's considerable energies, Imlay suggested that she travel to Scandinavia to deal with some of his business affairs. With her one-year-old daughter and a nurse, Wollstonecraft travelled through Norway, Sweden, and Denmark in 1795. It was an extraordinary journey. The literary result was that Wollstonecraft's letters to Imlay, written on the journey, were published as *Letters from Norway, Sweden, and Denmark*. Beautifully written and evocative, the letters combine political and social commentary with personal reflections and passionate descriptions of the wild northern landscape.

By 1796, Wollstonecraft had returned to London, accepted the break with Imlay, and resumed her work for the *Analytical Review*. She began a relationship with the radical philosopher William Godwin. After she became pregnant, she and Godwin married; they continued to conduct independent careers while developing a domestic life. In 1797 Wollstonecraft gave birth to a daughter, Mary Wollstonecraft Godwin, later to become the novelist Mary Shelley, author of *Frankenstein*. But Wollstonecraft suffered from infection. On September 10, 1797, at the age of thirty-eight, she died as a result of complications from childbirth.

Devastated, Godwin began almost immediately to write a biography of his wife, emphasizing her "intuitive" powers of understanding and her passionate nature. Despite his good intentions and genuine love for his wife, Godwin's work did considerable harm to Wollstonecraft's reputation. He underestimated the power of her intellect and stressed too much the intuitive and emotional side of her personality. People were unable to accept that a husband could acknowledge his wife's past loves, or that a woman who had written of reason and human perfectibility was also a sexual being. It was partly as a result of Godwin's memoir that Wollstonecraft was vilified as a prostitute. Even today, many writings about her pay more attention to her "scandalous" life than to her ideas.

Wollstonecraft was what we would call today an "applied philosopher." In analyzing social institutions and practices, she applied ideas about God, human nature, reason, and morality which were typical of the Enlightenment period, and which she adopted from Richard Price and others in Dissenting circles. Wollstonecraft was highly creative in the way that she used these ideas to interpret the society and politics of her time, and especially original in her analysis of the situation of women.

In her *Vindication of the Rights of Men*, writing against Edmund Burke, Wollstonecraft argued that human beings have rights because we have reason, which God has given to us. Human beings are reasoning beings who think, who can reflect on, evaluate, and reject the historical conditions in which we find ourselves. We can improve our circumstances by using our reason. These were classic themes of the Enlightenment: reason will bring insight; insight will bring progress, provided there is a willingness to alter customs and traditions. Wollstonecraft was convinced that reason, properly applied, would enable human beings to understand our situation in the world and give us the means to change it.

Writing of the early stages of the French Revolution, she expressed an optimism characteristic of the Enlightenment period:

> But these evils are passing away; a new spirit has gone forth, to organise the body-politic; and where is the criterion to be found, to estimate the means, by which the influence of this spirit can be confined, now enthroned in the hearts of half the inhabitants of the globe? Reason has, at last, shown her captivating face, beaming with benevolence; and it will be impossible for the dark hand of despotism again to obscure its radiance, or the lurking danger of subordinate tyrants to reach her bosom. The image of God implanted in our nature is now more rapidly expanding; and, as it opens, liberty with maternal wing seems to be soaring to regions far above vulgar annoyance, promising to shelter all mankind. . . . When courts [the nobility] and primogeniture are done away, and simple equal laws are established, what is to prevent each

> generation from retaining the vigour of youth? – What can weaken the body or mind, when the great majority of society must exercise both, to earn a subsistence, and acquire respectability?
> (*FR*, in Todd, 128)

Hereditary privilege was irrational; with the application of reason to social arrangements, improvements in society would result. If hereditary privilege were abolished, people would have to work to support themselves. It was not enough to have an educated and cultured aristocracy; to be valuable, improvements had to benefit people in all social ranks.

> But it is a palpable error to suppose, that men of every class are not equally susceptible of common improvement: if therefore it be the contrivance of any government, to preclude from a chance of improvement the greater part of the citizens of the state, it can be considered in no other light than as a monstrous tyranny, a barbarous oppression, equally injurious to the two parties, though in different ways. For all the advantages of civilization cannot be felt, unless it pervades the whole mass, humanizing every description of men – and then it is the first of blessings, the true perfection of man.
> (*FR*, in Todd, 134)

Here, Wollstonecraft is writing about all human beings; the words "man" and "men" are intended to refer to human beings of both sexes. By the exercise of reason, human beings can improve themselves and their society to the point of perfection.

As Wollstonecraft argued, traditional European institutions favored only certain groups – mainly upper-class men. Because of this gross injustice, she believed that common sentiments, opinions, and practices did not constitute a tradition worthy of preservation. They had no solid basis either in human feelings or in reason. From Wollstonecraft's point of view, something had gone wrong in the evolution of European societies. Progress had ceased because hereditary property, honors, and social practices prevented people from enjoying the true happiness and friendship that could only exist between social equals. In the corrupted societies of eighteenth-century Europe there was nothing like social equality. Like the French philosopher, Jean Jacques Rousseau, Wollstonecraft regarded so-called civilization as corrupted and an obstacle in the way of justice and reform. Because of the injustices of societies which privileged only a few men of the upper classes, men of other social classes and women of all classes were failing, emotionally and rationally.

> It is necessary emphatically to repeat, that there are rights which men inherit at their birth, as rational creatures, who were raised above the brute creation by their improvable faculties; and that, in receiving these, not from their forefathers, but, from God, prescription can never undermine natural rights.
> (*Vindication of the Rights of Men*, in Todd, 67)

> In what respect are we superior to the brute creation, if intellect is not allowed to be the guide of passion? Brutes hope and fear, love and hate; but without a capacity to improve, a power of turning these passions to good or evil, they neither acquire virtue nor wisdom. – Why? Because the Creator has not given them reason.
> (*Vindication of the Rights of Men*, in Todd, 73)

When he wrote against the French Revolution, the conservative philosopher Edmund Burke sought to defend tradition and the security of property. Wollstonecraft believed that Burke could only value tradition because he had ignored the interests of the vast majority of people, many of whom lived in desperate poverty. Alluding to the misery that "lurks in pestilential corners" and the heartbreaking idleness of the many thousands of unemployed people, she asked:

> Where is the eye that marks these evils, more gigantic than any of the infringements of property which you piously deprecate? Are these remediless evils? And is the humane heart satisfied with turning the poor over to *another* world, to receive the blessings this could afford?
> (*Vindication of the Rights of Men*, in Todd, 70)

Burke should have noticed the misery of the poor before he set out to defend the status quo. That misery was deplorable. Though she was a religious believer, Wollstonecraft was like Hume in believing that our attention should be devoted to affairs and conditions on this earth. She was convinced that earthly poverty and destitution should not be ignored on the assumption that they are inevitable facts of life; nor should they be rationalized away on the belief that the poor will somehow be compensated for their misery when they leave the earth and go to heaven.

Wollstonecraft firmly believed that people can do something to remedy human misery, if they will only pay attention to it and reflect on its causes.

> If society were regulated on a more enlarged plan; if man were contented to be the friend of man, and did not seek to bury the sympathies of humanity in the servile appellation of master; if,

> turning his eyes from ideal regions of taste and elegance, he labored to give the earth he inhabited all the beauty it is capable of receiving, and was ever on the watch to shed abroad all the happiness which human nature can enjoy; – he who, respecting the rights of men, wish to convince or persuade society that this is true happiness and dignity, is not the cruel *oppressor* of the poor nor a short-sighted philosopher. He fears God and loves his fellow creatures.
> (*Vindication of the Rights of Men*, in Todd, 82)

A Vindication of the Rights of Woman

It is difficult today to appreciate the originality and historical significance of Wollstonecraft's writings on women, because many of her ideas seem so clearly sound and would be accepted as such by most modern Western readers. Wollstonecraft's argument was, in essence, that women are human beings who can and should develop their capacity for rational thought and action. She believed in God and believed that God had created human beings to be creatures who could think, reflect, reason, evaluate, act rightly, and improve themselves. Wollstonecraft believed in the immortality of the human soul, and saw perfectibility as the purpose of this immortality. Our capacities for thought and reflection make us capable of improving ourselves and, eventually, perfecting ourselves. Women and men have rational souls, destined for immortality. For Wollstonecraft immortality was a fact – a fact that posed a question. Why are we born with immortal souls? Wollstonecraft believed that immortality had a definite purpose: we are immortal because we are intended by God to develop the capacities of our souls, thereby perfecting ourselves. Like Socrates, Wollstonecraft believed that the soul improves itself by thinking and reasoning.

Women are the equals of men in the absolutely fundamental respect that women are reasoning creatures. Whatever rights men have in virtue of their reason, women have as well. And these rights should be recognized.

> I shall first consider women in the grand light of human creatures, who, in common with men, are placed on this earth to unfold their faculties; and afterwards I shall more particularly point out their peculiar designation. . . . I wish to show that elegance is inferior to virtue, that the first object of laudable ambition is to obtain a character as a human being, regardless of the distinction of sex.
> (*Vindication of the Rights of Woman*, 8-9)

The absolutely fundamental thing to appreciate about women is that they exist as beings in their own right; they do not exist merely in order to be the wives and mothers of men. Wollstonecraft sometimes appealed to the nature of God the Creator to back up this insight; but there is an important sense in which it was not grounded in religious experience or belief. Her confidence in the status of women as human beings with needs and interests of their own was so great that she was willing to dispute established religious teachings to defend it.

> I may be allowed to doubt whether woman was created for man: and though the cry of irreligion, or even atheism, be raised against me, I will simply declare, that were an angel from heaven to tell me that Moses's beautiful, poetical cosmogony, and the account of the fall of man were literally true, I could not believe what my reason told me was derogatory to the character of the Supreme Being: and having no fear of the devil before mine eyes, I venture to call this a suggestion of reason, instead of resting my weakness on the broad shoulders of the first seducer of my frail sex.
> (*Vindication of the Rights of Woman*, 79)

If religion were to teach that God had created women solely to serve and please men, Wollstonecraft would not believe it; reason told her that a good God could never create one intelligent being solely to serve another. Unlike conservative thinkers of her time, Wollstonecraft did not believe that the story of the Garden of Eden gave a basis for understanding the nature of men and women. If a person is weak, she should not seek the explanation for her tendencies in the story of Adam, Eve, and the apple; rather she should reflect on herself and her situation and try to improve matters by her own understanding and action. It is reason and thought, not Scripture, that can equip human beings, both male and female, with ideas of what is right and what we should do. We are capable of exercising our minds, finding out what is right, and doing it. Wollstonecraft, a deeply religious woman, was nevertheless convinced that the story of Eve's sin in the Garden of Eden should be regarded as a myth. It was not a historical truth demonstrating that Eve was weaker than Adam, that women were inferior to men, or that women were responsible for original sin.

What Wollstonecraft says about Adam and Eve indicates that, like Plato and the Socrates of the *Euthyphro*, she regarded moral knowledge as independent of religious belief. Wollstonecraft was confident that God (the Supreme Being) was of morally good character and that no morally good God would be so cruel and irrational as to design a thinking creature solely to serve the needs of another. If God had done otherwise, Wollstonecraft would not have been prepared to believe it. As thinking beings, women are not, and were never designed to be, mere "helpmates" for men. Nor do they exist simply in order to be sexual playmates or even in order to be the mothers or companions of men. Women are persons, beings in their own right, conscious beings with minds of their own and reason permitting them to act and understand the world. They can do many things in this world and they can be of service to many people; like all human beings, they should be of service to others. But fundamentally they do not exist in order to serve others. They exist as beings in their own right, with their own needs, talents, and abilities.

This view of women stands in sharp contrast to the common eighteenth-century assumption that women were beings who existed only to please and serve men. The philosopher Rousseau, though quite penetrating in many of his criticisms of European culture, showed no independent insights on this subject. Rousseau, who behaved deplorably in his personal life – exploiting rich women for their patronage and poor women for their sexuality, having many affairs, and abandoning the resulting infants to orphanages – took the derivative status of women absolutely for granted. He wrote a widely-read treatise on education called *Emile,* describing how a young man, Emile, should be taught to develop his emotional and intellectual nature so that he could become a man, father, and citizen. Emile was to develop his capacities for independent thought and learn a variety of things. But his intended companion, Sophie, was to receive an entirely different education. Rousseau assumed, and boldly stated, that Sophie existed only to please Emile, to satisfy and control his sexual desires, and be a mother to their children. Rousseau said:

> The education of women should be always relative to [that of] men. To please, to be useful to us, to make us love and esteem them, to educate us when young, and take care of us when grown up, to advise, to console us, to render our lives easy and agreeable: these are the duties of women at all time, and what they should be taught in their infancy.
> (Quoted in *Vindication of the Rights of Women*, 79)

The view that women are not beings with goals and motives of their own could hardly be put more clearly. Emile, as a man, exists for himself; Sophie, as a woman, exists for Emile. Rousseau's language makes it clear that he assumed all his readers to be male. The pronoun "us" in this passage clearly refers to "us men" – those beings whom women are supposed to please and care for. Wollstonecraft lived and worked in circles where this way of thinking was absolutely normal and received virtually no attention or criticism. Seeing its ethical and logical limitations and its cruel implications for women, she struggled to write for an educated public of men and women whom she would lead away from those beliefs.

Wollstonecraft spared no words in criticizing Rousseau's ideas on Sophie and Emile. Women educated in the way Rousseau recommended would be servile and dependent. Taught to condone and endure injustice, they would themselves become unjust. Then, ignorant and thoughtless, they would be unfit for the very roles Rousseau had wanted them to play, those of wife and mother. Intentionally or not, Rousseau had been led to "degrade woman by making her the slave of love." In the late eighteenth century, women – especially upper-class women – were encouraged to spend their time flirting and arranging their hair and dress, and were taught to see their destiny in life as marriage, in which they would be subservient partners. The fundamental message of *A Vindication of the Rights of Woman* is that women are persons capable of independent thought and reason, and morality and custom should pay attention to that fact. Women have their own needs and abilities, and their own rights. They exist as beings who have souls destined for immortality, persons who are capable of developing their capacities for understanding and reflection and perfecting themselves.

> I will allow that bodily strength seems to give man a natural superiority over woman; and this is the only solid basis on which the superiority of the sex can be built. But I still insist that not only the virtue, but the *knowledge* of the two sexes should be the same in nature, if not in degree, and that women, considered not only as moral, but rational creatures, ought to endeavour to acquire human virtues (or perfections) by the *same* means as men, instead of being educated like a fanciful kind of *half* being.
> (*Vindication of Rights of Woman*, 39)

In her writing on the rights of women, Wollstonecraft addressed the many stereotypes of women that were common in her time: women were emotional, frivolous, weak and sickly, preoccupied with trivial concerns, unreliable, and intellectually less capable than men. She countered these ideas by acknowledging many of the criticisms but insisting that the faults of women were more attributable to custom and education than to their true natures. Yes, many women were emotional and incompetent. Yes, many women neglected their own children to spend their time and energy fussing over dress, indulging their pets, flirting, or having affairs. Yes, many women were ignorant and silly, irresponsible or dull. But Wollstonecraft was convinced that these characteristics of women emerged as a result of social practices and institutions, not female human nature. They were the results of restricted education and training and the extremely limited outlets for women's talents and energies.

According to Wollstonecraft, women's nature is human nature, and human nature is rational nature. Because women could think and reason, they could become capable of independent judgment and action, and in so doing, more effectively seek their own self-improvement and happiness. Independent thinking women would be competent citizens, workers, mothers and wives, and the whole society would benefit.

> Men complain, and with reason, of the follies and caprices of our sex, when they do not keenly satirize our headstrong passions and grovelling vices. – Behold, I should answer, the natural effect of ignorance! The mind will ever be unstable that has only prejudices to rest on, and the current will run with destructive fury when there are no barriers to break its force. Women are told from their infancy, and taught by the example of their mothers, that a little knowledge of human weakness, justly termed cunning, softness of temper, *outward* obedience, and a scrupulous attention to a puerile kind of propriety, will obtain for them the protection of man; and should they be beautiful, everything else is needless, for, at least, twenty years of their lives.
> (*Vindication of the Rights of Woman*, 19)

What women were taught was a lie – a discouraging and debilitating lie.

There is a clear distinction in Wollstonecraft's thought between the way women's nature appears to be and the way it is. Education and culture affect only the way human nature *appears*. Thus they give us no reliable indication of true human potential. Women who are not educated are likely to be ignorant; women who get no exercise are likely to be weak. Women who are taught that the purpose of life is to look beautiful and attract men are likely to be frivolous and flirtatious; and women who are never encouraged to think are likely to have silly ideas and seem purely emotional. But none of these cultural limitations reveals the *nature* of women or demonstrates that women would be incapable of undertaking important social functions or doing serious work. What human beings naturally are and may become cannot be known from how they appear in the limited circumstances of a corrupted and oppressive society. Wollstonecraft was absolutely confident that women were capable of more than they were allowed to do in eighteenth-century Europe – she saw no reason, for instance, why women could not become doctors.

Wollstonecraft drew an analogy between the growth of trees and the growth of the mind:

> Our trees are now allowed to spread with wild luxuriance, nor do we expect by force to combine the majestic marks of time with youthful graces; but wait patiently till they have struck deep their root, and braved many a storm. – Is the mind then, which in proportion to its dignity, advances more slowly towards perfection, to be treated with less respect? To argue from analogy, every thing around us is in a progressive state . . .
> (*Vindication of the Rights of Woman*, 108)

As trees grow and flourish over time, so will minds, if they are not inhibited and prevented from developing. The minds of men and women are at least as important as trees, and should be treated with as much respect.

> If wisdom be desirable on its own account, if virtue, to deserve the name, must be founded on knowledge; let us endeavour to strengthen our minds by reflection, till our heads become a balance for our hearts; let us not confine all our thoughts to the petty occurrences of the day, or our knowledge to an acquaintance with our lovers' or husbands' hearts; but let the practice of every duty be subordinate to the grand one of improving our minds, and preparing our affections for a more exalted state! Beware then, my friends, of suffering the heart to be moved by every trivial incident: the reed is shaken by a breeze, and annually dies, but the oak stands firm and for ages braves the storm!
> (*Vindication of the Rights of Woman*, 92)

Better to be the oak that braves the storm than a vulnerable reed: to stand as strong as oaks, women need to strengthen their minds, establishing a balance against the power of their passions. People can strengthen their minds by learning how to think critically and creatively, and actually engaging in thought. Wollstonecraft emphasized not the learning of a vast array of facts, but the development of critical and creative capacities of the mind. Education should be more than the accumulation of knowledge and practical skills. The most important thing is to know how to think for oneself.

A prominent theme in Wollstonecraft's work is that of marriage and motherhood. Unlike some contemporary feminists, who write as though women go through adult life unencumbered, finding sexual fulfillment only in temporary relationships, Wollstonecraft assumed that most women would be married and have children. She believed that most women would find their primary roles in life to be those of wife and mother. But that was no reason not to educate women. On the contrary, educated women would be better wives and mothers, and more responsible citizens.

Wollstonecraft was especially concerned about the tendency among many upper-class women to neglect their children, a phenomenon which, as a schoolteacher and governess, she had observed firsthand. It was common for upper-class women to send their children out to wet nurses as babies and later have them cared for by servants, governesses, or tutors. Against these practices, Wollstonecraft argued that women should breastfeed their own children and actively engage themselves with the children's upbringing and education. She believed that women could care for children in a sensible and responsible way only if they themselves had been educated to be serious, thoughtful beings. The advancement of women, something absolutely required for women themselves, would also benefit children. In this regard, Wollstonecraft's views have been strongly confirmed by modern experience. Current thinking about the alleviation of poverty in less-developed countries, for instance, understands the education and economic independence of women to be absolutely central in the progress of society because of the way women's empowerment benefits their children. Wollstonecraft also argued that acknowledgement of the rights of women and their status as rational beings would benefit men, who would gain wives who would become loyal partners and genuine companions instead of "mere lap dogs." Taught to think, to have independent goals in life, and to exercise their judgment, women would no longer indulge themselves in flirtation and affairs simply because they had nothing better to do.

Educating women to think would benefit their children, their husbands, and society at large. But the main and chief reason to recognize the rights and abilities of women was their status as thinking creatures, created by God as capable of independent reasoning and self-reflection. Wollstonecraft's answer to the question "for whom do women exist?" was clear and unequivocal; women exist for themselves and should be able to lead their own lives, whether within marriage or outside it.

Wollstonecraft called for changes in education and in economic and social institutions so that women could more easily support themselves without being married. Although she was not opposed to marriage as such, she recognized its dangers in any situation where women and men were not legal or social equals. When women are legally no more than a part of a family headed by a man who is granted legal authority over all its affairs, they run terrible risks of being victims of abuse. Wollstonecraft had witnessed domestic brutality and intervened with her own body to protect her mother from her father; she had rescued a sister from an abusive husband; and from her own experience she knew that women who were legally and economically dependent on men were terribly, appallingly, vulnerable. Even in good marriages, women and children were vulnerable to the death of the husbands and fathers who had been their sole means of economic support. If women could think independently and engage in productive non-domestic pursuits, their increased autonomy would help to protect them and their children. While marriage and motherhood were, in Wollstonecraft's view, natural and suitable roles for many women, she insisted as well on the importance of a woman's being able to choose not to be married. After considerable struggle, Wollstonecraft had become capable of supporting herself independently of her father, her brothers, or a husband. She made her own way in the world, and she argued that society should be changed so that other women could do the same if they chose to.

Thought and Reason

Though far in advance of her time in her ideas about women and the poor, Wollstonecraft was in other ways typical of her age. Her confidence in human reason and its power to liberate human beings from the weight of unreasonable tradition was absolutely characteristic of the Enlightenment period in which she lived. Wollstonecraft expressed the Enlightenment faith in reason and progress.

What is reason, and what does it do? How is reason related to sense, imagination, understanding, and memory? Does reason give people intuitions of self-evidence, like the Cartesian "light of nature?" Or is reason exercised only when we are reasoning, or arguing? For all Wollstonecraft's faith in the power of reason and stress on the importance of independent thinking, she had little to say about such questions. She was confident that reason would give a clear verdict on the merits of human institutions: feudalism and the exploitation of servants are wrong; men and women are fundamentally equal; the corrupt practices of the nobility should be eliminated; education develops the ability to think for oneself; human beings have immortal souls; the soul was made to perfect itself; men and women would have to overcome the many inequalities in European society in order to protect themselves. Unlike some radicals in her circle – including William Godwin – Wollstonecraft was a sincere religious believer. Her views about God are similar to those of the Deists, Enlightenment thinkers who believed in a Creator who had set the world on a predictable path but did not intervene directly in human history. Deists believed in a intelligent Creator who had made an orderly world, which could operate on its own according to natural laws and in which progress was possible and natural. Human beings could become aware of natural laws and use them to acquire knowledge of God himself; then their enhanced understanding would enable them to work towards a better world. Deists believed that religion was something that could and should be founded on reason. For this reason they did not regard the Bible or any other religious texts as literally true. For the Deists of the Enlightenment period, and for Wollstonecraft herself, there was no such thing as original sin. Human beings are not born evil. Rather, human nature is rational and human beings are capable of progress. The world is fundamentally a rational and comprehensible place, because God made it that way. Since human misery is a product of faulty institutions, it can be overcome.

Wollstonecraft's God was not a tyrannical creature, but a reasonable Being wanting His creatures to be virtuous and happy. This God respects the status of individual men and women, and provides the basis for human rights. Unlike the God of the Old Testament and established churches in the late eighteenth century, this God loves justice, freedom, and equality, and wants us to become happy by developing our individual capacities and talents. Wollstonecraft saw life as a preparation for immortality and the body as something that would give way to spirit. When in despair, she sometimes wrote longingly of a future world in which her problems would be solved. But her passion and energy led her to involvement in this world, where she applied her philosophical ideas to argue for women's rights, social justice, and progress for the masses of humanity.

Wollstonecraft's religious outlook, belief in a rational God and the immortality of the soul, and conception of the human being as a compound of body and mind/soul, serve as the grounds for her ethical and political analyses. She seems to have felt no sceptical doubts about such religious beliefs and did not explore their philosophical foundation. Had she wanted to, the pressures of her personal life and sweeping historical events would have left her little opportunity to do so. Wollstonecraft was a philosopher active in her age, engaged in making human history at a time of tumultuous change. Both *Vindications* were written and published hastily because they were responses to the developing events of the French Revolution.

So far as reason, morality, and virtue are concerned, Wollstonecraft's views are broadly similar to those of Socrates, and in detail close to those of her friend Richard Price. For most of her writing career, she was convinced that if people would only use their reason and think, they could come to know the right thing to do. Having obtained such knowledge, they would act in a virtuous way.

Richard Price's major work on the topic of moral knowledge was *A Review of the Principle Questions in Morals*, first published in 1758. In this work, Price argued that moral beliefs are not to be founded in a kind of emotional moral sense, or in love of the self, or in laws, or even in decrees of the divine will. Rather, they are grounded in human understanding – that is to say, in the human intellect or reason. Like Plato, Price claimed that we need abstract ideas in order to understand the world. Foremost among these abstract ideas are the ideas of right and wrong. According to Price, right and wrong are objective qualities of actions; right and wrong are real and fixed. Using our reason, we can intuitively apprehend these qualities. When we improve and strengthen our reason, we will better discern moral qualities and as a result we will become more virtuous.

Price was not entirely rationalistic in his conception of the human mind. He noted that we have perceptions, sensations, and instincts which bear significantly on our thinking, and give our intellectual ideas greater force and weight. To act morally, we need "both a perception of the understanding and a feeling of the heart." Our human feelings are important for our understanding of life and our decisions about what to do. These feelings often support reason; they are not opposed to it. On this topic, Wollstonecraft shared Price's view. Both were convinced that feeling counts for *something* when we are reflecting on moral problems. The main question about justifying moral judgments is whether feeling, or emotions, count for *everything* – not whether they count for something, which must be acknowledged as an obvious fact of life. Price and Wollstonecraft were convinced that reason had a large role to play in moral judgment even though our feelings are an important part of us and support us in our understanding and action. But the truth of moral judgments does not depend on how we feel or what we perceive. It depends, rather, on the real qualities of actions which we are able to grasp, not through feeling or perception, but through the intellect or understanding.

It is reason that should be our authoritative guide when we are deciding what to do and what is right or wrong. Reason provides insight into the rightness or wrongness of actions. If, after finding out the facts about a case, following our feelings, and thinking hard about the matter, we become convinced that some course of action is right, we ought to follow it. If we become convinced that some course of action is wrong, we ought not to follow it. "The intellectual nature is its own law. It has, within itself, a spring and guide of action which it cannot suppress or reject," Price wrote.

Price wrote rather abstractly and used few examples. His interest was in the abstract philosophical problem of moral knowledge. In contrast, Wollstonecraft's interests were in her turbulent social world and the wellbeing of many of the weaker members within it, including most notably women. In her writing on men's rights and women's rights, Wollstonecraft applied conceptions of reason, action, mind, and morality, which were essentially identical with those of Richard Price, to the disturbing phenomena of her social world. By doing so, she reached conclusions which should have been reasonable to any Enlightenment thinker but which were, nevertheless, novel and radical in her own time.

Wollstonecraft believed in co-education and in the value of exercise for maintaining health; she believed that sugar was bad for the teeth and skin; she argued that women should breastfeed their own babies; she claimed that women could safely get up and walk within a day or two of a normal childbirth. (She herself did this, to good effect, after the birth of her daughter Fanny.) She questioned the necessity for wars, and the blind obedience to authority that characterized military discipline, arguing that such discipline would prevent the development of good judgment and good citizenship. Wollstonecraft had a keen eye for inequity and injustice. She understood that women who were taught to be docile victims of injustice could not possibly communicate a sense of fairness and equity to their children. In her travel writings, she commented intelligently on variable practices and customs, distinctions of class, and varying attitudes to the French Revolution, without lapsing into ethnic or nationalist stereotypes. She distinguished human nature from its appearance in particular social contexts and observed in her travels the variety of customs and standards of living. Wollstonecraft showed considerable originality in applying philosophical conceptions to the troubled social world in which she lived.

Enlightenment and Romanticism; Reason and Emotion

The French Revolution is often cited as the beginning of the end of the Enlightenment outlook on the world. The Revolution that was supposed to bring liberty, equality, and fraternity led instead to brutality, repression, terror, and death. Enlightenment optimists had looked for reform and progress when the rational ideas of the philosophers were applied to politics, but they were horrified and shocked by the violence of the Revolution in the period of the Terror. In the face of the chaos and brutality of the Revolution, Wollstonecraft retained her conviction that there was something right about the Revolution because the old order had been unjust and had to change. But having witnessed the actions of desperate mobs and murderers who had risen to positions of political power, she qualified her faith in the power of human reason as an engine of progress. Still, Wollstonecraft's faith in reason and progress through activist politics was never entirely lost.

Wollstonecraft believed that the some of violence of the Revolution could be explained by the fact that the agents of terror were themselves products of a hungry and brutal society. Reason would eventually bring progress, but the process would be slow.

> Every nation, deprived by the progress of its civilization of strength of character in changing its government from absolute despotism to enlightened freedom, will, most probably, be plunged into anarchy, and have to struggle with various species of tyranny before it is able to consolidate its liberty; and that, perhaps, cannot be done until the manners and amusements of the people are completely changed.
> (*FRL*, in Todd, 213)

Although violence of the sword was awful and Wollstonecraft did not support it, there were worse abuses in human life, many completely legal and apparently without consequence to their perpetrators.

> During my present journey [in Scandinavia] and whilst residing in France, I have had an opportunity of peeping behind the scenes of what are vulgarly termed great affairs, only to discover the mean machinery which has directed many transactions of the moment. The sword has been merciful, compared with the depredations made on human life by contractors, and by the swarm of locusts who have battened on the pestilence they spread abroad. These men, like the owners of negro ships, never smell on their money

> the blood by which it has been gained, but sleep quietly in their beds, terming such occupations *lawful callings;* yet the lightning marks not their roofs, to thunder convictions on them, 'and to justify the ways of God to man.'
> (*Works*, Vol VI, 344)

Those who exploited slavery and economically gained from it were not punished, even by social reputation. They never drew a sword, and yet they had imposed terrible suffering on their fellow human beings. Apparently many felt not a pang of conscience.

Does reason itself provide insight into moral truth or the workings of the social and physical world? Can reason provide human beings with the power to reform their world? In the wake of the violence and chaos of the French Revolution, many thinkers were becoming doubtful. By the end of the eighteenth century, the Enlightenment period in European thought was yielding to the currents of Romanticism. In Romantic thought, passion and feeling are exalted as sources of insight, and there is an accompanying scepticism about the power of reason. The literature and art of the Romantic era are characterized by exaltation of feeling and emotion, a joy in personal freedom, and an intense awareness of the beauties of nature. In philosophy, there is a greater sensitivity to the need to say what reason is, and explore its limitations – a major theme of the late eighteenth-century philosopher, Immanuel Kant.

Many historians date the end of the Enlightenment period as 1789, the year of the French Revolution. Much of Wollstonecraft's work was completed in a kind of transition period between the Enlightenment and Romanticism. In so many ways a characteristically Enlightenment thinker, she was also in some respects an early Romantic. Her *Letters from Scandinavia* are widely regarded as the earliest expressions of Romanticism in English literature.

> Nature is the nurse of sentiment, – the true source of taste; – yet what misery, as well as rapture, is produced by a quick perception of the beautiful and sublime, when it is exercised in observing animated nature, when every beauteous feeling and emotion excites responsive sympathy in such an imperfect state of existence; and how difficult to eradicate them when an affection for mankind, a passion for an individual, is but the unfolding of that love which embraces all that is great and beautiful.
> (*Works*, Vol VI, 271)

We find in Wollstonecraft's letters a characteristically Romantic love of nature and exaltation of the human response to its beauties. Describing a walk to a waterfall in Norway, she says:

> Reaching the cascade, or rather cataract, the roaring of which had a long time announced its vicinity, my soul was hurried by the falls into a new train of reflections. The impetuous dashing of the rebounding torrent from the dark cavities which mocked the exploring eye, produced an equal activity in my mind: my thoughts darted from earth to heaven, and I asked myself why I was chained to life and its misery? Still the tumultuous emotions this sublime object excited, were pleasurable; and, viewing it, my soul rose, with renewed dignity, above its cares – grasping at immortality – it seemed as impossible to stop the current of my thoughts, as of the always varying, still the same, torrent before me – I stretched out my hand to eternity, bounding over the dark speck of life to come.
> (*Works*, Vol VI, 311)

Observations

Wollstonecraft's works are often labelled as rationalist. Wollstonecraft has been criticized on these grounds by some contemporary feminists who see her as a rationalist through and through, and believe that trying to be too rational isolates us from experience and represses significant aspects of ourselves. There is much of importance in the theory that we repress emotions at our peril – but as a criticism of Wollstonecraft, such attacks are misplaced. Even the casual reader cannot help but notice the strong and impassioned language Wollstonecraft uses. Her passion for justice and fairness, sympathy for the wretchedly poor, rage at the insults to women's intelligence, and zeal for reform call out from every page. Wollstonecraft's works show an impassioned application of reason to the issues of her own society, whose location in the transition between the Enlightenment and Romanticism makes the theme of reason and emotion an especially significant one.

The question of emotion and reason is posed by Wollstonecraft's life as well as by her work. Through most of the nineteenth and much of the twentieth centuries, critics found in Wollstonecraft a fundamental contradiction between theory and practice. Here was a woman who exalted the faculty of reason and called for its application to social problems, but who in her own life succumbed to feelings of love and longing at great cost to her personal security and reputation. Many critics saw Wollstonecraft as someone unable to live up to her own rationalist prescriptions – a woman more a creature of feelings than she was willing to admit, one great in pretensions, but lacking in self-knowledge and self-control.

Stereotypical thinking prominent in the eighteenth century, and still alive today, categorized women as purely emotional beings unable to discipline their feelings or their conduct. Wollstonecraft fell in love, had an illegitimate baby, attempted suicide, became pregnant a second time while unmarried, then married and enjoyed domestic life. Was all this "rational?" Critics did not think so: she was roundly attacked for flagrant immorality and (apparently) failing to live up to her own rationalist advice. Believing that a woman wanting independence and having intellectual interests and aspirations would have no longing for a sexual life or children, and assuming that reason and feeling were opposed, many saw Wollstonecraft's life as both immoral and a departure from her own teachings. The perceived contradiction was too delicious to resist. A full century after her death, Wollstonecraft was still attacked and satirized for it. Given stereotypical assumptions that women were (only) emotional creatures, it was easy to brand Wollstonecraft as a creature of passion, deluded in her pretensions of rationality.

Such commentary hits a low intellectual level, and it is largely irrelevant to the merits of Wollstonecraft's ideas. Whether or not she had an illegitimate baby, selected appropriate male partners, or felt lust or love, cannot establish the soundness or the unsoundness of Wollstonecraft's accounts of reason, human perfectibility, or the value of education. In fact, criticizing someone's theories and conclusions on the grounds that his or her personal life is faulty is such a well-recognized mistake in reasoning that it has a special name: the *ad hominem* fallacy, or fallacy of arguing against the man. (It would be more accurate to speak of the fallacy of arguing against the person, but tradition, begun when women had little or no role in public discussions, has established the *ad hominem* label.) Issues of Wollstonecraft's morality in her personal sexual life have no logical bearing on the validity of her philosophical ideas about women and men, rights, and equality; and they have little intellectual merit in their own right.

The persistence of such criticisms, right into our own century, points again to the question of reason and emotion. One thing critics simply assumed was that reason and emotion were opposed; a woman who appealed to reason in her analysis of social affairs would contradict herself if she gave in to powerful feelings.

What role do feelings play in thought? In the acquisition of knowledge? In moral judgment? Most philosophers, past and present, have tended to contrast thinking and feeling, regarding emotion as something that is likely to make us unreasonable and cause us to act unwisely. They have in this respect been more like Plato and Descartes than like Aristotle and Hume. Such polarized conceptions of reason and emotion are still held by many people today. We still tend, many of us, to believe that thought and rational argument will give us knowledge, whereas feeling tends to overcome us, or mislead us into doing silly things. Calling someone "emotional" has negative implications; in contrast, saying someone is "reasonable" or "logical" is typically a term of praise. The emotional and the rational are usually opposed.

Interestingly, however, this opposition of reason and emotion does not seem to have been assumed by Wollstonecraft herself – not even in the *Vindications* which are her most "rationalist" writings. In his theory of moral knowledge, Richard Price emphasized both emotion and reason, and allowed that emotions do and should affect moral judgment. Price never denied the relevance of feeling and emotion to moral judgment and action; our feelings are relevant to our moral situation although they do not dictate what we ought to do, because both intellect and feeling are required for proper moral judgment. Wollstonecraft seems to have held a similar view. She says, for instance,

> I am, indeed, persuaded that the heart, as well as the understanding, is opened by cultivation; and by, which may not appear so clear, strengthening the organs; I am not now talking of momentary flashes of sensibility, but of affections. And, perhaps, in the education of both sexes, the most difficult task is so to adjust instruction as not to narrow the understanding, whilst the heart is warmed by the generous juices of spring, just raised by the electric fermentation of the season; not to dry up the feelings by employing the mind in investigations remote from life.
> (*Vindication of the Rights of Woman*, 66)

Heart and mind should both be cultivated and should work together.

> *The world cannot be seen by an unmoved spectator*, we must mix in the throng and feel as men [people] feel before we can judge of their feelings.
> (*Vindication of the Rights of Woman*, 112; my emphasis)

> If we wish to render mankind moral from principle, we must, I am persuaded, give a greater scope to the enjoyments of the senses, by blending taste with them.
> (*Works*, Vol VI, 307)

Our emotions and feelings link us to the world and are fundamental in our responsiveness to situations around us. Wollstonecraft criticized Burke for not seeing, not noticing, misery, poverty, and degradation. Apparently, Burke did not feel sympathy for the downtrodden of the earth. He was unaware of their pitiful condition; he did not think about such things. So why did Burke not think about poor and destitute people? He was not sensitive to them; he either did not notice or did not acknowledge them, because of his limited sympathies. Wollstonecraft argued that emotional limitations lay beneath Burke's defense of the pre-revolutionary state of Europe. He did not feel sympathy; he barely noticed whole classes of people. Because of her life experience and her deep compassion and sympathy, Wollstonecraft noticed and felt things that Burke did not: abandoned young mothers having no recourse but to prostitution, neglected children, unemployed men, and poor people living on the streets.

In her writing and philosophizing, Wollstonecraft responded to the world she knew and the world she felt. She was in many ways a rationalist, because she regarded reason as a source of knowledge about the world and constantly appealed to reason to justify her negative judgments on the social order. But Wollstonecraft was not only a rationalist; it was her feelings and sentiments which allowed her to *take note* of situations ignored by many other thinkers and writers. Thus her feelings and sentiments contributed to her knowledge and the application of her philosophical ideas because they focused her attention on aspects of life that few other thinkers had emphasized.

Rousseau, 'great thinker' that he was, simply took it for granted that women were made to serve men. He found in his life and times no incentive to reflect on the status of women or children. Rousseau was able to seduce many a young girl, abandon the resulting children in orphanages, and pay no attention to such matters in his writings on the corrupted nature of civilized society. Wollstonecraft's life of responsibility for her sisters and brothers and, later, her infant daughter Fanny, meant that her experience and feelings were entirely different from those of Rousseau. This difference is dramatically apparent in their writings about men and women.

Though reason and emotion sometimes pull us in opposite directions, they need not be opposed. Reason and emotion can work together. A strong sense of anger, injustice, or pity can cause us to notice things, provide an incentive to learn about them, and give us a stronger motivation to undertake virtuous action. Thus emotion can inspire us to acquire knowledge and understanding. The relationship can also work the other way: a better understanding can affect the nature and quality of our emotions. In her writings on women's education, Wollstonecraft frequently commented on how limited knowledge and understanding led women to have limited preoccupations and sentiments. If we know more, we will appreciate more. Knowledge can open our minds and broaden our sympathies. With wider knowledge, we have a greater range of sympathies and a better understanding of why we should care.

> The woman who has dedicated a considerable portion of her time to pursuits purely intellectual, and whose affections have been exercised by human plans of usefulness, must have more purity of mind, as a natural consequence, than the ignorant beings whose time and thoughts have been occupied by gay pleasures or schemes to conquer hearts. . . . Make the heart clean, let it expand and feel for all that is human, instead of being narrowed by selfish passions; and let the mind frequently contemplate subjects that exercise the understanding, without heating the imagination, and artless modesty will give the finishing touches to the picture. (*Vindication of the Rights of Woman*, 124)

The polarization of reason and emotion, so common both in Wollstonecraft's time and in our own, is at best an over-simplification and at worst a mistake. Unlike so many of her critics, Wollstonecraft was aware of this fact. Both her life and her work expressed a passionate commitment to reason.

7

Kant: The Starry Skies and the Moral Law

Immanuel Kant (1724 - 1804), the greatest German philosopher, was born in the town of Konigsberg in East Prussia. His family was deeply religious, and this religious background was to have a lasting effect on his temperament and his philosophical ideas. Kant attended the small university in Konigsberg, where he was fortunate to have an excellent and generous teacher, Martin Knutzen, who was young, energetic and well-versed in the central disputes in the science and philosophy of the time. After completing his first degree Kant became a private tutor and served in the homes of several wealthy Prussian families.

In 1746 Kant was able to return to the university in Konigsberg to do further studies and become a lecturer. He is the first modern philosopher to have spent his working life as a professor in a university. Kant laboured long, teaching for four or more hours each day in geography and anthropology as well as philosophy. Until he was appointed to a Chair in 1790, at the age of 46, he was paid by the head. He was a good lecturer and attracted many students – which was fortunate because he was not a wealthy man.

While many philosophers and scientists of his day travelled widely and had contacts in the courts and great cities of Europe, Kant never left the area of Konigsberg, where he did all his teaching, thinking, and writing. In outward respects Kant's life was amazingly uneventful. He never married and lived alone, attended by several servants. He worked, on a regular schedule, and his daily solitary walk was so predictable that the citizens of Konigsberg said they could set the clocks by it. Kant's health was rather fragile and he protected it carefully. But all this does not mean that Kant was dull. He had many friends with whom he dined and visited frequently. He was apparently a brilliant conversationalist, and carried on an extensive correspondence with well-known philosophers and scientists on the key issues of the day. Kant's adventures were adventures of the mind.

Central among Kant's many philosophical works is *The Critique of Pure Reason*, which was first published in 1781, and deals with problems of knowledge. It is often referred to as the First Critique. Kant wrote two other Critiques: *The Critique of Practical Reason*, 1788, which is about reason in ethics, and *The Critique of Judgment*, 1790, which treats themes of art, beauty, and purposiveness in nature. They are commonly referred to as the Second and Third Critiques, respectively.

Though he was intellectually active, writing and teaching throughout his adult life, the peak of Kant's creative development and professional success came when he was in his fifties, sixties, and seventies. *The Critique of Pure Reason* launched Kant's "critical philosophy" and was so pivotal that his life and works are defined with reference to it. Before working out his own critical ideas, Kant had written a dissertation and many essays and books. These works, from the period 1746 to 1770, are called "pre-critical." During his "silent" period from 1770 - 1781, Kant was working out his original critical ideas for the First Critique and published nothing. Between 1781 and his death in 1804 he wrote many works based on the foundation he had set in the First Critique, applying his theory of knowledge and metaphysics to issues of ethics, religion, history, law, and international relations.

Kant's life and work fall largely within the period of the Enlightenment; indeed he wrote an essay called "What is Enlightenment?". But unlike most Enlightenment thinkers, Kant did not take the nature and power of reason for granted. He asked why the purely intellectual concepts of human reason applied to the natural world, and whether there were limits to their legitimate application. In exploring these questions, Kant developed a penetrating set of answers and launched a revolution in philosophy. To this day, some teachers of philosophy advise students that after they study Kant, the world may never seem the same again.

In his Second Critique, Kant wrote that two things filled his mind with awe: "the starry heavens above me and the moral law within me." This saying, which beautifully expresses Kant's wonder and desire to understand how reason can discover both laws of nature and moral truths, is written on his tombstone in Konigsberg, which is now called Kaliningrad and is a special region within Russia.

Kant's theory of knowledge can best be understood with reference to disputes in philosophy and science which were current during his time. One such dispute was that between rationalists and empiricists.

Rationalism, Empiricism, and Kant's Theory of Knowledge

Rationalists assumed that reason created purely intellectual concepts which could provide knowledge of the universe, including God and immortality. During Kant's lifetime the rationalism of Descartes was still influential; so too was that of Gottfried Leibniz (1646 - 1714). Rationalists were confident that the human mind had concepts and insights of its own, not derived from sensory experience. Empiricists, by contrast, believed that we gain our concepts and our knowledge only from experience. As an empiricist, Hume had been led to a form of scepticism; when he sought grounds in experience for some of our most fundamental beliefs, he was unable to find them.

Kant regarded neither rationalism nor empiricism as satisfactory. He could not rest content with the sceptical conclusions of the empiricists. And the rationalists, he thought, were too cavalier in their assumption that intellectual concepts, which were purely products of the mind, could apply to the physical world and serve to give knowledge. In addition, rationalists confidently applied these ideas to the "transcendental" realm, beyond any human experience. In the area of metaphysics, rationalists developed beliefs and conceptions which could not be validated and advanced their arguments and teachings with a false dogmatic confidence.

The rationalist philosopher Leibniz, for instance, had claimed that physical things are made up of absolutely simple items called "monads" which have no parts and cannot causally interact with each other. Leibniz argued that these monads exist in the world in a state of harmony which was pre-established by God. He had also stated The Principle of Sufficient Reason: for everything that is, there must be a sufficient reason why it should be so, and not otherwise. Using this principle, Leibniz had claimed to be able to prove that our world is "the best of all possible worlds". God had to have a sufficient reason for creating the world; had there been a possible better world than this one, God would have created that world instead. Thus, according to Leibniz, our world can be proven, independently of experience, to be the best of all possible worlds. If there is evidence of pain and tragedy, that does not refute the conclusion that ours is the best possible world, or even particularly trouble the rationalist metaphysician.

Kant argued in the First Critique that rationalist metaphysics was too dogmatic and had no solid foundation. But Kant was no more satisfied with the philosophy of empiricism as expressed by Locke, Berkeley, and Hume. Hume had shown that the notion of necessity which is contained in our concept of causation cannot be derived from experience. We cannot know that every event has a cause (a version of the Principle of Sufficient Reason) because we cannot prove it by logic; nor can we know it on the basis of past experience. Kant believed that Hume's sceptical arguments about causation posed a profound and central philosophical problem. The paradoxical nature of Hume's conclusions showed the inadequacy of the empiricist theory of knowledge. Empiricists ignored intellectual concepts and the activity of the mind, and it was because of these omissions, Kant believed, that they had been led to sceptical conclusions that no one could seriously accept. Kant was convinced that Hume's own empiricist theory of knowledge simply could not account for the knowledge that actually existed in mathematics, geometry, and natural science.

Kant's own theory of knowledge is neither rationalist nor empiricist: he moved beyond that debate by working out a third position. Like the rationalists, Kant believed that the mind contributed to human knowledge intellectual concepts and structures of organization which were its own and which were not acquired through sense experience. Like the empiricists, he believed that knowledge began with experience and was limited to the domain of experience. Kant's view was that knowledge begins with experience, as the empiricists had claimed, but its source is not only in experience, because there are concepts and structures which are within the mind and by means of which our experience is organized.

> There can be no doubt that all our knowledge begins with experience. For how should our faculty of knowledge be awakened into action did not objects affecting our sense partly of themselves produce representations, partly arouse the activity of our understanding to compare these representations, and, by combining or separating them, work up the raw material of the sensible impressions into that knowledge of objects which is entitled experience? In the

> order of time, therefore, we have no knowledge antecedent to experience, and with experience all our knowledge begins. But though all our knowledge begins with experience, it does not follow that it all arises out of experience.
> (B2, 42)

Kant distinguished sharply between thought and sensation. Sensation is something passive; when we sense, something is given to us as though "from outside". In contrast, thought is something active, something we ourselves do. For knowledge, we need both sensibility (which had been emphasized by the empiricists) and understanding (which had been emphasized by the rationalists).

> . . . there are two stems of human knowledge, namely *sensibility* and *understanding*. . . .Through the former, objects are given to us; through the latter, they are thought.
> (A16, B30, 61-62)

> If the *receptivity* of our mind, its power of receiving representations in so far as it is in any wise affected, is to be entitled sensibility, then the mind's power of producing representations from itself, the *spontaneity* of knowledge, should be called the understanding. . . . Without sensibility no object would be given to us, without understanding no object would be thought. Thoughts without content are empty, intuitions [single representations] without concepts are blind. . . . The understanding can intuit nothing, the senses can think nothing. Only through their union can knowledge arise.
> (A 52, B76, 93)

Knowledge requires something presented to us. For human beings, that means something given, usually from sensory experience, that appears to us in space and time. Kant argued that although knowledge does not all come from experience, knowledge is restricted to the domain of experience. Something outside our experience (life after death, for instance) cannot be known, because concepts can be known to apply only if we have something sensed, or given, to which we can apply them.

What we experience must be organized according to the mind's own intellectual structures. If the data of experience were not organized in this way, we could not experience them at all. For this reason, the intellectual structures of the mind are guaranteed to apply to everything within the bounds of experience. What we experience must be subject to all the conditions that our minds impose. Whatever *a priori* concepts and structures our minds have, we can be sure that everything we experience will conform to these concepts and structures. Thus we have intellectual sources of knowledge – provided that knowledge is restricted to the realm of experience.

To make this point, Kant distinguished between "appearances" (what we know in experience) and "things in themselves" (things as they are in and of themselves, considered independently from our experience of them). His view was that we have knowledge only of appearances; we do not have knowledge of things-in-themselves. What appears to us – what comes before our consciousness, what we are aware of – Kant called appearances or *phenomena*. Since we experience appearances, they must conform to the fundamental concepts and structures of our minds. Things-in-themselves – things that we have no consciousness or experience of – Kant called *noumena*. Of noumena we can have no knowledge. There is no guarantee that our intellectual concepts are applicable to things-in-themselves because by definition, such entities are never presented to our consciousness.

According to Kant, rationalist metaphysicians made the fundamental mistake of trying to transcend experience to make dogmatic claims about noumenal objects such as God, the beginning of the world, and life after death. That objects are made of simple monads, that there is a pre-established harmony in the order of monads, or that the Principle of Sufficient Reason applies to the world as a whole are, on Kant's view, things we can say and "think," but not things we can know.

Kant believed he had achieved a "Copernican Revolution" in philosophy. Copernicus had dramatically altered the picture of the universe by showing that the earth was not at its center; rather, the earth moved around the sun, which itself moved. What was central to the Copernican Revolution was looking at a problem from a different point of view, with a different set of assumptions. An analogous change of viewpoint led to Kant's critical philosophy. Instead of asking how, in knowledge, our minds can conform to objects outside themselves, Kant asked how and why those objects conform to the structures of our minds.

> But all attempts to extend our knowledge of objects by establishing something in regard to them *a priori*, by means of concepts, have on this assumption [the assumption that our knowledge conforms to objects] ended in failure. We must therefore make trial whether we may not have more success in the tasks of metaphysics, if we suppose that objects must conform to our knowledge.... We should then be proceeding precisely on the lines of Copernicus' primary hypothesis. Failing of satisfactory progress in

> explaining the movements of the heavenly bodies on the supposition that they all revolved around the spectator, he tried whether he might not have better success if he made the spectator to revolve and the stars to remain at rest. A similar experiment can be tried in metaphysics.
> (Bxvii, 22)

So far as Kant was concerned, this experiment worked; it led him to his theory of knowledge.

The mind has *a priori* structures and concepts, which do not come from experience. The mind imposes these structures on representations presented to it by the sensibility (in sensation). Nothing can be experienced unless it is subject to all the conditions imposed by the mind. Thus, of everything we experience (that is to say, of all appearances) we may obtain knowledge. There is a guaranteed "fit" between the objects of nature and the human mind, because we become aware only of what we can subject to the conditions of our minds. Knowledge of the objects of experience is possible because we order what we experience in the exact way that our minds require.

Empiricists had thought of the mind as largely passive, as simply receiving impressions of sense. Kant rejected this view, understanding the mind to be active. He argued that the mind organizes and connects the fluctuating impressions of sense so that what we experience are stable objects in a world. In that world, events are related to each other in law-like, predictable ways. In fact, so important was the organizing and connecting activity of the mind that Kant referred to the understanding as the lawgiver of nature. If the mind did not order colors, sounds, smells, tastes, and other impression, we could not experience objects or events. However, the *a priori* concepts and structures of our minds are only guaranteed to apply to what we experience. We never experience God, life after death, the world as a whole, or the moment of Creation; hence we can have no knowledge of these things. Kant's critical theory of knowledge led him to reject rationalist metaphysics. There was not, and never had been, any secure knowledge in metaphysics, Kant claimed. Kant thought he could explain this fact as follows: in metaphysics, people had tried to apply intellectual concepts in a domain where they had no legitimate application.

As he had done with rationalism and empiricism, Kant also placed himself in a third position with reference to dogmatism and scepticism. His position was not one of dogmatism: he questioned how and why concepts applied to the world, and claimed no knowledge of things-in-themselves. But neither was Kant's position one of scepticism: he did claim knowledge of appearances.

By limiting the powers of reason, Kant said that he had made room for faith. Given that we are not able to apply our concepts to obtain knowledge outside the bounds of experience, we cannot prove that God exists, that He created the world, or that He has provided for an everlasting life in which virtue will be rewarded by happiness. God and a future life are not objects of possible experience within this world; they are not and cannot be presented to us in sensibility. This transcendental territory, beyond experience, is one of which we can have no knowledge. Religious conclusions cannot be established by reason. In the First Critique Kant presented careful and original criticisms of all the traditional proofs for God's existence.

The fact that he criticized the arguments of natural theology did not mean that Kant had ceased to be a religious believer. What is distinctive about Kant's position on religion is that he thought that religion should be based on faith, not on reason. The supposed "proofs" for God's existence were not good arguments and did not make satisfactory bases for religious belief. Kant believed that his own theory of knowledge made faith secure, because it forbade all "proofs" about the supernatural. We can never come to know, by applying our reason and intellectual concepts, that God exists or that God does not exist. A consolation for the religious believer is that from critical philosophy there is a guarantee that God's existence will never be disproven. We can think of God as a creator who has made an organized system of nature and as one who provides for immortality and the rewarding of virtue by happiness. We can *postulate* these things; in fact, Kant believed that our inner rational sense of moral obligation requires these postulates. But they are not, and will never be, known truths of metaphysics.

Kant's Arguments

Two Distinctions

Many of Kant's central arguments are founded on two distinctions: that between the empirical and the *a priori*, and that between the analytic and the synthetic. The distinction between the empirical and the *a priori* may be applied to concepts, to statements, and to structures of the mind. The distinction between the analytic and the synthetic applies only to judgments, or statements.

A concept or claim is *a priori* if it cannot be derived from experience and is thus independent of experience. A cause is conceived to be something that necessarily leads to its effect. This "necessity" is not something we experience, because we can experience only that one thing does in fact follow another, not that it *must* follow. Thus, the concept of cause is *a priori*, according to Kant. By contrast, the concept of redness is an empirical concept; we have this concept because we have seen red things. When claims are known *a priori* that means that we do not require experience to know that they are true. For example, we can know *a priori* that a table is in space. We cannot know *a priori* whether a particular table is brown or blue, or is made of wood or marble. Such knowledge would require experience, and would be empirical. A structure of the mind that is *a priori* would be innate, or inborn; one which is empirically acquired would be the result of experience. Empirical judgments are also called *a posteriori*. They are known after (posterior to) experience.

Whether statements, or judgments, are analytic or synthetic depends on how their constituent concepts are related to each other. Kant thought of judgments as being in subject-predicate form. Consider a judgment of the form 'A is B,' in which A is the subject and B is the predicate. There are two possibilities:

> Either the predicate B belongs to the subject A, as something which is (covertly) contained in this concept A; or B lies outside the concept A, although it does stand in connection with it. In the one case I entitle the judgment analytic, in the other synthetic. (A7, B11, 48)

In an analytic judgment A and B are related as concepts; because of what A is, B is contained within it. For example, in the judgment, 'all mothers are female' the predicate B, "female", is contained in the subject A, "mother", because to be female is part of the concept of a mother. The judgment 'all mothers are female' is thus analytic. Kant's own example of an analytic judgment was 'all bodies are extended.' In analytic judgments we do not have to go outside concepts in order to connect the subject and the predicate. Thus we can know *a priori* that analytic judgments are true.

By contrast, in a synthetic judgment, the subject concept does not contain or imply the predicate concept. Kant gave as an example 'bodies are heavy,' saying that the mere concept of a body did not imply heaviness. Another example of a synthetic judgment would be 'all mothers are patient.' The concept of a mother does not imply patience. In synthetic judgments, the subject and the predicate are not linked by the nature of the concepts themselves; there must be something else (X) that provides the basis for linking them together.

Characteristically this third thing is experience: we have experienced heavy bodies, or have experienced patient mothers. Because we have had the relevant experience, we are able to judge that bodies are heavy, or that mothers are patient.

Considering these distinctions between the *a priori* and the *a posteriori*, and the analytic and the synthetic, we can see that there are four possible combinations.

(1) analytic a priori judgments. Example: A table is in space.
(2) analytic a posteriori judgments. Example: probably none.
(3) synthetic a priori judgments. Example: Every event has a cause.
(4) synthetic a posteriori judgments. Example: Grass is green.

It is the third category that Kant was interested in; if metaphysics exists, its propositions must be synthetic *a priori*.

Are Synthetic A Priori Judgments Possible?

There is a sense in which analytic judgments add nothing to our knowledge. The predicate concept was already contained in, or implied by, the subject concept before we made the judgment. Analytic judgments simply express relationships between concepts. They may be helpful in reminding us that these relationships exist, but they cannot really offer us any information about the world apart from concepts. Analytic *a priori* judgments (1) pose no special philosophical problem; they are true in virtue of the way concepts or meanings are related to each other. Analytic *a posteriori* judgments (2) are probably impossible; in any event Kant expressed no interest in them. Synthetic *a posteriori* judgments (4) are not philosophically problematic; these are judgments in which we link concepts on the basis of experience. Kant's interest was in (3), the synthetic *a priori*. Could there be such a thing as a synthetic *a priori* judgment?

Kant posed the question, 'Are synthetic *a priori* judgments possible?' It did not take him long to answer. Despite the lack of reliable knowledge in metaphysics, he immediately concluded that synthetic *a priori* judgments are possible. They are possible because they are actual. But how are they possible? In a synthetic judgment something, X, outside the concepts A and B, is required to connect them. What would X be, if a synthetic judgment were *a priori*? In the attempt to answer this question, Kant examined the nature of knowledge in arithmetic and geometry.

According to Kant, in mathematics we have *a priori* and necessary knowledge about the world. Both in arithmetic and in geometry, mathematical claims are synthetic *a priori*. Kant was convinced of this point because of the way he understood mathematics.

> We might, indeed, at first suppose that the proposition 7+5=12 is a merely analytic proposition, and follows by the principle of contradiction from the concept of a sum of 7 and 5. But if we look more closely we find that the concept of the sum of 7 and 5 contains nothing save the union of two numbers into one, and in this no thought is being taken as to what that single number may be which combines both. The concept of 12 is by no means already thought in merely thinking this union of 7 and 5; and I may analyse my concept of such a possible sum as long as I please, still I shall never find the 12 in it. We have to go outside these concepts, and call in the aid of the intuition [particular representation] which corresponds to one of them, our five fingers, for instance, or . . . five points, adding to the concept of 7, unit by unit, the five given in intuition. . . . Arithmetical propositions are therefore always synthetic. This is still more evident if we take larger numbers. For it is then obvious that, however we might turn and twist our concepts, we could never, by the mere analysis of them, and without the aid of intuition, discover what (the number is that) is the sum.
> (B16, 53)

Consider the sum of 672 and 549. The concept of this sum does not in itself give the answer; we have to work it out (1221). If the statement that 672 plus 549 equals 1221 were analytic, we would know it without doing any calculating.

The same sort of argument may be made for the propositions of geometry. That a straight line is the shortest distance between two points is true *a priori*; it is necessary and universal. And yet the proposition is synthetic, because the concept of "a straight line" does not contain anything about quantity. To know that the straight line is the shortest, we must call in intuition – making a singular representation by constructing the line so that we can show why, and see why, it is the shortest one. The geometric truth is not given merely by the concepts.

So some synthetic *a priori* judgments are true. But *how* is synthetic *a priori* knowledge in mathematics possible? This question led Kant to his theory of space and time.

Space and Time

Since synthetic *a priori* judgments form the core of arithmetic and geometry, there must be some X, which is itself *a priori*, which serves to connect the subject and the predicate in such judgments. This X, Kant argued, is time in the case of arithmetic, and space in the case of geometry. In arguing for this conclusion, Kant used a *transcendental* argument. Transcendental arguments arise in response to the characteristically Kantian question 'What makes knowledge possible?' Kant believed that arithmetic and geometry were synthetic *a priori* bodies of knowledge, and sought their presuppositions or requirements. In the case of arithmetical knowledge, Kant argued that time, as an *a priori* form of intuition, was required. In the case of geometrical knowledge, he argued that space, as an *a priori* form of intuition, was required. The nature of time makes arithmetic possible, and the nature of space makes geometry possible.

If a body of knowledge (K) does exist, and if K requires some condition or principle (P) in order to exist, we can conclude that P is true. To argue this way is to use a transcendental argument. The general form of a transcendental argument is:

(1) K exists.
K presupposes, or requires, that P is true.
Therefore,
P is true.

But the compactness of this summary is misleading. Because of the complexity of the relationship of "presupposing" or "requiring," there are two aspects to transcendental arguments. One side is purely *deductive*:

(1a) K exists.
P's being true is a necessary condition of the existence of K.
Therefore,
P is true.

The other side is more explanatory and is sometimes referred to as subjective or *psychological*.

(1b) K exists.
P's being true explains why K exists.
Therefore, it is a reasonable hypothesis that
P is true.

To speak of "making possible," or of "presupposing," or "requiring," is to imply both (la) and (1b). Since the deductive argument, (1a), is clearer and more conclusive, philosophers have tended to concentrate on it. I follow that practice here, in the interest of simplicity.

From the premise that there is synthetic *a priori* knowledge in arithmetic and geometry, Kant used transcendental arguments to arrive at his claims that space and time are *a priori* "forms of intuition." By this he meant to say that space and time were innate, or inborn, features of the structure of our minds. We can imagine the absence of particular objects and events, but we cannot imagine the absence of space and time. They are inborn, organizational features of our minds. Kant argued that space and time must be *a priori* in this sense, on the ground that synthetic *a priori* knowledge exists in arithmetic and geometry, and such knowledge could not be explained in any other way. The *a priori* nature of space and time – the fact that they are conditions of all our sense experience – explains how synthetic *a priori* knowledge in arithmetic and geometry is possible. Space and time provide an *a priori* X, an "intuition" in which particulars are exemplified and through which we are able to count or to construct geometric objects. It is this X which links the subject and predicate of the synthetic *a priori* judgments.

Space and time are *presupposed* or *required* by experience, not derived from it, Kant argued. Space and time are distinct from concepts, and they are also not empirical. Because space and time are in this way *a priori* they can serve the role of X in linking the subject and predicate in the synthetic *a priori* judgments of mathematics. The nature of space and time makes synthetic *a priori* knowledge possible.

The great physicist, Newton, had believed that space and time were absolute infinite substances, which had existed before God created the world of objects and before there were any events. In contrast, the rationalist philosopher Gottfried Leibniz argued that space and time were relational; they were aspects of the order of things and events. These two views were much in dispute in Kant's day, and he considered both to be unsatisfactory. According to Kant, the Newtonian view was metaphysically absurd because it was committed to the existence of "two eternal and infinite self-subsistent nonentities" which were supposed to exist before there was anything real. And the Leibnizian view was also inadequate. In claiming that space and time were nothing more than relations of objects and events, space and time were made too empirical and were thus unable to explain *a priori* certainty in mathematics. Kant understood his own view of space and time as offering a third alternative which would avoid the problems posed by the others. Kant's own view was that space and time are innate ordering structures of the human mind.

The Categories

Kant believed that we apply *a priori* concepts to what we experience in sense. The most fundamental *a priori* concepts he called Categories. These were:

unity
plurality
totality
reality
negation
limitation
substance
cause
community
possibility
impossibility
existence

Kant believed that these categories were purely intellectual, not derived from sense, and that they were required to make the judgments which express our knowledge. Because the categories did not arise from experience, there was a real question as to why they could be legitimately applied within experience.

In a highly complex transcendental argument called the "Transcendental Deduction of the Pure Concepts of the Understanding," Kant argued that we have to apply the categories in order to become conscious of objects. Diverse and disunified "data" are presented to us in sensations. If the understanding did not unify this data using *a priori* concepts, we could not be aware of objects and would have no experience at all. We know that the categories apply to experience, because if they did not play the role of unifying the data presented to our minds, we would not have any experience.

> The objective validity of the categories as *a priori* concepts rests, therefore, on the fact that, so far as the form of thought is concerned, through them alone does experience become possible. They relate of necessity and *a priori* to objects of experience, for the reason that only by means of them can any object whatsoever of experience be thought.
> (A 94, B126, 126)

The categories are not guaranteed to apply outside the realm of experience.

Any representation of which a human mind is aware is presented in time, and it has elements or parts which are given to that mind in different moments of time. But when the mind is aware of something (a house, for example) it is aware of the whole thing. The mind's awareness is possible because it can hold together the data, temporally separable parts of the representation, which must be made present to the mind at moments other than the precise moment at which they occur. Awareness of any representation presupposes that the mind is able to *reproduce* aspects of a representation. But that reproduction is of no use unless the mind can recognize something as a reproduction. That in turn presupposes that the mind must *recognize* at one time something which is a reproduction of a part which occurred at another time.

In order for recognition to occur, one and the same mind must be active throughout the period when the representation is given to it. Whatever is conscious of one aspect of a representation must be the same thing which is conscious of another aspect – otherwise the whole representation would not appear to a single consciousness. Underlying any person's knowledge, there must be one and the same underlying consciousness. Representation and knowledge presuppose a single consciousness. We are not directly aware of such a single consciousness. (Kant agreed with Hume that we cannot find a unitary self by introspection.) However, single unitary consciousness must exist in order to reproduce, recognize, and connect the diverse data given to us in sensibility. It is presupposed by our representations, so we know that it must exist.

Consciousness, which has an underlying unity, cannot tolerate data or representations that are chaotic and disunified. Consciousness therefore imposes a unity on the representations before it by connecting them together. This is where active thought enters the picture. The understanding is a faculty which connects things according to rules, and it makes judgments about the representations which it has helped to create. The categories are needed to make judgments. Thus every representation that a unified consciousness is aware of is subjected to the categories. Since experience would be impossible without the categories, they have a real application to all appearances.

From this series of presuppositions, we can see that a necessary condition of my having any representation as an object of consciousness is that I must myself be one unitary consciousness over time. If

I were not this sort of consciousness I would not apprehend, reproduce, and recognize what came before me so as to make it into one representation. It is this single unitary consciousness which generates the need for connected representations, and it is in virtue of this necessary condition, requiring that representations must be connected, that concepts are required. We can deduce that such concepts will be used, and their use will also help to explain how unified consciousness is possible. Because my consciousness is necessarily *one* consciousness, the representations which become its experience must be organized into a *connected whole*. All of my representations, however diverse they may be, are nevertheless contents of one consciousness. It is, after all, I who am aware of all of them. Thus, if there is any condition that must be fulfilled in order for them all to be ascribable to one self, I can be assured that they do fulfill it. And there is such a condition: it is that the representations must be *conjoined* or *connected* with each other. They are conjoined because I make judgments about them, using the categories.

A single consciousness could not hold within itself representations which were completely disordered and had no connection with one another. Suppose R_1, R_2, and R_3 are names of representations. Kant is saying, in effect, that given that I am aware of R_1, that I am aware of R_2, and that I am aware of R_3, there is necessarily some sense in which R_1, R_2, and R_3 are connected. And so it is for all my representations. To see a house I must relate various sensory impressions (of color, shape, and so on) to an object which I consider to be something in space. To perceive an event, such as the freezing of water, I think of two states of the water (fluidity and solidity) and I think of them as successive in time. To do this, I relate them in accordance with the concept of causality. (Cold causes fluid water to become solid ice.) I connect my representations by relating them to objects and events outside the mind, and I use *a priori* categories to do this, making judgments about objects, properties, and events. If my representations could not be connected in this way, they could not be my representations – which is just to say that I would not be aware of them at all. Kant anticipated the results of twentieth-century Gestalt psychology when he emphasized the order that we impose on our perceptions.

Without representations, I would have no experience. Space, time, and the categories, all innate features of the human mind, are what *make human experience possible*.

> We cannot think an object save through the categories; we cannot *know* an object so thought save through intuitions corresponding

> to these concepts. Now all our intuitions are sensible; and this knowledge, in so far as its object is given, is empirical. But empirical knowledge is experience. Consequently, there can be no *a priori* knowledge, except of objects of possible experience. But although this knowledge is limited to objects of experience, it is not therefore all derived from experience. The pure intuitions of receptivity [space and time] and the pure concepts of understanding [the categories] are elements in knowledge, and both are found in us *a priori*. . . . the categories contain, on the side of the understanding, the grounds of all the possibility of all experience in general. (B166-7, 174)

Kant answered his own question, 'How is synthetic *a priori* knowledge possible?' by arguing that space, time, and the categories are imposed *a priori* by the mind on the representations of sensibility. These structures make our experience possible; they are contributed by the mind; and for this reason, we can in some areas acquire synthetic *a priori* knowledge of appearances. We cannot have synthetic *a priori* knowledge of things-in-themselves, because such entities do not come come within the sphere of our consciousness. Mathematics and physical science can contain synthetic *a priori* truths, but there can be no synthetic *a priori* truths in metaphysics.

Metaphysics

As a source of knowledge of the universe, metaphysics is impossible because there is no X to provide the link between subject and predicate in a synthetic judgment. But this was far from being Kant's last word about metaphysics. Clearly metaphysics is possible in another sense, as a natural and inevitable human disposition. It is the nature of human reason to want to unify knowledge, to build systems, to arrive at ideas too sweeping to have a basis in experience. We human beings have an irrepressible tendency to ask metaphysical questions about such things as the cause of the world, whether there is free will, and whether there is life after death. To these questions we seek answers that are given nowhere in experience. We will inevitably ask ourselves what we can know, what we ought to do in this world, and what we can hope for. Our quest to understand the world and our place within it leads us to questions we cannot answer.

Did the world have a beginning in time and in space?
Does God exist?
Are human actions fully determined by natural causes?
Are material objects infinitely divisible into parts?
Is there a simple indivisible human soul that retains its identity over time?
Is the human soul immortal?

For all their difficulty, for all the risks of deception and illusion, humankind will never cease to pose such questions.

> We can therefore be sure that however cold or contemptuously critical may be the attitude of those who judge a science not by its nature but by its accidental effects, we shall always return to metaphysics as to a beloved one with whom we have had a quarrel. For here we are concerned with essential ends – ends with which metaphysics must ceaselessly occupy itself, either in striving for genuine insight into them, or in refuting those who profess already to have attained it.
> (A850, B878, 664-665)

Kant illustrated the fascinating temptations of metaphysics in four sets of opposed arguments called The Antinomies. These pairs of arguments are puzzling because in each pair, we seem to be able to prove both a conclusion and its opposite. In the First Antinomy, Kant offered an argument that the world has a beginning in time and another argument that the world has no beginning in time.

FIRST ANTINOMY.

THESIS: The world has a beginning in time.
Argument for Thesis:
If the world had no beginning, then before any given moment an eternity would have elapsed. But it is impossible for an eternity to have elapsed. Thus, if the world had no beginning, no given moment in time could have arrived and nothing would exist. Given that the world exists at all, it must, therefore, have had a beginning in time.

ANTITHESIS: The world has no beginning in time.
Argument for Antithesis:
If the world had a beginning in time, that beginning would have been preceded by an empty time. But the idea of an empty time would make no sense, because there would be nothing to distin-

> guish an empty time [time with no events happening and no objects] from nothing at all. Since empty time is impossible, the world cannot have a beginning in time. Therefore the world had no beginning in time; it must be infinite with respect to past time.

What has gone wrong here? We seem to have proven two contradictory propositions:

> B: The world had a beginning in time.
> and
> not-B: The world did not have a beginning in time.

These propositions cannot both be true; that would violate the Principle of Non-Contradiction so clearly defended by Aristotle. According to Kant, both the thesis and the antithesis in this conflict of reason are incorrect, and when we understand this, we can get rid of the contradiction by rejecting both B and not-B. The answer is that both B and not-B depend on the *false* assumption that the world as a whole can be an object of knowledge. The world as a whole cannot be an object of knowledge, because it is not within our experience. This is how Kant resolves the First Antinomy.

In any series of moments in time, a given moment is "conditioned" by moments which precede it, and is the "condition" of moments which come after it. Think of a simple series of temporal moments numbered from 1 to 10.

> 1 2 3 4 5 6 7 8 9 10

Now consider moment 5. It is conditioned by moments 1, 2, 3, and 4, which precede it. It is a condition of moments 6, 7, 8, 9, and 10, which follow it. In this series we *regress* if we go backwards from 5 to 4, 3, 2, and 1 and we *progress* if we go forward from 5 to 6, 7, 8, 9, and 10. A major cause of metaphysical illusion, Kant says, is that we have a strong compulsion to insist that any regressive series must somehow be completed. We have no such urge for the progressive series.

Consider an analogy: the case of ancestors. I tend to have a firm conviction that a regressive series of my ancestors – for example, myself, my mother, my grandmother, my great-grandmother, my great-great-grandmother, and so on must be complete. Otherwise how could I have come to exist? I do exist, so it would seem that the series of my female ancestors must be complete. Reasoning about this regressive series will lead me to the conclusion that either I had a First Female Ancestor or the series of my female ancestors along this line is infinite. But the same drive for completion does not come with the progressive series: myself, my daughter, my grand-daughter, my great-grand-daughter, my great-great-grand-daughter and so on. The difference is, unlike my female ancestors, my female descendents are not conditions of my own existence. Thus I feel no rational compulsion to insist that the progressive series must be complete because I exist.

Human reason will insist that any regressive series which conditions something given (for example, the present moment, or my own existence) must be complete. Otherwise, we are driven to ask, how could what is given have come to exist at all? What is given is *here*, and it is something conditioned; thus – we are compelled to argue – all its conditions must have been realized. Reason seeks completeness, leading us beyond the sphere of experience where our concepts have clear application. In the thesis of the First Antinomy the argument follows the urge for completeness in time by claiming that the whole time series is complete because it has a first member. In the antithesis, it follows the same urge by claiming the whole time series is complete because it is infinitely large. Both moves are wrong, Kant says. Though reason urges us to complete a regressive series, we are not entitled to do so, because that would require moving beyond experience to an area in which we can have no knowledge, and we would only delude ourselves.

Completing a regressive series is something we can never do. It is, rather something that is set for reason *as a task*. The quest must go on; there is no end to the series of conditions. I will not find my first female ancestor; but for any ancestor I do locate, I know that there will be one before her. The search can go on indefinitely – but that does not mean I have an infinite series of female ancestors.

The problem of regressive series also underlies the Third Antinomy, which is about free will and causation. Kant believed that in the realm of appearances every event has a cause; it is through causation and lawlike relationships between events that we organize our representations so that we perceive an ordered world. Empirically, we come to know a world in which events are causally related. However, when we act as moral agents, we presume that what we do is not merely the byproduct of antecedent natural causes. On the contrary, we tend to assume that we can make a spontaneous choice and initiate a new series of events through our own free action.

THIRD ANTINOMY

> THESIS. Natural causality is not the only causality explaining appearances in the world; there is also another kind of causality, the causality of freedom.
> *Argument for Thesis*:
> If there were only natural causality, there would be no first beginning in the sequence of events related as causes and effects. And without a first beginning, there would be no sufficient cause for anything that takes place. There must, therefore, be another sort of causality in which there is an absolutely spontaneous cause which begins "of itself." This is transcendental freedom. Without it, the series of appearances, on the side of causes, can never be complete.
>
> ANTITHESIS. There is no freedom; everything in the world takes place solely in accordance with the laws of nature.
> *Argument for Antithesis*:
> A completely spontaneous beginning would be an absolute beginning which would not emerge from a preceding state. Such a beginning would violate the law of causality and the unity of experience. Spontaneous causality would be blind and unintelligible and cannot exist.

Again, we seem to have proven contradictory propositions.

> C: Spontaneous causation exists.
> not-C: Spontaneous causation does not exist.

In this case, Kant resolves the contradiction differently from the way he resolved the First Antinomy. In this case, Kant argues that both C and not-C may be true, but they must be qualified to attend to the distinction between appearances and things-in-themselves. Not-C is true for the realm of appearances: within appearances, every event has a cause and there is no sponanteous freedom. But C may be true of things-in-themselves. Freedom [a spontaneous, undetermined cause of a human action] and causation in the realm of appearances may exist together. Properly understood there is no contradiction.

> Thesis (amended): Spontaneous causation may exist in the realm of things-in-themselves.
> Antithesis (amended): Spontaneous causation does not exist in the realm of appearances.

As amended, the thesis and the antethesis do not contradict each other; both can be true.

That freedom and natural necessity are possible together was fundamentally important for Kant because of his understanding of ethics and the moral life. He believed that in acting morally and reflecting on moral problems, we presuppose spontaneous freedom. We do not see our actions as emerging simply as the effects of natural causes. We assume that it makes sense to think that a person *ought* to have done something that he or she did not do, and *ought not* to have done something that he or she did do.

If someone tells a malicious lie which is harmful to society, we may be able to trace the causes of his action in his upbringing, the company he keeps, difficult circumstances, and so on. But we still nevertheless hold him accountable for doing something that he *ought not* to have done. In holding him responsible, we assume that he could have reasoned that the act was wrong and refrained from doing it.

> But although we believe that the action is thus determined, we none the less blame the agent . . . for we presuppose that we can leave out of consideration what this way of life may have been . . . just as if the agent in and by himself began in this action an entirely new series of consequences. Our blame is based on a law of reason whereby we regard *reason as a cause* that . . . could have determined, and ought to have determined, the agent to act otherwise. . . . in the moment when he utters the lie, the guilt is entirely his. *Reason*, irrespective of all empirical conditions of the act, *is completely free*, and the lie is entirely due to its default.
> (A555,B583, 477; my emphasis)

Morality presupposes that there are things we ought to do and things we ought not to do, and that in turn presupposes that we *can* act in ways we do not act. Thus morality presupposes freedom, which Kant understood to be spontaneous freedom, independent of natural causal laws.

Kant's view of morality was that by reason we can and should test the acceptability of "maxims" that underlie our actions. A person who lies is, in effect, basing his action on the maxim, 'Whenever it will be convenient for me, I will knowingly make false statements to other people.' Before acting on such a maxim, he should ask himself whether he could consistently accept that his maxim would become a universal law. If it were a universal law, then there would be universal acceptance of the principle that everyone may lie whenever it is convenient to do so. Such a law would be untenable: the very meaningfulness of language and the usefulness of communication, which are necessary for society, presuppose that people tell the truth. People who act immorally fail to apply reason to their actions because they do not apply a universal standard to what they do. Instead, they seek to make an exception of themselves and in this sense contradict themselves. The person who tells a malicious lie is relying on others to tell the truth, but implying by his action that it is morally permissible for him to tell a lie to them.

In explaining the Third Antinomy, Kant argues that this freedom of reason is possible; there may be spontaneous causality in the realm of things-in-themselves while there is at the same time natural necessity (empirical causality) in the realm of appearances. The world we know is the world of appearances. And yet when Kant discusses the causality of reason, he seems to allow that there is an aspect of human nature which is purely intelligible and partakes somehow of things-in-themselves.

> Man is one of the appearances of the sensible world, and in so far . . . must stand under empirical laws. Like all other things in nature, he must have an empirical character. This character we come to know through the powers and faculties which he reveals in his actions. In lifeless, or merely animal, nature we find no ground for thinking that any faculty is conditioned [affected by causes] otherwise than in a merely sensible manner. Man, however, who knows all the rest of nature solely through the senses, knows himself also through pure apperception [consciousness that he must be a single knowing subject] and this indeed, in acts and inner determinations which he cannot regard as impressions of the senses. He is thus to himself, on the one hand phenomenon and on the other hand, in respect of certain faculties the action of which cannot be ascribed to the receptivity of sensibility, *a purely intelligible object*. [Kant seems here to commit himself to the notion of a noumenal self.] We entitle these faculties understanding and reason. . . . That our reason has causality, or that we at least represent it to ourselves as having causality, is evident from the *imperatives* which in all matters of conduct we impose as rules upon our active powers. *Ought* expresses a kind of necessity and connection with grounds which is found nowhere else in the whole of nature.
> (A547, B575, 472)

The active spontaneity of understanding and reason suggests a side of human nature which is purely intelligible. In the acquisition of knowledge, the understanding is active in unifying representations. In moral life, the reason is active in guiding us by "oughts" and "ought nots" which are not to be found in nature itself.

Kant on Thinking

If we could bring Kant back to life and ask him about strategies for thinking, he would have some definite advice. He would urge us to reflect on our foundations, on how knowledge could be possible in the area in which we are reflecting. When we are about to make a judgment, we should ask ourselves whether it is analytic or synthetic. If it is analytic, we must recognize that it tells us only about the relationships between concepts. If it is synthetic, we need that X which provides the basis for linking the subject with the predicate, and we should be able to say what X is. Kant would say there are three possibilities. The X may be experience – as when we know that a table is blue because we have seen it. Or (as in Kant's own theory of knowledge) it may be a construction – as in geometry, when we make a figure according to a specification and then prove something about it. Or it may be the possibility of experience itself – if we can prove that a predicate, P, must hold true of a subject, S, in order for experience to be possible, we can know *a priori* that S is P, even when 'S is P' is a synthetic proposition.

If we cannot say what the X is that would provide a basis for connecting S to P in a synthetic proposition, we cannot know that S is P. We can of course think about things under such circumstances; we can wonder, imagine, hypothesize, and postulate – and such reflections may be very important. But we should be aware that thought without any definite object will not give us knowledge. In this way, we should be critical of our own use of reason.

Kant referred to the understanding as a faculty of rules, and emphasized the lawlike nature of knowledge in science. In the area of morality, Kant also emphasized universal principles or rules; a person who acts well acts only according to maxims that he or she could will to be universal laws of nature. An immoral person is one who wishes to make an exception of himself or herself and is unwilling to apply moral principles consistently. (An example would be the free rider, who uses services supported by other people's tax money but cheats on his own taxes.)

But for all his emphasis on rules and universal principles, Kant did not believe that thought progresses by rules alone. We need insight in order to apply rules properly; rules do not apply themselves. (In this respect, Kant's thinking is like that of Aristotle.)

> If it [general logic] sought to give instructions how we are to subsume under these rules, that is, to distinguish whether something does or does not come under them, that could only be by means of

> another rule. This in turn, for the very reason that it is a rule, again demands guidance from judgment. Thus it appears that, though understanding is capable of being instructed and of being equipped with rules, judgment is a peculiar talent which can be practised only, and cannot be taught. It is the specific quality of so-called mother-wit; and its lack no school can make good. For although an abundance of rules borrowed from the insight of others may indeed be offered to, and as it were, grafted upon, a limited understanding, the power of rightly employing them must belong to the learner himself, and in the absence of such a natural gift no rules that may be prescribed to him for this purpose can ensure against misuse.
> (A133, B172, 177)

There is a point when rules run out, and we must have enough insight to know what to do.

A doctor, judge, or political leader may have many rules at his or her disposal, but they will be of little use if that person cannot apply them properly. For example, if the rule says, 'All infected gall bladders should be removed,' applying it to a particular person involves correctly recognizing that that person's gall bladder is infected. To do this, the doctor will need to recognize signs of infection. He or she might have further rules in such a case. But at some point rules come to an end, and a person must simply be able to recognize the significant features of a situation. Rules are useless to us if we cannot understand which universal concept properly applies to a concrete case. This application requires matter of "mother wit," not rules. Practice and training can help in this area, Kant notes, but insight is also necessary. We are not computers, and there is no rule-governed program that can tell us how to think well; thinking and knowing require more than following rules. We need insight and good sense.

Kant emphasized the active nature of thought. Even in a simple matter such as seeing a house and coming to know that it has a red roof, our understanding is active, reproducing various representations, uniting them so as see a single object (the house) and making a judgment about it on the basis of experience. What we might assume to be a very simple case of knowledge turns out to be far from simple when we reflect on it. We are active when we are conscious of something. Throughout his critical philosophy, Kant emphasized that thought was active. We find out about nature by asking the right questions and performing appropriate tests and experiments; we do not wait until passive observations cumulate and the answer lands in our laps.

Kant alluded to experiments in physics, by Galileo, Torricelli, and Stahl, saying:

> They learned that reason has insight only into that which it produces after a plan of its own, and that it must not allow itself to be kept, as it were, in nature's leading-strings, upon fixed laws, but must itself show that way with principles of judgment based upon fixed laws, constraining nature to give answers to questions of reason's own determining. Accidental observations, made in obedience to no previously thought-out plan, can never be made to yield a necessary law, which alone reason is concerned to discover. Reason, holding in one hand its principles, according to which alone concordant appearances can be admitted as equivalent to laws, and in the other hand the experiment which it has devised in conformity with these principles, must approach nature in order to be taught by it.
> (Bxiii, 20)

We make observations for a purpose, because we have questions we are posing to nature. Kant advises that we should approach nature not as pupils waiting to be taught by it, but as judges who pose our own questions and reflect on the answers we receive. That is how progress is possible in science.

Human reason is also active in its quest for system. The desire for system leads reason to form ideas that have no basis in experience – one such idea being the idea of the world as a whole. We cannot know the world as a whole, but the idea of the world as a whole – a single connected world – nevertheless has an important regulative role in guiding our thought and construction of knowledge. Because we have this idea of the world as a unified, connected whole, we seek a complete system of knowledge. We seek to connect and systematize things – and to relate laws to each other. Of course we can never arrive at a complete and final system of knowledge: we will never understand and know the cause and effect of every event, the parts of every object, or the full set of motives of every person.

But despite this inevitable gap between our transcendental ideas and our experience, the idea plays an important role in propelling us forward in our quest for systematic knowledge. No theory or explanation is ever final or complete; we should always try to go further. When we have one scientific classification, we can always look for another more general one; when we make distinctions within a class or species, we can always look for further distinctions. When we find paradoxes and puzzles, as in the antinomies, we should not give up. The search must go on, and it is the search that is important. Though the whole world is not, in Kant's view, a possible object of experience, though a complete system of knowledge is something we will never have, completed knowledge is something that is *set for us as a task.* If we find something we cannot explain, we must simply keep on trying. We would never be able to discover that the world is an unsystematic place: we could know only that in some particular aspect, we have not yet found an explanation.

Like Socrates, Descartes, and so many other philosophers, Kant emphasized autonomy in thinking. We should not adopt rules or claims from some supposedly authoritative source and use them without critically evaluating them. The history of philosophy can be taught; a person can learn the philosophical system of Leibniz, or Descartes, or – for that matter – of Kant himself. But in learning what these people thought, we have not learned philosophy. To do that we must learn to think about philosophical topics by ourselves. Philosophy as such cannot be learned by a novice from a teacher. To have philosophical knowledge, a person must have understanding that has arisen out of his or her own use of reason.

> Philosophy can never be learned, save only in historical fashion; as regards what concerns reason, we can at most learn to *philosophize.*
> (A838, B866, 657)

There are many different paths by which people try to find a systematic philosophy. But the most important thing about philosophy is not its conclusions. It is learning to think philosophically oneself. Thinking carefully, struggling with deep problems, and criticizing one's own ideas on the basis of sustained reasoning are the central aspects of learning philosophy. Philosophy is not a matter of a set of truths that someone else has discovered and that we can learn from him or her.

Perhaps the one true path will be discovered, but

> Till then we cannot learn philosophy; for where is it, who is in possession of it, and how shall we recognise it? We can only learn to philosophise, that is, to exercise the talent of reason, in accordance with its universal principles, on certain actually existing attempts at philosophy – always, however, reserving the right of reason to investigate, to confirm or to reject these principles in their very sources.
> (A838, B806, 657)

In philosophical thinking, and indeed in all thinking, we should not simply submit to the verdicts of an outside authority. We must use principles that we ourselves can rationally accept, and not merely for reasons of authority. Nevertheless, in thought and knowledge, we must employ a standard that could be accepted by all. If we are tempted to use a rule or principle that we know others would not accept, we must ask ourselves why they would not accept it. Do they have reasons? We should hear those reasons and work with them to determine their merits.

An objective principle is one that human reason in general can support, not a principle favored merely by one or a few individuals. Urging people to think for themselves, Kant also urged them to think from the standpoint of everyone else. We must recognize that other people also have reason, and a point of view. For instance, a principle which insists that one individual or group is "the leader," or that one people or ethnic group has an especially favored role in history, could not be accepted by all reasoning human beings. The aspect of thinking from the standpoint of others as well as oneself was Kant's original addition to the idea of autonomous thinking. We think for ourselves, but at the same time, we think for everyone. In knowledge, just as in ethics, we should be able to will that our principles could be universal laws. In practice, the critical side of reason requires free and open public discussion, in which beliefs can be submitted to public scrutiny. Philosophical, moral, and historical matters cannot be resolved like questions of mathematics, but neither are they merely subjects for rhetoric and polemical discussion.

> Reason must in all its undertakings subject itself to criticism; should it limit freedom of criticism by any prohibitions, it must harm itself, drawing upon itself a damaging suspicion. Nothing is so important through its usefulness, nothing so sacred, that it may be exempted from this searching examination, which knows no respect for persons. Reason depends on this freedom for its very existence. For reason has no dictatorial authority; its verdict is always simply the agreement of free citizens, of whom each one must be permitted to express, without let or hindrance, his objections or even his veto.
> (A739, B767, 593)

Kant advocated free speech and free thought and saw no benefit in giving special credentials to people merely because they were powerful.

> ... there can be no manner of doubt that it is always best to grant reason complete liberty, both of enquiry and of criticism, so that it may not be hindered in attending to its own proper interests. These interests ... will always suffer when outside influences intervene to divert it [reason] from its proper path, and to constrain it by what is irrelevant to its own proper ends.
> Allow, therefore, your opponent to speak in the name of reason, and combat him only with weapons of reason. ... Reason is benefited by the consideration of its object from both sides, and its judgment is corrected in being thus limited.
> (A745, B773, 597)

Observations and Criticisms

Kant's philosophical system is intricate and hard to penetrate, and it is often difficult to detach his claims from his system. It may seem as though we cannot state Kant's ideas if we do not use his terminology; yet if we do use his terminology, we become so enmeshed in his philosophical system that we have neither the perspective nor the vocabulary to evaluate it. Despite these problems, there are some criticisms of Kant that can be stated reasonably simply.

Few modern philosophers would accept Kant's distinctions between analytic/synthetic and *a priori*/empirical in the strict way in which he formulated them. Many statements – including some of Kant's own examples, like 'Bodies are extended' (he called it analytic) and 'Bodies are heavy' (he called it synthetic) – strike modern readers as borderline cases. Nor is Kant's view of mathematics generally accepted today. Where Kant believed that mathematics was comprised mainly of synthetic *a priori* propositions, most contemporary theorists find instead analytic or purely formal propositions. In a formal system, statements are true by definition, or are axioms (accepted truths that establish the basis of a formal system), or can be deduced from axioms or definitions. If we ask whether a formal system applies to some area of reality, that turns out to be an empirical question. On these grounds, Kant's claim that there are synthetic *a priori* propositions in mathematics is often questioned. Arithmetical propositions are regarded as true by definition. As for geometry, there are a number of distinct systems of geometry in addition to the Euclidean geometry that Kant knew. Within each system, there are definitions, formal rules, and analytic truths based on the rules and definitions. Which system applies best to some area of physical reality, in a given scientific context, strikes modern thinkers as an empirical question. On this view, geometry is analytic in its formal context and the question of its application is empirical; thus geometry is not synthetic *a priori*.

Other major difficulties about the Kantian system concern the distinction between appearances and things-in-themselves. Whenever Kant says anything about things-in-themselves, he does so using categories which (according to his own restrictions) are appropriate only for the realm of appearances. Strictly speaking, this is an inconsistency. When he is writing carefully, Kant refers to things-in-themselves, or noumena, merely as possibilities, and holds back from saying anything about how they might be related to appearances. The concept of the thing-in-itself, or noumenon, is a purely limiting one – a way of pointing to what we cannot know. If there are noumenal objects, we do not know anything about them; in fact, they might not exist at all. We speak of a noumenon as a way of allowing that the phenomena we know may not exhaust everything that there is, and a way of acknowledging that when we conceptualize and organize representations to suit the structures of our minds, we may thereby fail to know some aspects of reality which we cannot categorize and organize in our own way.

Following through on his own conclusions about knowledge being restricted to appearances, Kant says early in the *Critique of Pure Reason* that we do not know even our own selves as noumena. We are aware of ourselves in time, and time is a form of our own sensibility. We know ourselves only as phenomena, and not as noumena, because all our self-awareness is in time. This restriction raises questions. Kant often goes beyond his own boundaries, suggesting that we do have knowledge of ourselves as purely intelligible, or noumenal, objects. For example, what about the sensibility, understanding, judgment, imagination and reason which Kant posits as faculties of the human mind, and which are the subject of so many of his arguments in the First Critique? Are these capacities only of our phenomenal selves, or are they also features of ourselves as noumena? Kant says knowledge of the self as a thing-in-itself is impossible, but he often wrote as though it were possible. In trying to reconcile freedom and causation, Kant speaks of the active nature of understanding and reason as indications that human beings are, in some aspects, purely intelligible beings. In saying this, he goes beyond the bounds of knowledge that he set for himself in his First Critique. Of such tensions in Kant's thought, his German successors, most notably Hegel, were very much aware.

8

Hegel: Negation and Progress

Georg Wilhelm Friedrich Hegel (1770 - 1831) was born in Stuttgart to a middle-class family. A conscientious and excellent student, Hegel entered a theological seminary at the University of Tubingen in 1788. After leaving the seminary, Hegel became a tutor to several aristocratic families. In 1800, he obtained a university teaching post at the University of Jena, where he began to work out the basis of his own philosophical system.

Hegel believed that Kant had been on the right path in his Copernican Revolution. But he rejected Kant's distinction between things-in-themselves and appearances. Throughout his philosophical career, Hegel was unwilling to accept divisions and dichotomies as final. Where there appeared to be a dichotomy, he sought an underlying reality or common ground which would reconcile opposites. Hegel did not like dualisms. His own philosophical position was a version of philosophical idealism: he believed that the knowing mind and the reality it knows must be inter-related and inter-dependent.

In 1806, Napoleon's army conquered the Prussian city of Jena, temporarily halting university life there, just as Hegel was completing the manuscript of his first major work, *The Phenomenology of Spirit*. At about the same time, his landlord's wife gave birth to a child, Ludwig, who was Hegel's first son. In this tumultuous situation, Hegel had to find another way to support himself. For a short time he was the editor of a newspaper. Between 1808 and 1816, he was the headmaster of a school in Nuremberg, where he taught philosophy at the high school level. In 1811, Hegel married. He and his wife had two sons, and were able to take Ludwig into their home.

In 1816 Hegel became a professor of philosophy in Heidelberg; then, in 1818, he moved to Berlin where he became, in effect, Germany's leading and "official" philosopher. Hegel's ideas about knowledge, logic, ethics, and politics dominated German philosophy in the 1820s and 1830s. In addition to *The Phenomenology of Spirit*, his major works are *The Science of Logic*, *Lectures on the History of Philosophy* (based on student notes from lectures given in Berlin), the *Encyclopedia of the Philosophical Sciences in Outline*, and *The Philosophy of Right*.

Hegel died in 1831. He was buried next to Fichte, another well-known German philosopher who had been his colleague at Jena. After his death, his colleagues compiled an edition of his works in eighteen volumes.

Hegel had a creative synthesizing mind, and he worked out an extremely ambitious and original philosophical system. He thought that philosophy should be systematic and form a unified whole: its fundamental purpose is to overcome oppositions and divisions. According to Hegel, the understanding of an element or part requires the understanding of the whole. Parts cannot ultimately be separated. Mind and matter, reason and feeling, thought and sensibility, individual and community, must be understood as interdependent phenomena; each aspect requires the other. Hegel believed that human history in general, and the history of philosophy in particular, were working toward a final goal in which ultimately Spirit will become fully aware of itself. The Hegelian Spirit is all human minds in inter-relation with each other in communities. In the Hegelian system of thought, all being, all life, all nature, and all personal feelings and ideas are regarded as expressions of a community of self-conscious beings which is Spirit. There are not just individual minds; there is a system of human individuals, all developing their potentialities. Art, religion, and philosophy are diverse manifestations of Spirit, or inter-related consciousnesses.

Absolute Idealism

The Hegelian Spirit is not an entity separated from human life and physical nature, as the Christian God is commonly thought to be. Rather, it is understood as a force within nature and human life. In keeping with Hegel's objection to dualisms, there is no separation in his system between a God and the world we know. Instead, the world is regarded as an expression of Spirit, which is characterized by complete unity or harmony. In the course of life, this Spirit cannot be expressed or encountered directly. Rather, it emerges in various incomplete manifestations, which conscious human beings can connect and reconcile. Hegel thought of human history as having an end or goal. Developing self-consciousness and freedom may be understood as the final goals of an ongoing temporal process which is human history.

For Hegel, the goal of human history was increasing rational self-consciousness, which meant, in effect, increasing human freedom. Hegel regarded human history as *progressive*; its later stages were developments of, and improvements on, its earlier ones. At the end of history, there will be no unreconciled oppositions. Practical and theoretical consciousness will be one; objects of consciousness will be understood (as philosophical idealists understand them) and comprehended within consciousness itself; selves will be inter-connected, not separate; and the finite and infinite will be united.

Hegel believed that self-consciousness and freedom are inseparable. Thought is better – more accurate – when it is free, because it can better grasp the way things are when it is not dependent on elements outside itself. A mind that is coerced and unfree cannot come to reliable knowledge of itself or anything else. Hegel was convinced that thought can grasp reality in a way that no other form of consciousness can, and that purity of thought makes for objectivity. Logic he understood to be "thought thinking about itself." In logic, form and content must be found together and should not be separated. Unlike many modern philosophers, Hegel did not think that logic was a purely formal subject. Rather, in logic we use thinking in order to examine how thinking works; we think about thinking itself. Thinking is a process of getting things fixed in our minds. We start with something indeterminate, and by attending to differences and relationships, we make it more determinate. Hegel believed that a primary task of thinking is to understand relationships and interdependencies. Often concepts or phenomena can be understood only when we are also aware of their opposite. For example, to understand a *part* we have to understand that there is a *whole* of which it is a part. Similarly, to understand something that is *inner*, we have to understand something else, which is *outer*, and with which it contrasts and to which it is related.

An especially important aspect of thought is that it progresses, noting differences and taking account of them to move forward.

Some thoughts lead to others in characteristic ways. We may recognize a limitation, notice a basic similarity or common ground, move to specifications from a general concept, or propose a solution to a problem we have noted. By thinking about our own thought, we can hope to avoid mistakes. As living, thinking beings, we express our thought in two ways: through knowing and through willing (choosing to do things). But either of these, taken alone, is one-sided. For complete thought, and for an accurate understanding of thought, knowing and doing must be integrated.

Like Kant, Hegel distinguished between reason and understanding. When we are thinking with understanding, we use fixed concepts. Using reason, we think more dialectically, acknowledging limitations in our views and revising our concepts as we go along. Unlike Kant, Hegel allowed a vast scope for speculative reason. With speculative reason, we survey and reflect on the whole of our thought and the world, seeking to achieve an overview. Hegel's full conception of thinking includes the processes of the understanding, reason, and speculative reason. As he understood them, these all fit together. When we employ a fixed category of the understanding, we come to think of its limitations and its opposite. We move from that stage to the dialectical thinking of reason. Then we survey the whole process, to reconcile our thoughts and put them in a more general context. Hegel did not accept Kant's distinction between appearances and things-in-themselves, or Kant's conclusion that we can have knowledge only of things which are within the realm of experience. Nor did he share Kant's view that we are unable to reason cogently about the whole of the world. Instead, Hegel confidently worked out theories about the direction of all of human history.

Hegel believed that self-consciousness is genuinely present in the world. As an idealist, he was willing to speak of thought as a part of the world which had become self-conscious. Logic is not something removed from nature and history, but rather a rationality expressed within them. What is real is, in this sense, rational. The relations inherent in thinking are so fundamental that they find expression in the world. What is rational is, in this sense, real. Hegel's idealist philosophy is often summed up in the saying, "The real is rational and the rational is real."

In *The Phenomenology of Spirit* Hegel describes various forms of consciousness which encounter problems and contradictions and move forward to a new stage of thinking and development in order to overcome these problems. A classic of philosophical idealism, Hegel's *Phenomenology* presupposes that the world of reality is to be defined in terms of whatever constitutes the true nature and foundation of the human self. There are tensions, difficulties, and oppositions in any developing self and analogously, there are conflicts in nature and in the course of human history. In a dialectical process, negative discoveries turn out to be positive discoveries, because they help individuals and societies to move forward to a new stage. Errors are partial views of the truth; without the partial truths, the total truth would be impossible. Both in the *Phenomenology* and in his *Logic* Hegel argued that commonsense beliefs and concepts lead us to "contradictions." These "contradictions" cannot be tolerated, and to avoid them we must move on to new beliefs and new stages of development. In fact, Hegel believed that every self and every object in nature will be "contradictory" in some sense if it is considered solely by itself. Things are integrally related to each other and comprehension requires connecting them systematically.

One area of modern science where a rather Hegelian view is plausible is that of ecology. We are still learning, often painfully, about the incredible interdependence in natural systems. Introduction of a new species to a territory – even an apparently trivial species such as a small plant or insect – often has sweeping consequences on a whole bio-region because of the intricate ways in which life systems are inter-related. A hard-learned ecological lesson about fertilizers, insecticides, and other agents which we may introduce into natural system is that they never have *only* the effects we originally intended – they have multitudinous other effects as well, because of the inter-relatedness of all the elements in an ecological system.

In human history, according to Hegel, Spirit will work its way through various stages until it finally encounters the light of reason. In any stage of history, there are problems and ideas that will work themselves out. When a process is near its end, we can look back and understand it, but we cannot predict what will come next. We might think of the end of history as the end of the stage in which we presently find ourselves – the time at which the preoccupations and difficulties of our present age have been resolved. After fifty years of Cold War politics, some analysts saw the end of the Cold War in 1989 as the "end of history." But presumably history will continue further after a particular phase comes to an end – though we may have little idea what the new phase will be like. Hegel believed that there could ultimately be such a thing as the lesson of the world's history, an absolute truth which will include, but surpass, all the forms of expression and self-expression which have been learned along the way. The self-consciousness of the Absolute Spirit, Hegel argued, will reach its most explicit form in philosophy. The final philosophy will be an Idealist one – not surprisingly quite a lot like Hegel's own!

Hegel on the History of Philosophy

Hegel loved to lecture on the history of philosophy. In his lectures, he devoted about two-thirds of his time to the Greek period with only one-third left for the medievals and the moderns. Hegel's presentation strikes the modern reader as informed and interesting on many points, but selective in its emphasis on trends that anticipated his own results. As an idealist, Hegel tended to praise any movement away from the sensible to the intelligible. Accordingly, he valued Plato's Forms; Aristotle's notion that intelligible form is present in what is observed; Descartes' Cogito; and Kant's Copernican revolution. He regarded the Middle Ages, when philosophers subjected their minds to the authority of a God outside the world, as an uninspiring period typifying a condition of unhappy consciousness in which human reason had lost its self-confidence and independence. Hegel gave short treatment to Hume, whose empirical work he regarded as a negative moment in the history of philosophy. Ultimately, Hegel believed, philosophy as a whole would reach the idealist conclusion that to think at all is to think thought, and to seek to know anything at all is to look for it in thought. Hegel predicted that the unity of thought and being, as understood by Idealists, would eventually be grasped as the ultimate lesson of the history of philosophy.

Hegel argued that philosophy in any given period presupposes the history of philosophy until that point. In order to understand a philosophical problem or thinker, we have to understand the historical context in which he or she emerged. At any given moment, philosophy will be the result of its whole past.

> Since Philosophy in its ultimate essence is one and the same, every succeeding philosopher will and must take up into his own all philosophies that went before, and what falls specially to him is their further development.
> (LHPII, 13)

In fact, Hegel identified philosophy with the history of philosophy. There is only one philosophy, according to Hegel, and its history shows how its logically related stages have developed.

Philosophy, Hegel thought, has a continuous life of its own, running through human history. It has various manifestations, none of which is exactly identifiable with philosophy itself. Individuals have thought and philosophized, and without them, there would be no history of philosophy. Thought must in this sense be individual. But there is also a crucial sense in which thought transcends individuals. Because of logical relationships, some thoughts will naturally emerge from others – whatever individuals exist and whatever may be the historical circumstances in which they find themselves. Thought must be the thinking of people in communities – and ultimately that of the universal Spirit which embraces all of humankind. To be sure, thought works through individuals. But if it were purely individual, it would get nowhere.

Thus the history of philosophy may be examined from two angles: one historical, the other logical. Parmenides, Heraclitus, Socrates, Plato, Aristotle, Descartes, Hume, Wollstonecraft, Leibniz, Kant, and hundreds of others lived and talked and did their work. The events of their lives and the details of their teachings and writings are the material of history – events that have happened over many centuries. We may study the history of philosophy as empirical history – the study of *what reason has said*. But the history of philosophy can also be regarded as a series of logical developments where the implications and consequences of thoughts are being worked out – as the study of *what reason must say*.

Hegel understood the story of Socrates as indicating that the individual must stand up for his own conscience, against the conscience of the people. He believed that free thought had first appeared in Socrates' Athens. In his theory of Forms and recollection Plato had implied that thinking is not merely a property of one individual soul. Thinking is the very substance of the soul, and in thinking, the soul takes part in something universal and shows that it has aspects which are universal and which cannot be confined to finite time.

> To Plato, accordingly, Philosophy is really the science of this implicitly universal, to which as contrasted with the particular, he always continues to return.
> (LHPII, 29)

Hegel did not praise Aristotle's syllogistic logic, believing that while it had a certain mundane usefulness, it was too dry and formal, detached things too much from one another, and showed nothing about how we do think or should think. He granted that the isolation of logical form in the Aristotelian syllogism was a brilliant discovery in its own time. But syllogistic logic cannot lead us to truth, Hegel claimed, because it is too dualistic and finite. Hegel commented (accurately) that Aristotle's own thought went far beyond the reaches of the syllogism. He greatly admired Aristotle as a thinker, referring to the "treasure" in his works, and calling his synthesis "great and masterly."

> Aristotle has the world of appearances before himself complete and in its entirety, and sets nothing aside, however common it may appear. All sides of knowledge have entered into his mind, all have interest for him, and he has thoroughly dealt with all.
> (LHPII, 131)

In Aristotelian philosophy, the individual thinker and the individual object are stressed, but the universality of reason is still emphasized. Aristotle argued that we need particulars to obtain knowledge, both in science and in ethics, but he nevertheless emphasized concepts and the universal form in things, as well as the inter-relationships and similarities between things in the world. Like Aristotle, Hegel accepted final causes. Hegel believed that history itself has a final cause, which is the self-consciousness of the Absolute Spirit.

According to Hegel, Descartes' work marked the beginning of modern philosophy.

> As regards his philosophic works, those which contain his first principles have in particular something very popular about their method of presentation, which makes them highly to be recommended to those commencing the study of philosophy. Descartes sets to work in quite a simple and childlike manner, with a narration of his reflections as they came to him. . . . Descartes started by saying that thought must necessarily commence from itself . . . the spirit of his philosophy is simply knowledge as the unity of Thought and Being.
> (LHPIII, 223-4)

Presumably Hegel meant that mind would come to know matter and would in this sense be united with it. (Unlike that of Hegel, Descartes' system was based on a resolute dualism between mind and matter.)

Hegel had little good to say about Hume the empiricist.

> Hume has thus destroyed the objectivity or absolute nature of thought determinations.
> (LHPIII, 371)

Hume's results provoke

> . . . astonishment regarding the condition of human knowledge, a general state of mistrust, and a sceptical indecision – which indeed does not amount to much . . . . Thus everything appears in the form of an irrational existence devoid of thought; the implicitly true and right is not in thought, but in the form of instinct, a desire. (LHPIII, 374-5)

As for Kant, Hegel saw him as the first in a great tradition of German Idealism. According to Hegel, Kant had understood how important thought was, but he had failed to complete his system because he insisted on such dualistic distinctions as those between thought and sensibility, matter and form, and appearances and things-in-themselves. Hegel did not accept Kant's views on the scope of metaphysics or his restriction of philosophical knowledge to the realm of possible experience. He believed that Kant had been wrong to insist that sensed particulars must be elements of knowledge, and further, that this mistake had led Kant to be too restrictive in describing the powers of Reason, and to incorrectly limit knowledge to the world of experience of sensed objects.

> It depends, however, on how the world is looked at; but experience and observation of the world mean nothing else for Kant than a candlestick standing here and a snuff-box standing there. (LHPIII, 444)

Hegel was sure that we human beings can know more than the realm of objects: we are spirits, and can know the infinite as Spirit. At one point Hegel seemed to appeal to common sense as one basis for rejecting Kant's distinction between appearances and things-in-themselves.

> There is no man so foolish as that philosophy; when a man feels hungry, he does not call up the imagination of food, but sets about satisfying his hunger.
> (LHPIII, 453)

Though he was greatly influenced by Kant's Antinomies in the Dialectic of the *Critique of Pure Reason*, Hegel did not accept Kant's view that we are inevitably led into difficulties when we try to prove conclusions about things-in-themselves or the world as a whole. Rather than showing the limitations of reason, as Kant thought,

Hegel believed that the Antinomies showed the power of reason: reason could overcome those limitations and resolve the dilemmas Kant had developed.

The Hegelian Dialectic

What is Hegel's Dialectic?

According to Hegel, every conception and theory – in fact, every state of consciousness – will contain within itself limitations and inadequacies. Over time, these are bound to emerge. Because of these "contradictions," we will be driven forward to new conceptions by a process of "negation." We realize a belief is inadequate and we "negate" it, arriving at a new belief. These new conceptions, however, will themselves never be fully adequate; we will find problems in them too, and will therefore "negate" again. From the rejection of the second position (called by Hegel "the negation of the negation") we will come to a third conception.

This third position will result from the first two; it will combine elements of both, but will be identical with neither. We will discover the limitations of our ideas in the working out of psychological processes, through logic, or in our encounters with reality itself. From these conflicts, we will move forward to something something new that is based on the old, but has amended it in constructive ways. We can think of a dialectical process in this way:

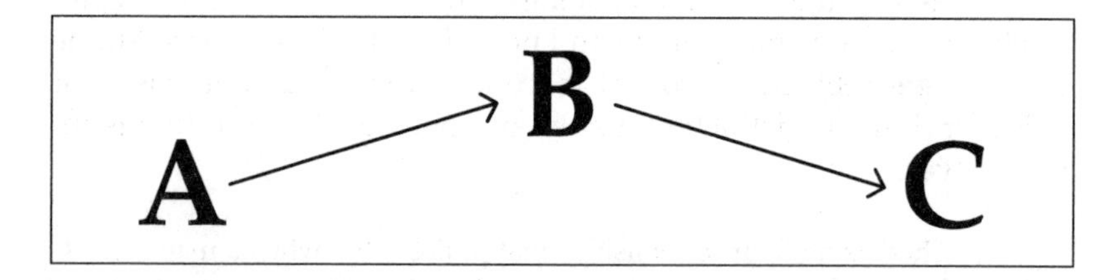

A is the first position; it turns out to be inadequate; then by understanding A and its inadequacies, we reach a new position, B. In reaching B, we have "negated" A. But B still retains elements of A. We later come to understand that B too is incomplete and has limitations. Appreciating these limitations and recollecting A and B, we arrive at a new position, C, which retains elements of A and B. C has been reached by "negating" B, which itself was a negation of A. We can refer to this third position as "the negation of the negation." The

Hegelian dialectic is often described as the process of "thesis, antithesis, synthesis" – though this terminology was popularized more by Marx than by Hegel. (In Hegel's idealist system, dialectic is different from what it is in Marx's materialist one.) In the model above, A would be the thesis; B would be the antithesis; and C would be the synthesis.

The labels, A, B, and C here suggest a fixity that may be misleading. Actually, B preserves elements of A, and C preserves elements of both A and B. Hegel believed that within the dialectical process our terms shift in meaning. The content of A, B, and C, then, is not fixed. It shifts as ideas develop. We can indicate this aspect by amending the diagram as follows:

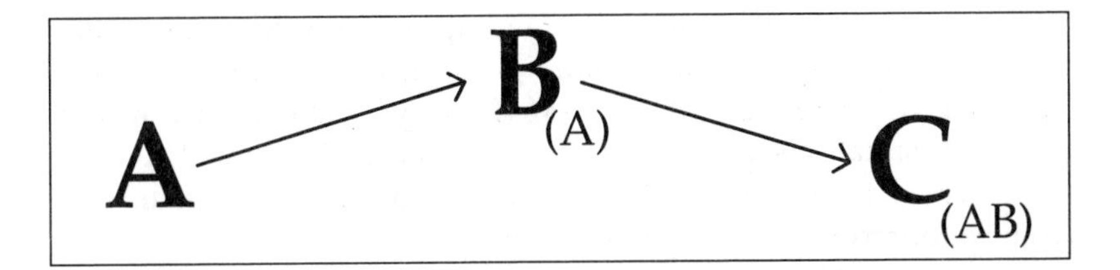

We can illustrate Hegel's theory using a present-day example. Suppose we begin by holding the view (A) that a sales tax should be avoided because it will be bad for the economy. Holding this view, we understand a sales tax to be an amount paid to the government whenever consumer purchases above a certain value are made; we do not think in terms of what the government does with funds it raises. We presume a fundamental distinction between consumer spending and government spending, and assume that consumer spending as such is good for the economy, whereas government spending is not. There are limitations in view (A) which will emerge over time. For example, when view (A) is accepted, we may find that there is insufficient government revenue to support what we agree to be necessary functions in areas such as public administration, health care, and education. The desirability of a sales tax will be regarded in a different light when these facts come to be understood. Coming to understand these exigencies, we then "negate" (A) to arrive at a different view (B) – that a sales tax is needed to support necessary government services.

We first held (A) that a sales tax should be avoided; we then rejected or "negated" that view, and came to the view (B) that a sales tax is necessary. There is a need to reconcile these opposed views. We do this partly by amending the concepts which underlie them. When we appreciate the limitations of (B) and "negate" (B), we come to a third view (C), which in this context is the synthesis of (A) and (B). This synthesis will involve a different understanding of what taxation is, what consumer purchases are, and how spending contributes to the economy. To reach the synthesis, we understand that money paid over to the government is not simply lost to the economy, because the government can decide to spend it in various worthwhile ways. Furthermore, not all consumer purchases contribute meaningfully to the economy, because many such purchases are of goods that are unnecessary or frivolous, or of goods made by workers outside the country.

View (A) has been "negated," leading to (B); then view (B) has been "negated," leading to (C). As the reconciling position, the third position reflects a different understanding of the purpose of a sales tax, the nature of government, and the effects of consumer spending from that of either view (A) or view (B). Hegel believed that as our positions, situations, and theories change, our concepts will change. For this reason, he believed that it is often a mistake to seek fixed definitions for terms.

Understood as an ongoing process, the Hegelian dialectic does not stop with any particular synthesis. The synthesis in one dialectical sequence will become the beginning of another dialectical sequence. Thus C, the early synthesis, can become a thesis with a "negated" position, D, as its antithesis, and E as the synthesis in a new series.

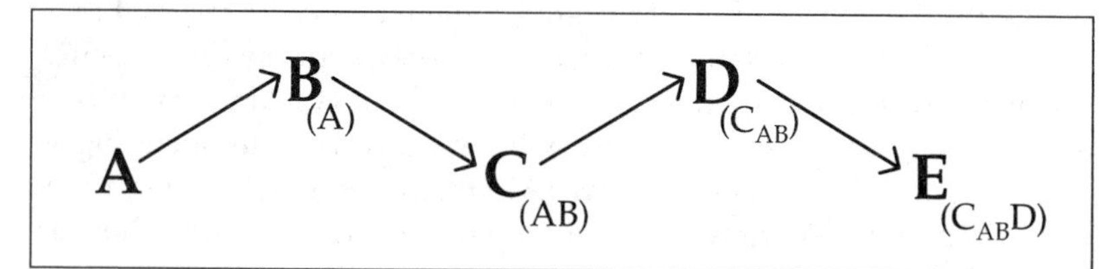

The dialectical process will not stop while human thought and human history continue. Error and opposition in views are inevitable, but they contribute to our growing awareness of the truth. As Hegel understood it, later stages in the dialectic incorporate earlier ones. We "negate" A to arrive at B, and we "negate" B to arrive at C. But the third stage, C, has not simply left A and B behind. On the contrary, elements both of A and of B are preserved within it. If we later move from C to D and E, the same thing will happen again. Elements of C – and hence of A and B – will be preserved in D and E. In the Hegelian dialectic, the resolution, or synthesis stage, is not something entirely new. Rather, it emerges from the earlier stages and our recognition of their limitations.

Early views are not merely abandoned; they continue to affect the later views to which they have given rise. With Hegel, the notion of intellectual development becomes important in philosophy for the first time. Our thoughts and beliefs are the result of cumulative developments and improvements. Believing in the dialectic, Hegel believed that human individuals, human history, and life itself move forward by reconciling opposites. The history of philosophy develops in the same way.

Dialectic in the History of Philosophy and Elsewhere

The idea that conceptions and beliefs change in a dialectical way is often quite plausible. It is especially attractive as a hypothesis describing developments in the history of philosophy. Parmenides argued that change was impossible (thesis); Heraclitus argued that change was happening all the time (antithesis); then Plato, attempting to reconcile the two views, argued that the world of sensation, which is in flux, is a reflection of a timeless and changeless world of forms (synthesis). Rationalism and empiricism provide another example. Rationalists argued that knowledge is intellectual (thesis); empiricists argued that it is sensory (antithesis); Kant then put forward a view in which knowledge requires both intellect and sense (synthesis). In the course of these historical developments, the understanding of key terms such as "change," "permanency," "sense," "intellect," and "knowledge" shifted in meaning along the way.

To think of meanings shifting as thought moves on also fits the context of human dialogue. Imagine a conversation in which two people are talking, listening to each other, and attending closely to each other. They are speaking and listening in turn. As their conversation continues, each thinks about what the other has to say, adapting and revising his views accordingly. Given that they truly attend and respond to each other, each person's understanding will integrate what the other has to say, and they will change in relation to each other as the dialogue goes on. (This, of course, is the kind of conversation which is a genuine interchange. Some supposed conversations are merely alternating monologues, and in these there would be no amendment of one person's view in response to that of the other.)

Hegel's view also seems to fit contemporary theories of conflict resolution. In these theories, there is considerable emphasis on the difference between a compromise and a creative resolution of a conflict. A compromise is a kind of average or cut between two existing views, whereas a creative resolution to a conflict embraces further possibilities. For example, suppose that Party A wants Party B to give him 100 dollars, whereas Party B thinks he should only have to give Party A 60 dollars. If they resolve their problem by compromising, Party B may give Party A 80 dollars; they split the difference. In a more creative resolution to their conflict, these parties would move beyond their original positions, considering other factors in addition to money. Like Hegel, advocates of creative conflict resolution believe that conflict often plays a positive role in moving us forward to a fresh view. The creative resolution or reconciliation of opposed parties takes into account, but then transcends, two opposed views.

In a creative resolution to a conflict, each party hears the other's case. They seek to understand each other's beliefs and feelings, find the common ground where they have shared interests, and select a solution which will reconcile their views by taking into account the needs and interests of both sides. In a resolution of a financial dispute, for instance, contending parties may realize that money is not the only thing underlying their dispute and that they can use other means (promises of cooperation, tokens of respect, exchanges of goods as opposed to money) to address their differences and reconcile. This creative resolution emerges from their expression of their conflict and is different from a simple compromise. This theory recalls the Hegelian view that dialectically we move to something new which is based on the old but has fresh elements.

Some Qualifications

In describing Hegel's dialectic, we have put the words "negation" and "negate" in quotation marks to indicate that the negation in question is not that of standard formal logic. In standard logic, if we negate A, we get not-A and if we negate the negation of A, we get not-not-A, which is A all over again. There is no movement from an antithesis to a synthesis. If A were 'We need a sales tax,' then the negation of A (not-A) in the standard formal sense would be merely 'We do not need a sales tax,' and the negation of that (not-not-A) would be 'We need a sales tax.' There is no movement or progress to a new view here, obviously. In Hegelian thought, the antithesis is not the purely logical negation of the thesis, and the synthesis is not its double negation. Thus Hegelian "negation" is not the same as standard logical negation.

How Hegelian "contradiction" should be understood is a controversial matter, and one which has contributed to the view among some contemporary philosophers that Hegel's philosophy does not make sense. If thought and reality are inseparable, and thought frequently contains "contradictions," does this commit Hegel to the view that reality itself is contradictory? Is Hegel willing to violate the Principle of Non-Contradiction and allow that statements of the form 'P and not-P' can truly describe the world? Some modern critics have thought so. But the interpretation is not plausible because Hegel is clearly committed to the view that there is something *wrong* with "contradictions;" it is our desire to avoid limitations, inadequacies, and "contradictions" that moves us forward in the dialectical process. When we find a "contradiction" we are moved to seek a new view of things in which the opposites are reconciled and the problem disappears.

To avoid this controversy about Hegel's philosophy, we do not interpret "contradiction" in the standard logical sense, which is why the word, as used here, is set in quotation marks. Often when Hegel speaks of "contradictions," he is saying only that there are inadequacies or tensions in our views, or that one conception needs reference to its opposite in order to be understood. (Hegel argued that this was the case for "parts" and "wholes," "being" and "nothing," "finite" and "infinite," and "particular" and "universal.") Hegel understood the thesis and antithesis as opposed and the synthesis as filling our need to reconcile these opposites. If he had no commitment to the Principle of Non-Contradiction, he would have been left without an impulse to drive the dialectic forward, because contradictions – and "contradictions" – would have been perfectly all right.

Examples of Dialectical Development in the *Phenomenology of Spirit*

In the *Phenomenology of Spirit*, Hegel tells the developmental story of a naive commonsense consciousness which, by going through many dialectical sequences, eventually reaches consciousness of objects, self-consciousness, then reason, and ultimately arrives at the brink of full-fledged philosophical idealism. Throughout, its progress is dialectical.

The initial stage in the development of this consciousness is one Hegel calls sense-certainty. (In describing the development of consciousness, he uses "I" to represent any human consciousness.) In this stage, the consciousness, I, does not raise issues about self or objects; I merely assume that I have direct immediate knowledge of something presented to me in sensation. This stage of sense-certainty will break down, Hegel argues. When I begin to think about it, I will use words, and even if the words are only indefinite pointers like "this," something universal enters the picture. "This" could apply to any other object of sensation. What seemed to be immediately known as a unique something presented in sensation turns out after all to be not capturable by thought in language. I move dialectically, from what seemed to be completely immediate sensory knowledge of a particular to a universal which could apply to anything at all.

Consider on the one hand complete particularity: I am immediately aware of this particular thing, say an orange. The orange is unique as a specific thing, before I classify it in any way. If I classify it (spherical, juicy) then other things can share those qualities too. Apparently I can keep to the level of the particular by just pointing and saying "this." But then, somewhat paradoxically, a kind of indefiniteness enters the picture, an indefiniteness that amounts to utter universality. Anything (an apple, a piece of paper, a tree) could be a "this." Because "this" can be used whatever I point to, "this" has no content. There is a conflict that needs to be resolved. To do so, the naive human consciousness will have to move on to a new stage, transcending sense-certainty.

> Because of its concrete content, sense-certainty immediately appears as the *richest* kind of knowledge, indeed a knowledge of infinite wealth for which no bounds can be found, either when we *reach out* into space and time in which it is dispersed, or when we take a bit of this wealth, and by division *enter into* it. Moreover, sense-certainty appears to be the *truest* knowledge; for it has not as yet omitted anything from the object, but has the object before it in its perfect entirety. But, in the event, this very *certainty* proves itself to be the most abstract and poorest *truth*.
> (PS, 58)

Now may be any time – day or night. *Here* may be any place – in front of the tree or beside the house. And *This,* which is immediately sensed, may be anything. What was at first absolutely particular and specific begins to disappear into an abstraction. I suppose myself to have sense-certainty when I am tasting an orange and "know" in an utterly immediate way what it tastes like. But when I reflect on this condition of supposedly certain knowledge, I find that there is nothing there. Even "I" does not represent anything specific. We might assume that

> . . . the vanishing of the single Now and Here that we mean is prevented by the fact that *I* hold them fast. 'Now' is day because I see it; 'Here' is a tree; but Another 'I' sees the house and maintains that 'Here' is not a tree but a house instead. Both truths have the same authentication, viz. the immediacy of seeing, and the certainty and assurance that both have about their knowing; but the one truth vanishes in the other.
> (PS, 16)

> Sense certainty thus comes to know by experience that its essence is neither in the object nor in the 'I,' and that its immediacy is neither an immediacy of the one nor of the other; for in both, what I *mean* is rather something unessential, and the object and the 'I' which I mean do not have a continuing being, or *are not*.
> (PS, 62)

From sense-certainty, I – or consciousness – move on to a phase of perception in which there is a distinction between the perceiving self and a perceived object which is a particular thing having universal properties. (The orange is spherical, juicy, sweet-tasting, has a rind with white underneath, and so on.) And the process continues, for that stage too reveals unresolved tensions which require further motion.

Later in the *Phenomenology* Hegel explores self-consciousness, and describes a dialectic of desire. When we get what we desire, there is a sense in which we kill the object of our desire, and a sense in which we ourselves die, because we lose the living impulse that was the desire. Somewhat paradoxically, the quest to move forward is destroyed when we are "satisfied." The activist is deflated when he finally achieves his goal. The writer feels only emptiness when her grand project has reached completion. The lover who finally fulfills his sexual passion is sated and depressed, having found the satisfaction less than the anticipation.

In Hegel, this theme is developed very abstractly. Self-consciousness, seeking a unity and seeking to discover itself, is led to desire living objects, which it wants to incorporate into itself. It seeks to know things; it desires things that are distinct from itself. But when this desire is satisfied, those things as living beings are destroyed; they are "negated." They are no longer independent beings, living and developing in their own right, and they cannot satisfy the self-consciousness which desired them and set out to absorb them in the first place. Self-understanding and self-recognition cannot be achieved by the sort of desire which, when satisfied, effectively abolishes the living object. The satisfaction of desire will lead only to the "death" of the desired object, and not to fulfillment.

Self-consciousness is possible only when there is recognition by another self-consciousness.

> A self-consciousness exists *for a self-consciousness*. Only so is it in fact self-consciousness; for only in this way does the unity of itself in its otherness become explicit in it. . . . A self-consciousness, in being an object, is just as much 'I' as 'object.' With this, we already have before us the Notion of *Spirit*. What still lies ahead for consciousness is the experience of what Spirit is – this absolute substance which is the unity of the different independent self-consciousnesses which, in their opposition, enjoy perfect freedom and independence: 'I' that is 'We' and 'We' that is 'I.' It is in self-consciousness, in the Notion of Spirit, that consciousness first finds its turning-point, where it leaves behind it the colourful show of the sensuous here-and-now and the nightlike void of the supersensible beyond, and steps out into the spiritual daylight of the present. (PS, 110-111)

What Hegel is saying here is that consciousness of oneself is necessarily tied to consciousness of others.

To be conscious of myself, I must be recognized by another human being, and I must in turn recognize her. I must understand that my self-consciousness depends on her recognition of me and her self-consciousness depends on my recognition of her. This is a delicate process in which things can easily go wrong. When a human consciousness becomes aware that it is facing another conscious human being, it goes forward to encounter that other – but then, feeling threatened by the fact that this really is another being capable of independence and "negation," it withdraws back into itself. I want to be a self and to be recognized as a self but somehow – and impossibly – I want to be *the only self*, the only center of consciousness capable of thinking, reflecting, and "negating."

When two such consciousnesses encounter each other, each feels threatened by the other, and is inclined to want to dominate, even destroy, the other, in order to preserve its own independence. The result is a "struggle to the death." Seeking recognition, each self at first seeks to destroy the other. The process of getting recognition from another self which truly is *another independent self* is a difficult one. I must be able to acknowledge that the other self really is *other* and has a capacity to think independently and "negate." Only from such an independent other self can I receive true acknowledgement.

One way that things can break down in the delicate process of mutual recognition is for one party to get all the recognition while the other is apparently reduced to a state of thing-like dependence. This situation of the lord and the bondsman – also referred to as the Master and Slave – has its own instability, and its dialectic leads to a surprising result. Hegel's description of this dynamic is frequently quoted and has been very influential.

The lord is able to dominate the bondsman; he has power over him and can tell him what to do. The vulnerable bondsman, in fear of the lord and dependent on him for his very life, must do as he is ordered. In this situation it would appear on the surface that it is the lord who has the advantage. Apparently, the lord has power, commands respect and recognition, and can get what he wants. However, the superiority of the lord is more apparent than real, because the lord depends on the bondsman for his sense of self. Furthermore, since the bondsman (or slave) is in a servile role, the master cannot in the full sense get recognition as a *self* from another self. The slave, a dominated being, is for that very reason unlikely to be open and honest with the master. Suppose, for example, that the master were to write a poem and asks the slave for his opinion of it, genuinely wanting to know whether or not it was good. If the slave said it was good, the master could not know whether the slave meant it, or whether he merely felt – due to his oppressed position – that he had to play along with the master and admire what he wrote. The bondsman's apparent recognition of the lord may be forced and thus not genuine.

The bondsman, because he is subservient to the lord, is not at this stage an independent consciousness and thus cannot give the lord the acknowledgement he needs to be a self. The lord, who does not in the full sense encounter another self, is thus unable to achieve consciousness of his own self. He does not know another independent human being, and as a result, he himself cannot come to know what it is to be a human being. Furthermore, the bondsman does all the lord's work, and as a result, the lord's encounter with material reality is only indirect. So far as self-consciousness is concerned, the lord can make no progress because he encounters no independent reality outside himself.

The paradox of this Master/Slave dynamic is that, as far as self-consciousness and self-development are concerned, the situation of the bondsman is better than that of the lord. The lord is the essential reality of the bondsman's situation. Desperate as his dominated situation is, the bondsman does experience a relatedness to another self, a self which is not dominated and servile. In the fearfulness of his situation, the bondsman has experienced dread and a sense that nothing in his world is stable. And the bondsman has work to do. Through work, he encounters and helps to shape a material reality and is thereby able to develop his mind and his capacities. He can develop a strong sense of self from looking at the products of his labor.

The dialectic can be even more subtle when we realize that the Master and Slave may both be represented in a single person. A single person may gain awareness of himself or herself as a distinct self, and of his or her own goals and wishes, through a dynamic internal relationship with another imagined self – an authoritative parent, for instance. (This conception of self-awareness has been extremely influential in the branch of contemporary psychology known as object-relations theory.)

In desire, we seek to consume an object, and preserve our preoccupation with our own state of satisfaction. But work is more than desire and its satisfaction. In work, we must go beyond the desires of the moment to commit ourselves to goals, and form and shape objects which are independent of ourselves and of our desires. As a worker, the bondsman will gain a sense of the reality of objects independent of himself, and in doing so, he will acquire a mind of his own.

> . . . the bondsman realizes that it is precisely in his work wherein he seemed to have only an alienated existence that he acquires a mind of his own.
> (PS, 119)

From servitude, the bondsman moves on to develop an independent consciousness.

Observations: Reflections on the Hegelian Dialectic

The dialectic played many roles in Hegel's thought. It was the basis of his system of logic: Hegel believed that basic categories such as Being contained "contradictions" and led to further categories. Within the Hegelian system, our thoughts, emotions, and beliefs develop dialectically; human history and the natural world also show dialectical processes. Thought and reality are inseparable in this system; thus we can use the structure of the dialectic to describe and explain changes both in thought and in reality. We can also use it to recommend how thought and knowledge should develop, provided we do not do so in a dogmatic way. Dialectic has a theoretical role in explaining developments in human situations as well as a practical role in recommending how they should occur.

Hegel also used the dialectical method in an argumentative way, to defend his own system against rival philosophical views. In alternative systems, there would be limitations and "contradictions;" the successive reconciliation of these conflicts would eventually lead to a Hegelian system. Hegel regarded his dialectical method as the true method of philosophy. But it was more than a method; it was based on a grand hypothesis about the shape of our categories, our consciousness, and natural and spiritual phenomena. Hegel related his view of dialectic to earlier argument styles of Socrates, Plato, and Kant. But his theory of dialectic is quite different from earlier ones.

Hegel used the dialectic throughout his philosophy in many different contexts: history of philosophy, logic, history, psychology, and argumentative defense. Indeed, the dialectic seems plausible and fruitful in many contexts today. If we understand thinking as dialectical, we should be encouraged to look for limitations in our present theories and beliefs, with the expectation that when we find these, our understanding of them will help us move forward to a fresh view. Thus, a dialectical conception of human thought should help to prevent dogmatism and function to encourage a critical attitude. It also suggests that there is value in opposition and controversy, which can serve a constructive role in propelling us forward to new ideas. This belief that conflict can be positive, and opposites can be reconciled, is one that can be immensely valuable in confrontational situations.

Hegel's understanding that later stages in history and in theory develop from earlier ones incorporated in them, serves to remind us of the importance of historical understanding. Ideas of the moment are not merely of the moment, and may well be misunderstood if we fail to consider their history. The dialectic can also be a fertile source of hypotheses about future intellectual and historical developments. What are the oppositions and "contradictions" in reality and in human theories, and what will the synthesis be?

However, there are some pitfalls in all this. One problem is that of *hypostatization*. Hypostatization is the mistake of speaking and thinking of an abstraction as if it were an independently existing and acting thing in its own right. Hegel tends to write of Consciousness, or Reason, or Spirit as moving forward on its own, and this style may lead us to forget that it is, after all, conscious human beings who reflect, find limitations or "contradictions," "negate," and reason further to arrive at alternate views. This is one of the aspects of Hegel's style that makes his work difficult for many people to read and understand. People who use Hegelian conceptions today are not, by and large, Hegelian idealists. Unlike Hegel, they distinguish between human minds and external reality. Unless we are willing to grant the idealist assumption that ultimately the movement of the world and the movement of human consciousness in the world are one and the same thing, we should be careful to recall that it is reflecting human beings who think, change their minds, and move forward to develop new ideas; it is not Reason, Spirit, or Consciousness. Nor is there a movement of Dialectical Forces which is a deterministic process. Contrary to what Hegel sometimes suggests, the results of "negation" and "negating the negation" are not inevitable. A particular "synthesis" does not necessarily result from a state of opposition. Often there are alternate possibilities and these depend on the choices of the human thinkers and agents who are engaged in the situation.

Especially when reduced to the pat triad, "thesis, antithesis, synthesis," the dialectic can seem a simplistic blueprint for interpreting and predicting human thought and history. It is all too easy to apply the blueprint to developments after the fact. If a series of events has happened, we find it easy to *look back* on them and interpret them as developments which fit the framework of Hegelian dialectic. But that does not mean that the dialectic has given us an insight we could have used to *predict* those developments. When Hegelian ideas are reduced to a formula which is applied routinely, they give little real insight, but some apparent insight. We can be misled and conclude that we understand more than we do. The danger in the Hegelian dialectic is not that it will apply to nothing, but that it will apply – all too readily, and misleadingly – to everything. Obviously, Hegelian conceptions have plausible applications in many contexts, as has been illustrated. But if Hegelian interpretations are applied simplistically, little or no insight will result. To make a dialectical interpretation useful, we must try to articulate the stages and the limitations in specific terms, recall that "negations" retain elements of previous views and that concepts may change along the way, and carefully ask ourselves how the synthesis emerges and whether it is Hegelian in nature.

Hegel believed that the synthesis would, *of necessity*, incorporate the best elements of earlier stages and would thus *of necessity* be an improvement on earlier stages. For Hegel, this conception of inevitable *progress* in thought and in history was a deep assumption, one which was absolutely central in his system of thought. In his assumption that history would necessarily involve progress, Hegel was typical of his time. That assumption had been deeply characteristic of the Enlightenment, which was coming to an end as Hegel wrote. But even when the Enlightenment gave way to the Romantic movement of the early nineteenth century, the assumption of progress remained a deep and unquestioned one. It has remained strong through much of the twentieth century, especially in contexts where technological development was being discussed.

Notwithstanding its pervasive influence in the modern era, the assumption of progress is open to serious dispute. Hume argued convincingly that we cannot prove – either by reason alone or on the basis of experience – that the future will resemble the past. Much the same can be said about a theory of inevitable progress. This is, in effect, a claim that the future will be an *improvement* on the past. Neither reason nor experience can conclusively support that claim. We do not know what will happen in the future, whether it will be good, bad, mixed, or indifferent, or how it will relate to what is happening today. Hegel is clearly right to insist that the future is affected by the past, and that future beliefs will emerge from amendments of our present beliefs, which in turn have been the result of amendments of past beliefs. We would like to believe that in making these amendments we are coming closer to the truth, but there is no logical or practical guarantee that this is the case. Nor is there is any guarantee, either in the physical world or in human nature itself, of the Hegelian notion that things will get better and better. Progress is possible, but not inevitable. In human affairs, progress will occur only if human beings work hard for it.

In fact, the arguments against our knowing that progress is inevitable are even stronger than Hume's arguments that we cannot know the future will resemble the past. The reason is that the idea of inevitable progress incorporates value judgments, which are themselves controversial. For example, if computer technology becomes more complex, operations can be done faster, and there is more and more automation of jobs formerly performed by human beings. Do such changes amount to *improvements*? Are they improvements in technology? Will they lead to improvements in the quality of human life? In the knowledge possessed by human beings? Many people assume without serious reflection that the answer to such questions is inevitably "yes." But the issues require serious analysis, and there are also important arguments to the contrary. To appreciate the distinction between *change* and *progress* (change for the better) is crucially important in understanding our potential for action in a world of almost constant change. Change does not necessarily amount to progress, and when we deem changes to be progressive, we are making value judgments for which we should attempt to have good reasons. Although the Hegelian conception of progress is extremely appealing and comforting from an emotional point of view, it has no solid intellectual foundation and is rendered implausible by the brutal realities of twentieth-century history.

The belief that progress is natural, even inevitable, that within human history things will get better and better, has not been a feature of all human cultures. Some cultures have believed in a Golden Age of the past, seeing later stages of human history as less exalted than its beginnings. Some regard history as cyclical, with sequences of rises and falls. Others find in history no systematic pattern of progression and regression. If we move outside the system of Hegelian idealism, there is no guarantee from logic or anywhere else that later stages in philosophical or historical developments are *better* than earlier ones.

After Hegel

Soon after Hegel's death, his system ceased to dominate philosophical thought in Germany. But its influence continued. Marx and Freud were in different ways deeply influenced by Hegel. Through Marxist theory, elements of Hegel's work had an enormous indirect impact on twentieth-century history, greatly affecting the politics of communism and socialism, and the methods and topics of philosophy in east-central Europe, Soviet Russia, and China. In the movements known as existentialism and phenomenology, Hegel's work influenced many twentieth-century philosophers. In England, aspects of Hegelianism lived on into the early twentieth century in the prominent work of Thomas Green, F.H. Bradley, and J.M.E. McTaggart – idealists who developed the Hegelian system in their own ways. In the United States, Josiah Royce was greatly influenced by Hegel.

G.E. Moore and Bertrand Russell, two of the most important British philosophers of the twentieth century, began their careers by rebelling against the English idealists and thus, indirectly, rebelling against Hegel. Wary of metaphysics, dubious about abstractions and sweeping generalizations, Moore and Russell saw little need for philosophy to offer a sweeping, grand-scale theory of the world and human history. To the contrary, they believed that philosophers should address more limited, specific questions, clarify meaning, and reason carefully from point to point. Moore and Russell sought clarity, rigor, and scientific precision in philosophy. Profoundly sceptical about the intellectual integrity of grand systems such as Hegel's, Moore and Russell regarded the idealism of Bradley and McTaggart as obscure and unclear, and urged close attention to logic and meaning.

In the twentieth century, especially in England and North America, there developed a growing awareness of the importance of language in thought and knowledge. Many philosophers have struggled to understand the relation between thought and language; logic and language; and language and the world. These themes were explored by the brilliant Austrian-British philosopher Ludwig Wittgenstein.

In Germany and France, Hegel's philosophy was influential in the work of the existentialist philosophers including Martin Heidegger, Jean-Paul Sartre, and Simone de Beauvoir. Sartre and Beauvoir were especially influenced by the Dialectic of the Master and Slave.

9

Beauvoir: More than Kings and Conquerors

Simone de Beauvoir (1908 - 1986) was born in Paris and educated at a Catholic girls school, where she was a brilliant and ambitious student. In 1929, she received her aggregate degree in philosophy from the Sorbonne, being one of very few women to complete it, and the youngest person ever to do so. At the same time, Beauvoir commenced the intellectual partnership central to her life – a relationship with Jean-Paul Sartre, a fellow student later to become the leading existentialist philosopher in France. In the period between 1930 and 1943, Beauvoir taught philosophy at a number of schools in various parts of France. At the same time, she began to write philosophical fiction, and worked closely with Sartre, developing the ideas for his *Being and Nothingness*. Her first novel was published in 1943.

Beauvoir lived in Paris when it was occupied by the Germans in World War II. In addition to teaching, writing, editing, and doing research for a radio station, she worked hard to scrounge food and cook, helping to support friends survive the hardships of the Occupation. With Sartre, Beauvoir was also involved in efforts to organize Resistance groups.

In 1944, Beauvoir worked with Sartre and Maurice Merleau-Ponty to found *Les Temps Modernes*, which became an influential literary-philosophical journal and the main public voice of the existentialist movement. For the rest of her life, she was closely involved with the journal as an administrator, writer, and editor. In the immediate post-war period, she wrote about existentialism and the need for sensitive moral choices in a politically troubled world. These discussions may be found in *L'Existentialisme et la Sagesse des Nations* (Existentialism and

Common Sense), *Pyrrhus et Cineas* (Pyrrhus and Cineas), and *The Ethics of Ambiguity*.

In the late forties, Beauvoir became interested in applying existentialist ideas to the situation of women. On the basis of considerable inter-disciplinary research, she wrote a massive work, *The Second Sex*, published in French in 1949 and in English in 1953. The first major exploration of women's situation since Wollstonecraft, and the most comprehensive ever, *The Second Sex* was highly original and received a huge amount of attention around the world.

Shortly after writing *The Second Sex*, Beauvoir commenced a novel, *The Mandarins*, which explores the situation and political dilemmas of left-wing French intellectuals in the period 1945 - 1950. Its themes of love, freedom, collaboration, and the deepening Cold War were tremendously significant to the French public at that time. In 1954 Beauvoir received the Prix Goncourt, a top literary award for *The Mandarins*. During the fifties and sixties, Beauvoir and Sartre supported a variety of left-wing political causes and travelled to Africa, China, the USSR, and Cuba. In 1970, Beauvoir allied herself with the women's movement in France and began to undertake public speaking and organizational work on its behalf. Sartre died in 1980 after ten years of ill-health. After his death, Beauvoir's own health began to decline. Nevertheless she continued to be active. In addition to writing, editing, and political activities, she worked with the Women's Ministry of the socialist Mitterand government.

Beauvoir died in 1986. Her funeral was a moving event attended by thousands of people. Messages were sent from women's groups around the world and the French feminist Elisabeth Badinter declared, "Women, you owe everything to her!" – a statement repeated by many who attended the funeral.

Beauvoir was a prolific writer. Her publications include eight works of fiction, four volumes of autobiography, a volume of edited correspondence, four volumes of philosophical essays, and six works of broadly philosophical non-fiction – including *The Second Sex* and a substantial book on aging, published in 1970. The discussion here is based on her philosophical essays from the forties and fifties and *The Second Sex*.

The existentialist ideas Beauvoir developed with Sartre during the thirties are central to all her work.

Existentialism

According to existentialism, the most significant metaphysical fact is that the world is not made up only of things. Objects such as mountains, trees, tables, and buildings have no consciousness or freedom. What is distinctive about human beings is that we are conscious and can make free choices; thus we can detach ourselves from nonconscious things. We can ask questions, some of which have a negative answer and in this way deny or step back from things in the world. Because we can separate ourselves from the world of things in which we are located, we are, in a sense, caught between being and nonbeing. As thinking human beings we are not exclusively defined by our bodies or our physical surroundings. Objects are beings-in-themselves (êtres-en-soi) and that is not what a human being is. As thinking creatures who can raise questions, find negative answers, and make free choices, we are beings-for-ourselves (êtres-pour-soi).

Consciousness is active, flickering, and unstable. It can move from moment to moment; it is never fixed. Things, on the other hand are simply what they are; they are inert. In parts of *Being and Nothingness* and in his well-known first novel, *Nausea*, Sartre expressed a kind of disgust for thought-less being. The dominant image of this novel is that reality is somehow viscous and horrible – it is slimy, sticky, and threatening. Sartre felt a kind of tension between being-in-itself and being-for-itself; the possibility that being-in-itself would absorb and destroy being-for-itself was for him a constant threat. He sometimes spoke of being as though it was lurking in readiness to absorb human consciousness, which would thereby lose its independence and be destroyed. The abundance of physical reality seemed horrifying to Sartre and to the central character of his philosophical novel because it was regarded as a threat to the possibility of meaning and truth.

The actual world is the basis of possibilities, and human consciousness may be considered as a bridge between the actual and the possible. As conscious human beings, we never simply find ourselves in a situation; we can interpret our situation in various ways and make various choices, from which we move forward. For conscious beings capable of reflection, even the past and the present are not fixed. They are sensed and felt in the light of future possibilities, which we select for ourselves. It is a serious philosophical mistake to think of ourselves as having a fixed character which has come to us from our genes, our personal past, or our situation, and to then rationalize and excuse our actions by appealing to that character or to "properties" we have. Sartre used the example of a hike. If someone says, "I cannot go on; I am too tired." he is rationalizing and excusing himself by ignoring the possibility of rallying his energies to continue. As a thinking person, he is a conscious being with the freedom to affect the way in which he experiences his fatigue and what he does in response. We often pretend to ourselves that we have no choice, that things must go in a certain way because of the way we "are." Usually, when we do this we are deceiving ourselves.

Beauvoir and Sartre called such self-deception *bad faith*. A person in bad faith has enough evidence to know something, but wilfully ignores or reinterprets that evidence, and believes something else. It is as though he knows one thing and believes another. The hiker knows he could go on, knowing that he is a thinking being who can make choices, is responsible for what he does, and could rally his energies to walk further – and yet he believes he is "too tired to go on." Like most of us most of the time, the hiker has more choices than he acknowledges. We can "transcend" the world, going beyond the things that are given, because we can ask questions about that world, perceive absences within it, and act to change it. Human beings are a blend of "facticity" (the world of things, the world as it is) and transcendence (the ability to go beyond the facts to create something new). Sometimes our freedom is something we do not wish to acknowledge. We pretend to ourselves that we are not free, that we have no choices to make, and are something less than we are. We may be tempted to back away from our responsibility by neglecting our possibilities for transcendence or by distorting the nature of our situation so as to misrepresent our freedom. This unclear consciousness is bad faith.

A waiter in a cafe who presents himself *only* as a waiter, only as one serving that social role, is in bad faith. A young woman flirting with a man and ignoring evidence that he wants to seduce her, pretending to herself that he is interested only in having an intellectual conversation with her, is in bad faith. (This was Sartre's example.) So too is a man who thinks he is courageous, while ignoring many circumstances in which he has failed to take an action because he was afraid to do so.

The existentialists denied the thesis of causal determinism, according to which all human actions are the inevitable result of antecedent causes. They also denied that there was any such thing as a natural moral law. Existentialists believed in what Kant called spontaneous freedom: we human beings have freedom, and we are morally responsible for what we are and what we do. As individual human beings, we define our own moral universe. According to existentialists, we create our own values. Often we want to give those values a "foundation" in being, in objective facts about the world. However, to do so would amount to bad faith because it would ignore the metaphysical fact that what we value emerges from our own free choices. As free beings we can isolate particular situations which we experience as incomplete and as calling for action on our part.

> If human beings are not naturally good, no more are we naturally evil. We are nothing, at the outset. Those aspects of human beings which are good or evil emerge from the way men and women assume their liberty or deny it. Good and evil do not emerge from nature; they are not given. There is nothing in bare factual reality to afflict us; it is neither sad nor gay. Facts are facts, nothing more, and what matters is the way in which men and women emerge from their situation.
> (ESN, 37)

There is no fact about the world of objects which amounts to a value requiring us to act in one way or another. Values emerge from free choice.

> It follows that my freedom is the unique foundation of values and that *nothing*, absolutely nothing, justifies me in adopting this or that particular value, this or that particular scale of values. As a being by whom values exist, I am unjustifiable. My freedom is anguished at being the foundation of values while being itself without foundation. . . . Anguish before values is the recognition of the ideality of values.
> (JPS, 127)

Every human being must seek to create a meaningful way of existing in the world. If life has meaning, it is because we give it meaning. There are no commandments written anywhere, telling us what to do in this world. We are thrown into the world, hurled into all this responsibility which, properly understood, may cause us anguish.

Although we are not just objects or things, we human beings have a strong tendency to think of ourselves as things. We often lapse into bad faith, deceiving ourselves, allowing ourselves to believe that there is some fixity in our nature or our situation which "makes" us act as we do. We value things, make commitments, and undertake projects – and this is all fine, provided we do not forget that these aspects of the world represent our own freely chosen undertakings. Sartre says:

> We discover ourselves, then, in a world peopled with requirements, in the heart of projects "in the course of realization." I write. I am going to smoke. I have an appointment this evening with Peter. I must not forget to reply to Simon. I do not have the right to conceal the truth any longer from Claude. All these trivial passive expectations of the real, all these commonplace, everyday values, derive their meaning from an original projection of myself which is my choice of myself in the world.
> (JPS, 128)

Consciousness is tied to the world and to the human situation in the world – but in such a way as to reinforce the distinction between it and the world. Constantly moving and shifting, consciousness should not be understood in terms of knowledge because knowledge is too fixed. There are three kinds of consciousness:

1. unreflective consciousness (example: I am aware of the wind blowing through the trees.)
2. reflective consciousness (example: I ask whether it will still be windy later in the afternoon and what I should do for the next few hours.)
3. being-for-others (example: I ask myself what my friends think of my marriage.)

Because we can always pose questions, we can move from unreflective consciousness (just absorbed in Being) to reflective consciousness (detaching ourselves, Nothingness) at any time. We may, then, think of ourselves as creatures suspended between Being and Nothingness.

When we see ourselves as we suppose ourselves to appear in the eyes of others, we may regard ourselves as fixed ("I am a philosopher; I am a mother; I am a peace activist; I am the author of four books, . . .") But such labels are misleading because they suggest that there is some definite "thing" that one is. Thinking of ourselves in terms of such categories, we may forget that we are thinking creatures, beings-for-ourselves. We can redirect our consciousness at any time, define the world in new ways, and launch ourselves into the future by undertaking new projects.

The human mind is not an unobservable something (X) hidden underneath the skull. Nor is it reducible to its outward manifestations in the behavior of a person. As conscious beings, we have a capacity to grasp and understand situations in various ways and to define ourselves by the way we project ourselves into the future. Philosophy can teach us to understand our nature as free and conscious beings who have no fixed essence and are responsible for defining our position in the world of being. Philosophy is a kind of systematic purifying reflection on ourselves and our world. Practised properly, it should help us to emerge from a condition of bad faith.

Sartre and Beauvoir repeatedly emphasized that our life tasks and projects cannot be known to us by a study of things. Values are not written in the sky or engraved on the ceiling of heaven. Rather, the existentialists claimed, values are constructed by human beings who make choices about how to live. To value something is to seek through it to achieve a certain stabilization of one's own being. For instance, if I value the grain elevators that have for many decades characterized the prairie landscape, I may set out to photograph them. I thus devise a project for myself, make a free choice to undertake this activity, because of a value I have given to these old buildings. The value I place upon them comes from me; it is not a fact about them. There is a sense in which what I undertake emerges from my opposition to certain facts. I decide to act because I perceive a certain lack in the world as it is. Other people, deeming the grain elevators inefficient in the contemporary economy, are threatening to tear them down. My project represents my own interpretation of the past and present; in undertaking it, I become active in the world, trying to effect change, moving into the future on the basis of my own values and choices.

Inter-personal relationships are a prominent theme in French existentialist works. On this topic, Beauvoir and Sartre were influenced both by Cartesian philosophy and by Hegel's Master/Slave dialectic. They believed that we are unable to prove by a strict logical argument that other people are conscious. However, this conclusion did not commit them to philosophical solipsism (the idea that "I" is a solitary consciousness, alone in the universe with its own ideas). Rather, they believed that our own personal existence has features that presuppose the existence of other human beings. My own state of mind could not be what it is, were I not a human being living among other human beings with whom I interact and to whom I try to respond. Emotions such as shame and pride presuppose that other people are aware of me and that I am aware of them being aware of me. When I feel ashamed or proud, I see myself and react to myself, much as I think I am seen by other people. Being seen just as I am by other people is somewhat threatening, because what they see is my body, not my conscious self.

Sartre may be accused of a kind of emotional solipsism, because his philosophical works and his fiction give a confrontational depiction of inter-personal relations. In *Being and Nothingness* other people appear as threatening and imperfectly understood adversaries. (Beauvoir's work differed significantly from Sartre's in this respect.) Following the early stages of Hegel's Master/Slave dialectic, Sartre described encounters with other people as confrontational; each self tries to dominate or destroy the other. A central problem in personal relationships is the human tendency to see other people as objects and not credit them with their true metaphysical status as subjective thinking beings. Each human being tends to objectify other human beings, turning them into things, and neglecting the fact that they are conscious and free subjects. In an encounter with another person, there is always the implicit threat that he will label me, fix me in some way, and in that sense turn me into an object. I am a conscious, free subject, capable of choice; but for him I can so easily be only one object among others – an in-itself rather than a for-itself. Knowing that my existence is jeopardized in this way, I feel threatened, and may try to dominate the other person in an attempt to prevent him from dominating me. With this mutual risk of objectification, personal relationships may imply a kind of ongoing warfare.

In *Being and Nothingness* Sartre describes seeing a man in a garden and realizing that this man, the Other, is himself a conscious being. The phenomenon makes a kind of gap in Sartre's world, because he cannot be conscious of the garden scene as the other man is.

> The grass is something qualified; it is *this* green grass which exists for the Other; in this sense the very quality of the object, its deep, raw green is in direct relation to this man. This green turns toward the Other an aspect which escapes me. I apprehend the relation of the green to the Other as an objective relation, but I cannot apprehend the green *as* it appears to the Other. Thus suddenly an object [the man] has appeared which has stolen the world from me. Everything is in place – everything still exists for me – but every-

> thing is traversed by an invisible flight and congealed in the direction of a new object. The appearance of the Other in the world corresponds therefore to a congealed sliding of the whole universe, to a decentralization of the world which undermines the centralization which I am simultaneously effecting.
> (JPS, 192)

The fact that Sartre's perceived world, the garden, is also a world for this other person means that his perceived world is no longer simply *his* world. The man is a measurable distance away from him, and within this space is the "disintegration" of "his" universe.

> We are not dealing here with a flight of the world toward nothingness or outside itself. Rather it appears that the world has a kind of drain-hole in the middle of its being and that it is perpetually flowing off through this hole.
> (JPS, 192)

The grass and trees that appear to Sartre appear also to this other man, and Sartre cannot know how they appear to the Other; it is as though that man's presence creates a gap in Sartre's world. Worse yet, the Other can see Sartre and make Sartre into an object of his consciousness, thus treating Sartre as a thing and not as a conscious person. The look of the Other, who cannot comprehend Sartre's subjective consciousness, but only his physical being in the world, can reduce Sartre to a thing.

> For the Other, I *am seated* as this inkwell *is* on the table; for the Other, I *am bending over* the keyhole as this tree is *bent* by the wind. Thus for the Other I have stripped myself of my transcendence.... My original fall is in the existence of the Other.
> (JPS, 201)

If the Other categorizes Sartre with some label, he reduces him, ignoring that fact that he has many possibilities. Thus Sartre comes to say that the Other is "the hidden death of my possibilities." On this view, what is alarming about the Other is that the Other's consciousness means that aspects of Sartre's world (how it appears to the Other) and Sartre's very self (how he appears to the other, how he may be labelled or categorized by him) are removed from Sartre's control. Sartre is a conscious and free being, but since the Other is also a conscious and free being, Sartre's freedom is not total.

> With the Other's look the "situation" escapes me. . . . I *am no longer master of the situation*. Or more exactly, I remain master of it, but it has one real dimension by which it escapes me, by which unforeseen reversals cause it *to be* otherwise than it appears for me. . . . The appearance of the Other, on the contrary causes the appearance in the situation of an aspect which I did not wish, of which I am not master, and which on principle escapes me since it is *for the Other*.
> (JPS, 203-4)

What is disappointing for Sartre, and what leads to his emotional distancing from other people, is the fact that *other people entail his own lack of control over a situation*. Interestingly, and very significantly, this theme of anticipated control and disappointment with the loss of control does not appear in Beauvoir's own work, where accounts of inter-personal relations are quite different.

Jean-Paul Sartre and Simone de Beauvoir

Beauvoir is sometimes labelled as a disciple of Sartre's rather than as an original philosophical thinker in her own right. She did rely heavily in all of her writings on the existentialist ideas described in Sartre's *Being and Nothingness*, but this is not to say that she was merely Sartre's disciple. Beauvoir was closely involved with the development and editing of all of Sartre's ideas between 1930 and 1960. During most of those years she spent several hours each day discussing philosophical, literary, and political problems with him. She helped him with research, spending hours in the library pouring over Hegel. Throughout his life Sartre published virtually nothing that she had not closely edited first. Given this substantial participation, Beauvoir was no disciple; she was Sartre's partner and colleague.

In the decades when Beauvoir was doing this work, many people naturally assumed that a woman in a partnership would take on many mundane chores for no recognition, and that all the original ideas would emerge from the man. Beauvoir contributed to this interpretation herself when she insisted that it was Sartre who was the philosopher, that she herself was a writer, and that Sartre and not she had created an original philosophical system. To be sure, Beauvoir was a writer, but her essays and books, as well as her contributions to the work regarded as Sartre's own, show clearly that she was also a philosopher. For fifty years, Beauvoir was Sartre's closest colleague, the person on whom he was most dependent for ongoing philosophical discussions, the one who worked with him to develop the ideas for which he became known. For those ideas, Beauvoir also deserves credit. Simone de Beauvoir was a literary and intellectual figure in her own right, as witnessed by her accomplishments as a widely-read columnist and fiction writer, prize-winning novelist, and active, world-renowned feminist.

Interestingly, even prior to the publication of *The Second Sex*, Beauvoir's existentialism differed from that of Sartre in subtle ways. Whereas Sartre and a number of other existentialists wrote of life as being absurd because human beings have to create their own values and choose their own path in life, Beauvoir never said this. For her, the human situation was not absurd, but rather *ambiguous*. Human situations can be given many different meanings, and from the many possibilities we make choices to create meanings for ourselves. Our lives make sense when we act in the world according to our own choices, undertake projects which launch us into the future, and assume responsibility for our actions. Rather than regarding the existentialist analysis of the human situation as a basis for anguish, Beauvoir saw it as a foundation for optimism. She argued that because existentialism emphasizes human freedom and the many choices open to us, it should not be regarded as a pessimistic philosophy.

Beauvoir also differed greatly from Sartre in her attitude toward the physical world. A keen hiker and traveller, she passionately appreciated the beauties of the natural world. Her attitude to nonconscious being was never one of disgust; she never feared that her consciousness would be absorbed or sucked into a slimy hole, or a viscously demanding world of things. On the contrary, Beauvoir sometimes expresses an almost mystic appreciation of nature.

> There is an original type of attachment to being which is not the relationship "wanting to be" but rather "wanting to disclose being." Now, here there is not failure, but rather success. . . . By uprooting himself from the world, man [the human being] makes himself present in the world and makes the world present to him. I should like to be the landscape which I am contemplating, I should like this sky, this quiet water to think themselves within me, that it might be I whom they express in flesh and bone; and I remain at a distance. But it is also by this distance that the sky and the water exist before me. My contemplation is an excruciation only because it is also a joy. I cannot appropriate the snow field where I slide. It remains foreign, forbidden, but I take delight in this very effort towards an impossible possession. I experience it as a triumph, not as a defeat.
> (EA, 12)

The beauties of the world are so wonderful that she would like to absorb them within herself. She cannot; they are outside her. But this distinctness, the very fact that such things are impossible for human beings to possess, is part of their delightfulness. There is no sense in Beauvoir of the Sartrean wish to *master* the world.

Sartre is occasionally prone to peculiar leaps of logic. For example, in *Being and Nothingness* he argues in effect:

> We can ask questions that have negative answers.
> Therefore,
> Nonbeing exists.
> And
> Humans are placed between Being and Nothingness.

As Sartre's colleague and frequent editor, Beauvoir may bear some responsibility for overblown statements of this type – but it is important to note that they rarely appear in her own philosophical essays.

Nor is Beauvoir trapped in the emotional solipsism which is such a prominent feature of Sartre's thinking. Unlike Sartre, she emphasizes the importance of relationships. Other people are not a threat to one's own subjective existence, but rather a necessary dimension of it. Genuine love and fully reciprocal relationships may be difficult, but they are possible.

Beauvoir's Existentialist Essays

In denying that human beings have a fixed nature, existentialism says that there is neither a good human nature nor an evil one. People become good or evil depending on what they make of themselves and their situations. Reality itself is neither sad nor cheerful; it depends on what we make of it.

> One cannot start by saying that our earthly destiny *has* or *has not* importance, for it depends upon us to give it importance. It is up to man [the human being] to make it important to be a man, and he alone can feel his success or failure.
> (EA, 16)

History is not something that flows along no matter what human beings do about it. We can, and must, act in history. Beauvoir says that there are people whose lives slip by in an almost infantile way – many women are among them. Such people never stop to reflect on themselves and their situations, and do not try to make choices as to how to act in the world. As human agents, we can invest the world with meaning. The world can be a source of joy, and we can be happy when we live with vitality, sensitivity, and intelligence. But these qualities are not ready-made, awaiting discovery by human beings. They emerge from the way we engage ourselves in the world and discover what is there. A truly human existence requires a thrust toward transcendence, a movement from the past and present into the future on the basis of chosen projects and values. In everything we do there is a passing beyond a concrete situation, and we are re-inventing our actions which carry our justifications with them. We choose something that does not exist in the present, and we work toward it.

Moral codes cannot do this work for us. For example, conventional morality tells us to "serve our country" but it does not provide or give us any idea of the sort of country we would choose as ours; nor what would count as serving it; nor what would amount to justice or peace within it. When the Germans invaded France in 1940, French officials had to decide how to respond, and there was no pre-established system of morals to tell them what they should do. Morality is not a collection of rules or commandments; it is a movement from which values have been created. It is this movement that the authentically moral person should make for himself or herself.

> Great moralists have not been virtuous souls, who docilely submitted to a pre-established code of good and evil: they have created a new universe of values from words which were acts, from acts which criticized the world; and they have modified the face of the world more profoundly than kings and conquerors.
> (ESN, 81)

In political action, it should never be forgotten that the only reasonable end or goal is the freedom of human beings as conscious beings. It is absurd to conduct politics as an indefinite set of sacrifices of present generations for the future. If the present had no value, neither could the future have value – because when the future arrives, it will (at that time) be present.

The separation of minds is a metaphysical fact: I am not directly conscious of another's feelings, nor he of mine. But this metaphysical fact can be surmounted. It is possible for people to love each other, to have deeply meaningful friendships, and to stand in relations of solidarity with other people. It is only through relationships with others that we will find the basis of our own being. Beauvoir sought to develop an ethic based on existentialist foundations but insisted *personal freedom* be exercised with concern and respect for the freedom of others. Alluding to Hegel and Sartre, she notes that we may find the existence of the Other threatening initially; we might even start to resent or hate the Other. But such attitudes are naive. If the world were to be taken away from other people, it would be taken from me as well. Beauty provides an example. Beauty in the natural world and in objects of art is more than something to be *possessed* by *me*. Beautiful things could not be what they are were it not for the fact that other people too can experience them as beautiful; they are sources of many possible experiences for others.

> If a man prefers the land he has discovered to the possession of this land, a painting or a statue to their material presence, it is insofar as they appear to him as possibilities open to other men. Passion is converted to genuine freedom only if one destines his existence to other existences through the being – whether thing or man – at which he aims, without hoping to entrap it in the destiny of the in-itself.
> Thus, we see that no existence can be validly fulfilled if it is limited to itself. It appeals to the existence of others.
> (EA, 67)

There is a fundamental distinction between things (the in-itself) and consciousness (the for-itself), but granting this distinction, objects are nevertheless not wholly divorced from consciousness. We respond to them and are aware that other people will do so too; beauty and value appeal to others, not only to ourselves.

The fact that other people exist as free conscious beings helps to prevent us from becoming rigid; they react to us and we in turn react to them.

> Only the freedom of others keeps each one of us from hardening in the absurdity of facticity.
> (EA, 71)

Emotionally and ethically, human beings cannot be separated.

> I concern others and they concern me. There we have an irreducible truth. The me-others relationship is as indissoluble as the subject-object relationship. . . . To will oneself free is also to will others free. This will is not an abstract formula. It points out to each person concrete action to be achieved.
> (EA, 72-3)

Beauvoir refers to the ancient Stoic distinction between things that are within our control and things that are not within our control. (The Stoics were philosophers during the turbulent period that the Roman empire was beginning to decline; they argued that, to retain their peace of mind, people should train themselves not to care about things that were outside their personal control.) She argues that this distinction is ill-founded. It presumes an overly-simple opposition because it ignores the fact of human interdependence in what we do. If I think of myself as a solitary agent, I may conclude that the wellbeing of the poor in my country does not depend on me: there is, after all, little or nothing that I, as an individual, can do about poverty. However, if I understand that actions can be collaborative and collective, I may conclude that the wellbeing of the poor in my country does depend on me, in the sense that it depends on *us* (me and others). We could affect it, were we to work together. During the Second World War, if all European countries had been resigned to Hitler's triumph, Hitler would have triumphed. But because some refused to conform, defined him as an enemy rather than an ally, and fought together against him, Hitler was eventually defeated.

To be free is not to have the power to do anything I like, but rather to be able to surpass the given, to choose how I will move into an open future. Beauvoir offers a moving image of the open future: the sight of children laughing and playing in the midst of poverty and oppression, which she says shows a "living affirmation of human transcendence."

The Second Sex

Beauvoir used existentialism as a foundation for her analysis of the situation of women. The work was not exclusively philosophical; it was based on extensive historical reading, literature, sociological and economic data, and on interviews with women in France and the United States. A central message of the work is already implied in the title. Why are women the second sex, and men the first? Adam was created before Eve in the Biblical story of Creation. The male sex has been first in importance in most human societies. And throughout recorded history, the dominant assumption has been that men just *are*, whereas women are different from men, defined with reference to a male norm.

Beauvoir claims that "Man" is commonly regarded both as the positive (normal and best) pole and as the neutral. (In fact, Beauvoir herself was led by the conventions of the French language to conform to this custom; she often uses "l'homme," the French word for "man," to mean both "male" and "human being.") Throughout human history men have had the power to shape and define the world, and they have defined women as beings Other than the male "norm."

> Man defines woman not in herself but as relative to him; she is not regarded as an autonomous being. . . . She is defined and differentiated with reference to man and not he with reference to her; she is the incidental, the inessential as opposed to the essential. He is the Subject, he is the Absolute – she is the Other.
> (SS, xxii)

Beauvoir distinguishes between *immanence*, those aspects of human life where we are caught in the flow of life and do not reflect or make free choices to undertake projects, and *transcendence*, the human capacity to reflect, choose, and direct ourselves.

> There is no justification for present existence other than its expansion into an indefinitely open future. Every time transcendence falls back into immanence, stagnation, there is a degradation of existence into the "en-soi," the brutish life of subjection to given conditions – and of liberty into constraint and contingence. This downfall represents a moral fault if the subject consents to it; if it is inflicted upon him [or her], it spells frustration and oppression.
> (SS, xxxv)

Like all human beings, women are potentially free and autonomous. But by regarding women as Other, men try to fix them as objects and doom them to a life of immanence. Women's situation is one of conflict between their aspirations as free beings and the tendency of men to treat them as useful sexual and domestic objects, ignoring the fact that they can think and are potentially free and equal human beings. These themes in Beauvoir's work echo Wollstonecraft's complaints a century and a half earlier. Women are so accustomed to this treatment, so isolated from each other, and so easily rendered victims of biology and circumstances that they often submit to the oppression with relatively little resistance.

It is difficult for women to succeed in living the lives appropriate to human beings. The female Other is defined as passive, confronting the active male being; she is regarded as matter as opposed to form; disorder as opposed to order; evil as opposed to good. When there is a distinction, and one side is valued more than the other, women are identified with the aspects of "lower" value. Men's attitude toward women is deeply ambivalent. Men need women for biological and economic purposes; they need and want them for sexual and emotional companionship. In some respects what men need and want is another human being, a conscious being with a free working mind, able to think and act independently. Yet in many other ways, men benefit from women's subservience and oppression. Many want "their" women to be passive and unquestioning, to serve as producers of children, meals, and clean houses while at the same time being objects of sexual passion. Many men want a woman in the role of *wife* (Beauvoir was writing in the late forties) to be both servant and companion.

> Woman thus seems to be the inessential who never goes back to being the essential, to be the absolute Other, without reciprocity. This conviction is dear to the male, and every creation myth has expressed it, among others the legend of Genesis, which through Christianity, has been kept alive in Western civilization. Eve was not fashioned at the same time as the man; she was not fabricated from a different substance, nor of the same clay as was used to model Adam: she was taken from the flank of the first male. Not even her birth was independent; . . . She was destined by Him [God] for man; it was to rescue Adam from loneliness that He gave her to him; in her mate was her origin and her purpose; she was his complement on the order of the inessential. Thus she appeared in the guise of privileged prey. She was nature elevated to transparency of consciousness; she was a conscious being, but naturally submissive. And therein lies the wondrous hope that man has often put in woman: he hopes to fulfill himself as a being by carnally possessing a being, but at the same time confirming his sense of freedom through the docility of a free person. No man would consent to be a woman, but every man wants women to exist.
> (SS, 141)

Throughout most of human history, men have had the power to define women and to shape women's lives. The prevailing assumption among men has been that women should submit to men. In doing so, women will be unfree – but what men want, ironically, is the submission of a free person. Men's expectations about women are demeaning: they reduce women to objects functioning to serve male needs while ignoring women's potential for original action. Men's expectations are also contradictory: men want companions who are servile but equal – and wives who are companions, but servants.

Consistently with her existentialist premises, Beauvoir rejected the suggestion that it is biological factors that keep women in a subordinate position. Beauvoir notes that both men and women have hormones which may affect their behavior. She describes female bodily experience in rather negative terms, emphasizing the unpleasant, painful, and hazardous aspects of menstruation, pregnancy, childbirth, nursing and menopause. These aspects of their physiology have caused women discomfort and tragedy, and have been used to rationalize their inferior status in society. With no legal birth control or abortion in France or the United States at the time *The Second Sex* was written, and limited power over sexual activity within marriage, women were vulnerable to repeated pregnancies, dangerous childbirths, and onerous responsibilities for child-rearing. They were in jeopardy of being slaves to the reproduction of the species, sacrificing their creative and intellectual potential to reproductive functions, falling into lives of immanence and missing their possibilities for transcendence. Wollstonecraft's premature death from complications due to childbirth at the age of thirty-eight was a tragic example.

But for all this, it is the social interpretation of biological differences, not those differences themselves, which are significant for the status of women.

> [T]he facts of biology take on the values that the existent bestows upon them. If the respect or the fear inspired by woman prevents the use of violence toward her, then the muscular superiority of the male is no source of power. If custom decrees – as in certain Indian tribes – that the young girls are to choose their husbands, or if the father dictates the marriage choice, then the sexual aggressiveness of the male gives him no power of initiative, no advantage. The close bond between mother and child will be for her a source of dignity or indignity according to the value placed upon the child – which is highly variable – and this very bond, as we have seen, will be recognized or not according to the presumptions of the society concerned.
> (SS, 36)

For all the biologically-founded discomforts and hazards of life as a female, it is not a woman's body that dictates for her a life organized around deference to men, sex, reproduction, and childcare. It is not the nature of her body that dooms a woman to secondary status in society, but rather the assumptions and practices of that society. Biology alone will not provide the answer to the question: why is woman the Other?

Nor did Beauvoir find a satisfactory explanation of woman's situation in Freudian psychoanalysis. According to Freud, girls notice that they differ from boys in not having a penis. They have no external sex organ that they can treat as a thing with a life of its own – and they want one. Thus girls suffer from "penis envy." Girls eventually seek to satisfy this desire by having babies; the baby is a substitute for the penis. Beauvoir argued against this theory, pointing out that in presuming that girls naturally assume that a penis would be a good thing to have, the theory assumed the inferiority of women rather than explaining it. A penis would be something relatively trivial, hardly worth missing were it not for the much higher status of boys and men within society. What matters for women and girls is not the lack of a penis as a physical body part but the lack of the freedom and power enjoyed by boys and men. If the father were not "sovereign," if boys were not more free than girls, a penis would be nothing to envy.

> In particular, psychoanalysis fails to explain why woman is the *Other*. For Freud himself admits that the prestige of the penis is explained by the sovereignty of the father, and, as we have seen, he confesses that he is ignorant regarding the origin of male supremacy.
> (SS, 49)

What explains the fact that men have almost always and almost everywhere dominated women? Marx's colleague Engels had suggested that it was the institution of property that had led to the subordination of women. Men wanted to pass on their property to their own offspring; to know which children were biologically theirs, they attempted to control the sexuality of women. But the problem with this account is that it presupposes what it attempts to explain: the subordination of women. Engels took for granted that it was *men* who owned property and *men* who sought to limit the freedom of *women* in order to control the transfer of that property to their biological offspring. In these ways he assumed that men were more powerful than women – which was the very thing he purported to explain.

Throughout human history men have been in a position to define women as Other.

> Never have women constituted a separate caste, nor in truth have they ever as a sex sought to play a historic role. The doctrines that object to the advent of woman considered as flesh, life, imma-

> nence, the Other, are masculine ideologies in no way expressing feminine aspirations. The majority of women resign themselves to their lot without attempting to take any action; those who have attempted to change it have intended not to be confined within the limits of their peculiarity and cause it to triumph but to rise above it. When they have intervened in the course of world affairs, it has been in accord with men, in masculine perspectives.
> (SS, 129)

Beauvoir believed that the institution of marriage has served to keep women in a subservient position. In the older ideology of marriage, the woman is a thing to be transferred, to be possessed. In some parts of the world, one man gives a woman to another man in marriage. Such marriages are rarely founded on love. Upon marriage, a woman becomes the vassal of her husband. She swears lifelong sexual fidelity to this partner whose body she has not known before the ceremony; she takes his name, becomes economically dependent on his earnings, and allows her place of residence to be determined by his. Within marriage, men are likely to take the labor of their wives for granted and to rationalize their unhappiness and physical discomfort as inevitable.

According to Beauvoir, after the traditional marriage in which man and wife become a "we" that is in reality a "he," there seems to be no future for a woman. Characteristically, married women have lost their independence. They are likely to be lonely, because the husbands who limit the wive's activities and friendships are often sexually disloyal and provide little meaningful companionship. The predicted path for a married woman is a life of immanence where she is caught in the flow of sex, reproduction, childcare, household management, and meeting the needs of other people. Beauvoir believed that women who have not cultivated the habit of reflection and have never been taught or encouraged to think for themselves are all too easily dominated by their husbands. Many women of talent, engulfed and subordinated in traditional marriages, have been submerged in a world of immanence and lost to humanity. Despite her lifelong partnership with Sartre, Beauvoir never wanted to marry him.

There is a fundamental inequality underlying the traditional marriage. The husband has an opportunity to develop himself through work and action; the wife does not. The notion that Motherhood should be enough to crown a woman's life was not convincing to Beauvoir; nor did she believe that every child was bound to be happy in its mother's arms. Motherhood will be experienced as a worthwhile activity only if children are valued by the surrounding culture and society and only if a mother's work is socially supported in appropriate ways. Beauvoir had harsh things to say about domestic work as a life occupation for women. Cooking can be satisfying on occasion but not when it is a constant labor, and housework is even less satisfying.

> The magic of the oven can hardly appeal to Mexican Indian women who spend half their lives preparing tortillas, identical from day to day, from century to century. And it is impossible to go on day after day making a treasure-hunt of the marketing or ecstatically viewing one's highly polished faucets. The male and female writers who lyrically exalt such triumphs are persons who are seldom or never engaged in actual housework. It is tiresome, empty, monotonous, as a career. If, however, the individual who does such work is also a producer, a creative worker, it is as naturally integrated in life as are the organic functions; for this reason housework done by men seems much less dismal; it represents for them merely a negative and inconsequential moment from which they quickly escape. What makes the lot of the wife-servant ungrateful is the division of labor which dooms her completely to the general and the inessential. Dwelling-place and food are useful for life but give it no significance: the immediate goals of the housekeeper are only means, not true ends.
> (SS, 453-4)

Employing someone else to do the housework and remaining idle is no better. What women need is to be active in the world and to gain some economic independence through meaningful work. Thinking and acting are tied together.

Beauvoir believed that women have not understood their own possibilities. Rarely encouraged to reflect on their situation and rebel against it, many have carelessly and in bad faith accepted the assumption that reproduction, child-rearing, and housework are their lot in life. They have failed to recognize their own freedom and possibilities; they may even convince themselves that they are happy in positions of subordination. In societies with strong traditions of male domination, women have been taught to accept male authority without thinking or reasoning independently, and to put their faith in male heroes. In many love relationships, men are able to retain a sense of individual self and identity, but women are not. They become people who *wait*. As unmarried women, they wait to be absorbed into the emotional and sexual life of a man, and as married women, they wait for that man to come home and have time for them.

Yet even such women, even those who are apparently the most docile creatures, are conscious human beings capable of reflective thought and free action. For all that men may degrade and objectify them, women are not things. A dominated woman is likely, in subtle ways, to deceive and manipulate her man. Like Wollstonecraft, Beauvoir argued that what appeared to be woman's "feminine character" (trivial, lacking in seriousness, vain, oriented towards love, seeking a dominant partner, occasionally deceptive and manipulative) resulted from the choices made in limiting and oppressive situations.

Beauvoir raised the issue of why so very few geniuses in world history have been women. Women, she speculated, are easily reconciled to moderate success; they do not dare aim too high. Often even relatively independent women have so many commitments to other people and household affairs that they do not passionately lose themselves in great projects. Passionate dedication is necessary to accomplish great things. To devote ourselves to original and profound projects, we need to forget ourselves. But to be able to forget ourselves, we need to be firmly assured that for now and for the future we have found ourselves. We need to feel rooted and acknowledged as free and potentially creative beings.

To improve their situation, women must see it clearly and cease to live in bad faith.

> The fact is that the traditional woman is a bamboozled conscious being and a practitioner of bamboozlement; she attempts to disguise her dependence from herself, which is a way of consenting to it. To expose this dependence is in itself a liberation; a clear-sighted cynicism is a defense against humiliations and shame; it is the preliminary sketch of an assumption. By aspiring to clear-sightedness women writers are doing the cause of women a great service; but – usually without realizing it – they are still too concerned with serving this cause to assume the disinterested attitude toward the universe that opens the widest horizons. When they have removed the veils of illusion and deception, they think they have done enough; but this negative audacity leaves us still faced by an enigma, for the truth itself is ambiguity, abyss, mystery; once stated, it must be thoughtfully reconsidered, re-created. It is all very well not to be duped, but at that point all else begins. Woman exhausts her courage dissipating mirages and she stops in terror at the threshold of reality.
> (SS, 709-10)

Because of their discouraging and limiting situation, women thinkers have tended not to ask enough questions of the world. Women need to understand how social customs and male ideologies have objectified them and encouraged them to ignore their potential as free and creative beings. Women need to struggle against the bad faith in themselves that makes them ignore their own possibilities. To begin with, women should not be duped by themselves or others. To go further, they must have the courage to approach reality in all its mystery and ambiguity, and take on great projects.

To produce great art, literature, or philosophy, a person must unequivocally assume the status of a free being and interpret the world from that position. It is hard for women to do this because it is hard for them to find a firm position in the world. A thinker needs a secure location in the world in order to strive to get away from that location.

> The men that we call great are those who – in one way or another – have taken the weight of the world upon their shoulders; they have done better or worse, they have succeeded in re-creating it or they have gone down, but first they have assumed that enormous burden. This is what no woman has ever done, what none has been *able* to do. To regard the universe as one's own, to consider oneself to blame for its faults and to glory in its progress, one must belong to the caste of the privileged; it is for those alone who are in command to justify the universe by changing it, by thinking about it, by revealing it; they alone can recognize themselves in it and endeavor to make their mark upon it. It is in man and not in woman that it has hitherto been possible for Man to be incarnated. For the individuals who seem to us most outstanding, who are honored with the name of genius, are those who have proposed to enact the fate of all humanity in their personal existence, and no woman has believed herself authorized to do this.
> (SS, 713)

Beauvoir is not defending economic or class privilege here – indeed, when she wrote *The Second Sex*, she was a socialist. Rather, she is acknowledging that circumstances pose obstacles to achievement. As an existentialist, Beauvoir continues to emphasize choice and freedom, but in exploring the real situation of women, she has had to recognize that freedom is not absolute. Custom and circumstance restrict what we can do, making some things impossible and others very difficult. It is those who are relatively privileged who have the confidence and the opportunity to reflect on the world as a whole. Until women and others who have been disadvantaged can gain such opportunities, they are unlikely to take responsibility for the state of the world. We do not know what the free woman will produce, because she is just being born.

Consistently with her position that people are interdependent and must concern themselves with each other, Beauvoir did not posit an inevitable rivalry between men and women. Men and women should recognize each other as peers and collaborate in their activities. It is not the nature of men and women themselves, nor their physiology, that makes for evil and bad feeling between the sexes; it is custom, economic arrangements, and poor choices. For the future, Beauvoir predicted new friendships and more equitable relationships between men and women. She insisted that reciprocity between the sexes was possible.

> To emancipate woman is to refuse to confine her to the relations she bears to man, not to deny them to her; let her have her independent existence and she will continue nonetheless to exist for him *also*: mutually recognizing each other as subject, each will remain for the other *another*. The reciprocity of their relations will not do away with the miracles – desire, possession, love, dream, adventure – worked by the division of human beings into two separate categories; and the words that move us – giving, conquering, uniting – will not lose their meaning.
> (SS, 731)

The "miracles" Beauvoir refers to here are those of classic romance. Despite the fact that her work was revolutionary in its time, Beauvoir tends to describe sexual attraction and sexual intercourse in what would now be regarded as old-fashioned terms (giving, conquering, uniting). She is saying that when relations between men and women have become truly reciprocal, men and women will still want to "possess" each other, will still desire each other and dream together.

> [W]hen we abolish the slavery of half of humanity, together with the whole system of hypocrisy that it implies, then the "division" of humanity will reveal its genuine significance and the human couple will find its true form.
> (SS, 731)

Reflecting and thinking about alternatives is the first and most important step towards women's freedom and independence. If human beings lack imagination, we will "depopulate the future," failing to appreciate all our possibilities. What women need and want is not a penis, nor a monopoly over the goods and opportunities enjoyed by men, but to be acknowledged as free human beings who are able to choose projects in the world and move into a future of multiple possibilities.

Thinking

Fiction and Philosophy

In an essay called "Literature and Metaphysics" Beauvoir explored the relationship between philosophical thinking and literature. The fascination of a novel is that in it an imaginary, but concrete, world is developed. As readers we can become immersed in this fictional world, experiencing for a time an alternate reality created by the author. Fiction offers an enrichment of experience: fresh worlds experienced by other minds. To have philosophical doctrines and arguments in a novel would be to risk destroying this imaginative reality. Nevertheless, Beauvoir argued that the metaphysical novel (a form both she and Sartre employed) had much to offer, provided that it was not the didactic presentation of a single philosophical system.

Some metaphysical feelings and attitudes are part of life, as for instance, when a child discovers his body, or when we try to understand our inevitable mortality. There are various ways of making such themes explicit; writing philosophical essays and treatises is by no means the only one. The relation between philosophy and fiction takes us back to a powerful duality in Plato, which Beauvoir beautifully describes. When metaphysics is devoted to defending the reality of Ideas, or Forms, of which the real world is only a deceptive degradation, we find Plato the metaphysician. Plato even argued that poets and storytellers should be banned from an ideal republic because he thought they told false stories about things that were not real. But there is the other side of Plato; he was a poet and dramatist himself, and when he described the dialectical movement that carries us toward the Forms, he integrated his philosophizing with everyday human life. The characters in his dialogues are in realistic situations: at bedsides, in the marketplace, at the law courts, or in the garden.

Beauvoir argued that because there are metaphysical aspects to life as it is lived, philosophical reflections can be successfully integrated into fiction without turning the novel into a dogmatic treatise. In fact, novels can show an aspect of metaphysical experience which would not be manifested in any other way. They can show the subjective, singular, and dramatic character of philosophy-in-life, as a straightforward philosophical treatise cannot. Reality is not perceptible by only one intelligence; different people perceive and respond to it in different ways. In a novel, the author has the means to reflect this plurality by approaching reality through several distinct points of view not her own; several characters may narrate events, as is the case in *The Mandarins*. A novelist is dependent on her readers to follow the narrative and to try to participate in the experiences she offers – including the metaphysical ones. Honestly read and honestly written, a metaphysical novel carries an unparalleled opportunity.

> It emphasizes man and human events in their rapport with the totality of the world; because it alone can succeed in doing what pure literature and pure philosophy both fail to do, and that is to evoke the living unity and living, fundamental ambiguity – this destiny which is ours, and which is written at once in time and in eternity.
> (ESN, 106-7)

Observations: Applying Philosophy

A philosophical theory or outlook may be applied to a new subject, as Wollstonecraft sought to apply the ideas of Richard Price and the Enlightenment generally to the situation of women and the poor at the time of the French Revolution. When Beauvoir wrote *The Second Sex*, she used an existentialist framework to approach the situation of women in the twentieth-century industrialized world. Beauvoir included information from history, anthropology, sociology, and economics; she also described and reflected on the conceptions and myths about women expressed in literary works. Both for *The Second Sex* and for her book on aging (1970), Beauvoir did an astounding amount of empirical research. The situation of women and that of old people cannot be described only with the resources of philosophy; Beauvoir recognized the need for inter-disciplinary research. A vast amount of information is relevant, and that information must be organized and interpreted. In both cases, the result is a synthesis. Beauvoir's approach was inter-disciplinary. Yet at the same time it is correctly described as philosophical due to its synthetic "overview" character and because its interpretive framework was existentialist philosophy. As fundamental concepts in interpreting the situation of women, Beauvoir used such existentialist terms as "being-in-itself," "being-for- itself," "immanence," "transcendence," "freedom," "ambiguity," and "responsibility."

Such an application of philosophical ideas presents opportunities for discovery and change because the phenomena one is trying to describe may not fit the theory. Suppose that one holds a theory, T, that has plausibly described some data, D, and one finds new data, D*, that cannot plausibly be described in terms of T. In this situation, one should re-examine T to determine whether it can reasonably be amended so as to describe both D* and D. When this approach is taken, applied philosophy is not merely a matter of taking theoretical principles and applying them to empirical data. The data can reflect back on the theory and lead one to change it. Thus, interpreting data according to a theory can be a challenging task, posing critical questions and posing opportunities for creative thought.

To a certain extent, this happened with Beauvoir's work on women and the existentialist emphasis on freedom. In examining women's situation, Beauvoir was led to recognize the significance of cultural and economic factors for their freedom; this in turn should have led to qualifications in her convictions about human freedom and possibilities. To a certain extent, it did. She saw women as handicapped by custom, circumstance, and their relative inability to earn their own livelihood, and in these ways "oppressed." However, if they came to understand their situation and realized the sense in which they were free beings, women could make choices and realize other possibilities.

Existentialism is a useful theory for describing some aspects of women's situation – as when Beauvoir wanted to stress that women could choose to live their lives differently. She sought to inspire women to make choices about their own lives and adopt projects in the non-domestic world to give their lives meaning. But existentialism is, at the same time, a peculiar theory for discussing women's "oppression" because it does not acknowledge causal influences on life choices, and the punitive consequences that some choices can have for some people.

Consider, for instance, the case of a battered wife. If she is married to a physically dominant man on whom she is economically dependent, if she has four young children to care for, if that man abuses her sexually and physically, and if she has no independent earning power, what are her options in life? Reading the early existentialism of Sartre and Beauvoir, one might take them to be implying that there is never nothing such a person could do; she is, despite all, responsible for her fate because she is in a situation partly of her own making, and she can simply choose to walk out of it. Such an account seems harsh, inaccurate, and insensitive. Suppose that the battered wife is a person who wishes to be a responsible mother and keep her children fed and sheltered, that she wants to be with them and protect them. Then her range of realistic alternatives may be very small. Some choices may carry with them harsh material consequences – a life of poverty for her and her children; others may bring severe risks – her husband may be so furious at her leaving that he murders her. Such a person is in very difficult circumstances and her ability to shape her own life is limited in significant respects.

In *The Second Sex* Beauvoir acknowledged that socio-economic factors and myths about women did serve to hold women back, that men had assumed the power to define women, that women had been oppressed by male-defined institutions and ideologies, and that they were handicapped by their history and position in society. Given such circumstances, women are nevertheless thinking beings, capable of reflecting and posing questions about the world, and able to make *some* choices. But, to be sure, they are not able to define their own situations or to transcend the world in freedom in quite the way that Beauvoir and Sartre had suggested in their early writings, when they spoke so grandly of people being able to transcend the world of facts to establish their own values and determine their own future.

If people are free to emerge from their situations and circumstances, how is oppression possible at all? Do not the presuppositions of existentialism contradict the very notion that people can be oppressed? The matter seems paradoxical. But perhaps a solution can be found. Oppression is possible because many people are in circumstances from which it is very difficult (though not in every sense impossible) to emerge, and from which their escape is risky and may cost them dearly; and they are in this situation because of law, custom, and practice, as implemented by other people. Oppressed people are still conscious beings, capable of reflective thought and independent action. But that capacity for reflection and independence is compromised by circumstances. Oppressed people still have human freedom, but because of their restricted circumstances, some choices and actions will carry an extraordinarily high cost and may be so difficult as to be, for all practical purposes, impossible.

To some extent, recognizing oppression as a fact of life requires qualifying the existentialist view that all human beings choose how to lead their lives. Nevertheless, existentialism has much to contribute to the analysis of oppression. Most people, even the downtrodden, have in some ways accepted their situation; some have even encouraged it. Many have seen their situation as inevitable, as one to which there is no alternative. Examining our situation from an existentialist perspective can be revealing; there will be aspects to which we have acceded, and aspects we can interpret in various ways; possibilities for witholding consent and different ways – albeit sometimes small – of interpreting our situation and moving forward. It is never literally true that there is absolutely "no choice," even in desperate situations. Even in the worst case, there is one alternative to going on, that of suicide. If we do not choose this, we have chosen to remain alive, and can seek ways of moving forward. The battered wife may remember a helpful neighbor or friend, phone a crisis line, or seek a job as a housekeeper at the other side of the continent. With four children to care for, living in fear, and with limited funds, her options are indeed tragically limited. But there are *some* alternatives that can be considered. A woman who does reflect on her situation is more likely to discover such alternatives, and to understand that she may escape what appeared to be a *fate*.

To think that there is, in a literal sense, *no choice* is to be in bad faith. An existentialist account of oppression is powerful and inspiring on the subject of reflecting on situations from various perspectives, recognizing our own contributions to them, and finding possibilities of acting. As an existentialist, Beauvoir warns that we should not lapse into bad faith and rationalize inaction by telling ourselves we have no choice, using our energy finding the causes of our "fate" and complaining. This warning is as timely and accurate today as it ever was.

Despite her lifelong loyalty to existentialist principles, Beauvoir was not primarily a philosopher with a system. She was rather sceptical of systems and liked to respond to concrete situations. Her writing was generally careful and sensitive to detail. Consistently with her existentialism, Beauvoir rarely applied abstract or general principles to yield dogmatic conclusions about what to do in this or that case. She stressed that we have the power to think, the power to reflect, and to choose a new path. In *The Second Sex*, Beauvoir's most important recommendation for women was that they should seek transcendence through projects they would undertake in the world. Thinking should not be a matter of sitting in an armchair, pondering the fate of ourselves or the world. Rather, it means seeking to understand the world and our situation in order to *act* in response to it, according to our values. Thinking expresses itself in doing, in action, when we use our conscious freedom in attempts to shape our world and our own future. Human thinking will express itself in human work, and it is in this way that men and women will create meaningful lives for themselves.

10

Wittgenstein: Duck-rabbits and Talking Lions

Ludwig Wittgenstein was born in Vienna in 1889, to a wealthy and highly cultured Austrian family. He was the youngest of eight talented children. As a youth Wittgenstein was interested in religion and philosophy and read the German idealist philosopher Schopenhauer. After completing high school in Vienna, Wittgenstein studied engineering in Berlin; from there he went in 1908 to the University of Manchester as a research student in aeronautics. He found his interests shifting to logic and the philosophy of mathematics. When Wittgenstein discovered the logical work of Gottlob Frege and Bertrand Russell, he was captivated by several unresolved problems and paradoxes, and went to study philosophy with Russell at Cambridge.

After several years at Cambridge, Wittgenstein moved to Norway, where he built a small house near Bergen. To this place he returned at several points in later life. When World War I began in 1914, Wittgenstein enlisted in the Austro-Hungarian army, where he served on a ship, in the Austrian artillery, and as an attache to an engineering unit. He was later in an Italian prisoner-of-war camp. Throughout his adventures and ordeals, he continued to work on philosophy and logic, writing his thoughts in notebooks which he carried with him. Those notes were the basis for his first philosophical book, *Tractatus Logico-Philosophicus*, published in German in 1921 and in English in 1922. In this work Wittgenstein sought to describe a fundamental logical language that he believed was implicit in everyday language.

Believing that there was no work remaining in philosophy after the *Tractatus*, Wittgenstein left philosophy at the end of the war. Having given away the considerable fortune he had inherited from his father, he attended teachers' college in Vienna. He taught elementary school in several remote Austrian villages, worked as a monastery gardener, and collaborated with architects to design a house for his married sister in Vienna.

While Wittgenstein was living in isolation in rural Austria, the *Tractatus* was making a considerable impact on the philosophical world. The Vienna Circle, a group of scientifically minded philosophers, had been greatly influenced by the work, and Wittgenstein had extensive conversations with several of its members. In 1929, Wittgenstein returned to Cambridge and was awarded the Ph.D. degree. He began to revise the ideas of the *Tractatus*. In his later work, he shifted to a view of language which emphasized the connection between linguistic rules, meaning, and human customs.

At Cambridge Wittgenstein offered highly unorthodox lectures in which he wrestled aloud with his thoughts. Attendance was restricted to only a few dedicated students. Wittgenstein was driven to philosophize: he was seldom happy unless he was working hard on some new problem about logic and language, and discussing his work with someone who could respond to it. He was determined to develop and express his personal genius, which lay in philosophy and nowhere else. Wittgenstein's compelling personality, moral seriousness, and total commitment to his subject matter had a tremendous impact on many of his students.

When Austria became a part of Hitler's Germany in 1938, Wittgenstein accepted a professorship at Cambridge and took out British citizenship. During World War II, he worked as a medical porter at a hospital in London and assisted a medical research unit in Newcastle-upon-Tyne. At the end of the war, he returned to Cambridge for several more years, lecturing to a new generation of fascinated students. But he grew increasingly unhappy at Cambridge. To teach philosophy was not to philosophize; Wittgenstein called the life of a philosophy professor artificial and a living death. In 1948, he left Cambridge and went to work in Ireland. There, despite declining health, he finished the notes for his second great work, the *Philosophical Investigations*. During the last two years of his life, when he suffered from cancer, Wittgenstein was cared for by friends at Oxford and Cambridge. He continued to struggle with philosophical themes and ideas, and wrote his last notebook entry the day before his death in 1951. Wittgenstein's last message for his loyal friends was, "Tell them I've had a wonderful life."

From his extensive notebooks, embodying many years of labor, Wittgenstein's literary executors have published many works, including *On Certainty, Zettel, Remarks on Colour, Culture and Value,* and *Remarks on the Foundations of Mathematics.*

Wittgenstein developed two quite distinct theories of logic and language. Both were highly influential during and after his life.

The Early Philosophy of the *Tractatus*: Propositions and Pictures

In his early work, Wittgenstein sought to answer the question of how language can make true statements about the world. When he worked out his answer, Wittgenstein was greatly influenced by an account he had read about a court case in Paris, where motor vehicle accidents were reconstructed using toys and dolls to make a model. Wittgenstein came to believe that language can make a true or false statement about the world because it offers a picture of the world.

> 2.19 Logical pictures can depict the world.
> 2.2 A picture has logico-pictorial form in common with what it depicts.
> 2.201 A picture depicts reality by representing a possibility of existence and non-existence of states of affairs.
> (TLP)

If X is a proposition and Y is a state of affairs, then X can be a picture of Y if and only if X has features which are related in the appropriate way to the features of Y. For X to depict Y, there must be something in common between them. This is their common pictorial form or logical form. There is a correlation between the signs used to for-

mulate X and the objects in the world, in just the way that in a model of a traffic accident, there is a correlation between the toys used to make the model and the cars and people in the real event.

When he wrote the *Tractatus* Wittgenstein did not wonder how signs and objects were connected. Later this question was to bother him enormously.

If X is the proposition 'The blue truck hit the brown car' and Y is the state of affairs in which the blue truck hit the brown car, then the words in X are correlated with the objects in Y in such a way that X offers a picture of Y. Because it is expressed in words, the proposition makes thought expressible in a manner accessible to the senses. We can see or hear words; our thought is manifest in them. The names in the proposition are correlated with the objects in the world; if the proposition is true, it pictures the state of affairs in the world. If it is false, it does not, but it still pictures a possible state of affairs in the world. The word "car" may be regarded as a physical entity, and as such, the word is a *sign*. When a sign is used in a proposition which is thought, it represents an object (the word "car" represents a car) and it is then a *symbol*.

Because we *think*, we are able to use signs as symbols; words can represent things, and propositions can depict situations in the world. Thought connects language to the world. But language does not always reveal the nature or form of our thoughts, which connect language to reality. Sometimes our language disguises the real logical form which underlies the appearances of our ordinary speech.

> 4.002 . . . Language disguises thought. So much so, that from the outward form of the clothing it is impossible to infer the form of the thought beneath it, because the outward form of the clothing is not designed to reveal the form of the body, but for entirely different purposes.
> The tacit conventions on which the understanding of everyday language depends are enormously complicated.
> (TLP)

Consider, for instance:

> Peabody is in the auditorium.
> Nobody is in the auditorium.

"Peabody" is the name of a person. "Nobody" may appear at first glance to play a similar naming role, because it is a noun-like word occupying the position of subject of a sentence. This superficial grammatical similarity may lead us to ask, "Who is Nobody?" Does the word "Nobody" name a peculiar kind of object, in much the same way in which the word "Peabody" names a person? A superficial consideration of the grammar might lead us to think so, but that would be a mistake. "Nobody" is not the name of any person or being! One way to reveal the mistake is through logical interpretation.

> Peabody is in the auditorium = There is someone called Peabody and that person is in the auditorium.
> Nobody is in the auditorium = There is no person who is in the auditorium.

Sartre's argument that because we can answer a question negatively there is such a thing as nonbeing or nothingness seems to have been based on this sort of mistake; "nonbeing" is treated as the name of a certain "thing."

There is no ideal language in which every element corresponds to an object in the world. But in his early philosophy, Wittgenstein believed that implicit in everyday language there must be a language which has the structure described in the *Tractatus*, in which each name refers to an object in the world, and propositions picture states of affairs. Only in this way can language picture the world and have meaning.

Logical words like "not," "and," "or," "if," and "all" do not point to objects in the world. Such words serve as structural devices which allow us to make complex propositions from simple ones. 'The car is blue' and 'The truck is brown' are simple propositions; 'The car is blue and the truck is brown' is a complex proposition formed by combining these two simple propositions, using "and" as the linking word. The role of "and" can be defined *truth-functionally* (in terms of whether the component statements are true or false): the compound statement 'The car is blue and the truck is brown' is true when, and only when, the car is blue and the truck is brown. If either or both of the elementary propositions is false, the compound statement is false.

B	U	B.U
T	T	T
T	F	F
F	T	F
F	F	F

Wittgenstein invented a device called the truth-table to display such relationships. In the example that follows, "B" represents 'The car is blue;' "U" represents 'The truck is brown;' and "." represents "and." When B is true and U is true, B.U is true. When B is true and U is false, B.U is false. And so on.

An elementary proposition combines two names, and is either true or false. Complex propositions have meaning because they are formed from elementary ones. We can calculate the truth or falsity of any other propositions from these elementary ones because all complex propositions are (on this theory) truth-functional compounds of elementary propositions. If we had a list of all the elementary propositions and could compare each one with the world to determine whether it was true or false, we would be able to derive a complete description of the world. Names in language are signs for simple objects.

In the *Tractatus*, Wittgenstein understood a proposition to be a set of physical marks on the page arranged according to rules which reflect logical form. Consider, for instance, the proposition 'John is taller than Fred.' Taken individually, the words used to point to John and Fred represent objects in the world. Taken together with the relation "is taller than," they state a proposition which provides a picture: they say what the world is like or might be like. For a proposition to have "sense" it must say how something is or could be in the world and be capable of being true or false. A proposition depicts the facts that it describes. If it is true, it depicts a situation in the world. If it is false, it offers a picture of what the world would be like if it were true.

> 4.023 A proposition must restrict reality to two alternatives: yes or no.
> In order to do that, it must describe reality completely.
> A proposition is a description of a state of affairs.
> . . .A proposition constructs a world with the help of a logical scaffolding, so that one can actually see from the proposition how everything stands in logic *if* it is true. One can *draw inferences* from a false proposition.
> (TLP)

Whether a proposition is true or false can be known only when it is compared with reality. If it agrees, or corresponds, with reality, it is true; if it does not, it is false. According to the *Tractatus*, each fact has just one logical form and can correctly be depicted by only one proposition. Although there are thousands of languages in the world, underlying all this variety is one and the same logical language. Logic is wholly present in any language that makes sense. A language that does not make sense is no language at all.

We cannot just invent logic. At a deep level, our logic must reflect the logical structure of the world. At the surface verbal level, we have choices about signs. For example, the word "Socrates" would not have to name Socrates; that very man, the teacher of Plato, might have been called Zeno instead. And the word "snub-nosed" would not have to refer to the sort of nose Socrates had. We could have used "bub" to mean what "snub" means and "wose" to mean what "nose" means. But given that "Socrates" and "snub-nosed" have been selected as signs to symbolize that person and that sort of nose, it is not an arbitrary matter that there is a thought and a proposition, 'Socrates is snub-nosed,' and there is no thought and no proposition, 'Snub-nosedness is Socrates.' Logical form underlies the rules of language and guarantees that symbols will be used to make sense.

Saying and Showing

When he wrote the *Tractatus*, Wittgenstein believed that a proposition has "sense," or says something, only when it pictures a fact and can be determined to be true or false on the basis of a comparison with reality. Interestingly, the propositions of logic itself do not, on this definition, have "sense." They do not say anything. Consider, for instance, the Principle of Non-Contradiction: that no proposition can be both true and false. Using "-" to represent "not" and "." to represent "and," we may state this principle as "-(P.-P)". We can make a truth table to represent it.

P	-P	P.-P	-(P.-P)
T	F	F	T
F	T	F	T

If P is true, P.-P is false and -(P.-P) is true. The compound propositions have the same values when P is false. The Principle of Non-Contradiction, stated in this way, turns out to be a *tautology*. A tautology is an expression which does not depict any situation in the world and which is "true" regardless of what the world is like. Being "true" in all circumstances, a tautology does not give us any information about how things are in the world; we do not have to check with the world to see whether it is true. Thus it "says nothing." A *contradictory* proposition (for example, 'The cat is on the mat and the cat is not on the mat') would turn out to be "false" no matter what the world was like, as does 'P.-P' on the truth table.

Because they do not depict anything, neither tautologies nor contradictions have "sense," in the technical way in which Wittgenstein understood this term in the *Tractatus*. They do however "show something," much as the truth table above shows that -(P.-P) is a tautology and P.-P is a contradiction.

> 4.4611 Tautologies and contradictions are not, however, nonsensical. They are part of the symbolism, just as '0' is part of the symbolism of arithmetic.
>
> 4.462 Tautologies and contradictions are not pictures of reality. They do not represent any possible situations. For the former admit *all* possible situations, and the latter *none*.
> (TLP)

Thought and language cannot depict logic itself, because logic is a matter of pictorial form and no picture can depict its own pictorial form. The proposition 'The cat is on the mat' says that the cat is on the mat. But it does not, and cannot, *say* that it says the cat is on the mat. It *shows* this. A proposition cannot say what its own logical form is, though it can show this form. A tautology does not present a picture of reality and should therefore not strictly be called true; a book about logic will include tautologies which *say* nothing but *show* something about logic.

> 6.12 The fact that the propositions of logic are tautologies *shows* the formal – logical – properties of language and the world.
> (TLP)

In German, English, and other natural languages, there are sentences which look as though they should state propositions but do not, because they do not depict any states of affairs. They do not say how things are. These sentences include the sentences of logic, mathematics, ethics, and philosophy. Since they do not picture facts or states of affairs, they do not in this way have a "sense." They are attempts to SAY what can only be SHOWN.

The Mystical

According to Wittgenstein, when we want to express our attitudes and feelings about religion, art, and metaphysics, we run up against the limits of language. It is as though we encounter the realm of the transcendental; there is something inexpressible that we want to express. What we want to say cannot be said, because there are no facts to be pictured; it can only be shown. This is the mystical.

> 6.522 There are, indeed, things that cannot be put into words. They *make themselves manifest*. They are what is mystical.
> (TLP)

Good and evil may show themselves in the world, but we cannot use factual propositions to make statements about value. In ethics, there are no true or false propositions, because ethics does not deal with facts. Ethics is about the significance of facts, and this is inexpressible.

> 6.41 The sense of the world must lie outside the world. In the world everything is as it is, and everything happens as it does happen: *in* it no value exists – and if it did exist, it would have no value.
> If there is any value that does have value, it must lie outside the whole sphere of what happens and is the case. For all that happens and is the case is accidental.
> What makes it non-accidental cannot lie *within* the world, since if it did it would itself be accidental.
> (TLP)

Beauvoir, Sartre and other existentialists did not believe that values were to be found in facts. Interestingly, Wittgenstein had a similar view on this issue: he believed that we could not get our values from facts. Unlike the existentialists, however, Wittgenstein did not believe that values could be created by human choices.

> 6.42 And so it is impossible for there to be propositions of ethics.
> Propositions can express nothing that is higher.
> 6.421 It is clear that ethics cannot be put into words.
> Ethics is transcendental.
> (TLP)

Wittgenstein wrote much of the *Tractatus* while he served as a soldier in World War I. Knowing this, it is especially moving to read his remarks about death.

> 6.431 Death is not an event in life: we do not live to experience death.
> If we take eternity to mean no infinite temporal duration but timelessness, then eternal life belongs to those who live in the present. Our life has no end in just the way in which our visual field has no limits.
>
> 6.4312 Not only is there no guarantee of the temporal immortality of the human soul, that is to say of its survival after death; but, in any case, this assumption completely fails to accomplish the purpose for which it has always been intended. Or is some riddle solved by my surviving forever? Is not this eternal life itself as much of a riddle as our present life? The solution of the riddle of life in space and time lies *outside* space and time.
> (TLP)

Facts cannot tell us what life means. If the meaning of life is a riddle, it would not be solved by facts, even if we were to live forever.

Wittgenstein felt religion and ethics intensely. He was a profoundly spiritual person, haunted throughout his life by his personal imperfections, constantly struggling to lead a life of integrity. What he is trying to say in the *Tractatus* about ethics is that the attitudes and actions that are right for a person are not to be found in the world of facts. Within this life, there is no factual solution to the problems of life. So what is the "answer?"

> 6.521 The solution of the problem of life is seen in the vanishing of the problem.
> (TLP)

The only way in which we will find a solution to our questions about the meaning of life is that we may some day not concern ourselves any longer with them.

The *Tractatus* itself was a work of logic and philosophy and was thus, on Wittgenstein's own view, a body of propositions "without sense." He recognized and faced this problem in his dramatic ending to the work. The correct method in philosophy, Wittgenstein suggested, would be to say only things that could be said with sense. (At this stage of Wittgenstein's philosophizing, though not later, this meant propositions of natural science.) Then, when someone wanted to say something more metaphysical, one would demonstrate to him that he had not given a meaning to certain signs he was trying to use. Such a method might be felt by the respondent to be unsatisfying, but it would be strictly correct. Rightly understood, philosophy is not a body of propositions but an activity of clarification. It should come to an end when language and logic are correctly understood. As for his own work in the *Tractatus*, Wittgenstein said:

> 6.54 My propositions serve as elucidations in the following way: anyone who understands me eventually recognizes them as nonsensical, when he has used them – as steps – to climb up beyond them. (He must, so to speak, throw away the ladder after he has climbed up it.)
> He must transcend these propositions, and then he will see the world aright.
> What we cannot speak about we must pass over in silence. (TLP)

If we begin by treating the statements in the *Tractatus* as true propositions, we will come to understand the way in which they are without sense (they do not depict any possible state of affairs in the world) and we will then be able to move beyond the stage where we have any need for them. It is as though the *Tractatus* serves as a temporary ladder; after we have climbed it, we will understand that we no longer need it, and we can throw it away.

One may compare this conception of philosophical understanding with the case of a young person searching for the meaning of life. She asks herself, "What does life mean? What is it all about?" Let us suppose that she eventually reaches the conclusion that her question is not a genuine one because it does not make sense to attempt to find something that constitutes "the meaning of life." It is not that life has meaning or has no meaning, but rather that the question, 'What does life mean?' is ill-founded if it leads to an attempt to find a fact, or set of facts, that constitute that meaning. She may decide that there is no answer to the question, but the process of arriving at this conclusion will nevertheless have been enlightening. The process *shows* something that cannot be stated in words.

Thinking, According to the *Tractatus*

In the *Tractatus* Wittgenstein believed that thought could serve to link language to the world. He believed that the fundamental logic he was describing in his work was the language of thought, a basic language underlying natural languages and guaranteeing their sense. At this stage Wittgenstein had no interest in how we are able to connect words to reality, save to say that we do this by thinking. He regarded the process of connecting words to the world as a purely psychological one which was of little importance to logic and philosophy.

In his early work, Wittgenstein's conception of thought is curiously limited on the one hand, curiously split on the other. It is limited because thought is only about simple or compounded states of affairs; we think only about *facts* or *truth-functional arrangements of facts*. It is split because there are factual propositions on the one hand and a vast range of "mystical" topics on the other. The latter category included many matters of intense personal importance to Wittgenstein, such as religion, ethics, and art.

Another oddity in the *Tractatus'* view of thought is that there seems little role for any movement or progress. The *Tractatus* consists mostly of conclusions, announced as from on high – almost as though God himself were telling us how things are. It contains little argument. Yet we know from Wittgenstein's notebooks and letters that he struggled intensely with problems of logic and life during the decade before the work was published. If we were to read the *Tractatus* knowing little of this background, we would find much of it incomprehensible – as did many of Wittgenstein's contemporaries.

The Vienna Circle and Logical Positivism

The Vienna Circle was a group of scientists, mathematicians, and philosophers based in Vienna during the twenties. Their goal was to offer an account of scientific knowledge that would do justice to the central roles of mathematics, logic, and science in human knowledge, while maintaining the view that the fundamental aim of science is to describe the world as experienced. The Vienna Circle included many men who later became eminent: Morris Schlick, Friedrick Waismann, Herbert Feigl, Rudolph Carnap, Otto Neurath, Hans Hahn, and Kurt Godel. The British philosopher A.J. Ayer was also connected with the group. All these people wrote important works and had a lasting impact – persisting to this day – on subsequent philosophy and natural and social science. Their influence has been greatest in the United States, Britain, Canada, and northern Europe. Members of the Vienna Circle studied the *Tractatus* and were influenced by it. Wittgenstein had extensive discussions with Schlick and Waismann and attended some papers in Vienna, but he was never formally a member of this group.

When the Vienna Circle was formed, idealist philosophy in the style of Hegel still dominated philosophical teaching, research, and writing in Germany and Austria. The members of the Circle regarded idealist philosophy as fuzzy, vague, and unscientific. They wanted philosophy to shed its metaphysical trappings and become scientific. According to their doctrine of *logical positivism*, knowledge was either logico-mathematical or empirical and scientific. There was nothing in between. (This idea had been put forward by Hume, whose empiricist philosophy influenced the logical positivists.) Wittgenstein's view, in the *Tractatus*, that the only meaningful propositions were those that described facts in the world, seemed to the logical positivists to be close to their own ideas. According to logical positivism, meaningful thought will be either logical or empirical (scientific) and there is nothing else – no metaphysics, no ethics, no religion, no poetry. When people think that they are making meaningful claims in such areas as religion, ethics, and metaphysics, they are deceiving themselves. Mathematics, logic, and science are all there is so far as knowledge and meaning are concerned, and philosophers should be content to describe the structure of logical and scientific knowledge.

The logical positivists formulated the Verification Principle, which they regarded as an articulation of their theory of meaningfulness. According to the Verification Principle, a proposition is meaningful if and only if we can verify or disconfirm its truth. Its meaning is determined by our method of verifying it. Statements in poetry, religion, and ethics cannot be verified or disconfirmed; thus, according to logical positivism, they have no meaning. They are either nonsense or, at best, expressions of emotional responses. The logical positivists applied this theory to religious claims and to idealist and existentialist metaphysics, with dramatic results. On their account such claims as 'God created the world;' 'Being may absorb me;' 'Nothingness exists;' 'Mankind is thrown between Being and Nothingness;' and 'The Absolute is beyond time and history' are neither true nor false. They are strictly meaningless. What people regard as propositions of ethics serve at best to express attitudes and emotions; they do not make claims which could be true or false.

The Verification Principle is now regarded as crude and unsatisfactory. There are many problems with this principle. A major one is that it cannot account for its own meaningfulness. The Verification Principle is neither a truth of logic and mathematics, nor an empirical principle verifiable by sense experience. So according to its own standard for meaningfulness, the Verification Principle turns out to be meaningless! Nevertheless, logical positivism is still discussed by philosophers and social scientists, if only because they are so determined to convince themselves that it is an incorrect view of meaning and knowledge. Many influential members of the Vienna Circle left Germany and Austria during the Nazi period and moved to North America and England, where they became leading philosophers in the immediate post-war period. It was partly due to their influence that the positivist desire to make philosophy more scientific has had a tremendous impact on twentieth-century philosophy.

Although Wittgenstein's early work was of great interest to the members of the Vienna Circle, he was not a member of the Circle and it would be a mistake to regard him as a logical positivist. Wittgenstein never accepted the view that the claims of ethics, religion, and metaphysics are meaningless. He emphasized the mystical, and argued that there are important aspects of thought and life that can be "shown," even if they are not "said." Despite its link between meaning and describing facts, the philosophy of the *Tractatus* is not that of logical positivism. The differences between logical positivism and Wittgenstein's later work are even more pronounced.

Wittgenstein's Later Philosophy

In the late twenties Wittgenstein began to move away from the picture of logic and language that he had stated in the *Tractatus*. He came to understand that there were problems in his early notion that propositions could "picture" facts by having names that corresponded on a one-to-one basis with objects in the world. There are at least three difficulties here. The first lies in the notion of "picture," which is metaphorical and not particularly explanatory. The second is that there are many functions for language; not all words name things, and not all statements depict or purport to depict facts. The third problem concerns the assumption that by thinking we can establish lines of projection connecting words to the world. Wittgenstein later argued that such "projection" was no simple matter.

In the *Tractatus* a declarative sentence gets its meaning by virtue of its truth conditions – that is to say, its correspondence to facts that must hold if it is true. In Wittgenstein's later philosophy, the talk of truth conditions is replaced by talk of the role of language, and the utility of certain social practices. Instead of looking in the world for a fact to correspond to a proposition, Wittgenstein asks: Under what sorts of circumstances is it appropriate to assert this proposition, and of what use is it to us to do so?

Wittgenstein begins the *Philosophical Investigations* by objecting to the view that the individual words in a language name objects, and sentences are combinations of such names. He says that the view that words name objects might accurately describe an extremely simple language – but it is not correct for our language, in which words have many functions. He imagines such a simple language.

> 2. . . . A is building with building-stones: there are blocks, pillars, slabs, and beams. B has to pass the stones, and that in the order in which A needs them. For this purpose they use a language consisting of the words "block," "pillar," "slab," "beam." A calls them out; – B brings the stone which he has learnt to bring at such-and-such a call. – Conceive this as a complete primitive language. (PI)

We may call this small language a simple *language game*. When A calls out "pillar," B brings him a pillar, and thus B is able to help A in his work. In such a case, we might accurately say that words function as names, but "pillar" could also be said to mean 'Bring me a pillar.' But this is a primitive case, without the resources of more complex languages, in which there are many words and many other functions.

Even in an apparently simple case, setting a relationship between a word and the sort of thing it names is more complex than one might think. The most obvious way to define a name is by *ostensive definition*. We point at the object – a pillar for instance – and say "pillar." Then the child learning the language is to make the connection between the thing and the word, and know what the word means. However, many interpretations are possible. The child might attend to the color of the pillar, its location, its lower segment, its "holding up" function, or whatever. What will make a child concentrate on the "right" aspect so that he can learn what "pillar" means? What makes one aspect right and another wrong? It is a matter of social practice and training.

Somehow, children do learn language. They live with adults in a culture which selects some kinds of things for attention, and they learn to use words correctly. Even in the most simple case, where a word is a name, establishing the naming relation cannot be done *only* by pointing. The relationship requires a context in which people use the word in a systematic way. Given the proper circumstances, any sort of word can be taught ostensively – but it is also true that any act of ostensive teaching can be misunderstood.

Understanding is not a matter of having the right mental image. It depends on the circumstances, on the form of life shared by the teacher and the pupil. Ostensive teaching explains the meaning or use of a word only when the overall role of the word in the language becomes clear. Even if there is a characteristic image, feeling, or experience that the child has whenever she hears a word, this mental "something" is not the meaning of the word. Whether a child understands the word is shown by whether she can go on and use it as others do.

In the *Tractatus*, thought was supposed to serve as a kind of ghostly intermediary between a sentence and reality, connecting language to reality.

TRACTATUS	Objects		Names
	O_1	← Thought	N_1
	O_2	← Thought	N_2
	O_3	← Thought	N_3
	O_4	← Thought	N_4

In the *Investigations*, Wittgenstein took the view that language connects thought to reality, because it is only by using language that we are able to think in the first place.

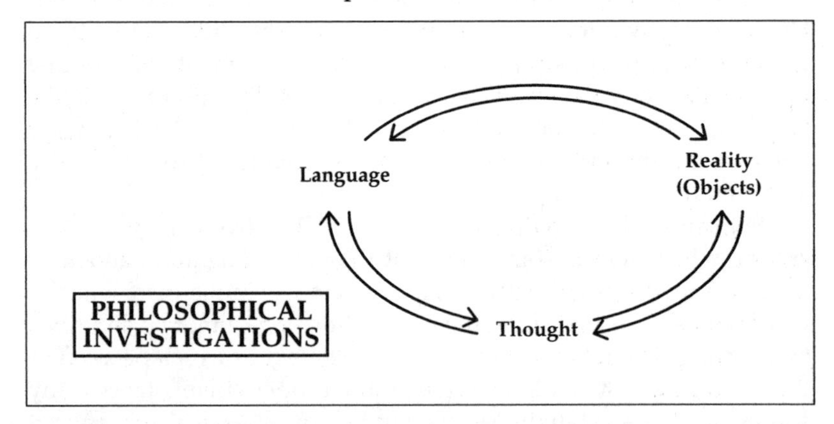

We use words to react and respond to reality, and we understand reality through language. It would be a tremendous over-simplification to say that the function of language is to depict facts. To think about how language is related to the world, we have to look at and appreciate the many functions of language.

> 23. But how many kinds of sentence are there? Say assertion, question, and command? – There are *countless* kinds: countless different kinds of use of what we call "symbols," "words," "sentences." And this multiplicity is not something fixed, given once for all; but new types of language, new language-games, as we may say, come into existence and others become obsolete and get forgotten. . . . Here the term "language-*game*" is meant to bring into prominence the fact that the *speaking* of language is part of an activity, or of a form of life. . . .
> (PI)

The many purposes for which language is used include giving orders, describing objects, stating the measurements of objects, reporting, speculating, play-acting, praying, telling jokes, translating, cursing, greeting, and many more. Logicians and philosophers – including the Wittgenstein of the *Tractatus* – had failed to consider many of these functions.

A Sceptical Problem and its Resolution

When he wrote the *Tractatus* Wittgenstein had assumed that by thought we could make a word mean something, connecting a word to an object. In his later philosophizing, Wittgenstein came to see *meaning* as far more complicated than this. He asked, 'How does a word mean something?' and struggled long and hard to work out the answer. The problem is that there does not seem to be any "fact" – either in the mind or in objects in the world – that can guarantee what a word or sign means.

Consider the simple arithmetic operation of adding. We all know how to add. When we add, we assume that "+" indicates that we are to add and that we know what adding is. We can add properly and get the right answers: 2 + 3 equals 5; 6 + 11 equals 17; 257 + 13 equals 270; and so on. For simple questions we may count on our fingers. For longer ones we have established procedures of carrying that give us the correct results. But what is it, Wittgenstein asks, that guarantees that "+" means just what would make those answers the *right* answers? What "+" means cannot be identified with experiences or mental images that we have when we add. There is no experience or image that is present to us every time we add and serves to mark out what adding is. And even if such an experience did exist, no such experience or image could stipulate a procedure that was to hold for all the *future* cases of addition. No process or state or disposition of the mind guarantees the meaning of "+" either. Even if such a mental process were to exist, it would not show us how to operate in future cases. Nor can the meaning of "+" be guaranteed by a formula: formulas are open to different interpretations. If God himself could look into our minds or heads, he would not be able to see anything that was the meaning of "+".

Thus there is no *fact* that guarantees the meaning of a sign or word. What establishes the fact that a sign means something, and what makes it mean one thing rather than another? There must be some solution to the puzzle because we do use words to speak and communicate; we have a whole way of life in which language has a central role; we know our words mean something. We know how to add; we know that "+" means something definite, and we know what "+" means. But what makes it true that "+" has this meaning?

Wittgenstein imagines a case where a teacher wants his pupil to write down a series of numbers based on adding 2.

> 2 4 6 8 10 12 14 16 18

The pupil continues the series in the way the teacher expects, up to the number 1000. But then – contrary to what the teacher expects – he continues as follows:

> 1000 1004 1008 1012 1016 1020

When the teacher tells the pupil this was not how he was *meant* to do it, the pupil replies that he thought this was what was *meant*, and says, "But I went on in the same way." Suppose that the old examples are repeated and the pupil continues to understand them in his own way. In the pupil's responses, there is a pattern and a system but it is not the same pattern and system as his teacher wanted him to learn.

> 185. . . . In such a case we might say, perhaps: It comes natural to this person to understand our order with our explanations as *we* should understand the order: "Add 2 up to 1000, 4 up to 2000, 6 up to 3000 and so on."
> Such a case would present similarities with one in which a person naturally reacted to the gesture of pointing with the hand by looking in the direction of the line from finger-tip to wrist, not from wrist to finger-tip.
> (PI)

Is there any fact which would make it true that such people would be making a mistake and *misunderstanding* the teacher's directions? Wittgenstein's sceptical paradox is about *what counts as being in accord with the directions*. Who is to say that it is the teacher who understands what "+ 2" means and his pupil who does not? What *does* the symbol "+" mean? What makes it have this meaning rather than another? The pupil has an interpretation and procedure which has its own pattern. There is nothing we can point to – no feeling, sensation, thought, mental process, or formula – that can prove the teacher right and the pupil wrong.

The only solution to this problem is to admit that what makes the normal ordinary interpretation right is just that it is the normal ordinary interpretation. When we add, we use procedures to get the answers we do; we do not amend the pattern every 1000 numbers. The teacher is "right" just because he adds the way most people do. Adding is a social practice that serves us well and involves using the signs for "+" and "2" in just this way – the recognized, acknowledged way that most people do it. If someone does not do it this way, we will not acknowledge him as a person who knows how to add. And it is for this reason that in order for the pupil to learn to add, he must learn to do it *this way*. This is what knowing how to add amounts to.

After a certain point, no more justifications can be given. Wittgenstein says we "follow the rule blindly" – meaning that we follow the rule without having any further rule that instructs us what to do at every stage. When we add 2 to 1000, we get 1002, not 1004, as the right answer. That is how it is done. The sceptical paradox of meaning can be resolved by appealing to custom and practice.

> 201. . . . This was our paradox: no course of action could be determined by a rule, because every course of action can be made out to accord with a rule. The answer was: if everything can be made out to accord with a rule, then it can also be made out to conflict with it. And so there would be neither accord nor conflict here. [If everything were in accord with the rule, then there would be no such thing as following a rule and also no such thing as failing to follow a rule. Anything goes.]
> . . . there is a way of grasping a rule which is *not an interpretation*, but which is exhibited in what we call "obeying the rule" and "going against it" in actual cases.
> (PI)

If someone who has been told to add 2 to 1000 gets 1002, he is said to have done as he was told. If he gets 1004, he is told that he has got it wrong. What it means to add 2 is seen in these social facts. We don't acknowledge that it is right to get 1004 by adding 2 to 1000; and it is just this lack of acceptance that makes that response wrong.

> 202. And hence also 'obeying a rule' is a practice. And to *think* one is obeying a rule is not to obey a rule. Hence it is not possible to obey a rule 'privately;' otherwise thinking one was obeying a rule would be the same thing as obeying it.
> (PI)

> 206. Following a rule is analogous to obeying an order. We are trained to do so; we react to an order in a particular way. But what if one person reacts in one way and another in another to the order and the training? Which one is right?
> Suppose you came as an explorer into an unknown country with a language quite strange to you. In what circumstances would you say that the people there gave orders, understood them, obeyed them, rebelled against them, and so on?
> The common behaviour of mankind is the system of reference by means of which we interpret an unknown language.
> (PI)

If a solitary person were to wish to establish his own private practice of adding, he could make that practice whatever he wanted it to be, and he could go on after 1000 to add 4, getting 1004, 1008, and so on. Apparently, he could make up his own rules. But the problem in this case would be that anything at all would be consistent with those rules. There is no one to say that after 1020, he cannot continue 1028, 1036, 1044 . . . or whatever might strike his fancy. A purely private rule would not be a rule at all, because one could do anything one wanted with it. We might think we could construct a purely private language, but this notion turns out not to make sense.

Private Language and the Egocentric Predicament

The sceptical paradox about meaning can be resolved when language is used in a community, because we can appeal to public practice to say when a rule is followed and when it is not. Thus, rules about words become possible; signs and words are able to mean something and serve as symbols. For one person by himself to set up a language in which words had a regular use and a meaning would be impossible, because there would be no such thing as "regular use." There would be no basis for distinguishing between a correct use and an incorrect use. Anything he wanted to do with his own private word would count as right.

If we consider the context of our own thoughts and experiences, we would at first be inclined to think that there should be nothing easier than to to name something within our own personal experience – to attach a word to a particular sensation, for instance. I might try to give myself a private ostensive definition; say I have a particular sensation of delight and then call it "oof." Isn't this simple enough?

But there is a problem here. For "oof" to mean "TG's particular sensation of delight" there would have to be a regular connection between its correct use and my experiencing just that sort of delight. A regular connection must be systematic; the *same* word must be used for the *same* sensation. But when I have various sensations, who is to say which ones are "the same" as that sensation of delight that was supposed to be called "oof"? There is no one but me to say. I feel various things: pleasure, anticipation, glee, joy, expectation, a sense of success – and only I am to judge which if any of these inner sensations is the same as that sensation of delight. I can make any interpretation or classification at all and there is nothing to say whether my classification is right or wrong. The word "oof" is my word and I use it as I will, to refer to delight, pleasure, joy, expectation, anticipation, or whatever. As my private word, "oof" could mean anything at all – there is no rule underlying its use, and that is just to say that it means nothing.

> 378. "Before I judge that two images which I have are the same, I must recognize them as the same." And when that has happened, how am I to know that the word "same" describes what I recognize? Only if I can express my recognition in some other way and if it is possible for someone else to teach me that "same" is the correct word here.
> For if I need a justification for using a word, it must be one for someone else.
>
> 380. . . . I could not apply any rules to a *private* transition from what is seen to words. Here the rules really would hang in the air; for the institution of their use is lacking.
>
> 381. How do I know that this colour is red? – It would be an answer to say: "I have learnt English."
> (PI)

I have many feelings, images, sensations, and flashes of thought – but these cannot constitute the meanings of words. Language must be public; and in a public language, people have to agree about how words are used. Because a rule gets its content only from general public agreement about what counts as following it, there can be no such thing as a private language. No language could exist in which the meanings of words were an image, sensation, or thought experienced by only person.

This conclusion has dramatic philosophical implications, which we can appreciate if we think back to the philosophy of Descartes. After the arguments of his First Meditation, Descartes was committed to the implication that a person might be a solitary mind, the only thing in the world. Such a mind's solipsistic consciousness would contain ideas, thoughts, and beliefs alluding to an external world, but that external world might be only a figment of his imagination. Other people, the community, and the whole material world might not exist; there might be only the solitary mind with its thoughts and ideas. Wittgenstein argued, in effect, that there is no such possibility. The philosophical fiction of a solipsistic consciousness is founded on a mistake, because it presupposes that a private language is possible. The solipsistic mind could have no language and could not think; it could not even think through the argument of the Cogito.

For a solitary mind to think, it would have to use symbols; signs would have to represent things. Representation requires a rule-governed relationship between a sign and what that sign represents, and a rule-governed relationship requires a community of people using the rule. Thus my consciousness, and use of language to represent the world, is possible only because there are other conscious beings who use language to represent the world. Only in this way is there a difference between what counts as following the rule and what counts as departing from it. If a private language is impossible, the solipsistic consciousness is impossible. Thus the Egocentric Predicament does not arise as a problem for philosophy.

In the Cartesian philosophy, after the Cogito, there is a need for a guarantee that the external world is not illusory. Descartes tried to give that guarantee by offering a proof (an unsuccessful one) for the existence of a good and non-deceiving God. If there is no Egocentric Predicament in the first place, the sceptical problems raised by Descartes in his First Meditation never arise. They do not need to be solved, because they have been dissolved. Wittgenstein dissolved the sceptical problems about material objects and other minds by arguing that they are ill-founded, based on a mistaken understanding of meaning.

To have meaning, words must be used in a community which establishes, by its practices, which uses are correct and in accord with rules; language must be public. For language to be public, there must be people using words in a publicly perceptible world. Human beings in human communities are presupposed by meaning itself. From his resolution of meaning scepticism, Wittgenstein gained a basis for avoiding the Egocentric Predicament and rejecting Cartesian scepticism without appealing to arguments about God. Wittgenstein achieved a kind of certainty in his arguments for conforming with social custom. It should be noted, however, that this was not the kind of individual rationally grounded certainty that Descartes had been looking for.

What is Thinking?

In the *Philosophical Investigations*, Wittgenstein moved away from the conception of thinking underlying the *Tractatus*. He relinquished his earlier conviction that there was a purely absolute logical order in thought, and that this order is the essence of meaning in a logical language. On his later view, language, thought, and experience can be many things in many circumstances. It is not the essential function of language to state facts, and there is no logical essence that enables propositions to picture facts.

It is because we know and use language that we are able to think; language is the vehicle of thought. Given his conclusions about private language, Wittgenstein was naturally sceptical about the suggestion that deaf-mutes might have complicated thoughts. The American philosopher William James had cited the case of a deaf-mute, Mr. Ballard, who had written that before he could speak, he had thoughts about God and the world, asking himself how the world came into being.

> 342. . . . – Are you sure – one would like to ask – that this is the correct translation of your wordless thought into words? Why does this question – which otherwise seems not to exist – raise its head here? Do I want to say that the writer's memory deceives him? – I don't even know if I should say *that*. These recollections are a queer memory phenomenon, – and I do not know what conclusions one can draw from them about the past of the man who recounts them.
> (PI)

One might suppose that since people sometimes think without speaking, they could think even if they did not talk at all. But this notion, Wittgenstein argues, does not make sense. Suppose that a person can speak, and on many occasions we know what he thinks because he has told us. Then on some particular occasion we may have good reason to say he is thinking something that he has not expressed. But that supposition makes sense only because we have spoken to him on other occasions and because he is a user of a public language, which we know that he can speak.

> 344. . . . Our criterion for someone's saying something to himself is what he tells us and the rest of his behaviour; and we only say that someone speaks to himself [silently] if, in the ordinary sense of the words, he *can speak*. And we do not say it of a parrot; nor of a gramophone.
> (PI)

People talk to us, and act in certain ways, and share our way of life. We understand their words and much of their behavior, and we sometimes credit them with unexpressed thoughts. Without a common way of life, we could not understand the words of another. This is the basis of Wittgenstein's charming but puzzling remark, "If a lion could talk, we could not understand him."

Characteristically, when we speak or write we are thinking, but we are not conscious of our thought as something separate. We do not experience thinking as a distinct process which is neither speaking or writing but lies somehow behind them. In ordinary life, we have little reason to conceive of thought as an ethereal or spiritual something going on in a "thinking part." Rather, we think using language, and language provides the form of thought. It is through language that a sign can represent something, and it is this relationship of representation that is necessary for thought. Wittgenstein believed that to imagine thought as an interior spiritual process is to fall prey to an illusion. Of course we have feelings and experiences, we dream, have images, and so on. Wittgenstein was not a behaviorist: he did not argue that there is no inner experience, only that inner experience did not explain our meaningful use of language. Wittgenstein is sometimes called a *linguistic* or *logical* behaviorist, because he argued that our understanding of the language of thoughts, desires, intentions, and beliefs is based on our understanding of behavior and customs. We are aware of the world – we think while talking and acting; we think while writing. And we are sometimes aware of thinking, of thinking hard. (In fact, one of the things that is likely make us aware of thinking very hard is reading Wittgenstein's *Philosophical Investigations*!) To understand thinking, to appreciate what thinking is, Wittgenstein recommends that we look at the various circumstances when we would use the word "thinking" to describe what people do. If we try to understand thinking by looking inside ourselves to discover an extra, mysterious "something," we will get nowhere.

At one point, Wittgenstein considers the peculiar feeling that comes over a person when he contemplates the idea that his thinking might be produced by a process in the brain. He calls it "the feeling of an unbridgeable gulf between consciousness and brain-process" and says that it is likely to occur when we consider certain scientific or philosophical theories.

> 412. . . . When does this feeling occur in the present case? It is when I, for example, turn my attention in a particular way on to my own consciousness, and, astonished, say to myself: THIS is supposed to be produced by a process in the brain! – as it were clutching my forehead. – But what can it mean to speak of "turning my attention on to my own consciousness"? This is surely the queerest thing there could be! It was a particular act of gazing that I called doing this. I stared fixedly in front of me – but *not* at any particular point or object. My eyes were wide open, the brows not contracted (as they mostly are when I am interested in a particular object). No such interest preceded this gazing. My glance was vacant, or again *like* that of someone admiring the illumination of the sky and drinking in the light.
> (PI)

Such introspection is an unpromising way of trying to find out what thinking is.

When we are simply thinking, in daily life, such puzzling matters do not trouble us. We speak, we write, we act – and in doing so, we think. Our words speak our thoughts, and we feel no temptation to postulate an interior mysterious "something" which is going on inside us to guarantee the meanings of those words. It is only when we move away from the particular circumstances in which we act and speak, and forget about how we function in the everyday world, that we are inclined to make assertions like, 'There is always a thought behind the sentence' or 'Pure thought ties language to the world.' Wittgenstein believed that it is because we seek the wrong kind of general understanding that we are led to *hypostatize* thought as a mysterious something that lies behind words. If we think of ourselves as *translating* more primitive thoughts into our thoughts in English we are making a mistake.

> 598. When we do philosophy, we should like to hypostatize feelings where there are none. They serve to explain our thoughts to us.
> '*Here* explanation of our thinking demands a feeling!' It is as if our conviction were simply consequent upon this requirement.
>
> 606. "The expression in his voice was *genuine.*" If it was spurious we think as it were of another one behind it. – *This* is the face he shews the world, inwardly he has another one. – But this does not mean that when his expression is *genuine* he has two the same. (PI)

To understand the difference between a genuine expression in someone's voice and an expression suggesting falsity or hypocrisy, we have to look at the circumstances in which the person is speaking and hear the voice itself. The difference lies in those aspects of the context or circumstances, not in postulated thoughts that are supposed to be inside the person's mind or head.

Towards the end of the *Investigations,* Wittgenstein introduces questions about the relationship between thinking and seeing. There are cases in which we can see the same thing in different ways, seeing it "under different aspects." Here is the famous duck-rabbit:

If we see the figure as a rabbit, the long appendages are ears; if we see it as a duck, they are the duck's bill. The figure is the same, as a rabbit or as a duck; yet it is quite different, because it is seen under different aspects. Thinking and seeing seem bound together in such cases. There is a sense in which we have a new perception when we have seen a rabbit and then begin to see a duck – but there is also a sense in which we have the same perception. We are seeing the same thing, yet not the same thing. Theorizing that althought there is just one figure, there are two different mental images (one of a duck and the other of a rabbit) that we experience does not help to explain matters, according to Wittgenstein. There is just one figure, and we can see it in different ways.

Seeing a real rabbit in a natural landscape requires some organization and knowledge of what we are seeing and its background. When we describe our perception by saying we see a rabbit – "A rabbit!" – we are also expressing our *thoughts.* To understand thinking and perceiving as *distinct* will, in many contexts, be an over-simplification, because much perception presupposes familiarity and knowledge.

> Now, when I know my acquaintance in a crowd, perhaps after looking in his direction for quite a while, – is this a special sort of seeing? Is it a case of both seeing and thinking? or an amalgam of the two, as I should almost like to say?
> (PI, p. 197)

When we spot an acquaintance, we see the crowd, the same crowd as before, but now we see it in a new way.

To understand this phenomenon, Wittgenstein suggests that we must accept that the word "see" is used for many different sorts of cases. We can see various aspects, organize what is seen in different ways, and come to see the same thing quite differently. Consider this figure of a triangle.

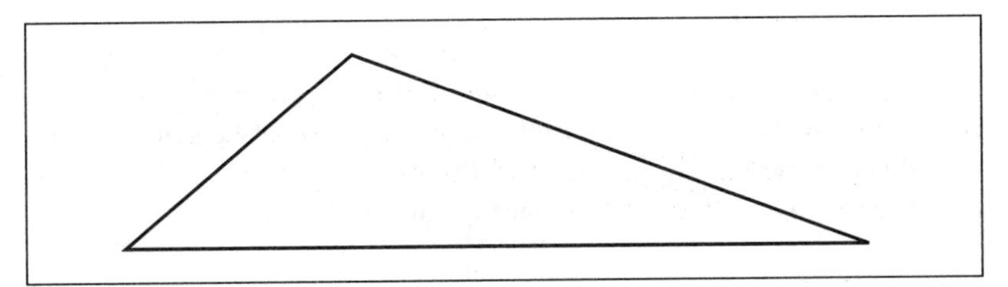

We can see the triangle in different ways. Perhaps there is a triangle-shaped hole. Perhaps it is a geometric solid standing on its base. Perhaps it is an arrow, or pointer. We may be even more imaginative: the triangle could be hanging from something, or we could see it as having fallen over. What we know and expect, and the context we assume as background for this picture, affect our interpretation. This is not to say that there is a separate "act of interpretation" that we are performing when we see something. When we see the triangle as this or that, we simply see it as this or that.

> A triangle can really be *standing up* in one picture, be hanging in another, and can in a third be something that has fallen over. . . .
> This is how we react to the picture.
> Could I say what a picture must be like to produce this effect? No.

> There are, for example, styles of painting which do not convey anything to me in this immediate way, but do to other people. I think custom and upbringing have a hand in this.
> (PI, p. 201)

There is a kind of sensation that is, in a sense, tied to knowledge, concepts, and attitudes. What we *see* presupposes training and beliefs. A similar thing may be said of other senses, such as hearing. It takes a certain understanding to hear a melody as sad. If we hear a melody as sad, we do not first hear it and then superimpose an interpretation, according to which it is sad. We simply hear a sad melody.

> Think of this too: I can only see, not hear, red and green, – but sadness I can hear as much as I can see it.
> Think of the expression "I heard a plaintive melody." And now the question is: "does he *hear* the plaint?"
> And if I reply: "No, he doesn't hear it, he merely has a sense of it" – where does that get us? One cannot mention a sense-organ for this 'sense.'
> Some would like to reply here: "Of course I hear it!" – others: I don't really *hear* it."
> We can, however, establish differences of concept here.
> (PI, p. 209)

There is a sense in which we can see that faces are happy and hear that tunes are sad. There is something in common between such cases and those in which we understand the meaning of a word. Because of our culture, we find some meanings and not others.

How Wittgenstein Makes Us Think

The *Investigations* are demanding reading; they are expressed in many voices and move through questions, allusions, imagined situations, and analogies. The reader must supply many of the thoughts. For Wittgenstein philosophy was an activity of struggling to resolve or dissolve problems, and to see things clearly. It is appropriate that, reading his philosophical works, we ourselves should have to struggle to follow his thinking and work out our own responses.

In the *Investigations* there is no single *voice*. Yes, it was Wittgenstein who struggled to write this work, over a period of nearly twenty years – but the *Investigations* contains many statements and questions that do not directly express his own views. Often Wittgenstein suggests an idea only to criticize and reject it. A suggestion put forward may be that of a philosophically naive person – someone who began to consider a problem and gave his first instinctive response to it. It may be that of a more sophisticated person (perhaps someone influenced by Descartes and his conception of the solipsistic consciousness) who is nevertheless inclined or tempted to hold a naive view. It may be Wittgenstein's own mature voice – or the voice of his earlier self of the *Tractatus*. Wittgenstein often seems to be posing questions to himself, then trying to answer them, and then expressing dissatisfaction with his answers. There is the voice of the interlocutor, who questions Wittgenstein about his views. Something is stated; there is a response; a questioning of that response; then a further response. The whole process is intensely dialectical. Through the tangle of voices, it is a real challenge to us as readers to follow what is being said. We might wonder: why doesn't Wittgenstein just say what he thinks? An obvious answer is that we as readers are not going to be spoon-fed; we have to do a lot of the work ourselves. So far as the *Investigations* are concerned, to read is to think.

Sometimes an authoritative, apparently knowledgeable voice of "correction" is speaking, and the philosophically naive person seems to be answered; this voice, we assume, is Wittgenstein's mature voice. Sometimes a side of Wittgenstein's mature self seems to be speaking; occasionally the temptations of this speaker seem to coincide with those of the philosophically naive person. Wittgenstein often tells us what he is tempted or first inclined to say, only to go ahead and correct himself. He then moves ahead again to raise further questions or offer a fresh example. In the midst of all this, there are themes from other philosophers – Socrates, Plato, Augustine, Descartes, Hume, James, Russell, and Moore – and references to Idealism and Realism. We have to think as we read, posing questions to ourselves, and trying to sort out which voice is speaking. As Wittgenstein questions himself, we have to question ourselves, trying to follow Wittgenstein's words to grasp his intense thinking while at the same time we ask ourselves what is going on. What voice is speaking?

In the following passage Wittgenstein is exploring the question of whether there is an inner object or experience which a person *has* when he imagines something.

> 398. "But when I imagine something, or even actually *see objects, I have got* something which my neighbour has not." [comment from philosophically naive person] – I understand you. You want to look about you and say, "At any rate only I have got THIS." [Wittgenstein, restating view of the philosophically naive person] – What are these words for? They serve no purpose. – Can one not

> add: "There is no question of a 'seeing' – and therefore none of a 'having' – nor of a subject, nor therefore of 'I' either"? Might I not ask: In what sense have you *got* what you are talking about and saying that you have got it? Do you possess it? You do not even *see* it. Must you not really say that no one has got it? [Wittgenstein posing critical questions to the philosophically naive person] And this too is clear: if as a matter of logic you exclude other people's having something, it loses its sense to say that you have it. [Wittgenstein in his authoritative voice]
> (PI)

We follow through this intensely personal dialectic, thinking with Wittgenstein. If we stop to analyze the passage, we as readers must keep track of which voice is speaking – something which is by no means an easy task.

The passage illustrates another prominent aspect of Wittgenstein's style in the *Investigations* and other later writings: the predominance of questions. One scholar counted the questions in the *Investigations* and found 784. Of these only 110 were answered and 70 of these answers were meant to be wrong. So Wittgenstein poses 784 questions, and only answers 40 of them! To complicate matters further, there are many kinds of questions.

Some questions are intended to lead us to an answer, as when Wittgenstein asks the philosophically naive person, "Do you possess it?" He intends a definite answer (no) but does not supply it in the text. Some are questions in the voice of the interlocutor, who implicitly criticizes a view that has been put forward – Wittgenstein's own or another's. Such questions are sometimes answered, sometimes not. When they are not, the reader is left to think about them, trying to work out her own answer. Some questions are genuinely exploratory, formulating a problem which Wittgenstein will try to answer. In other cases, a question is raised as a prelude to a comment on that question itself. Sometimes one question expresses a response to another. A natural response when reading the *Investigations* is to try to answer all the questions. If we do this, we will often find that Wittgenstein's next remark is a comment on our own answer. It is as though there is a dialogue between the text and ourselves. The following is just one of many examples where there is an intense dialectic, in different voices, expressed in Wittgenstein's writings.

> 184. I want to remember a tune and it escapes me; suddenly I say "Now I know it" and I sing it. What was it like to suddenly know it? [Here an exploratory question is posed in the voice of philosophically naive person, which may at this point be his own]

> Surely it can't have occurred to me *in its entirety* in that moment! [Here Wittgenstein responds to this person] – Perhaps you will say: "It's a particular feeling, as if it were *there*" [*Here Wittgenstein imagines the person* speaking back] – but *is* it there? [Here Wittgenstein questions the response; the implicit suggestion is that the answer should be no] Suppose I now begin to sing it and get stuck? – [Wittgenstein proposes another exploratory question] But may I not have been *certain* at that moment that I knew it? [This question puts forward the philosophically naive person's response to the exploratory question] So in some sense it was *there* after all! – But in what sense? [Wittgenstein is questioning that response] You would say that the tune was there if, say, someone sang it through, or heard it mentally from beginning to end. I am not, of course, denying that the statement that the tune is there can also be given a quite different meaning – for example, that I have a bit of paper on which it is written . . .
> (PI)

Another striking feature of Wittgenstein's philosophy and writing style is his use of analogies. Wittgenstein was extraordinarily imaginative in his use of analogies, which are vivid and original, often humorous and charming. Analogies usually function to highlight similarities. When one thing is compared to another, we begin to see it in terms of the other, and we notice aspects we might not have noticed before. Analogies have many functions: they may add interest, offer a vivid and memorable description, explain, or serve as the basis of an argument. To grasp the point of an analogy, we have to think it through, making the comparison that the analogy points to, noting similarities and differences, sometimes really beginning to look at one thing in terms of another.

In one famous analogy, Wittgenstein compared language to an old city. One might wonder whether a language which consisted only of orders was a complete language; this thought leads to the question: what does it take for a language to be complete? But that question is not quite right: there are no clear standards for completeness. Was our language complete before the symbolism of chemistry was incorporated into it? (We are supposed to ask ourselves and answer "yes.") Beginning a comparison between a language and a town, Wittgenstein calls the symbolism of chemistry one of the "suburbs of our language" and asks, again rhetorically, "How many houses or streets does it take before a town begins to be a town?" The point is supposed to be that there is no precise answer. There is no general model specifying when a language is complete, or when one language becomes two.

> 18. . . . Our language can be seen as an ancient city: a maze of little streets and squares, of old and new houses, and of houses with additions from various periods; and this surrounded by a multitude of new boroughs with straight regular streets and uniform houses.
> (PI)

We are to think of language as an ancient city, and its various parts or "games" as streets or areas that grew in irregular ways and are made up of combinations of old and new. (The analogy is most striking if we think of old cities, such as Boston, Montreal, or Athens, in which there is an extremely crowded central core, with outlying modern suburbs.) Since there is no standard of completeness for cities, which grow in various ways, thinking of language in these terms will help us to understand that there is no standard of completeness for language; it is something that grows in various ways, just as an ancient city grew into a modern one with new suburbs.

Thinking through Wittgenstein's analogies will help us to understand his point – or, if we spot a flaw in the analogy – to disagree with him.

> 268. Why can't my right hand give my left hand money? – My right hand can put it into my left hand. My right hand can write a deed of gift and my left hand a receipt. – But the further practical consequences would not be those of a gift. When the left hand has taken the money from the right, etc., we shall ask "Well, and what of it?" And the same could be asked if a person had given himself a private definition of a word; I mean, if he has said the word to himself and at the same time has directed his attention to a sensation.
> (PI)

We cannot give things to ourselves, because anything we could give, we would already have. Our apparently private transaction would have no point. With this analogy, Wittgenstein amusingly states his rejection of private definition and private language. Defining a word to myself would be as useless as my right hand giving my left hand money.

Another striking Wittgensteinian analogy is that of the beetle in the box.

> 293. . . . Now someone tells me that *he* knows what pain is only from his own case! – Suppose everyone had a box with something in it: we call it a "beetle." No one can look into anyone else's box,

> and everyone says he knows what a beetle is only by looking at *his* beetle. – Here it would be quite possible for everyone to have something different in his box. One might even imagine such a thing constantly changing. – But suppose the word "beetle" had a use in this people's language? – If so it would not be used as the name of a thing. The thing in the box has no place in the language-game at all; not even as a *something*: for the box might even be empty. – No, one can 'divide through' by the thing in the box; it cancels out, whatever it is.
> That is to say: if we construe the grammar of the expression of sensation on the model of 'object and designation' the object drops out of consideration as irrelevant.
> (PI)

If the thing in the box were purely private, the word "beetle" in the public language could not refer to it. "Beetle" would just mean "whatever is in the box" – and whether there was anything there or not would not matter. Wittgenstein's curious analogy leads us to think this through. Just how are these beetles in boxes similar to private sensations? We might regard mental terms as referring to purely private sensations but if we did so, the consequence would be that it would not matter what private sensation anyone had when he was angry, or fearful, or happy, or whatever. If the sensation was purely private, known only to the one who had it, the use of words like "angry," "afraid," and "happy" could not possibly be based on its presence or absence. If we tried to make "happy" mean "whatever a person feels when he is called happy," we would get nowhere. Happiness would be like the beetle in the box.

Often Wittgenstein explicitly asks us to do things, imagine things, or perform "thought experiments." When we do this, we are actively thinking; anticipating our results, Wittgenstein moves on to draw a conclusion or pose further questions.

> 610. Describe the aroma of coffee. Why can't it be done? Do we lack the words? And *for what* are words lacking? – But how do we get the idea that such a description must after all be possible? Have you ever felt the lack of such a description? Have you tried to describe the aroma and not succeeded?
> (PI)

If we try to describe the aroma of coffee, we will find that we cannot do it. Wittgenstein makes us think about what causes our inability. Is it lack of words, or something else? He implies by his questions that it is not a lack of words, that there is no basis for our feeling that a description of an aroma should be possible. We will find out that we have no practical need to put the "quality" of an aroma into words.

> 279. Imagine someone saying: "But I know how tall I am!" and laying his hand on top of his head to prove it.
> (PI)

That would be a joke: placing his hand on his own head does not amount to measuring his height. The point of the joke is that measuring requires a standard independent of the person measuring and the thing to be measured. But Wittgenstein will not state this outright; he wants us to imagine something and discover it for ourselves.

Some thought exercises are quite difficult – readers may begin to appreciate the intense struggles Wittgenstein himself experienced with philosophical questions.

> 501. "The purpose of language is to express thoughts." – So presumably the purpose of every sentence is to express a thought. Then what thought is expressed, for example, by the sentence "It's raining?"
>
> 502. Asking what the sense is. Compare:
> "This sentence makes sense." – "What sense?"
> "This set of words is a sentence." – "What sentence?"
> (PI)

The thought expressed by 'It's raining' is the thought that it is raining. But saying this seems redundant, and somewhat useless – as is suggested by the analogous examples offered in the next passage. Again, Wittgenstein does not state the point directly. We have to think it through for ourselves.

Wittgenstein on the Nature of Philosophy

Wittgenstein had an absolutely distinctive manner of philosophizing. He was wary of generalizations, wanting to attend to particular cases and examples in context, and to note similarities and differences. He believed that philosophers had made mistakes in raising such abstract and general questions as 'What is courage?', 'What is knowledge?', and 'What is time?' Socrates, Plato, Augustine, and many others had been on a wild goose chase when they sought definitions which could capture a "common essence." When we seek to understand a word such as "courage," we will make progress by looking at cases where the word is used and seeking to understand the work it does in those circumstances. We should not assume that that there is some "essence" [a Platonic Form, an Aristotelian universal, or a single verbal definition] which will provide the answer. Cases of courage will resemble each other to varying degrees and differ from each other in various respects. Often, attending to differences will be as important as attending to similarities.

For all his talk of language games, Wittgenstein saw no element common to all games.

> 66. Consider for example the proceedings that we call "games." I mean board-games, card-games, ball-games, Olympic games, and so on. What is common to them all? – Don't say: "There *must* be something common, or they would not be called 'games'" – but *look and see* whether there is anything common to all. – For if you look at them you will not see something that is common to *all*, but similarities, relationships, and a whole series of them at that. To repeat: don't think, but look! – Look for example at board-games, with their multifarious relationships. Now pass to card-games; here you find many correspondences with the first group, but many common features drop out, and others appear. When we pass next to ball-games, much that is common is retained, but much is lost. – Are they all 'amusing'? Compare chess with noughts and crosses [Xs and Os]. Or is there always winning and losing, or competition between players? Think of patience. In ball games there is winning and losing; but when a child throws his ball at the wall and catches it again, this feature has disappeared.... And we can go through the many, many other groups of games in the same way; can see how similarities crop up and disappear. And the result of this examination is: we see a complicated network of similarities overlapping and criss-crossing: sometimes overall similarities, sometimes similarities of detail.
>
> 67. I can think of no better expression to characterize these similarities than "family resemblances;" for the various resemblances between members of a family: build, features, colour of eyes, gait, temperament, etc. etc. overlap and criss-cross in the same way. — And I shall say: 'games' form a family.
> And for instance the kinds of number form a family in the same way.
> ... we extend our concept of number as in spinning a thread we twist fibre on fibre. And the strength of the thread does not reside in the fact that some one fibre runs through its whole length, but in the overlapping of many fibres.
> (PI)

Wittgenstein spoke of the "craving for generality" as something that can make us pose the wrong questions and accept simplistic answers. He thought that philosophers had been led astray by asking flawed questions and setting forth to find answers without pausing to see whether those questions made sense. There is a danger in philosophy of getting into a state of hazy abstraction and building one failure to understand upon another. Wittgenstein sought *clarity* above all; he seems to have believed that if we thought long enough and hard enough, we could achieve a state of "complete clarity" in which the philosophical questions that "troubled us" would go away. Often clarity is to be found by moving away from abstractions and generalizations to look at particular cases. Instead of asking whether pain is a sensation, for instance, we may consider a particular case in which someone has a toothache, and how he might express that saying, "It hurts." Instead of asking "What is time?" we might consider how we measure time.

Wittgenstein argued that there is no need in philosophy for a grand system in the style of Sartre, Hegel, or Kant. We need not assume that all problems should be solved at once. If one had a library and the books were in no decent arrangement, it would be a worthwhile achievement to arrange some of them. Even if the others remained in disorder, that would be a good beginning. In philosophy too, we have to start in some particular place; we should not assume that no problem can be resolved unless all problems are resolved. Wittgenstein believed that philosophy can proceed "piecemeal," in small steps. If we can bring generalities and abstractions to bear on the world of our real experience, and use words as they are commonly used in ordinary life, we can hope to *see how* things are, and thus get rid of some of the problems that worry us. Wittgenstein often implied that if we could just learn to *see* how words work in ordinary circumstances, and what function they have in real life, matters would become "completely clear" to us, and we would cease to be "tormented" by philosophical questions.

Wittgenstein regarded philosophical questions as fundamentally conceptual – dealing with the application and function of concepts, and the use of words in various contexts. To approach such questions scientifically would be to make a fundamental mistake. Whatever else it might be, philosophy is not, and never should be, a science. We know our language, and we live within our own form of life. We do not need scientists postulating and investigating peculiar mental mechanisms to tell us what is going on. We can say with some authority what we would say in certain circumstances, because we are speakers of our own language and participants in our own way of life.

> 109. It was true to say that our considerations could not be scientific ones. It was not of any possible interest to us to find out empirically 'that, contrary to our preconceived ideas, it is possible to think such-and-such' – whatever that may mean. (The conception of thought as a gaseous medium.) And we may not advance any kind of theory. There must not be anything hypothetical in our considerations. We must do away with all *explanation*, and description alone must take its place. And this description gets its light, that is to say its purpose, from the philosophical problems. These are, of course, not empirical problems; they are solved, rather, by looking into the workings of our language .... The problems are solved, not by giving new information, but by arranging what we have always known. Philosophy is a battle against the bewitchment of our intelligence by means of language.
> (PI)

How can our intelligence be "bewitched" by language? Wittgenstein believed that one thing that misleads us is the basic sense in which all words look alike. When written, they all appear in a script or typeface. This superficial similarity tends to make us think that all words serve the same purpose. We may carelessly lapse into silly assumptions about words – such as the assumption that all have the same function: to name objects. And there are surface grammatical similarities which disguise the fact that another level of grammar, the depth grammar, is very different.

Compare:

> I have a solid chair.
> I have a terrible toothache.

The phrases, "a solid chair" and "a terrible toothache" are similar at the level of surface grammar: both are noun phrases, containing an indefinite article, an adjective, and a noun. In both the noun phrase is the object of the verb "to have," used in the first person. This similarity at the level of surface grammar may encourage us to mistakenly compare a toothache with a chair (a material object out there in public space for anyone to see or touch), leading us to conclude that a toothache is a private object in inner space (a very special object; only the person who "has it" can feel it). But according to Wittgenstein, such an assimilation would be a mistake. We make this mistake only because we are misled by *surface grammar* and fail to understand the *depth grammar* in these expressions. If we thought harder about the analogy, we would realize that it is only a superficial one. Wittgenstein argued that we believe in *inner objects* only because we have been misled by this sort of grammatical analogy.

Another case:

> All roses have thorns.
> All rods have length.

Here too a surface similarity hides a fundamental difference. The first statement is empirical but the second is not. By definition, a rod has length; if it did not, it could not be a rod. A further striking example:

> It is five o'clock in London.
> It is five o'clock on the sun.

These sentences are grammatically parallel. The first surely has a use and a meaning, and that fact may lead us to assume that the second has a use and a meaning. But to think so would be a mistake: our measurements of time are based on the motion of the earth around the sun and have no meaning for the sun itself. Language is "on holiday" if we talk about what time it is on the sun, because it cannot do any work in such a case. One way to think, and think hard, is to reflect on the expressions we use and make sure that we are not misled by superficial similarities in grammar.

Observations

While appreciating Wittgenstein's intense struggle to achieve clarity, we must realize that it is impossible to just *look and see*, and it is equally impossible to achieve *complete clarity*. Both depend on perspective. We cannot just look at a particular case – we look at it for some reason, and bring some set of concepts to bear on it. If we compare it with some other case, we do so for a reason. In Wittgenstein's own philosophical practice there are elements of implicit generality and an urge to explain, as we can see from the instructive character of some of his own analogies. For all his scepticism about general answers to general questions, Wittgenstein himself put forward substantive theories about universals, sensations, meaning, culture, and the foundations of mathematics. He was also developing a general theory of philosophy itself. We speak and write, but know not what we speak and write, because we fail to think hard enough about what we say and what we mean. As a result we are "bewitched by language" and pose these queer and peculiar philosophical problems. Wittgenstein sometimes suggested that all philosophical questions arise for all philosophers in the same way – as a result of "our bewitchment with language." But this would seem to be just the kind of rash generalization that he warned against. There are many different philosophers and many different philosophical problems; it is most likely that different problems have arisen for different people in different ways.

Wittgenstein seems not to have studied the historical genesis of specific philosophical problems and solutions, offering instead an *a priori* theory that diagnosed all philosophical problems in the same way (arising from language) and sought the solution to all in the same place (understanding ordinary language in the context of the practices and customs of ordinary life). It is perplexing to find that Wittgenstein, whose genius lay in philosophy more than anywhere else, sometimes suggests that philosophy has nothing to it after all. And it is ironical, in that if he did believe this, Wittgenstein would have done so after falling victim to the very craving for generality that he had criticized in others and sought to overcome.

Is philosophy founded on a misunderstanding of language? Would the world be a better place if there had never been any such thing as philosophy – if people were never "confused" by language in the first place? Would human history be in some way "better" if Socrates' intellectual children had never existed at all? As a hypothetical question about the history of Western culture, this question is impossible to answer. And there is a deep sense in which the supposition is likely impossible – not just false. If these particular individuals had not existed, questions about immortality, the meaning of life, the nature of knowledge, the relation between concepts and particular things, doubt, and the existence of a God would have occurred to other people, who would have spoken and written as philosophers, developing a tradition that would almost certainly have been different, but would have treated many of the same themes. As Kant so clearly recognized, as human beings we are driven to ask such questions and we do our best to construct reasonable answers to them. For all his desire to be "cured" of philosophical "troubles," it is hard to believe that Wittgenstein would have said the world would be a better place without philosophy.

> 123. A philosophical problem has the form: "I don't know my way about."
> (PI)

What, after all, could be more important than finding one's way about?

> 109. What is your aim in philosophy? – To shew the fly the way out of the fly-bottle.
> (PI)

A fly trapped in a bottle will buzz around, captured and frustrated. It wants desperately to escape. The analogy, presumably, is that a man or woman troubled deeply by philosophical problems will want desperately to "get rid of them." One may do this by dissolving the problems, convincing himself or herself that these problems do not really arise, because some sort of mistake was made when we came to formulate them. Or one may do it by constructing a theory that offers a solution, and trying to get the best arguments and evidence to support that theory. In much of his later philosophizing, Wittgenstein suggests that only the first approach (dissolving the problem) is appropriate. Wittgenstein sometimes seems to say that all the philosophical problems that had so occupied him and others were founded on false analogies and misunderstandings of language, and will disappear if we understand language properly. Certainly many of Wittgenstein's students and disciples adopted that view, which was widely discussed in Britain, Canada, and the United States during the fifties and early sixties. The implication is that a philosopher who takes a long hard look at language will achieve clarity and learn that everything is just fine as it is. Some of Wittgenstein's followers came to believe that by approaching language in a quest for clarity and understanding of the ordinary contexts in which words are used, the philosopher will learn that, in the end, there are no philosophical questions.

> 124. Philosophy may in no way interfere with the actual use of language; it can in the end only describe it.
> For it cannot give it any foundation either.
> It leaves everything as it is.
> (PI)

What Wittgenstein seems to be saying here is rather puzzling. It recalls, in a peculiar way, the themes of logical positivism. Why engage in philosophy, if it will leave everything as it is? What is the "everything" that is left as it is?

Whatever Wittgenstein's ultimate view of philosophy might have been, in the end two things are certain. One is that Wittgenstein was the foremost philosophical genius of the twentieth century. The other is that there is one thing philosophy does not leave as it is: the man or woman who has struggled to think things through and achieve clarity. The philosopher is certainly affected by the struggle.

11

Contemporary Voices

Philosophers today explore many topics, historical and non-historical, and their methods and conclusions are diverse. An overview of current philosophy especially pertinent to themes of thinking and knowledge may be gained from a consideration of four trends prominent since 1970. These are artificial intelligence projects; the Informal Logic - Critical Thinking movement; deconstruction; and feminist epistemology.

Artificial Intelligence

Many researchers and scholars are currently trying to understand the nature and strategies of human thinking by exploring what computers can do. Much of this work is inter-disciplinary. Over the past twenty years, research in artificial intelligence has been burgeoning not only in philosophy but also in psychology, computer science, engineering, and mathematics. The most ambitious orientation from a philosophical point of view is called Strong Artificial Intelligence, or Strong A.I. The word "strong" is used not as pre-judging that the claims made are all true, but as alluding to the metaphysically and scientificially ambitious nature of these claims. Strong Artificial Intelligence research seeks confirmation for a materialist (non-dualist) account of the mind by demonstrating that computers can think.

The general line of argument behind Strong A.I. is something like this. Suppose that a computer can be programmed to do an activity such as proving mathematical theorems, playing chess, or creating poetry. Suppose that this computer can produce a result comparable to that of many human subjects. When a human being is able to play a good game of chess, or prove a mathematical theorem, we regard that performance as evidence that he or she is intelligent, can think, and is thinking. So, by parity of argument and to be consistent, we should reason in the same way about the computer. If we make this intellectual move, then we have in effect allowed that thinking can be embodied in a complex physical mechanism, a machine. Such a conclusion undermines mind-body dualism. The computer is able to perform in an "intelligent" way, and yet it has no *mind* in the Cartesian sense. We have no reason to believe that the computer is conscious or that it has feelings or sensations. Proponents of Strong A.I. argue that thinking without a conscious mind is possible, using the development of successful computer programs as the main basis for their case. If thinking can take place "in" a machine, then surely it can also be embodied in a brain. Thus, A.I. research is taken to confirm a materialist philosophical view and to refute the dualistic view that the mind is a thinking thing which is distinct from the body.

Clearly, human beings are not computers, and human minds or brains are not machines. However, the brain is a physical organ. The human brain is understood by most proponents of Strong A.I. as a physical *mechanism*. We have brains, and it is because we have brains that we can think. If computers can produce products of intelligence on the basis of their hardware and software, then, it is argued, the brain produces them in much the same way. There are two fundamental aspects of Strong A.I. research. One is the over-riding materialist hypothesis that human beings are purely physical and material beings. The other is the belief that computer modelling can give specific guidance as to how human brains perform various thinking tasks.

Proponents of Strong A.I. seek detailed confirmation for a materialist hypothesis. Such theorists as Patricia Churchland, Paul Churchland, Fred Dretske, Margaret Boden, and Paul Thagard see themselves as taking a scientific approach to the study of human thought and intelligence. They do not regard dualism as a promising hypothesis for science. They would say that thinking clearly goes on in the brain, and suggest that a promising way to find out how the brain works when we think is to attempt to model human mental activities on computers.

An important conception in artificial intelligence research is that of the Turing Test, proposed in 1950 by Alan Turing. To understand this test, imagine sitting in a room where you are connected both with a computer and with a human being. The computer and the human being are in another room. You cannot see them, but you can ask them questions; you get the answers in a typed form. Turing claimed that if you ask questions of a certain type (pertaining to chess, mathematics, knowledge of French, or conversation, for instance) and you cannot tell the difference between the human responses and those of the computer, the computer has "passed the test." Judging from the behavioral responses you have in such a situation, the computer is as intelligent as the human.

Although the merits of the Turing Test are taken for granted in many areas of artificial intelligence research, the assumptions underlying the test are highly debatable from a philosophical perspective. They are debatable for two reasons. The first reason is that, even if human and computer responses in this restricted situation are indistinguishable to some observers, that fact does not show that the same cause (intelligent thought) underlies the result in each case. The second reason is that if human testers did not know very much about programming computers, they might be overly impressed by a superficial performance and misjudge the results of the test.

Researchers in Strong A.I. have studied chess and chess playing, worked out an account of successful and unsuccessful moves in chess, and programmed computers to play a good game of chess. Of course, the fact that a computer with a certain kind of hardware can play a good game of chess when it is programmed in a particular way does not *prove* that human chess players have brains comparable to the hardware, or thought strategies comparable to the software. Proponents of Strong A.I. acknowledge this point. What they say in response is that the manifestation of intelligent activities in machines proves that thinking and intelligence (capacities for intelligent behavior) *can* emerge from the activities of a machine. The source of intelligence, then, need not be anything mental or spiritual.

A.I. research can be a source for suggestions or hypotheses about how the brain works. What does the brain do when we experience an optical illusion? Or translate a document from Japanese into English? Make up a new series of plots for a situation comedy series? Strong A.I. research is based on the assumption that the cognitive (knowing) activities of the brain will be better understood when they are modelled on computers. Typically A.I. research involves formalizing human knowledge and thinking strategies, and then trying to create programs to duplicate the procedures. The conceptual, programming, and engineering research associated with this program is also called Cognitive Science.

In A.I. research there is first an attempt to describe the human activity (whether this be mathematics, chess, creative writing, explanatory reasoning, understanding analogies, recognizing patterns, or whatever) followed by work to develop programs aimed at making a computer capable of doing the same thing. Eventually, experiments may be done to determine whether the human brain follows the same sorts of procedure which are exemplified in the computer program.

Human beings can recognize letters of the alphabet written in a great variety of script styles.

a a a a a a a

All these letters are instances of the letter "a" and would be recognized as such by virtually all literate people who use the Roman alphabet. Researchers have worked to devise computer programs to similarly recognize many variations on a theme. (This turns out to be very difficult.) Another complex and difficult case is the following: human beings have background knowledge which they can bring to bear on stories, enabling them to understand connections which are never explicitly mentioned in the stories. If computers are going to be artificially intelligent with respect to showing understanding of stories, they will need a vast store of background knowledge – one might call this common sense – and some mechanism for applying it when needed. The philosophical task of trying to specify and formally represent human "common sense" or "background knowledge" in such cases is a massive chore in its own right, quite apart from the programming seeking to connect the appropriate elements of such knowledge with a specific task or story.

Using a cognitive science approach, researchers within philosophy and elsewhere have explored such central aspects of thinking as induction, deduction, analogy, and explanation. Whatever one thinks about the materialist orientation of Strong Artificial Intelligence Research, it is unquestionable that this work has exposed many difficult and important questions about thinking and knowledge.

As a matter of fact, not all A.I. researchers have the metaphysical ambition of supporting materialism or even of finding out how the brain works. Some have more qualified or restricted goals: to store knowledge of particular types or to get computers to perform tasks which are "thinking tasks." These less sweeping research programs are typically classified as Weak A.I. The adjective "weak" does not mean that the projects are weak, but rather that the purpose of the research is a limited practical one; such research is not done in an attempt to corroborate materialism or make claims about how the human brain operates. The "expert systems" projects are a case in point. In such systems, a great deal of human knowledge is organized so that a user can access it conveniently, almost as though the user had a vast library, or a knowledgeable human expert beside him or her. Expert systems have important uses, and many have been developed for practical and commercial reasons. One important area is that of diagnostic medicine. A doctor can enter in a description of a patient's background, symptoms, and circumstances and elicit from the system suggestions for diagnosis and treatment. The computer is not thinking; it is not developing medical knowledge. Rather it is able to print out suggestions about how to apply knowledge that has been cultivated by scientists and medical researchers, because relevant knowledge and beliefs have been efficiently stored within it so as to be available in response to questions. No one claims that computers programmed with expert systems *think* the way a doctor does: in fact, such systems are so comprehensive that no human doctor could think this way. These experts systems are nevertheless extremely helpful, especially for doctors in isolated areas who may have few colleagues and limited access to libraries. In the early eighties the development of expert systems was often linked with Strong A.I. Presently, it tends to fall within Weak A.I., in recognition of the fact that these systems represent and store knowledge.

A prominent critic of Strong A.I. is Hubert Dreyfus, whose book *What Computers Can't Do*, appeared in two editions and has been widely discussed. Although his background is largely in existentialist philosophy, Dreyfus has carefully studied artificial intelligence projects over many years. Dreyfus argues that human thinking involves sensitivity to context, intuition, emotion, judgment, and a vast amount of common sense and background knowledge. Because computers are not living, sensing creatures, they cannot acquire background knowledge and a sense of context. For this reason, Dreyfus contends, computers will never be able to be intelligent in anything like the way human beings are. Proponents of Strong A.I. regard this approach as mystifying and pessimistic. They generally argue, against Dreyfus, that the fact that something has not *yet been successfully programmed* does not mean that it will *never* be successfully programmed.

The Informal Logic - Critical Thinking Movement

This movement within philosophy is largely based in North America and strongly identified with the Socratic educational goal of encouraging people to think for themselves. Over the last thirty years, many philosophers have looked sceptically at the teaching of formal logic, questioning its practicality. They have shifted from teaching technical formal logic to teaching the analysis and evaluation of argument expressed in natural languages. This shift has been motivated largely by the desire to use philosophy courses, those in logic in particular, to cultivate critical thinking skills in students.

Philosophers in the Critical Thinking - Informal Logic movement argue that education should not be indoctrination. Students should be enabled to think for themselves rather than being trained in some kind of orthodoxy, or taught to unquestioningly follow authorities. A person who thinks critically is one who can follow, understand, and evaluate arguments; recognize and avoid fallacies; reason carefully; and judiciously estimate the credibility of claims. He or she values clarity and accuracy. Not only is a critical thinker capable of careful and accurate reasoning and judicious assessment of claims, he or she values reason and truth. A critical thinker is disposed to employ reasoning and thinking skills on a regular basis. The purpose of the Critical Thinking movement is not to encourage facile scepticism. Nor is the theory of Critical Thinking based on the Cartesian policy of doubting everything and trying to re-build human knowledge from scratch. Rather, questioning is valued when the questions fit into a context, have a specific basis, and are raised responsibly. Philosophical work has been used in efforts to incorporate critical thinking in all subjects and for all grade levels, for kindergarten through college.

A critical thinker is one who can assess reasons and wants to use this ability to think hard and think well. He or she is willing to conform judgments and actions to rational principles and standards. Educated people should be able to see through manipulative commercial and political messages, and conquer their own biases and prejudices. With its long tradition of sustained responsible questioning, philosophy can make important contributions to this goal. Like Wollstonecraft, philosophers who participate in the Informal Logic - Critical Thinking movement show a kind of practical idealism; they seek to apply philosophy not only to the academic materials studied in universities and colleges, but to the arguments and problems of life outside the academic environment. They hope, by cultivating rationality and responsible autonomous thought in students, to further educational reform. Influential proponents of critical thinking as a means to enlightenment include Richard Paul, Harvey Siegel, and Mark Weinstein in the United States; Alec Fisher in Britain; and Anthony Blair, Ralph Johnson, Douglas Walton, David Hitchcock, and the present author in Canada. Related work on argumentation has been pursued in the Netherlands by Frans van Eemeren, Rob Grootendorst, and numerous others.

Informal logic is the study of arguments as they appear in ordinary writing and speech and not (as in the case of formal logic) as they are translated into the symbols of formal systems. The study of natural argument has led philosophers to raise and explore issues not treated in formal logic, and interest in those issues has inspired papers, journals, books, and conferences. In its present form, informal logic is a relatively new branch of philosophy, related to formal logic but having a different and more practical focus. Philosophers working in informal logic seek to develop criteria and procedures for the interpretation, evaluation, and construction of arguments in natural language. They understand argument as primarily a phenomenon involving several people, either two speakers or a writer and the intended audience of his or her work. When people argue back and forth, in effect they think together, reasoning together, trying to persuade each other of claims they are making and considering. The Informal Logic - Critical Thinking movement understands reason as practical and social.

In an important paper on informal logic and politics, Ralph Johnson describes features that a theory of argument would need, in order to be a useful tool for describing and evaluating arguments about political issues. It would have to allow that there can be good arguments both for and against the same claim; it would have to allow that there are stronger and weaker arguments; and it would have to incorporate standards clear and straightforward enough that an ordinary person could determine whether they were satisfied. A major goal of informal logicians is to develop a theory which would meet these conditions, would be applicable to arguments from diverse fields and contexts, and would be philosophically adequate in other respects. Since the teaching of argument is a core aspect of the teaching of critical thinking, work in informal logic contributes directly to the study and teaching of critical thinking.

An argument is an attempt at rational persuasion. We may argue with ourselves, thinking by attempting to persuade ourselves of something, or exploring a question in our minds by seeing whether we can persuade ourselves of something. But the most characteristic context of argument is social. We present arguments to other people – either orally, when we talk with them, or in writing, when we write for an audience. In an argument some claims (the premises) are put forward as reasons or evidence for another claim (the conclusion). The goal is to lead the audience from the premises to the conclusion. The premises are intended to provide rational support for the conclusion and make it acceptable. Informal logicians have replaced this classic conception of a sound argument with a conception more sensitive to practical contexts. One model in an influential textbook about practical argument assessment is the following:

> An argument is cogent if, and only if:
> A. its premises are rationally acceptable to the audience to whom it is addressed;
> R. its premises are relevant to its conclusion;
> and,
> G. its premises, taken together, provide sufficient grounds for its conclusion.

In other words, a good or cogent argument is an ARGument that satisfies ARG. (The formula was devised to be memorable.) Of course, these ARG conditions of argument cogency need to be filled in to be fully understood. Filling them in is a major part of the research agenda of informal logic. The ARG conditions can be used to pose questions that we think through in order to evaluate an argument; thus they provide important thinking tools. We evaluate arguments by asking ourselves whether good enough reasons or evidence are supplied to justify the conclusion; then using the ARG structure, we go on to seek answers to those questions.

The ARG analysis is restricted to premises and conclusions. Johnson suggests a second level of assessment for argument, one which explores the merits of an argument or position in the more complete context of social and intellectual debate. He suggests that, in addition to reflecting on how well the premises support the conclusion, we ask the following questions:

1. How well does the argument or position address alternate positions?
2. How well does the argument or position deal with objections?
3. How well does the argument or position handle consequences?

For most important questions and issues, more than one answer has been proposed. To think through the adequacy of a particular claim or theory, we must ask ourselves what its proponents would say about alternative positions. Have they considered alternative positions? Do they understand them? Have they any objections to them? Significant objections? Compelling objections? From the standpoint of alternative positions, a conclusion will seem controversial, inadequately supported, or false. Those who dissent from a conclusion or position are likely to have objections to it. Can these be answered in a plausible way? Finally, what are the practical and theoretical implications of accepting the conclusion? If those consequences are objectionable in some way, we should look at the argument and the theory again.

The second level of argument assessment is truly dialectical because it concerns responses to controversy. It requires knowledge of the context in which an issue arises and of what other people are saying about it. Until now, informal logic and critical thinking have concentrated more on the first level than on the second.

Philosophers within the Informal Logic movement see important intellectual benefits from the careful study and analysis of argument. Attending to the structure, interpretation, and evaluation of arguments will help people be more careful and accurate thinkers. Benefits from the careful study of argument include greater clarity, an ability to concentrate and focus on important details, respect for evidence and reason, recognition of the need to understand a theory or argument before criticizing it, open-mindedness, respect for opposing points of view, a recognition of the need to review our own views in the light of criticism, and sound intellectual and practical judgment.

Critical thinking is an ethical matter as well as an intellectual one, because it is founded on humility, respect for other people, respect for the truth, and a kind of faith that in the long run better reasoning will prevail over worse. In popular culture and in some theories, argument is conceived as a kind of war in which opponents struggle with each other. On this view, arguing is a matter of asserting oneself: people want to "learn to argue" because they want to convince others and get their own way. Who will "win" the argument? Who will "prevail" in the dispute, convincing the other that he is right, claiming the intellectual victory? The adversarial model of argument, in which we see argument as a kind of contest for intellectual dominance, has been quite prominent in the Western intellectual tradition and in popular thinking. Its attendant militaristic metaphors – holding your ground, defending your position, winning the debate, tactics and strategy – have been influential in informal logic as well. But the adversarial model is no longer seen as inevitable. Rather, there is a shift toward a conception of people arguing with and for each other, and collaborating by correcting each other to arrive at a common conclusion, appropriately checked and modified. Learning to argue well and to *critically* evaluate arguments is a core skill in Critical Thinking. But for all this, trust is involved – trust in the other person and in the dialectical process of arguing back and forth. The other person, to whom the argument is directed, need not be regarded as an opponent to be conquered. Rather, he or she can be seen as a companion in a journey of thought and inquiry.

One criticism sometimes launched against the Informal Logic - Critical Thinking movement is that its orientation is too negative and insufficiently creative – that it encapsulates the philosopher's tendency to criticize and question everything, to be picky and fuss and tear things apart, rather than to create new ideas. Critical thinking seems analytic, rarely synthetic. Those who evaluate and analyze claims and arguments usually begin their work with material provided from elsewhere: newspapers, televisions shows, classic texts, recent books and pamphlets. The grist for their sceptical mill has been created by others; it is rarely their own product. Informal logic and critical thinking are more a matter of questioning and evaluation than of creation.

A compelling response to this objection is that critical thinking and creative thinking often go hand-in-hand. Criticism itself has creative aspects: we must creatively construct the counter-example (instance that refutes a generalization), the *reductio ad absurdum* argument, or the fresh analogy that rebuts a standard analogy. Any reader of the later Wittgenstein should be able to testify to the fact that criticism can be creative. In addition, critical thought is often the first step to creative thought. When we find flaws in an accepted account, it is often our reflection on those very errors that can inspire us to think of new ideas. Critical thinking is not all of thinking, to be sure – but it is an important part and one which is frequently the stimulus to creativity.

Another criticism of Informal Logic is that it is insufficiently rigorous and scientific. In some circles, such as those of A.I. research, the idea that logic should be formal retains considerable influence. Key terms in informal logic – such as "credibility," "authority," "argument," "explanation," "assumption," "relevant," "acceptable," and "sufficient grounds" – are not definable in a formal way, as are terms in a rigorous mathematical system. Unlike cognitive scientists, informal logicians believe that thinking requires sensitivity to context and shades of meaning, and an ability to make fine judgments. They do not regard such matters as being formal, or formalizable, abilities. There is not a full consensus among informal logicians on standards for a cogent argument. If the ARG model – or anything like it – is used for argument evaluation at the first level, prospects for formalization are poor. And at the second level, having to do with criticism and consideration of alternative views, formalization would clearly be impossible.

Aristotle is a resource for replying to this line of criticism. We have only to look to his well-known statement that in seeking knowledge we should expect only as much precision as a subject matter permits. Arguments can be evaluated; reasons can be put forward for saying some arguments are cogent and others less so; philosophical theories about those reasons have been developed and are being discussed. Yet it would be wrong-headed to look for a *science* or a formal theory that would tell us whether one natural argument about politics, morality, or day-to-day problems is better than another. In these areas what is needed is to develop clear thinking as a better basis for *judgment* and discretion. We cannot expect universal formal standards for the evaluation of thinking about such problems, when there are many pertinent principles and perspectives, and evidence that is open to diverse interpretations.

Of course philosophy and logic (formal or informal) do not provide all the resources for critical thinking. Critical thinking needs many resources from outside philosophy. But the point remains that there are central logical concepts (argument, premise, conclusion, fallacy, analogy, assumption, definition, and so on) that cross various disciplines, are discussed and refined within philosophy, and are absolutely central in the evaluation of our thinking and our arguments. There are related principles and criteria (such as ARG) which are broadly applicable. Informal logic cannot develop *everything* we need for critical thinking but it can and has developed *some* important concepts and tools that apply across the disciplines. For critical thinking, we need both general concepts and standards, and the specific knowledge and tools of particular disciplines.

Deconstruction

The "deconstructive" style of philosophy and criticism was originated by the French philosopher Jacques Derrida, who was influenced by Freud and Heidegger, among others. Like Wittgenstein, Derrida stresses the importance of language in thought. He emphasizes our tendency to be misled by language and to construct overly-simple theories of meaning and interpretation. Derrida argues that language outwits philosophers. In close studies of philosophical texts, he points to ambiguities, puns, metaphors, and indeterminacies of meaning that have escaped notice in the philosophical tradition.

Derrida has been resistant to define what "deconstruction" is, warning that all attempts to explain it in a sentence or two are bound to miss the point. In the Western philosophical tradition, the conviction that meaning is more directly expressed in speech than in writing has been a fundamental assumption. Derrida questions this view, branding it a philosophical illusion. He argues that neither in speech nor in writing is meaning anything straightforward, clear, or immediately expressive of personal intentions. Every text – whether literary, scientific, or philosophical – can be interpreted or read in various ways; there is no single authoritative version of its meaning. After struggling with the phenomenon of alternative interpretations, Wittgenstein insisted that explanations and justifications must come to an end somewhere. His end point for interpretation was tied to contexts of ordinary life and common social practice. From the premise that words are open to multiple interpretations, Derrida moves in a different direction from Wittgenstein, arguing that no context is so "normal" that it sets a foundation for interpretation.

In contrast to Wittgenstein, who wanted to reach the point of complete clarity so as to be able to stop philosophizing, Derrida exults in the possibility of reading a text in various ways. He delights in making things more puzzling and less clear. Derrida enjoys demonstrating that we do not understand what we thought we understood. Often this involves making something that formerly seemed serious, or even sacred, look funny. Derrida says that things are not simple; if they were, problems would easily be solved and we would know it. Whereas Wittgenstein sought to explain the fact that people use words in regular ways and do understand each other, Derrida emphasizes the perpetual and constant possibility of misunderstanding. On his view, there is no one regular way in which people use words; people often *do not* understand each other. Derrida acknowledges that we can put a stop to a seemingly endless play of undecidable meanings, as Wittgenstein did. But there is no philosophical justification for stopping – or beginning – at one point rather than another.

Derrida questions much in the Western philosophical tradition by reading classic texts in alternate ways. Characteristically, he discovers fundamental oppositions (serious/nonserious, soul/body, intelligible/sensible, natural/cultural, masculine/feminine) and identifies assumptions on which these polarities rest. He then poses the Kantian question of what makes these oppositions possible. There is an all-or-nothing aspect to every distinction we make using language. For example, in using contrastive words, we assume and imply that it is all or nothing: if a person is black, he is not white, and if he is male, he is not female. But reality is more fluid than this. Things and situations differ by degrees, and there are always "unusual" or "marginal" cases which are misleadingly characterized by our sharply contrastive terms. (There are shades of grey; there are males with high levels of female hormones; there are people born with some male and some female sexual organs.) In "deconstructing" texts, Derrida notes cases which do not fit the polarized distinctions very well, and then criticizes fundamental concepts so as to "destabilize" oppositions underlying the text. In language, we rely on polarities and contrasts that are questionable because there are shared properties and borderline cases. Think of speech and writing: speech has some of the uncertainties of writing; writing has some of the directness of speech. Or think of male and female: some males have soft breasts like females; some females have narrow pelvises like males.

Often the basis for questioning central polarities may be found in texts themselves and in this way, a text can be turned against itself or "deconstructed." Texts both employ distinctions and provide within themselves the grounds for denying exactly those distinctions. The deconstructive method takes thought and language to their limits, Derrida claims. In commenting on traditional texts in this way, Derrida introduces new terms of his own, at the same time warning his readers that they are all inadequate for his purposes.

Derrida argues against four common philosophical assumptions about the nature and role of philosophy. First, he denies that writing is a means of expression that is subordinate to speech for communicating knowledge. Second, he denies that matters of philosophical style can be separated from, and are secondary to, matters of logic and meaning. Third, he denies the Hegelian notion that we pass, in the history of philosophy, through stages that are bringing us progressively closer to the truth. And fourth, he questions the idea that philosophy and philosophers are uniquely qualified to clarify meaning, establish values, and validate claims to knowledge.

To think *deconstructively* is to question distinctions by seeking to comprehend how they function, what values they presuppose, and what cases are borderline, marginal, or left out. Dichotomies, Derrida argues, are not value-neutral. An opposition between concepts is never merely a contrast between two equally balanced terms; it is a hierarchy and order of subordination. One side of the dichotomy is valued more highly than the other; for instance, reason is typically valued more highly than emotion, and male more highly than female. Derrida believes that the classical oppositions must be overturned and displaced. In deconstruction, a conceptual order is overthrown and displaced. Because we think about reality in words, that upheaval affects reality as well as language. But there are no objective standards which we could use to show that the account which remains after such an upheaval is an improvement on what came before it.

Since dichotomies presume hierarchies and hierarchies presume values, when we question dichotomies, we will also question values. In this way, decontruction can provide the basis for radical analysis. It has been so used by feminists, anti-racists, and anti-colonialists. (However, deconstruction gives an unstable basis for analysis, since it refuses to recognize any foundations.) The deconstructive method need not be radical in its implications; those may be conservative, Derrida argued. Inherently, deconstruction is neither conservative nor radical; its implications will depend on the context in which it is used. One might read a radical account and "overturn" its distinctions as a prelude to proposing an account based on more conservative language. However Derrida insists that deconstructive thinking can never be used in a value-neutral way. When we "deconstruct" a discourse, we seek to understand it, analyze its presuppositions and context, detect key conceptual distinctions, and redescribe the phenomena. Such activities will always have evaluative and implicitly political implications.

A central term in Derrida's work is "différance." It is a pun on the French verb "différer" which means both to differ and to defer. Derrida uses this term to refer to the perpetual slippage (ongoing slight alterations) of meaning of signs as they are used again and again. The meaning of a word depends on its context of use. No two contexts are identical. No word has meaning alone, and there is no fixed point or foundation which makes meaning stay the same. All objects, elements, or categories are "differentially constituted." That is to say, what makes them what they are is their relations to other things from which they are distinguished. Any thing or element depends for its status as an individual and for its meaning on its differential interrelation with other elements. According to Derrida, what any thing *is* is a function of what it *is not*. For example, Cartesian mind is understood in a certain way because of the way it is distinguished from – and thereby related to – Cartesian matter. Women are understood in a certain way because of the way they are distinguished from and related to men; men in turn are understood as they are because of the way they are distinguished from and related to women. In a way reminiscent of Hegel, Derrida argues that identity presupposes difference, and difference leads back to identity.

Another central notion in Derrida's deconstructionist philosophy is that of the trace. Words and things are defined and must be understood with reference to a system of interconnected elements within which they are located. For this reason, each element has a trace of other elements. For example, when we seek to understand thinking, we are led to mind and then to body, to language and then to writing and speech. There is no foundation to make meanings clear and determinate. There are, Derrida says, "only everywhere differences and traces of traces." Traditional concepts of speaking, he argues, depend upon a "trace" of writing.

Derrida argued that there is no useful conception of thinking in the Western tradition, because we are caught in a basic circularity from which we seem unable to escape. We first define thinking as speaking (silently) to oneself. But when we come to say what speaking is, we define speaking as communicating one's thinking to another person, in words. Derrida argued that this is a vicious circle which needs to be deconstructed.

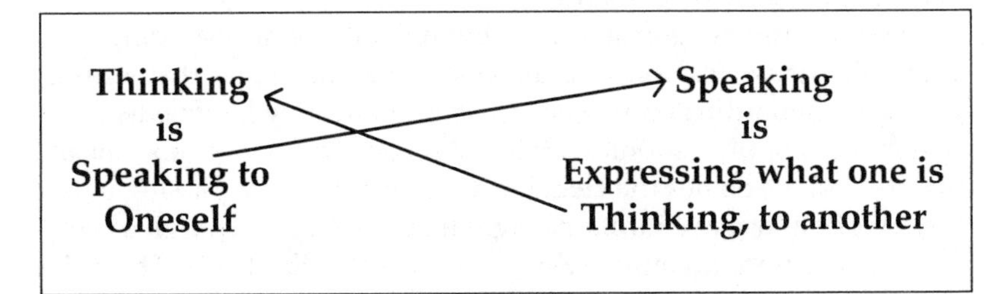

Derrida claims that when we deconstruct these concepts, we will realize that we do not understand either thinking or speaking. The implication he draws from this paradox is that we should work with written texts; we know we have texts but we do not know that reality or thought provide a foundation for understanding them. When we read texts closely, we will see that they reveal tensions. If we allow these tensions to increase, they will run their natural course and our "ailment" (presumably our sense that the text should say something clear and consistent) will pass. Like Wittgenstein, Derrida believes that people can have intellectual ailments; unlike Wittgenstein, he does not look to clarity for the cure.

Derrida argues that problems of interpretation and meaning, possibilities of jokes, puns, and surprising allusions are as much a feature of language in philosophy as they are of literature and everyday life. At the same time, all language is affected by its metaphysical history which, in the Western philosophical tradition, carries a heritage of polarities such as body/mind, reason/emotion, inner/outer, and masculine/feminine. Philosophy and philosophical language are not privileged or unique. Philosophy has no special authority to analyze and clarify meanings; it does not work in a Platonic heaven of pure concepts, Derrida says. Philosophy should not be blind to its own reasons and motives. We cannot expect philosophy to discover reliable foundations for knowledge. But nor can we avoid philosophy. Those who inherit the Western cultural tradition are all, in a sense, the children of Socrates; the influence of philosophy and philosophers on our language and thinking goes very deep. If we try to go "beyond" philosophy, we will only end up rehearsing old moves and making mistakes diagnosed centuries ago. Nor is reason something disdained in deconstruction, however anarchistic that movement might seem to be. Derrida said that one cannot advance even a single proposition without rejoining the discourse of reason. When we make a claim, we put it forward as true, acceptable, and reasonable; thus we commit ourselves to its making sense and being supportable by evidence.

Derrida argues against three common philosophical assumptions about the nature and role of philosophy. First, he denies that writing is a means subordinate to speech for communicating knowledge, and that matters of philosophical style are secondary to logic and meaning. Second, he denies the Hegelian notion that we are passing in the history of philosophy through stages that will lead us, progressively, to more accurate accounts which are closer to the truth. Third, he questions the idea (common among philosophers especially) that there is something particularly authoritative about philosophy – that philosophy and philosophers are uniquely qualified to clarify meaning, establish values, and validate claims to knowledge.

Derrida has in effect proposed a new way of thinking based on questioning distinctions and assumptions, and looking for subtle inter-relations and connections. His deconstructionist methods have been tremendously influential in literary criticism. They have had far less impact in his original discipline of philosophy, where deconstruction is criticized for its apparent implication that "anything goes" so far as interpretation and meaning are concerned. Many philosophers are impatient with Derrida's deliberately paradoxical and puzzling statements, blatantly obscurantist language, apparently non-serious playing with texts, and love of the enigmatic. They find Wittgenstein's response to the paradoxes of meaning far more sensible than that of Derrida. Nevertheless, through literary criticism, Derrida has had a tremendous influence on intellectual culture, one which has seeped back into some areas of philosophy itself.

Feminist Epistemology

In the decades since 1970 the number of women philosophers in most Western countries has grown considerably. In addition to exploring the historical issues, traditional problems, and themes pertaining to women's equality, many of these philosophers have done original and thought-provoking work on topics concerning logic, knowledge, and the philosophy of science.

Some feminist philosophers have argued that classical Western philosophy is predominantly *masculine*. Because most philosophers in the Western tradition have been male and many have been outright misogynists, standard accounts often fail to seriously consider the work and role of women, adopting instead philosophical ideals and theories which incorporate cultural norms of masculinity. In some cases philosophical theories seem to be premised on the subordination of women and turn out to be incompatible with viewing women as equal to men.

In ethics, feminists have criticized what they see as excessive abstraction in many mainstream theories. They deny absolutely that it could be right to sacrifice lives in the pursuit of some great cause. Feminist moral theorists tend to be sceptical of large-scale theories of justice and value, and insist that the small personal values of women's lives should be taken into account when public priorities are established. They have emphasized the ethical importance of empathy, nurturing, and caring. Feminists point to the importance of relationships in human life and argue that because many central relationships (that between child and parent, for instance) are not chosen, choice should not be the central concept of morality. We find ourselves in situations; we attend to aspects of those situations; and they make demands on us. Unlike Sartre and Beauvoir, contemporary feminists do not endorse a sharp distinction between fact and value.

In the areas of epistemology (the study of knowledge) and the philosophy of science, feminist philosophers have taken a distinctive approach and raised many new questions. There are many different versions of feminist epistemologies; however certain themes stand out as prominent in virtually all of them. Like the later Wittgenstein, feminist epistemologists stress the importance of paying attention to individual concrete cases and understanding those cases in context. Also like Wittgenstein, they emphasize the social aspects of knowledge, denying the individualistic view that one can construct or validate claims to knowledge on one's own. Intellectual autonomy is important, but it must be interpreted so as to allow for the fact that in constructing and acquiring knowledge, we rely and depend on other people. Some feminist theorists have argued that it is a community of people, not an individual by himself or herself, that constitutes the knowing subject.

We think using language, and we learn language from other people. We build up a world picture incorporating beliefs about times and places we have never experienced, and we do this by relying on the testimony of other people whom we trust. Research in natural and social science also presupposes trust because it requires that people collaborate with each other. In working to state and corroborate our hypotheses and theories, we need honest dialogue, based on mutual confidence and aimed towards the goal of consensus. In epistemology as in ethics, feminist theorists argue that human beings develop and live in relationships with each other; we do not think by ourselves.

Like deconstructionists, feminist theorists tend to be sceptical of dichotomies and to dispute hierarchies. Many express scepticism about absolute objectivity and universality. Feminist epistemologists argue that knowledge is constructed by human beings who are inevitably influenced in their curiosity and assumptions by such characteristics as gender, position in society, culture, class, age, race, and sexuality (homosexual or heterosexual). Knowledge – and theories of thinking and knowledge – does not emerge from the point of view of God, who would be totally knowledgeable, capable of seeing and understanding everything, and devoid of bias. These theories are constructed by human beings who occupy a particular historical position in the world. Everyone has a viewpoint, and every viewpoint is located in a body (male or female), a culture, a place, and a time. To make our knowledge more reliable, we should take account of our subjective position in the world and do our best to collaborate with others. Any claim to be completely neutral and impartial should be regarded with suspicion.

Claims to knowledge should be recognised as approximate and provisional: we may not know exactly; we may not know for sure. Feminist epistemologists question such traditional goals in epistemology as neutrality, impartiality, and universally applicable knowledge of an object distinct from the knowing subject. Often in the Western tradition mind has been strictly distinguished from matter. Knowledge has been seen as something minds could possess and use to "master" or dominate nature. (These assumptions are especially prominent in the work of Descartes and Sartre.) Conceptions of separation, domination, and mastery have been rejected by most feminists, who regard human beings as creatures within nature and do not wish to connect knowledge with control and domination.

Feminist epistemology is broadly empiricist, stressing the importance of experience in thinking and knowledge. But feminist empiricists do not understand experience in the way that Hume did. Experience for them is less a matter of sights and sounds, tastes and smells, than a question of what we go through in life. Feminists urge that what is personally experienced is important in the construction of knowledge and should not be neglected or argued away. Emotion and reason are not polar opposites. Feminist epistemologists usually adopt the view of reason and emotion implicit in Wollstonecraft's work: heart and mind should go together, because feeling can help us think and thinking can help us feel. Most feminist epistemologists think that women's experiences are different from men's because women and men have different bodies, experience different social expectations, and are assigned or undertake different roles in life. These aspects of gendered experience are significant for thought and knowledge. What questions we explore, what assumptions and interests we bring to bear on those questions, and what applications of knowledge we find useful will depend on what role we play in the social world. Thus they will depend on gender – and also on class, culture, age, sexuality, and race.

According to most feminist epistemologists, thinking, knowledge, and power cannot be separated. To think more creatively and accurately, we need to make research communities diverse and egalitarian: when people have varied interests and assumptions, they have a better chance of checking each other's biases, prejudices, quirks, mistakes, and hasty inferences. Critical thinking will be facilitated by having a diverse group of people who respect each other and can work together in a democratic and egalitarian way. Domination by an "authority" or powerful in-group will lessen the rationality of a community.

Feminist epistemologists such as Sandra Harding, Lorraine Code, Nancy Hartsock, and Helen Longino have reframed traditional questions about thought, knowledge, and justification. Who is the subject of knowledge – the individual or the community? Does the social position a person occupies affect what he or she comes to know? If so, how? Is knowledge given to us, or is it something we construct? What is the influence of gendered experience and sexuality on human knowledge? Are some standpoints in the world advantageous for achieving knowledge and others less so? How does a system of thoughts or beliefs come to qualify as "knowledge?" Who authorizes it to be knowledge, and what gives that person or group the authority to do so? Is objectivity possible? How should objectivity be understood? Our values affect our interests, our curiosity, our relationships with each other, and our handling of differences; thus our values affect our thinking, our beliefs, and what we come to know. The traditional devaluing of what has been deemed feminine (caring for the young, the old and the sick; household tasks; emotion; empathy; nurturing) has led to a distortion of values both in philosophy and in the Western culture at large. Feminist epistemologists argue that to be adequate, a theory of knowledge must pay attention to these ways in which social values influence knowledge. It must also pay attention to its own values, which should be democratic and egalitarian.

Some feminist epistemologists have argued that because of their situation in the world, women tend to have a better standpoint for understanding social reality than do men. An influential version of this "feminist standpoint" theory was put forward by Nancy Hartsock in the early eighties. Her view is an adaptation of Marxist theory, and as such shows the influence of Hegel's Master/Slave dialectic. Marx argued that the material structures of life affect and limit our understanding of social relationships. If material life is structured around the interactions of two groups (for Marx, capitalists and workers; for Hartsock, men and women) each group will have a view of the world and of the other group. These visions will tend to be inversely related; each taking off against the other. The dominant group will have a partial and perverse view of the social world because it will tend to ignore the interests and perspective of the subordinate group. The dominant group is in a position to structure the material relations in which all parties must participate; because its view of the social world plays a large role in constructing that world, that dominant view is bound to correctly describe the world, to some extent. But the dominant view will omit the perspective and interests of the oppressed group. These people will have to struggle to work out their own view of the world and to do so, they will have to look beneath the surface of ordinary social relationships. In the process, they will produce an activist vision which will show how real relationships among human beings are often unjust and inhumane.

Simplifying this theory, we might say that what and how people think depends on the sorts of people they are, and the sorts of people they are depends on what they do. As Beauvoir emphasized in *The Second Sex*, there has been a sexual division of labour, which is reflected not only in the family and home but in institutionalized social practices and policies. There are many important exceptions, such as Beauvoir herself, but generally women's lives have been characterized by the work of bearing and rearing children, cleaning and maintaining a household, and providing the means of life within the home. These roles have meant that women are closer to concrete bodily life than men who work producing objects to be exchanged. What women produce has primarily "use value," not "exchange value," Hartsock says. She argues that their role as oppressed domestic workers gives women a distinct standpoint, more distanced from power and dominance, closer to the concrete realities of actual living than the point of view associated with men and characteristically male activities. Women's standpoint, Hartsock argues, is an epistemically privileged one. From it we may expect better insights about values, politics, and social and economic relationships than those that would emerge from the dominant standpoint, namely that of men.

An illustration of this sort of approach may be found in Sara Ruddick's essays on maternal thinking. Ruddick claims that all thought arises out of social practice; the way we think depends on what we do in life. People occupy certain roles and respond to a reality that appears to them as given. The maternal role is shaped by interests in preserving, reproducing, directing and understanding individual and group life. Ruddick argues that those who fulfill this role well have a characteristic way of thinking, arising from the interests and goals that define mothering. Mothers who are seriously carrying out this role seek to preserve and maintain a child's life, to foster his or her physical, emotional, and intellectual growth, and to turn the child into an adult who can function within the cultural group. If they care well for their children, mothers are characteristically flexible and humble. They maintain a kind of resilient cheerfulness which enables them to cope with adversity or sudden change. Children are continually growing and changing, often in unpredictable ways, and mothers are called upon to respond to their needs and demands in a constructive way. To do so, good mothers learn to be tolerant of ambiguity and uncertainty. They must resolve conflicts, offer hopeful encouragement, sometimes against all odds, and adapt to the many changes in their children and their circumstances.

Ruddick claims that there are many fights and feuds to resolve and arbitrate among children and that mothers, despite their superior physical force, generally do this without resorting to physical force. Ruddick sees non-violence as a constitutive principle of maternal thinking. In such thinking, means and ends are intertwined. We cannot bring up a child to be just using unjust methods; nor can we bring up a child to be democratic using undemocratic practices. Maternal thinking is concrete and practical, flexible and adaptable, attentive and empathetic. It includes a realistic sense of threats and yet shows a balance of optimism and pessimism. There are of course temptations in the role; there are many ways mothers can easily go wrong. Mothers may control too much, may overly favor their own child, or blind themselves to important problems. But effective mothers manage to resist these temptations most of the time. Maternal thinking is not a by-product of female hormones or bodily structure; it emerges from the activities of caring for children. Men who do this, and do it well, will also practice maternal thinking.

According to Ruddick, the thinking in maternal practice is holistic (qualities and events are understood in context), concrete, and practical. It is field-dependent: different beliefs and concepts are brought to bear on different contexts and situations. It is open-ended; because children change and develop quickly and unpredictably, mothers learn not to make definitive judgments on what their children are like or will become. It is realistic; children cannot be sustained and preserved by a parent who does not acknowledge the concrete obstacles and threats that confront her and her children. It acknowledges the particularity and uniqueness of each child. It does not seek mastery or domination and is non-violent. It is hopeful and preserving.

Ruddick argues that maternal thinking should be brought into the public realm, where its constitutive values could greatly improve our political life. She says that mothers have a tradition of peacefulness and conflict resolution that should be brought to bear on public thinking, where it could support a diminution of militaristic values and a general desire for peace. The empathy, attentive love, cheerfulness, and hopeful persistence characteristic of maternal thinking and maternal practice provide a distinctive approach to conflict and a distinctive way of caring and knowing. Ruddick argues that maternal thinking is superior to the power-oriented and often manipulative thinking so characteristic of national and international politics.

Inspiring though it may be, this account is open to criticism insofar as it necessarily discounts some of the negative facts about mothers and motherhood. Although maternal thinking in Ruddick's sense no doubt exists, her description is highly idealized. There are mothers who seek to dominate and control their children; mothers who neglect their children; mothers who abuse their children; even mothers who kill their children. Clearly, playing the role of mother does not always bring forth the kind of practical creative thinking that Ruddick describes. Another criticism is that the maternal role has been used to justify limiting opportunities for women, keeping them in the home and restricting their participation in public life. Feminists who exalt the virtues of motherhood and the special characteristics of "maternal thinking" risk playing into the hands of traditionalists who have argued that women should, above all else, be mothers – and who have used that doctrine to restrict opportunities for women.

In fact, the notion of a female or feminist standpoint is open to serious objections, if we understand it as implying a kind of superiority or privilege. Hartsock argues that people gain a more accurate view of the world because they are oppressed. Is this true? The best answer would seem to be, "It depends." What is the subject: astronomy, child-rearing, slavery, or particle physics? Which oppressed person or group are we talking about? Some oppressed people may more intensely feel and more accurately understand certain aspects of social relationships, but many are handicapped by lack of education and opportunity, and others are blind to their own oppression.

Another problem with Hartsock's version of standpoint theory is that there are many different people and groups who can claim to be oppressed – not just women but native Canadians, African-Americans, other visible minorities, the poor, the disabled, gay men, lesbians, children, and so on. To take seriously the view that simply being oppressed gives one a stronger, privileged basis for thought and understanding is to open the door to bizarre competitions between various groups. Who has the best standpoint from which to understand dominance in the society? Who is more oppressed, a gay African-American man, an elderly Chinese-Canadian woman, or a blind lesbian? Who dominates? It is not enough to say "white males;" that ignores poverty, class, age, and context. In some contexts and respects, wealthy older women hold power over young white men. Who has the "best" standpoint for understanding "dominance?" Attending to such absurd questions is unlikely to improve our thinking because it distracts from issues of substance.

There are various versions of feminist standpoint theory and, in any event, that theory is not endorsed by all feminist epistemologists. Many feminist theorists do not like the idea of claiming a kind of privileged access to knowledge. They argue that evidence, suggestions, and theories should be evaluated on their merit rather than by reference to the degree of oppression of the person or group putting them forward. This is not to deny that democratizing thinking and research are central and worthy goals. It is important to hear many voices; diversity can facilitate critical thinking and lessen the prevalence of sexism, racism, and classism in research, politics, and everyday life. Valuable questions for research are likely to emerge when the lives of marginalized people are taken seriously. But many people can raise and address such questions. Hegel thought through the Master/Slave relationship from the point of view of a slave – but Hegel was not a slave.

Elizabeth Anderson offers an interpretation of feminist epistemology which values both reason and objectivity. Thought and reason enable us to amend our beliefs, attitudes and practices. We reflect on evidence and reasons to see whether they are cogent, whether we would still endorse an argument after careful analysis. When social relationships are egalitarian and well arranged, there is a better chance for people to correct each other's mistakes. Thus bringing more women and other previously disadvantaged groups into research can be justified on intellectual grounds. There is no need to appeal to a privileged feminist standpoint. Diversity is defensible intellectually, as well as ethically and politically, because it will serve the interests of reasonableness. Also, diversity will make science more empirically adequate because of the broader range of experience included. Neither in science nor in politics should either gender set the agenda and standards for the other.

Feminist epistemologists have raised important questions about the influence of subjective conditions on knowledge and have argued convincingly for the intellectual and political benefits of democratizing thought. Every person and every group tend to have biases and special interests which potentially distort their thinking; we all have a tendency to think that the world must be just as it appears to us. The only way we can hope to correct this and approach objectivity is to work together, from diverse points of view.

Concluding Comments

This survey has revealed many themes about thinking, knowledge, meaning and value in Western philosophy from the time of Socrates and Plato to the present. In Socrates, we find thinking as arguing and critical thinking displayed in argument. For Plato, the main goal of thinking was to reach an understanding of the Forms, or timeless universals, to establish reliable and permanent standards for theoretical knowledge and practical wisdom. Aristotle sought universals in particulars, invented formal logic, and recognized that styles of thinking and types of knowledge could vary with the subject matter. In Descartes, we see doubt and analysis as philosophical methods directed to the goal of certainty. Thought should be rigorous above all else, and we should precede in small steps, with indubitability as our primary goal.

Wollstonecraft exemplifies the Enlightenment faith in reason and confidence that progress will result from the application of reason to human affairs. In Hume and Kant, we find a more qualified confidence in the ability of human reason to understand and change the world. Hume's conception of thinking is naturalist and empiricist. The paradoxes that emerge from his work show the need to amend the empiricist approach, to acknowledge intellectually grounded concepts and the activity of the mind. The active, connecting role of the human understanding in thinking and the role of ideas of reason in pushing thought forward are major themes in Kant's philosophy. In different ways and for different reasons, Hume and Kant raise the problem of limits to human thinking and knowledge. Both argue that although we can think about themes beyond experience, we can have no knowledge outside the world of experience. So far as such topics as God and immortality are concerned, we can only think. We may have faith, but we cannot know.

Hegel emphasizes change, history, and development in thinking. His dialectic offers a model of how beliefs encounter problems, in response to which they change, only to encounter more problems and change again. He too confidently assumed progress, believing that what was later would necessarily be better. Hegel's philosophy illustrates the synthetic aspects of thinking; in contrast to the analytic reductionism of Descartes, it provides a model for systems in which parts affect and depend on the whole. In Beauvoir and Sartre, we find an account of thinking as the human capacity to turn away from material reality, to step back, reflect, and initiate a fresh course. Thought and choice ground the freedom of human action; because we are free, thinking creatures, we can create for ourselves values and meanings. Wittgenstein's later philosophy demands that we interpret concrete phenomena in contexts of actual human life, question abstractions and generalizations, and struggle for clarity.

Our ability to think is a fundamental, defining quality of human life. It can liberate us from our circumstances, connect us with each other, and create new possibilities. Our critical thinking allows us to reject fallacies and shallow doctrines. We doubt, analyze, reflect, spot contradictions, discover paradoxes, then try to move on. Our creative thinking is the source of art, beauty, play, and explanatory theory. It is by thinking that we take things apart and put things together, by thinking that we make meanings.

We do not find in the history of Western philosophy any single message about human life and knowledge. There is no one message as to how we should think; nor is there any such blueprint in the mosaic of contemporary philosophy. In addition to their differing theories of knowledge, meaning, and value, each philosopher has his or her own characteristic style of thinking, used to arrive at theories and responses to pressing issues. In both historical and contemporary philosophy we have a rich intellectual resource, a wealth of overlapping, fascinating theories of thinking, knowledge, and value. It is true what the critics say: from the time of Socrates, philosophers have done vast amounts of critical thinking. But in addition, philosophers have had much to say about the nature of thinking and – if we read between the lines – about the highly practical and related question of how to think.

NOTES

Notes for Chapter One, Socrates

The metaphor of the sting ray is taken from Plato's dialogue, the *Meno*. When Meno is unable to define virtue to Socrates' satisfaction, he says:

> Socrates, even before I met you they told me that in plain truth you are a perplexed man yourself and reduce others to perplexity. At this moment I feel you are exercising magic and witchcraft upon me and positively laying me under your spell until I am just a mass of helplessness. If I may be flippant, I think that not only in outward appearance but in other respects as well you are exactly like the flat sting ray that one meets in the sea. Whenever anyone comes into contact with it, it numbs him, and that is the sort of thing that you seem to be doing to me now. My mind and my lips are literally numb and I have nothing to reply to you.
> (80a)

The effects of a sting ray were powerful enough to knock over a full-grown adult if he stepped on the flat fish in shallow water.

Quotations from Plato's early dialogues are taken from *Plato: Collected Dialogues*, edited by Edith Hamilton and Huntingdon Cairns (New York: Bollingden Foundation, Pantheon Books, 1961). In this collection *Socrates' Defense (the Apology)* and the *Crito* were translated by Hugh Tredennick; the *Laches* was translated by Benjamin Jowett; the *Meno* was translated by W.K.C. Guthrie and the *Euthyphro* was translated by Lane Cooper. The *Phaedo* (usually regarded as a middle dialogue) was translated by David Gallop (Clarendon Plato Series: Oxford, 1975).

The article on pronoia was written by Maggie Scarf, who seems herself to have been slightly sceptical about the claim that happiness is a mental disorder. Scarf's essay originally appeared in *The New Republic*; it was reprinted in the *The Globe and Mail* December 31, 1994.

A challenging, though somewhat unorthodox, interpretation of Socrates' trial and conviction is offered by I.F. Stone in *The Trial of Socrates* (New York: Doubleday Anchor, 1988). Stone argues that Socrates was anti-democratic and elitist and that it was these aspects of his thought and life that got him into trouble in Athens. He also suggests that for various reasons Socrates did not launch the kind of defense that would have served him well. Stone believes that Socrates was unwilling to appeal to principles of free speech because he did not fully believe in them. (Not everything is worth saying.) Stone acknowledges that Socrates' sentence and death were a black mark against democratic Athens: Socrates gained from this persecution a reputation as a "secular saint." Stone suggests that the ultimate explanation for Socrates' death is that at seventy, he had decided that it was time for him to die.

Excellent background on Greek culture and ideas is given in Terence Irwin, *Classical Thought* (Oxford, U.K.: Oxford University Press, 1989). Source materials on Socrates, including Aristophanes' play, *The Clouds*, are collected in Richard Levin, *The Question of Socrates* (New York: Harcourt Brace and World, 1961). Hugh Tredennick and Robin Waterfield have translated and collected materials pertaining to Socrates from Xenophon, in *Conversations of Socrates* (London: Penguin, 1990). A thorough and useful account is that of W.K.C. Guthrie in *Socrates* (Cambridge: Cambridge University Press, 1971). The eminent classical scholar, Gregory Vlastos, offered a comprehensive and careful account of Socrates in *Socrates: Ironist and Moral Philosopher* (Ithaca, N.Y.: Cornell University Press, 1991). Another helpful discussion is Terry Penner, "Socrates and the Early Dialogues," in *The Cambridge Companion to Plato* (121 - 169) edited by Richard Kraut (Cambridge, U.K.: Cambridge University Press, 1992).

Discussions of Socratic questioning and the quest for definitions in particular may be found in essays by Richard Robinson, George Nakhnikian, and Marc Cohen in Gregory Vlastos (ed.) *The Philosophy of Socrates* (New York: Anchor Books, 1971) and by Gregory Vlastos and Richard Kraut in *Oxford Studies in Ancient Philosophy* (Volume 1, 1983). (Oxford, U.K.: Oxford University Press, 1983.) A clever satire of Socrates, Plato, and scholarly writing in general, based on the characters of Socrates' wife, Xanthippe, and Plato's mother, Perictione, is presented by Roger Scruton in *Xanthippic Dialogues* (London: Sinclair-Stevenson, 1993).

Notes for Chapter Two, Plato

The *Meno* was translated by W.K.C. Guthrie; the *Phaedo* by David Gallop (Clarendon Plato Series: Oxford, 1975); the *Symposium* by Alexander Nehamas and Paul Woodruff (Indianapolis: Hackett, 1989); and the *Republic* by Paul Shorey. The *Meno* and the *Republic* appear in *Plato: Collected Dialogues*, edited by Edith Hamilton and Huntingdon Cairns. An extremely helpful overview article on Plato is that of Gilbert Ryle in *The Encyclopedia of Philosophy* edited by Paul Edwards (New York: Macmillan and Free Press, 1967) Volume 6, 314-333. Useful introductory works include R.M. Hare, *Plato* (Oxford: Oxford University Press, 1982); G.C. Field, *The Philosophy of Plato* (second edition; Oxford: Oxford University Press, 1969); G.C. Rowe, *Plato* (Brighton, Sussex: The Harvester Press, 1984); Julia Annas, *An Introduction to Plato's Republic* (Oxford: Oxford University Press, 1981) and Nicholas P. White, *A Companion to Plato's Republic* (Oxford: Blackwell, 1977).

The analogies of the Line, Sun, and Cave are extremely famous, and the Divided Line especially has inspired much commentary. The notion that Knowledge should be twice as large as Belief is my own. Plato does not give a ratio; in fact he does not say that Knowledge should be the larger segment. Knowledge is clearer than Belief; and the Forms are, for Plato, more real than material things; the greater size of the line segment in my drawing is intended to reflect these aspects which make Knowledge more valuable than Belief. But it could be argued that, on the contrary, Knowledge should be represented by a shorter segment of the line than Belief because it is rarer than Belief.

Another question about Plato's theory of knowledge is whether we can have any knowledge of things in the ordinary material world or whether, to the contrary, material things are always merely objects of opinion. Plato sometimes seems to say that the Forms are the only objects of knowledge. If this were so, it would be hard to explain why the philosopher who has seen the form of the Good would know more than other people when he or she returns to the everyday, or mundane, world. If *only* Forms can be known, knowledge of the Forms will not alter the fact that even the philosopher who has grasped the Good will merely have beliefs (not knowledge) when he or she returns to the mundane world. I follow arguments by Gail Fine to the effect that after knowing the Forms one will understand objects in the material world for what they are and have, in a sense, knowledge at this mundane level.

The word "dialectic," which will be important in the philosophies of Kant and Hegel as well as that of Plato, is still widely used. In theories about argument and discussion, "dialectical" is commonly used now in a somewhat Platonic sense: a dialectical view of argument is one in which attention is paid to the beliefs and challenges of the audience and the ability and obligation of the arguer to respond to challenges. Present-day dialectical theories of argument emphasize that argument is social, much as Plato and Socrates did. (See Chapter Eleven, Critical Thinking – Informal Logic Movement.) As for the preference for speech over written works, W.K.C. Guthrie points out that books in Plato's day were papyrus rolls which were awkward and inconvenient to use. There was a lack of punctuation, paragraphing, and indexes, and sometimes even lack of space between words. In addition, Plato had reasons to prefer spoken dialogue over the written word, which he explored in his dialogue *Phaedrus*. (This preference is contested by the contemporary philosopher, Jacques Derrida. See Chapter Eleven.)

Why should one Form, the Form of the Good, be supreme over others, and why should it be this Form that one must behold in order to achieve *nous*, the final state of knowledge? The matter is indeed mysterious; one answer may be that understanding other things requires knowing what they are *good for*, and that is why knowing the Good enables one to know how all the other Forms, and other things, fit together.

I was greatly assisted in preparing this chapter by various articles and commentaries, including Gail Fine, "Knowledge and Belief in Republic V-VIII" in Stephen Everson (ed.) *Companions to Ancient Thought I: Epistemology* (Cambridge: Cambridge University Press, 1990); Mary Margaret McCabe, "Myth, Allegory and Argument in Plato" in *The Language of the Cave* (*Apeiron* XXV no. 4; December 1992, pp. 46-67); Nicholas P. White, *Plato on Knowledge and Reality* (Indianapolis: Hackett, 1976), chapters I - IV; Richard Robinson, *Plato's Earlier Dialectic*. Second Edition (Oxford: Clarendon Press, 1953); W.K.C. Guthrie, *A History of Greek Philosophy IV: Plato: the Man and His Dialogues – Earlier Period* (Cambridge: Cambridge University Press, 1975); Anders Wedberg, *Plato's Philosophy of Mathematics* (Stockholm: Almqvist and Wiksell, 1955); Ian Mueller, "Mathematical Method and Philosophical Truth," in Richard Kraut (ed.) *The Cambridge Companion to Plato* (Cambridge: Cambridge University Press, 1992); Konrad Gaiser, "Plato's Enigmatic Lecture on the Good," *Phronesis* 25 (1980), pp. 5 - 37; and David Gallop, "Image and Reality in Plato's Republic," *Archiv fur Geschichte de Philosophie* 47 (1965), pp. 113 - 131.

Plato's views on women have provoked considerable debate. In the *Republic* Plato argues that because the soul is distinct from the body women's souls are unaffected by their "weaker" bodies and women could, in principle, be intelligent enough to be educated to be Guardians (rulers) in the ideal state. He also argues that even though most men may be superior to most women, some women will be more intelligent, and thus, by Plato's standards superior, to most men. Despite these views, which stand out as radical and enlightened in the context in which he wrote, Plato reflected the subordinate view of women in Athenian culture. He considered the love of men for each other to be superior to love between men and women, and his dialogues contain a number of misogynist remarks. For a general discussion of these isues, and a clear argument that Plato should not be regarded as an early feminist, see Julia Annas, "Plato's Republic and Feminism," in *Philosophy* 51 (1976) 17 - 321. In *Engendering Origins: Critical Feminist Readings in Plato and Aristotle* edited by Bat-Ami Bar On (Albany: State University of New York Press, 1994, p. 35) Christine Peirce claims interestingly (but without documentation) that a few women attended Plato's Academy and one who did wore man's clothing.

The figure of Diotima is of considerable interest. Part of her speech seems to echo a pre-Socratic view of the world similar to that of Heraclitus or even, possibly, to the matriarchal goddess religions of Crete, of which vestiges survived in Plato's time. In *A History of Women Philosophers, Volume I: Ancient Philosophers* (Boston: Nijhoff, 1987) Mary Waithe argues that Diotima was a real person. Her grounds are that Plato virtually never created fictional characters, and elsewhere in the Dialogues represents Socrates as consulting a priestess for guidance. In addition, an archaeological remain – a bronze relief depicting the *Symposium* banquet – shows Socrates conversing with a woman who was probably Diotima. Waithe notes that commentators apparently did not begin to question Diotima's existence until about the fifteenth century, when they apparently did not do so on the basis of any new evidence.

The idea that the dialogues may be seen as images of the Forms and might have been seen in this way by Plato himself comes from David Gallop, who suggests that the dialogues contain verbal images by which the Forms may be recollected, through their embodiment in the characters and dramatic action. Gallop suggests that some characters in some dialogues portray the very characteristics they are discussing. In the *Euthyphro*, for instance, Euthyphro might be thought to display piety and Socrates impiety. In the *Symposium* the speakers both display, and discuss, love and beauty. In the *Phaedo*, death and immortality are discussed when Socrates is about to die. The idea that Plato's myths may be regarded as having the role of counter-arguments in a dialectical process is taken from Mary McCabe.

Notes for Chapter Three, Aristotle

All quotations from Aristotle's works are taken from *The Complete Works of Aristotle*, the Revised Oxford Translation edited by Jonathan Barnes (Princeton, N.J.: Princeton University Press, 1984; two volumes). The *Metaphysics* was translated by W.D. Ross; the *Nichomachean Ethics* was translated by W.D. Ross and revised by J.O. Urmson; *De Interpretatione* was translated by J.L. Ackrill; *Prior Analytics* by A.J. Jenkinson; *Posterior Analytics* by Jonathan Barnes; *Topics* by W.A. Pickard-Cambridge; *Physics* by R.P. Hardie and R. K. Gaye; *Parts of Animals* by W. Ogle, and *Generation of Animals* by A. Platt.

An excellent introductory overview of Aristotle's thought is *Aristotle the Philosopher* by J.L. Ackrill (Oxford: Oxford University Press, 1981). Also extremely helpful are D.J. Allan, *The Philosophy of Aristotle* (Oxford: Oxford University Press, 1970, second edition); G.E. R. Lloyd, *Aristotle: The Structure and Growth of His Thought* (Cambridge: Cambridge University Press, 1968); Marjorie Grene, *A Portrait of Aristotle* (London: Faber and Faber, 1963) and Jonathan Barnes *Aristotle* (Oxford: Oxford University Press). In preparing this chapter I found *The Cambridge Companion to Aristotle* edited by Jonathan Barnes (Cambridge: Cambridge University Press, 1995) to be indispensable. It contains many clear and helpful overview articles, and a useful bibliography. I also benefitted from Nancy Sherman's *The Fabric of Character: Aristotle's Theory of Virtues* (Oxford: Clarendon Press, 1989).

There is considerable contemporary discussion about Aristotle's philosophy, both from an interpretive and from a substantive point of view. The problem of how universal concepts and particular things are related was a major topic throughout the whole medieval period and is still debated today. Another issue which has been central throughout the entire history of Aristotle interpretation and has, by necessity, received relatively little emphasis here is that of materialism and immaterialism. As contrasted with Plato, Aristotle seems close to materialism: he emphasized observation, the centrality of individual observable substances, and the interdependence of matter and form; he viewed the soul as the form of the body. Yet there are aspects of Aristotle's thought which are clearly immaterialist. He argued for the existence of the Unmoved Mover, a non-physical being whose sole activity was contemplation and who was ultimately the source of movement in the natural world. In places, he seemed to allow that the soul, at least so far as its active reason was concerned, was independent of the body and could exist without it.

To what degree Aristotle should be regarded as an empiricist is also debatable. He accumulated vast amounts of scientific material based on observations and understood philosophy as having to take phenomena into account. But Aristotle has been criticized for too easily reading his own values into nature. He was convinced that right was better than left, light better than darkness, and male better than female. These were not exactly judgments based on careful observations. Whether Aristotle's phenomena were data in a modern scientific sense is unlikely. They seem to have been more like beliefs based on experience, or even in some cases common opinions. As for the principle of the Excluded Middle, Aristotle was less clear that this was a basic principle of thought than he was for the Principle of Non-Contradiction. He expressed uncertainty as to whether it should apply to statements about "future contingencies" such as 'There will be a sea battle tomorrow.'

Pertinent articles on some of these themes are: T.H. Irwin, "Homonymy in Aristotle," (*Review of Metaphysics* 34 (1981), 523 - 44); G. Ryle, "Dialectic in the Academy" in G.E.L. Owen, ed., *Aristotle on Dialectic* (Oxford: Oxford University Press, 1968); Martha Nussbaum, "Saving Aristotle's Appearances" in M. Schofield and M.C. Nussbaum (eds.) *Language and Logic* (Cambridge: Cambridge University Press, 1982); W. Leszl, "Knowledge of the Universal and Knowledge of the Particular in Aristotle," *Review of Metaphysics* 26 (1972-3) 278-313; and T. Lowe, "Aristotle on Kinds of Thinking," *Phronesis* 28 (1983), 17-30.

Aristotle had many shocking things to say about women. In virtually all respects, he regarded the female as less excellent than the male. Women, he thought, were defective men, defined by a "certain lack;" they were incomplete beings; they played only a passive role in reproduction and contribute only matter, not form, to their offspring. Women, Aristotle reported, had fewer teeth than men. (He did not check this belief by counting the teeth of his wife or his daughter.) Aristotle regarded male and female virtue as different.

Still more alarming, and especially pertinent to the theme of thinking, is the fact that Aristotle seems to have held that women do not, or cannot, reason and think in the same way as men. At one point he remarks that women have deliberative ability, but in an immature form. They need male guidance. The good life was to include contemplation and leisure and it is unlikely that women would have been able to participate in this; their work within the household would prohibit them from doing so.

When such remarks appear in the work of a famous and profound thinker, there are various responses, among which four stand out. We may fail to notice or take seriously such remarks; we may dwell on them and attack the work accordingly ("muckraking") using our present political and ethical values as the basis for appraising theories of the past; we may charitably adapt the system, assuming in effect that "male" means "human;" or we may explore whether the system logically *requires* the bias in question, or could be coherent and plausible without it. The first policy is common among scholars; the second and fourth have been popular with contemporary feminist thinkers and writers. In general I favor the fourth approach. But here, due to limitations of space, I have adopted the third. I have assumed that what Aristotle said about particulars and universals, induction and deduction, demonstration, judgment, deliberation, dialectic and the like is applicable to, and usable by, women as well as men – whether Aristotle himself would have thought this or not. Textual evidence, unfortunately, suggests that Aristotle himself would not have welcomed this adaptation. But I fail to see any reason why women cannot judge, deliberate, deduce, induce, argue, and so on and so forth in just the way Aristotle described.

Those wishing to pursue this topic further might consult F.E. Sparshott, "Aristotle on Women," *Philosophical Enquiry* 7 (1985), pp. 177 - 200. Another relevant source is *Engendering Origins: Critical Feminist Readings in Plato and Aristotle* edited by Bat-Ami Bar On (Albany: State University of New York Press, 1994), especially the very helpful and balanced article, "Nourishing Speculation: A Feminist Reading of Aristotelian Science" by Cynthia A. Freeland (pp. 145 - 188). Suggestions for further reading may be found therein. Especially noteworthy are Genevieve Lloyd, *The Man of Reason: "Male" and "Female" in Western Philosophy* (Minneapolis: University of Minnesota Press, 1984), and Sandra Harding and Merrill B. Hintikka (eds.) *Discovering Reality: Feminist Perspectives on Epistemology, Metaphysics, Methodology, and Philosophy of Science* (Dordrecht: D. Reidel, 1983).

Notes for Chapter Four, Descartes

Quotations from the Meditations and Objections and Replies are taken from *René Descartes: Meditations on First Philosophy with Selections from the Objections and Replies* edited and translated by John Cottingham (Cambridge: Cambridge University Press, 1986). The quotation on free will being something we can know by looking inside ourselves is from Descartes' conversation with Burman, as presented in John Cottingham, editor and translator, *Descartes: Conversations with Burman* (Oxford: Clarendon Press, 1976). Quotations from the Rules for the Direction of the Mind and Discourse on Method are from *Descartes: Philosophical Writings* translated and edited by Elizabeth Anscombe and Peter Geach (London: Thomas Nelson, 1954).

Pierre Gassendi (1592 - 1655), was a French sceptical philosopher and critic of Aristotelian philosophy. Author of one of the six sets of Objections which were published with the Meditations, Gassendi later went on to expand his criticisms and reflections into a large book on metaphysics. The Princess Elizabeth of Bohemia (1618 - 1680) was an extremely accomplished woman with considerable philosophical ability. She was a close friend and frequent correspondent of Descartes. Selections from her correspondence are as presented in Margaret Atherton *Women Philosophers of the Early Modern Period* (Indianapolis: Hackett, 1994).

An especially clear and helpful book is *Descartes: A Study of His Philosophy* by Anthony Kenny (New York: Random House, 1968). More complex, but also helpful, is Bernard Williams *Descartes: the Project of Pure Enquiry* (Hassocks, Sussex: The Harvester Press, 1978). I benefited as well from Peter A. Schouls, *Descartes and the Enlightenment* (Kingston and Montreal: McGill- Queen's University Press, 1989) especially Chapter II, on reason and free will. An older book, still useful, is Norman Kemp Smith, *New Studies in the Philosophy of Descartes* (London: Macmillan and Company, 1952). Interesting critical essays on Descartes may be found in *Meta-Meditations: Studies in Descartes* by Alexander Sesonske and Joel Fleming (Belmont, CA: Wadsworth, 1965) and Willis Doney, *Descartes: A Collection of Critical Essays* (New York: Anchor, 1967).

Many twentieth-century philosophers have rejected the Egocentric Predicament. Notable among these are Ludwig Wittgenstein in the *Blue and Brown Books* (Oxford: Basil Blackwell, 1958), *Philosophical Investigations* (Oxford: Basil Blackwell, 1963), and *On Certainty* (Oxford: Basil Blackwell, 1969); and Gilbert Ryle in *The*

Concept of Mind (London: Hutchinson's University Library, 1949). Wittgenstein's views are described in Chapter Ten.

A strong link between the Cartesian separation of mind from nature and humanity's often destructive attempts to dominate nature is drawn by Carolyn Merchant in *The Death of Nature* (New York: Harper and Row, 1980).

Notes for Chapter Five, Hume

Quotations from the *Treatise of Human Nature* are from the classic L.A. Selby-Bigge edition (Oxford: Clarendon Press, 1965). Quotations from the *Enquiry Concerning Human Understanding* are from the Open Court printing (La Salle, Ill.: Open Court Publications, 1963). As for quotations from Thomas Reid, they are taken from *The Works of Thomas Reid,* with Preface and Notes by Sir William Hamilton (Edinburgh: Maclachlan and Stewart, 1863; sixth edition). The passage from Kant is from his *Prolegomenon to any Future Metaphysics* (New York: Library of Liberal Arts, 1951; edited by L.W. Beck; translated by Richardson, Carus, and Mahaffy), page 6.

Three useful books on Hume, of a reasonably introductory nature, are Terence Penelhum, *Hume* (London: Macmillan, 1975); A.J. Ayer *Hume* (New York: Hill and Wang, 1980) and John Passmore, *Hume's Intentions* (London: Duckworth, 1980; third edition). Penelhum's work is especially clear and helpful. I am endebted to his discussion of Descartes and Hume with regard to the relationship between knowing and being unable to doubt. Passmore's book contains an appendix on Hume and the Ethics of Belief, treating the question of how one can conform one's belief to the evidence if belief is an entirely involuntary matter. He argues that Hume is inconsistent on this matter.

Other pertinent books on Hume include Donald W. Livingston, *Hume's Philosophy of Common Life* (Chicago: University of Chicago Press, 1984) and Anthony Flew, *Hume's Philosophy of Belief* (London: Routledge and Kegan Paul, 1961).

Two useful collections of essays on Hume's philosophy are V.C. Chappell, *Hume: A Collection of Critical Essays* (New York: Doubleday Anchor, 1966), and Alexander Sesonske and Joel Fleming, *Human Understanding: Studies in the Philosophy of David Hume* (Belmont, CA: Wadsworth, 1965). Richard H. Popkin's essay "David Hume: His Pyrrhonism and his Critique of Pyrrhonism" in Chappell is especially good. A recent more advanced book on Hume is Annette Baier, *A Progress of Sentiments* (Cambridge, Mass: Harvard University Press, 1991).

Hume made one qualification to his principle that every simple idea had to be derived from a simple impression. He allowed that if one had seen many shades of blue, and arranged them (mentally) on a kind of scale, one could detect a gap if a particular shade were missing. In such a case, one would be able to imagine the shade without experiencing it; one would then have an idea of this missing shade of blue without having first had an impression of it. But for some reason, Hume did not think this "singular" example was a serious exception to his empiricist principles.

In the *Dialogues on Natural Religion* there are three characters, Demea, Cleanthes, and Philo. Demea combines a sort of mysticism or negative theology (the nature of God is unknowable to man) with emphasis on religious authority. Philo and Cleanthes, the main characters, agree that if God is to be known, it must be through experience. They debate the merits of the Argument from Design. Cleanthes defends natural theology – the view that human beings, through their natural reason and experience of the world, can come to know that God exists and know something of his nature. Philo takes a sceptical stance and puts forth many criticisms of the Argument from Design. So balanced are these characters that commentators still argue as to whether it is Cleanthes or Philo who best represents Hume's own views. My comments on Hume's views of religious knowledge assume that Philo represents Hume's view.

Notes for Chapter Six, Wollstonecraft

Quotations from *A Vindication of the Rights of Woman* are from the Norton Critical Edition edited by Carol H. Poston (New York: W.W. Norton, 1975). This book also contains several essays on Wollstonecraft by other writers, including a beautiful piece by Virginia Woolf. Quotations from the *Letters from Norway, Sweden and Denmark* are from *The Works of Mary Wollstonecraft* edited by Janet Todd and Marilyn Butler (London: William Pickering, 1989), Volume 6. Quotations concerning the French Revolution, and from the *Vindication of the Rights of Men*, are taken from *A Wollstonecraft Anthology* edited by Janet M. Todd (Bloomington: Indiana University Press, 1977).

Richard Price's *A Review of the Principal Questions of Morals* may be found in L.A. Selby-Bigge (editor), *British Moralists* (Indianapolis: Bobbs Merrill, 1964).

At the time of her death, Mary Wollstonecraft was writing a novelized treatment of women's vulnerability in marriage. This work, *Maria or The Wrongs of Woman*, is now available, edited and with an introduction by Anne K. Mellor (New York: W.W. Norton, 1994).

Three useful biographies of Mary Wollstonecraft are Ralph Wardle, *Mary Wollstonecraft: A Critical Biography* (Lawrence, Kansas: University of Kansas Press, 1951); Claire Tomalin, *The Life and Death of Mary Wollstonecraft* (London: Weidenfelt and Nicolson, 1974); and Emily W. Sunstein, *A Different Face: The Life of Mary Wollstonecraft* (New York: Harper and Row, 1975). An overview of Wollstonecraft's writings is offered by Harriet Devine Jump in *Mary Wollstonecraft, Writer* (New York: Harvester Wheatsheaf, 1994). Useful articles on aspects of Wollstonecraft's thought and work include Mervyn Nicholson, "Sex and Spirit in Wollstonecraft and Malthus," *Journal of the History of Ideas* 51 (1990), 401 - 421; Moira Gatens, "Rousseau and Wollstonecraft: Nature versus Reason," *Australian Journal of Philosophy*, Supplement to Volume 64 (June 1986), 1 - 15; and Alison Ravetz, "The Trivialization of Mary Wollstonecraft: A Personal and Professional Career Re-Vindicated," *Women's Studies International Forum* Volume 6, no. 5 (1983).

The theme of the relationship between reason and emotion, which arises so naturally from Wollstonecraft's life and work, is prominent today, especially among feminist writers. There are literally hundreds of pertinent works. Among them are Louise M. Anthony and Charlotte Witt (editors), *A Mind of One's Own: Feminist Essays on Reason and Objectivity* (Boulder: Westview, 1993); Alison

Jaggar, "Love and Knowledge: Emotion in Feminist Epistemology," in *Women, Knowledge, and Reality* edited by Ann Garry and Marilyn Pearsall (Boston: Unwin Hyman, 1989); Hilary Rose, "Hand, Brain, and Heart: A Feminist Epistemology for the Natural Sciences," *Signs* 9 (1983) 73 - 90; and Sara Ruddick, *Maternal Thinking: Towards a Politics of Peace* (New York: Ballantine Books, 1987). A recent book arguing on biological grounds that emotions are essential to rational thinking is Antonio R. Damasio, *Descartes' Error: Emotion, Reason and the Human Brain* (New York: Avon Books, 1994).

Notes for Chapter Seven, Kant

All quotations from Kant are taken from Norman Kemp Smith's translation of Kant's *Critique of Pure Reason* (New York: St Martin's Press, 1969; first published by Macmillan in 1929). The citations are from Kemp Smith's blend of the first (A) and the second (B) editions, followed by the page number. Kant's Transcendental Deduction of the Categories was altered quite considerably in his second edition. The summary of Transcendental Deduction is my own; it combines themes from both editions.

The analytic/synthetic and *a priori*/ empirical distinctions have been discussed exhaustively in twentieth-century philosophy. The prevailing current opinion is that the lines cannot be drawn as neatly as Kant did. An especially influential article on the subject has been W.V.O. Quine's "Two Dogmas of Empiricism," in From a Logical Point of View (Cambridge, Mass: Harvard University Press, 1953).

For the beginning student, one especially easy and attractive approach to Kant's philosophy is that of Robert C. Solomon in *Introducing the German Idealists: Mock Interviews with Kant, Hegel, and others, and a letter from Schopenhauer* (Indianapolis: Hackett, 1981). Two extremely clear introductory books on Kant and his philosophy are Justus Hartnack's *Immanuel Kant* (Atlantic Highlands, New Jersey: Humanities Press, 1974) and *Kant's Theory of Knowledge*, translated by M. Holmes Hartshorne (New York: Harcourt Brace, 1967). A reliable general account is also offered in Volume VI *From the French Enlightenment to Kant* of Frederick Copleston, S.J., *A History of Philosophy* (New York: Image Doubleday, 1994; first published 1965).

Other useful works on Kant include Stephan Korner, *Kant* (Harmondsworth: Penguin Books, 1955); Robert Paul Wolff (editor), *Kant: A Collection of Critical Essays* (Garden City, N.Y.: Doubleday Anchor, 1967); T.M. Penelhum and J.J. MacIntosh, *The First Critique: Reflections on Kant's Critique of Pure Reason* (Belmont, CA: Wadsworth, 1969); Onora Nell (O'Neill), *Acting on Principle: An Essay on Kantian Ethics* (New York: Columbia University Press, 1975); Onora O'Neill, *Constructions of Reason: Explorations of Kant's Practical Philosophy* (Cambridge: Cambridge University Press, 1989); Lewis White Beck, *Studies in the Philosophy of Kant* (Indianapolis: Bobbs-Merril, 1965); and Frederick C. Beiser, *The Fate of Reason: German Philosophy from Kant to Fichte* (Cambridge, Mass: Harvard University Press, 1987). Beiser offers a fascinating account of criticisms of Kant made during the first decade after the publication of the First Critique.

Important reconstructions of Kant's ideas in our century include P.F. Strawson, *The Bounds of Sense* (London: Methuen, 1966); Robert Paul Wolff, *Kant's Theory of Mental Activity* (Cambridge, Mass: Harvard University Press, 1963); and Jonathan Bennett, *Kant's Analytic* (Cambridge: Cambridge University Press, 1966), and *Kant's Dialectic* (Cambridge: Cambridge University Press 1974).

In preparing the chapter, I was greatly helped by *The Cambridge Companion to Kant* (Cambridge, U.K.: Cambridge University Press, 1992) edited by Paul Guyer, especially by the essays by Frederick Beiser, Thomas Wartenburg, and Onora O'Neill.

Knowing how disappointed Hume was with the reception of his philosophical ideas in England and Scotland during his lifetime, it is fascinating to see how seriously Kant and his German contemporaries took Hume's sceptical arguments. Kant did not know English. But he had read Hume's *Enquiry Concerning Human Understanding*, other essays by Hume, and all or substantial parts of the *Dialogues on Natural Religion*, which were available in German translation. In addition, Kant had access to excerpts from Hume's *Treatise on Human Nature* as they were quoted by James Beattie, whose superficial common sense attack on Hume in *An Essay on the Nature and Immutability of Truth* was available in German.

Leibniz's rationalist "proof" that this is the best of all possible worlds was brilliantly satirized by Voltaire in *Candide*, a work still widely studied in its original form and popularized in a Broadway musical of the same title.

Apart from the *Critique of Practical Reason*, Kant's moral philosophy is best studied in his *Grounding for the Metaphysics of Morals* (translated by James W. Ellington; Indianapolis: Hackett, 1993). In addition to what he says in his Critiques, Kant wrote several essays especially relevant to the specific topic of thinking. One is "An Answer to the Question: What is Enlightenment?" which was published in 1784 and can be found in Ted Humphrey translator and editor, *Immanuel Kant, Perpetual Peace and Other Essays* (Indianapolis: Hackett, 1983). The other is "What Does it Mean to Orient Oneself in Thought?" (1786), available in L.W. Beck, translator and editor, *Kant's Critique of Practical Reason and Other Writings on Moral Philosophy* (Chicago: University of Chicago Press, 1949). The relevance of these essays for Kant's view of reason is described in Onora O'Neill in "The Public Use of Reason," in *Constructions of Reason*; in her essay in *The Cambridge Companion to Kant*, and in "Enlightenment as Autonomy: Kant's Vindication of Reason," in Peter Hulme and Ludmila Jordanova (editors), *The Enlightenment and Its Shadows* (New York: Routledge, 1990).

Kant called his view that we can know appearances, but not things-in-themselves, "transcendental idealism." He said that material things in space and time are quite real, and we can have objective knowledge of them. Our knowledge is objective because we share it with other people, who use public standards to order experience according to synthetic *a priori* principles. Kant did *not* want to be classified with idealists like the empiricist Berkeley, who had argued that objects are nothing more than collections of ideas in our minds. Against Berkeley, Kant insisted that the world was empirically real. However it is "transcendentally" ideal, because when we inquire into the conditions of knowledge, we discover that all appearances are conditioned by the structures of our minds. Whether Kant's transcendental idealism is ultimately different from Berkeley's idealism is one of many issues discussed by scholars and readers.

Notes for Chapter Eight, Hegel

Quotations marked as LHPII and LHPIII are from Hegel's *Lectures on the History of Philosophy*, Volumes II and III. (Translated by E.S. Haldane and Frances H. Simson; London: Kegan Paul, 1894; reprinted 1955 by Routledge Kegan Paul.) Quotations marked as PS are from Hegel's *Phenomenology of Spirit* translated by A.V. Miller (Oxford: Oxford University Press, 1977). Because Hegel's writing is often difficult, quotations from other works were not used. Hegel's philosophical system is sweepingly ambitious and, of necessity, many of its aspects have not been mentioned in this chapter. For a fairly reliable overview at an introductory level, see F.C. Copleston's chapters IX to XI in Volume VII of *A History of Philosophy* (New York: Doubleday Image Edition, 1994). The *Encyclopedia of Philosophy* also offers a general summary. An older work, Josiah Royce, *Lectures on Modern Idealism* (New Haven: Yale University Press, 1919; reissued 1964) is well-written and readable, and offers an attractive synopsis. In addition, R. C. Solomon's *In the Spirit of Hegel* (New York: Oxford University Press, 1983) is more accessible to relative beginners than most studies of Hegel.

I found the *Cambridge Companion to Hegel* (Cambridge, UK: Cambridge University Press, 1993) edited by Frederick C. Beiser indispensable in preparing this chapter. Especially helpful were articles by John Burbidge, Frederick Beiser, Michael Forster, Paul Guyer, and Peter Hylton. From Burbidge and Forster, I have borrowed several key points about thought and the dialectic. Other useful articles were Quentin Lauer, "Hegel as Historian of Philosophy" in *Hegel and the History of Philosophy* edited by Joseph J. O'Malley, Keith W. Algozin, and Frederick G. Weiss (The Hague: Martinus Nijhof, 1974), 21 - 46; K.R. Popper, "What is Dialectic?" Mind 49 (1940), 403 - 426; Karl Ameriks, "Hegel's Critique of Kant's Theoretical Philosophy," *Philosophy and Phenomenological Research* 45 (1981), 1 - 35; and Gustav Mueller, "The Hegel Lend on 'Thesis/ Anthithesis/Synthesis'" *Journal of the History of Ideas* 19 (1958), 411- 414. I have also benefited from Charles Taylor, *Hegel* (Cambridge, UK: Cambridge University Press, 1975) and Alasdair MacIntyre, editor, *Hegel: A Collection of Critical Essays* (New York: Doubleday Anchor Books, 1972).

Notes for Chapter Nine, Beauvoir

I follow Toril Moi and Deirdre Bair, two recent biographers of Simone de Beauvoir, in using "Beauvoir" rather than "de Beauvoir." Quotations marked SS are from Simone de Beauvoir, *The Second Sex*, translated and edited by H.M. Parshley (New York: Random House, 1989), first published in French in 1948 and in English in 1952. Those marked EA are from Simone de Beauvoir, *The Ethics of Ambiguity*, translated by Bernard Frechtman (New York: The Citadel Press, 1968), first published in French in 1947 and in English in 1948. Those marked ESN are from Simone de Beauvoir, *Existentialisme et la Sagesse des Nations* (Paris: Nagel, 1948), translated by me. Beauvoir's prize-winning novel, *The Mandarins*, is available in English, translated by Leonard M. Friedman (New York: The World Publishing Company, 1956). Quotations marked JPS are taken from *The Philosophy of Jean-Paul Sartre*, edited and introduced by Robert Denoon Cumming (New York: Random House, 1965). A useful introduction to Sartre's philosophy is that of Iris Murdoch in *Sartre: Romantic Rationalist* (New Haven: Yale University Press, 1953).

Works helpful for understanding existentialism generally include Albert Camus, *The Rebel* (New York: Random House, 1954); Gabriel Marcel, *The Philosophy of Existentialism* (New York: The Citadel Press, 1961); Marjorie Grene, *Introduction to Existentialism* (Chicago: University of Chicago Press, 1984); and Robert G. Olson, *Introduction to Existentialism* (New York: Dover Publications, 1962).

An excellent and readable biography of Simone de Beauvoir is that of Deirdre Bair, *Simone de Beauvoir* (New York: Summit Books, 1990). Toril Moi's *Simone de Beauvoir: The Making of an Intellectual Woman* (Oxford: Blackwell, 1994) combines biographical and critical material. Toril Moi offers a less sympathetic view of Beauvoir than Bair. I have chosen to concentrate on Beauvoir's philosophical ideas and to omit considerations of the merits of her personal life and the issue of whether her relationship with Sartre was an appropriate one for a feminist. I believe that in almost all cases philosophers should be discussed for their intellectual ideas and not on the basis of their personal and sexual lives. Toril Moi does not always take this view. Michele le Doeff in *Hipparchia's Choice: An Essay Concerning Women, Philosophy, Etc.* (Oxford: Basil Blackwell, 1991; translated by Trista Selous) offers many interesting comments on Beauvoir's position as a philosopher and intellectual at a time when there were still relatively few women intellectuals. LeDoeuff argues that existentialism, with its emphasis on freedom, makes oppression inexplicable and that for that reason, it was an unpromising framework for analyzing the situation of women.

Much of the critical discussion of Beauvoir concerns her fiction rather than her philosophical essays. Within philosophy, she is discussed primarily for her feminist ideas. An overview with some comments on Beauvoir's philosophical work is that of Catharine Savage Brosman, *Simone de Beauvoir Revisited* (Boston: Twayne Publishers, 1991). A collection edited by Elaine Marks *Critical Essays on Simone de Beauvoir* contains essays by a variety of interpreters. A philosophical collection is that of Margaret A. Simons, *Feminist Interpretations of Simone de Beauvoir* (University Park, Penn.: Pennsylvania State University Press, 1995).

Beauvoir has been harshly criticized by some contemporary feminists – for being philosophically and personally subservient to Sartre, for her negative interpretation of such female bodily functions as menstruation, pregnancy, nursing, and for seeming at times to classify herself as being so exceptional that she scarcely fell into the category of 'woman.' I deliberately do not address such criticisms, partly for lack of space, but mostly because I believe that it is a mistake to approach thinkers of the past (even the fairly recent past) with the expectation that they should reach ethical and political conclusions we would judge to be appropriate today. Re-reading *The Second Sex* while preparing this chapter, having known the book more than thirty years ago, I was fascinated to find mention of many themes still under discussion in contemporary feminism – including goddess religions, roles in lesbian relationships, and the relation between morality and gossip.

Relevant articles in recent philosophical journals include Monika Langer, "A Philosophical Retrieval of Simone de Beauvoir's *Pour Une Morale de l'Ambiguite*," in *Philosophy Today* (Summer 1994); Margaret A. Simons, "Sexism and the Philosophical Canon," *Journal of the History of Ideas* 51 (1990), 487 - 504; Margaret A. Simons, "Two Interviews with Simone de Beauvoir," *Hypatia* (1989), 11 - 27; Andrea Nye, "Preparing the Way for a Feminist Praxis," *Hypatia* (1989), 101 - 116; Donald Hatcher, "Why It's Immoral to be a Housewife," *Journal of Value Inquiry* (1989), 59 - 68; Joseph Mahon, "Existentialist Feminism and Simone de Beauvoir," *History of European Ideas* (1993), 651 - 658; Eva Lundgren-Gothin, "Simone de Beauvoir and Ethics," in *History of European Ideas* (1994), 899 - 903; and Debra B. Bergoffen, "The Look as Bad Faith," in *Philosophy Today* (1992), 221 - 227.

Notes for Chapter Ten, Wittgenstein

The chapter is based primarily on Wittgenstein's two greatest and most influential works: the *Tractatus Logico-Philosophicus* and the *Philosophical Investigations*. Passages marked TLP are from the *Tractatus Logico-Philosophicus*, translated by D.F. Pears and B.F. McGuinness (London: Routledge & Kegan Paul, 1961). Passages marked PI are from the *Philosophical Investigations* translated by G.E.M. Anscombe (Oxford: Basil Blackwell, 1963). I have also used ideas from Wittgenstein's *On Certainty*, edited by G.E.M. Anscombe and G.H. von Wright, translated by Denis Paul and G.E.M. Anscombe (Oxford: Basil Blackwell, 1969); and *Zettel*, edited by G.E. M. Anscombe and G.H. von Wright, translated by G.E.M. Anscombe (Oxford: Basil Blackwell, 1967).

The best single book about Wittgenstein is Ray Monk's superb philosophical biography, *Ludwig Wittgenstein: The Duty of Genius* (London: Jonathan Cape, 1990). This extraordinarily readable and fascinating work describes Wittgenstein's life and background, integrating these with his philosophical ideas in a lively way. An older biographical account by a devoted student is that of Norman Malcolm in *Ludwig Wittgenstein: A Memoir* (London: Oxford University Press, 1958). Justus Hartnack's *Wittgenstein and Modern Philosophy*, translated by Maurice Cranston (New York: Doubleday Anchor, 1965), is a helpful introductory work. An excellent philosophical overview of Wittgenstein's work may be found in Anthony Kenny, *Wittgenstein* (Middlesex, England: Penguin Books, 1973). Additional reliable sources are David Pears, *Wittgenstein* (London: Fontana, 1971); Robert J. Fogelin, *Wittgenstein: The Arguments of the Philosophers* (London: Routledge, 1987; second edition) and P.M.S. Hacker, *Insight and Illusion: Themes in the Philosophy of Wittgenstein* (Oxford: Oxford University Press, 1986; revised edition).

For my account of the *Tractatus*, I was assisted by Kenny's discussion and by H.O. Mounce, *Wittgenstein's Tractatus: An Introduction* (Chicago: University of Chicago Press, 1981). In my understanding of Wittenstein's paradox of meaning I have been greatly influenced by the work of Saul Kripke on rules and private language. I heard Kripke speak on this topic twice – in London, Ontario in 1976 and in Banff, Alberta in 1977. In preparing this chapter I benefitted again from his work as presented in *Wittgenstein on Rules and Private Language* (Cambridge, Mass.: Harvard University Press, 1982).

The analogy between a young person seeking the meaning of life and the reader of the *Tractatus* who realizes he can throw away the ladder when he has finished the book is taken from K.T. Fann, *Wittgenstein's Conception of Philosophy* (Berkeley and Los Angeles: University of California Press, 1971). Fann says, "The 'question' of the meaning of life is strictly speaking not a question – but the process of raising it, trying to answer it, and finally realizing the non-sensicality of the question *shows* the meaning of life to the one who has gone through this process. He is better off for it; the sense of life becomes clearer to him" (38). Fann is also my indirect source for the statistics about questions posed in the Investigations; he attributes the figures to Anthony Kenny.

Two central works of logical positivism are A.J. Ayer *Language, Truth, and Logic* (New York: Dover Publications, 1946; first published in London in 1936), and Rudolph Carnap, *The Logical Structure of the World*, translated by Rolf George (London, 1965). The standard anthology of writings by logical positivists is A.J. Ayer, *Logical Positivism* (Glencoe, Ill: Free Press, 1959).

Writings about Wittgenstein are extraordinarily extensive. Writing in 1990, Ray Monk reported that one bibliography listed 5868 books and articles about Wittgenstein's work. Needless to say, the present chapter was not based on a complete survey! Potentially useful sources about Wittgenstein are simply too numerous to mention. In addition to those already listed, some pertinent works are: M.B. Hintikka and J. Hintikka, *Investigating Wittgenstein* (Oxford: Basil Blackwell, 1986); George Pitcher (editor), *Wittgenstein: The Philosophical Investigations* (New York: Doubleday Anchor, 1966); Peter Winch, *Studies in the Philosophy of Wittgenstein* (London: Routledge & Kegan Paul, 1969; see especially the introduction and essay by John W. Cook); and Thomas Morawetz, *Wittgenstein and Knowledge: The Importance of On Certainty* (Amherst: University of Massachusetts Press, 1978).

Notes for Chapter Eleven, Contemporary Voices

Useful for an introductory understanding of artificial intelligence research is Douglas Hofstadter and Daniel Dennett's anthology *The Mind's I* (New York: Basic Books, 1981). Discussions of the Turing Test and of various philosophical objections to Strong A.I., including those of John Searle, may be found in that volume. Hubert Dreyfus' book *What Computers Can't Do* (New York: Harper and Row, 1972 and 1979) is highly readable and still important. Two very useful works offering a cautious interpretation of the field are Margaret Boden *Artificial Intelligence and Natural Man* (New York: Basic Books, 1977) and Margaret Boden *The Creative Mind: Myths and Mechanisms* (New York: Basic Books 1991). A more technical survey may be found in John Baker's article, "Philosophy and Artificial Intelligence in Canada," which appeared in the journal *Eidos* (1994), 87 - 160.

The discussion of the Informal Logic - Critical Thinking movement is based in part on my own participation in that movement. The essays by Ralph Johnson are found in Ralph Johnson, *The Rise of Informal Logic* (Newport News, Virginia: Vale Press, 1996). A helpful survey article is Ralph H. Johnson and J. Anthony Blair, "Informal Logic: The Past Five Years," in *American Philosophical Quarterly* (1985), 181 - 196. A useful overview of critical thinking from the perspective of education is Harvey Siegel's *Educating Reason: Rationality, Critical Thinking and Education* (New York and London: Routledge, 1988). The best way to investigate work in informal logic is to read the journal *Informal Logic* which is available from the Philosophy Department, University of Windsor, Canada. Influential textbooks include R.H. Johnson and J.A. Blair, *Logical Self-Defence* (Toronto: McGraw-Hill Ryerson, 1993; third edition) and Trudy Govier, *A Practical Study of Argument* (Belmont, CA: Wadsworth, 1997; fourth edition). The ARG account is my own, and is developed in *A Practical Study of Argument*. A highly relevant psychological study, emphasizing the connection between thinking and arguing, is Deanna Kuhn, *The Skills of Argument* (New York: Cambridge University Press, 1991).

The discussion of deconstruction is based on selections from Derrida in Peggy Kamif (editor), *A Derrida Reader: Between the Blinds* (New York: Columbia University Press, 1991), and Jacques Derrida, *Limited Inc.* (Evanston Ill.: Northwestern University Press, 1977). In addition, I benefitted greatly from *Redrawing the Lines: Analytic Philosophy, Deconstruction, and Literary Theory*, edited by Reed Way Dasenbrock (Minneapolis: University of Minnesota Press, 1989). Especially pertinent and helpful were the essays of Jules David Law and Steven Winsput, relating themes in Derrida to some of Wittgenstein's ideas.

The exploration of themes in feminist epistemology is based on Jean Grimshaw, *Philosophy and Feminist Thinking* (Minneapolis: University of Minnesota Press, 1986); Linda Alcoff and Elizabeth Potter (editors), *Feminist Epistemologies* (New York and London: Routledge, 1993); Sara Ruddick, "Maternal Thinking," and "Preservative Love and Military Destruction: Some Reflections on Mothering and Peace," both in *Mothering: Essays in Feminist Theory* edited by Joyce Trebilcot (Totowa, NJ: Rowman and Allanhead, 1984, 213-230 and 231 - 262); and Nancy Hartsock, "The Feminist Standpoint: Developing the Ground for a Specifically Feminist Historical Materialism," in Sandra Harding and Merrill Hintikka (editors), *Discovering Reality* (Dordrecht: D. Reidel Publishing, 1983). Sara Ruddick's ideas about maternal thinking and peace are further developed in her *Maternal Thinking: Towards a Politics of Peace* (New York: Ballantine Books, 1989).

Elizabeth Anderson's essay, "Feminist Epistemology: an Interpretation and a Defense" appeared in *Hypatia* (1995), 50 - 84. That whole volume of *Hypatia* is pertinent to themes of feminist epistemology. Relevant to arguments that epistemic individualism is impossible are John Hardwig, "Depending on Experts," in Trudy Govier, *Selected Issues in Logic and Communication* (Belmont, CA: Wadsworth, 1988); C.A.J. Coady, *Testimony* (New York: Oxford University Press, 1991); and Trudy Govier, "Trust and Testimony: Nine Arguments on Testimonial Knowledge," *International Journal of Moral and Social Studies* (1993), 21 - 39.

INDEX

SOCRATES' CHILDREN

SOCRATES' CHILDREN

Thinking and Knowing in the Western Tradition

Trudy Govier

broadview press

Canadian Cataloguing in Publication Data

Govier, Trudy
Socrates' Children

Includes bibliographical references and index
ISBN 1-55111-093-8
1. Philosophy – History. I. Title.

B72.G684 1997 190 C97-930774-0

Broadview Press
Post Office Box 1243
Peterborough, Ontario, Canada, K9J 7H5

in the United States of America
3576 California Road, Orchard Park, N.Y. 14127

in the United Kingdom
B.R.A.D. Book Representation & Distribution Ltd.
244A, London Road, Hadleigh, Essex SS7 2DE

Broadview Press gratefully acknowledges the support of the Canada Council, the Ontario Arts Council, the Ontario Publishing Centre, and the Ministry of National Heritage.

Cover design and book layout: Alvin Choong Design Studio

PRINTED IN CANADA
10 9 8 7 6 5 4 3 2 1 97 98 99

Contents